MANAGING THE DEVELOPMENT OF DIGITAL MARKETPLACES IN ASIA

Edited By Cyn-Young Park, James Villafuerte, and Josef T. Yap

DECEMBER 2021

ASIAN DEVELOPMENT BANK

ADB

Notes:
In this publication, "$" refers to United States dollars, unless otherwise stated; CNY = Chinese yuan;
₱ = Philippine peso; and RM = Malaysian ringgit.
ADB recognizes "China" as the People's Republic of China; "Hong Kong" as Hong Kong, China;
"Korea" and "South Korea" as the Republic of Korea; "Vietnam" as Viet Nam; and "Macau" as
Macau, China.

Cover design by Jasper Lauzon.

Contents

Tables, Figures, and Boxes

Tables

Figures

Boxes

Foreword

Digital platforms continue to accelerate development across Asia and the Pacific. This book describes how they transform the way we work, socialize, and create economic value. The ongoing pandemic is helping fuel this digital transformation. Yet, it also underscores the importance and urgency of putting in place policies and regulations that can maximize gains from the rapidly advancing digital economy. These range from widening access to promote digital inclusion, e-health, and online learning, to fostering digital ecosystems, ensuring data privacy and security, and preventing cyberattacks, to name but a few. While coordinating national agencies is critical, regional cooperation will also grow in importance on issues such as data transfer, taxation, and the financing needed to boost support for sustainable and inclusive digital development.

Digital platforms use data, search engines, and algorithms to reduce the cost of acquiring and applying information, bypass intermediaries, reduce trade barriers, ease customs clearance, and use idle assets to lower production and distribution costs. They also lower the cost of services to households and businesses—everything from food delivery to banking and e-commerce. They enhance market efficiency and, if used effectively, can help improve diversity and inclusion in the market and workplaces.

But just like any new technology, digital platforms disrupt existing markets and force market players to adapt. As they create new marketplaces where producers, service providers, workers, and consumers interact, some platforms that create massive networks tend to amass extraordinary market power. Access to big data and their exclusive use allow digital platforms to innovate and create new products and services. But they can also grow monopolistic. Privacy and cybersecurity issues increasingly impact both users and consumers.

Thus, it is critical for governments to nurture digital entrepreneurship and innovative ecosystems by providing rules and guidelines to ensure fair and competitive digital marketplaces for better economic and social outcomes. They also need to attract sufficient investment in digital infrastructure—both hardware and software—to narrow the digital divide and ensure no one is left behind.

This book contributes to the rapidly growing body of literature and policy debate on digital platforms. It includes the background papers prepared for the Asian Development Bank's *Asian Economic Integration Report 2021*. Chapters detail the scope, benefits, disruptions, and implications of digital platforms across Asia and the Pacific. The book will help policy makers better grasp the challenges of digital platforms and the ongoing digital transformation, in general. What we need are effective strategies that guarantee accessibility of this evolving technology to everyone—rich and poor, urban and rural—to help fulfill our goal of a prosperous, inclusive, resilient, and sustainable Asia and Pacific region.

Bambang Susantono
Vice-President for Knowledge Management
and Sustainable Development
Asian Development Bank

Preface

The coronavirus disease (COVID-19) outbreak has accelerated the pace of digital transformation as severe mobility restrictions to control its spread prompted people globally to use, adopt, and trust in digital technology marketplaces. People have shifted to working from home, online education, telehealth, e-commerce, and reliance on digital media. And digital platforms helped ensure that essential socioeconomic activities and transactions could continue even during the peak of the pandemic. Indeed, most activities can now be conducted effectively, safely, and affordably through digital platforms. This transformation is expected to remain a key feature of the new economy and society post-COVID-19.

Even before the pandemic, digital technology and platforms were growing rapidly. This is an integral part of the Fourth Industrial Revolution fueled by rising computational power and greater affordability of computing and smart devices. As digital platforms such as Amazon or Alibaba as well as Facebook or Zoom have proliferated, it has revolutionized how people work, socialize, and create economic value. These digital platforms use data, search engines, and algorithms to (i) lower information costs, (ii) circumvent intermediaries, (iii) weaken trade barriers, and (iv) use idle assets to create new economic values. They also opened new opportunities for small firms, households, and individuals, using their spare assets, to participate in economic activities.

Recognizing the growing penetration and increasing economic importance of digital platforms, the Asian Development Bank commissioned background papers to examine their key features. These papers were consolidated and presented as the theme chapter of the *Asian Economic Integration Report 2021*, "Making Digital Platforms Work for Asia and the Pacific." Eight of these background papers were selected for this volume's chapters.

An important cross-cutting issue among the chapters is the set of opportunities and challenges digital platforms present to existing markets and market players. There will be winners and losers, and the eight chapters analyze the evolution of this process. One chapter suggests that the expansion of digital platforms favorably impacts trade, employment, and output. At the microeconomic level, e-commerce is supported by fintech payments or, more generally, financial services transacted through digital platforms. E-commerce, in turn, leads to greater trade in goods and services. Another chapter notes, however, that a significant digital divide exists and prevents equal access to new economic opportunities. Meanwhile, the massive network externalities generated by digital platforms may allow a few Big Tech firms to dominate the new marketplaces. Taxing digital platforms is also challenging given elusive digital profits and cross-border tax fraud, which arise because of difficulties in identifying taxable digital activities as companies develop their businesses without a physical presence within a specific tax jurisdiction, among many other issues.

The chapters also propose measures and policies to realize the potential benefits and maximize social and economic gains while alleviating adverse effects. For example, competition policy has to be attuned to how digital platforms wield their market power. With increasing cross-border digital transactions, it is crucial to strengthen international tax cooperation to plug loopholes and capture profits generated by the digital economy—even more so in the post-pandemic era, with digital platforms expected to remain important after the crisis has passed.

We hope this volume will contribute to better understanding of the issues emerging from the ongoing transition to the digital economy and considering how the region's policy makers must respond to harness the potential.

Cyn-Young Park
Director, Regional Cooperation and Integration Division
Economic Research and Regional Cooperation Department
Asian Development Bank

James Villafuerte
Senior Economist, Southeast Asia Department
Asian Development Bank

Josef T. Yap
Consultant, Regional Cooperation and Integration Division
Economic Research and Regional Cooperation Department
Asian Development Bank

Acknowledgments

This publication was prepared by the Regional Cooperation and Integration Division (ERCI) of the Economic Research and Regional Cooperation Department (ERCD) of the Asian Development Bank (ADB), with support from Technical Assistance 9914: Strengthening Knowledge Alliance for Innovation, Technology, and Regional Cooperation, financed by ADB's technical assistance special fund.

The editors would like to thank all contributors to this book volume, namely, Thomas Abell, Jose Ramon Albert, Ma. Diyina Gem Arbo, Rolando Avendano, Sylwyn Calizo, Jr., Kimberly Diet, Jessmond Elvina, Yueling Huang, Ryan Jacildo, Aiko Kikkawa, Philip Libre, Badri Narayanan, Francis Mark Quimba, Maureen Ane Rosellon, and Peter Rosenkranz. The editorial team is thankful for the collaboration with the Philippine Institute for Development Studies led by its President Celia Reyes, and Senior Research Fellow Ramonette Serafica. The editors are also grateful for the helpful comments and suggestions provided by the participants of the following workshops and events: "The Emergence of the Platform Economy: Challenges and Opportunities in Developing Asia" held on 5–6 December 2019 in ADB headquarters, Manila; "Virtual Conference on Making Digital Platforms Work for Asia" held on 25–26 June 2020, ADB headquarters, Manila; "AEIR 2021 Theme Chapter Internal Workshop on Making Digital Platforms Work for Asia and the Pacific" held on 24 August 2020, Manila; and "Workshop: Asian Economic Integration Report 2021" held on 9 September 2020, Manila. Further contributions and excellent research support from Ryan Jacildo are greatly acknowledged.

Rogelio Mercado (economist, ERCI/ERCD); Kijin Kim (economist, ERCI/ERCD); and James Villafuerte (senior economist, Southeast Asia Department, ADB) led the coordination of all contributors in this publication, with the support of Paulo Rodelio Halili (senior economics officer, ADB); Aleli Rosario (senior economics officer, ADB); Maria Josephine Duque-Comia (senior programs officer, ADB); and administrative assistance from Marilyn Aure Parra (senior operations assistant, ADB) under the overall guidance and supervision of Cyn-Young Park, director of ERCI/ERCD. The editorial team is also grateful to all those who helped in the production of this edited book volume, including Eric Van Zant for editing the book chapters, Jasper Lauzon for creating the cover design, Joe Mark Ganaban for typesetting and layout, Lawrence Casiraya for proofreading, and Marjorie Celis for page proof checking, with assistance from Carol Ongchangco. The editors, likewise, acknowledge the printing and publishing support by the Printing Services Unit of ADB's Corporate Services Department and the Publishing team of the Department of Communications.

Editors

Cyn-Young Park is Director of the Regional Cooperation and Integration Division in the Economic Research and Regional Cooperation Department of the Asian Development Bank (ADB). In her current capacity, she manages a team of economists, who examine economic and policy issues related to regional cooperation and integration (RCI) and develop strategies and approaches to support RCI. She has been a main author of and contributor to ADB's major publications; and has published extensively in peer-reviewed academic journals. She has also conducted lectures about the Asian economy and financial markets and participated in various global and regional forums. Prior to joining ADB, she served as economist at the Organisation for Economic Co-operation and Development. She received her doctor of philosophy (PhD) in economics from Columbia University. She holds a bachelor's degree in international economics from Seoul National University.

James Villafuerte is Senior Economist at the Southeast Asia Department of ADB, where he leads the Policy Network of Economist. He previously served as Senior Economist in the Economics Research and Regional Cooperation Department and Team Leader of the Asia Regional Integration Center—both at ADB—where he contributed regularly to the ADB's flagship publications. His advisory and research expertise covers economic outlook and risk assessment, policy and development issues, regional integration, macroeconomic surveillance, and early warning systems. Prior to joining ADB, he was a senior economist at the Department of Treasury and Finance in Victoria, Australia, and an economist at the World Bank Office in Manila. He obtained his master's and bachelor's degrees in economics from the University of the Philippines.

Josef T. Yap is Consultant at the Regional Cooperation and Integration Division in the Economic Research and Regional Cooperation Department of ADB. He was previously the President of the Philippine Institute for Development Studies, where he served for 26 years until his retirement. He was the regional coordinator of the East Asian Development Network and was involved in the establishment of the Economic Research Institute for ASEAN and East Asia. He has also published extensively on national and regional cooperation and integration issues and has been the Editorial Adviser of the Asian Economic Journal. He obtained his bachelor's degree in industrial engineering and PhD in economics from the University of the Philippines Diliman. He also attended a postdoctoral program at the University of Pennsylvania.

Authors

Thomas Abell is Advisor, Sustainable Development and Climate Change Department, Asian Development Bank (ADB), and the Chief of ADB Digital Technology for Development Unit

Jose Ramon Albert is Senior Research Fellow, Philippine Institute for Development Studies

Ma. Diyina Gem Arbo is Analyst and Project Coordinator, International Trade Centre, and previously a Consultant, ADB Economic Research and Regional Cooperation Department

Rolando Avendano is Economist, ADB Economic Research and Regional Cooperation Department

Sylwyn Calizo, Jr. is Research Specialist, Philippine Institute for Development Studies

Kimberly Diet was the Chief-of-Staff of the Commissioner, Philippine Competition Commission

Jessmond Elvina is Economist, Philippine Competition Commission previously; and Senate of the Philippines Committee on Energy currently

Yueling Huang is PhD in Economics candidate, New York University

Ryan Jacildo is Consultant, ADB Economic Research and Regional Cooperation Department

Aiko Kikkawa is Economist, ADB Economic Research and Regional Cooperation Department

Philip Libre is Consultant, ADB Economic Research and Regional Cooperation Department; and Lecturer, Ateneo de Manila University School of Social Sciences

Badri Narayanan is Founder and Director, Infinite Sum Modelling Inc. Seattle; and Consultant, ADB Economic Research and Regional Cooperation Department

Cyn-Young Park is Director of the Regional Cooperation and Integration Division in the Economic Research and Regional Cooperation Department of the Asian Development Bank

Francis Mark Quimba is Senior Research Fellow, Philippine Institute for Development Studies

Maureen Ane Rosellon is Supervising Research Specialist, Philippine Institute for Development Studies

Peter Rosenkranz is Economist, ADB Economic Research and Regional Cooperation Department

James Villafuerte is Senior Economist in Southeast Asia Department at the Asian Development Bank

Josef T. Yap is Consultant, ADB Economic Research and Regional Cooperation Department, and former President, Philippine Institute for Development Studies

Introduction and Overview

Cyn-Young Park, James Villafuerte, and Josef T. Yap

1.1. Background

Globally, the Fourth Industrial Revolution is fundamentally shifting the way we live, work, and create value. New technologies and applications are connecting individuals, organizations, and machines at unprecedented scale and speed. And this greater interface across the physical, digital, and biological worlds has been made possible by advances in artificial intelligence (AI), robotics, the Internet of Things, 3D printing, genetic engineering, quantum computing, and other technologies (Figure 1.1).

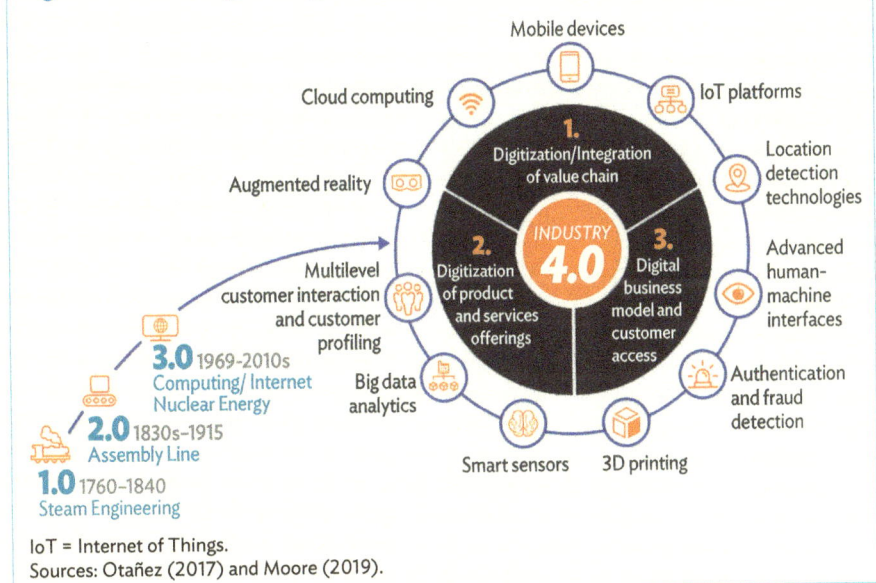

Figure 1.1: Situating the Digital Economy in the Fourth Industrial Revolution

Mobile devices

Cloud computing

IoT platforms

Augmented reality

Location detection technologies

1. Digitization/Integration of value chain

INDUSTRY 4.0

2. Digitization of product and services offerings

3. Digital business model and customer access

Advanced human-machine interfaces

Multilevel customer interaction and customer profiling

Authentication and fraud detection

3.0 1969–2010s Computing/ Internet Nuclear Energy

Big data analytics

2.0 1830s–1915 Assembly Line

Smart sensors

3D printing

1.0 1760–1840 Steam Engineering

IoT = Internet of Things.
Sources: Otañez (2017) and Moore (2019).

The revolution is transforming the services sector with wide-ranging applications in retail markets, financial sector, manufacturing, and agricultural production and value chain. Digital apps are matching supply and demand in real time, data analytics are improving credit scoring, the application of AI is improving crop yields, and automation in manufacturing is enhancing efficiency, among many others. The coronavirus disease (COVID-19) pandemic has also accelerated the adoption and application of digital and Fourth Industrial Revolution technologies, which offers essential tools for survival and business continuity while mitigating the risk of physical contact. The potential economic benefits are vast and, if harnessed properly, will contribute to inclusive and sustainable development.

A key component of the Fourth Industrial Revolution is the digitalization of economic transactions and markets, underpinned by big data, data analytics, and Internet of Things. This digitalization, along with software development and application, has fueled the transition from the Third Industrial Revolution, which saw computers and the internet emerge.

This volume analyzes digital platforms or marketplaces, a segment of this emerging digitalized economy. Figure 1.2 shows that the digital economy has core, narrow, and broad scopes. The latter includes digital technologies for undertakings such as automation, AI, and e-commerce, as well as sharing and gig economies. Generally, digital platforms exhibit three defining characteristics: they (i) are mediated through technology, (ii) link user groups, and (iii) allow these groups to perform varied tasks.

A digital platform or a digital marketplace is defined as an intermediary and infrastructure that brings together different parties through the internet to interact, matching supply and demand in a multisided market. As a virtual matchmaker, the digital platform provides a mechanism for consumers and suppliers of products and services to conduct various value-creating transactions, including information exchange, demand matching, payment and receipt, and delivery of said goods and services.

Digital platforms are transforming how people work, socialize, and create economic value. Examples of successful social media digital platforms include Facebook, Instagram, LinkedIn, TikTok, and Twitter. In search and marketing, notable names are Google, Yahoo!, and Baidu. As regards video sharing and music streaming, popular platforms include YouTube and Spotify. In e-commerce,

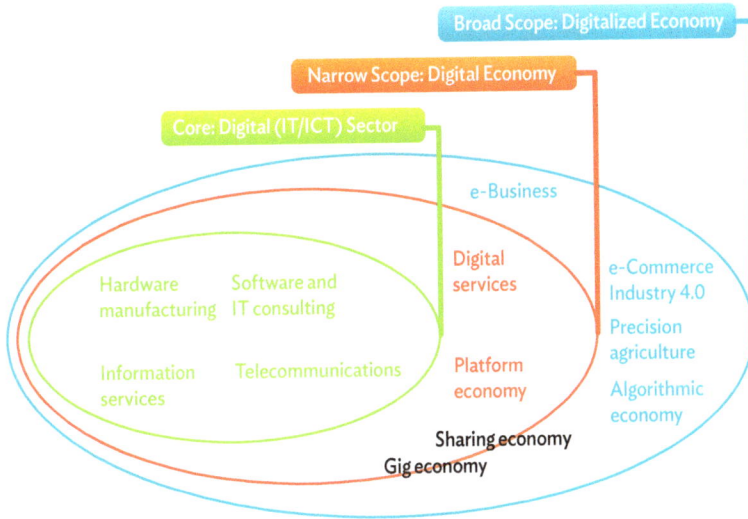

Figure 1.2: Three Scopes of Digital Economy

Broad Scope: Digitalized Economy

Narrow Scope: Digital Economy

Core: Digital (IT/ICT) Sector

e-Business

Hardware manufacturing

Software and IT consulting

Information services

Telecommunications

Digital services

Platform economy

e-Commerce Industry 4.0

Precision agriculture

Algorithmic economy

Sharing economy

Gig economy

ICT = information and communication technology, IT = information technology.
Source: Bukht and Heeks (2017).

Amazon and Alibaba are two of the well-known platforms. And in service-sharing segment, the prominent players include Airbnb, Grab, Uber, and GrubHub. These digital platforms use data obtained from their search and tracking facilities and algorithms to (i) lower the cost of obtaining and applying information, (ii) circumvent intermediaries, (iii) effectively weaken trade barriers, (iv) bundle the ordering of goods with efficient payment and delivery conduits, and (v) use idle assets to reduce production and distribution costs.

Like any "revolution," digital transformation will create winners and losers. Specifically, digital platforms are a disruptive force in existing markets and to the incumbent players. Disruptive innovations are transforming business process, value chain structure, and employment arrangements. They are also a significant challenge for all market participants, particularly smaller businesses with fewer resources, as they adapt to new orders and changes. To cope with disruptive transformation, businesses need to better understand forces at work and form effective strategies and systems in a timely manner to continuously manage them.

This volume considers possible disruption in several areas:

Competition: There are ample merits for authorities to craft policies that encourage healthy competition and ease barriers to entry. They should also promote interoperability and sharing of data across platforms to encourage collaboration among market players and promote innovation for consumers' benefits.

Labor issues and social protection: As traditional labor conditions and arrangements may no longer be applicable to the jobs market that digital platforms create, online workers are typically categorized as contractors or self-employed. This leaves them with little job and income security, possible deterioration of working conditions, or uncertain social protection. Efforts are needed to strengthen employment protection for gig workers and strengthen social protections by making them digital, flexible, and portable.

Data access, privacy, and security: As the data value chain depends on data access, use, and sharing, substantial premium should be placed on regulations that foster greater transparency in using and sharing the collected data as well as in creating value from them. It is vital to uphold data privacy and at the same time ensure that access to data and information is secure. It is just as crucial to have safeguards against the use of data to discriminate against any specific group. Continuous cross-border policy coordination is equally important to ensure cybersecurity and fight cybercrimes.

Taxation: Taxing digital platforms and the activities within is a big challenge. There are regulatory gaps that make it difficult to identify taxable digital activities, especially as companies develop their businesses in a manner that does not necessarily entail having a physical presence within a specific tax jurisdiction, among many other issues. Preventing tax avoidance and evasion of national and multinational technology companies will ensure that benefits are fairly distributed both domestically and internationally.

The eight subsequent chapters in this volume deal with (i) defining digital platforms and measuring their aggregate economic contribution, (ii) assessing their benefits to other sectors and ensuring a more equitable distribution of these benefits, and (iii) identifying the areas of disruption and proposing measures to cope with these and mitigate adverse effects.

1.2. Measuring the Platform Economy: Concepts, Indicators, and Issues

Delineating the scope and features of digital platforms can lead to estimating their turnovers, purchases, employment costs, and marketing expenditures, as well as the use of online technologies by platform-enabled firms, in comparison with non-platform businesses. Many typologies are used in discussing platforms. They are either based on the type of interactions, roles, participation strategies, overall scope and structure, or profit motive. Nevertheless, it is challenging to have categories that are mutually exclusive given that some platforms, especially "superplatforms," have features from several types. Furthermore, functional typologies get archaic as platforms evolve quickly, thus necessitates periodic adjustments in the typologies.

In Chapter 2, Albert presents possible approaches to obtaining data and indicators for measuring the digital platform economy using existing business and household surveys, dedicated surveys, and a process known as web-scraping. The chapter presents a case study of measurements of the platform economy in the Philippines using a household survey on the use of information and communication technology (ICT). It emphasizes that national statistics offices should incorporate various data sources into their national accounting system. For example, the household sector should not only be considered from the expenditure side, but also from the production side, given the rising incomes and production arising from their participation in platforms. Policy implications for the measurement of the digital platform economy in areas such as data privacy, competition, decent work and innovation policy, and taxation are also discussed in the chapter.

1.3. Digital Platforms, Technology, and Their Macroeconomic Impact

In Chapter 3, Villafuerte, Narayanan, and Abell present and analyze data showing the global reach of digital platforms. In 2019, digital platform business-to-consumer revenues reached $3.8 trillion, equivalent to 4.4% of global gross domestic product (GDP). Asia and the Pacific accounted for about 48% ($1.8 trillion; equivalent to 6% of regional GDP); the United States for 22% ($836.7 billion; 3.9%); and the euro area 12% ($445.3 billion; 3.3%). Within this region, the People's Republic of China (PRC) is the biggest market for digital platforms, accounting for about $1.2 trillion in revenue or

68.2% of Asia's total (about 8.8% of the country's GDP). Figure 1.3 shows the distribution of these revenues across the six major types of digital platforms: digital media, e-commerce, e-services, online travel, advertising technology, and transportation.

The digital economy in the region is expected to expand, providing opportunities to boost economic growth, create new businesses and jobs, and address various socioeconomic challenges. In order to estimate the impact on the macroeconomy of increased digital technology usage, the authors use a recursive-dynamic GDyn model developed by Ianchovichina and Walmsley (2012). The GDyn Model is the dynamic extension of the standard Global Trade Analysis Project (GTAP) model, a multi-region, and multi-sector Computable General Equilibrium (CGE) model. The dynamic CGE model used combines aspects of financial assets and associated income flows, capital accumulation, and investment theory.

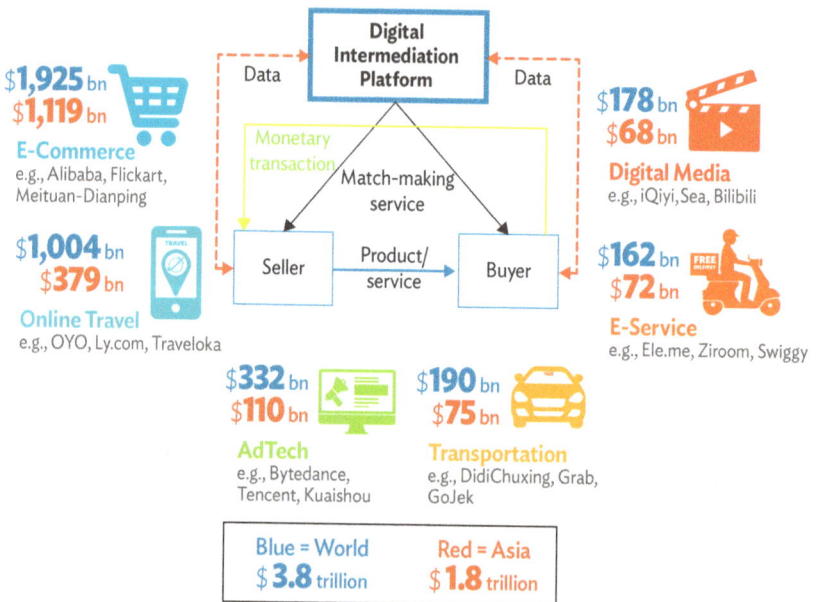

Figure 1.3: Digital Platform Revenues, World and Asia, 2019

AdTech = advertising technology, bn = billion.
Note: Refer to Figure 8.4 in ADB (2021) for the country composition and the detailed sources.
Source: ADB (2021).

The dynamic CGE model is calibrated to represent the relevant changes during the COVID-19 outbreak. These include the shift to work from home, online education, and telehealth, as well as the increased patronage of e-commerce and reliance on digital media, among others. In particular, investment in the digital sector has increased, which in turn contributes to higher output of sectors that use digital inputs more intensively, raising overall economic productivity. The simulation results reveal that the size of the global digital sector is expected to rise by an average of about $617 billion annually from the baseline levels, which total to $3.1 trillion from 2021 to 2025. In comparison, Asia's digital sector size is forecast to increase by about $184 billion per year from baselines, which translate to about $919 billion in 5 years. This expansion will substantially impact economic growth, exports, and employment.

Globally, if the size of the digital sector expands by 20% by 2025 from the baseline, global GDP is estimated to increase by about $4.3 trillion per year, which is roughly about 5.4% of the baseline 2020 GDP. Given this average annual gain, the total increase in global output will run up to $21.4 trillion in 5 years. The increased size of the digital sector accounts for about a third of the GDP increase, while productivity enhancement accounts for the rest. Similarly, global trade is projected to increase by close to $2.4 trillion annually to the baseline levels from 2021 to 2025, which represents about 5.5% of the 2020 baseline total trade. With this average markup, over $11.8 trillion of additional trade value can be expected in the 5-year period to 2025.

Global employment will accordingly increase by almost 140 million jobs per year during the period, which is about 5.0% of the 2020 baseline global employment. Given this rate of expansion, the cumulative job generation will be about 698 million by the end of 2025.

Realizing potential gains from the growth of the digital economy, however, requires critical policy support and reforms in various areas. First, digital sector investments will have to increase substantially to provide a solid base that will support this projected expansion in digital sector output. Also crucial are better trade and logistics processes and infrastructure to address existing bottlenecks to goods delivery. Investing in digital skills and literacy of workers and the general population will also allow people's access to the economic opportunities of digital technologies and encourage their economic empowerment. Developing a digital, safe, and secure payment system is likewise critical. It is important to put together a robust, smart, and transparent regulatory system to prevent illegal activities, protect personal data, and strengthen cybersecurity.

1.4. Trade and E-Commerce in Asia: Policy Considerations

E-commerce—buying and selling of goods and services over the internet—comprises the bulk of transactions under the auspices of digital platforms. Global e-commerce sales to businesses and consumers are estimated to have breached $25 trillion in 2018, or about 30% of GDP of the countries included in the assessment (UNCTAD 2020). The business-to-business segment accounts for about 83% of the sales, according to the report, and the rest by business to consumer sales.

In Chapter 4, Jacildo provides empirical evidence of the positive association between e-commerce development and consumer goods trade, with the linkage having strengthened in recent years. Poisson pseudo maximum likelihood estimations of gravity-model equations indicate that combined internet retailing activity of trading economies is positively and significantly associated with their bilateral consumer goods trade.

Cross-border e-commerce transactions highlight three important policy areas: (i) cross-border taxation, competition, and customs administration issues; (ii) the role of multilateral initiatives and trade agreements in resolving policy disconnects; and (iii) the responsiveness of free trade zone or economic processing zone strategies in light of the increasing role of platforms and other digital media in trade.

In this context, it is essential to strengthen official statistics for better monitoring of e-commerce development. Fostering e-commerce in line with the economic inclusion and development agenda also requires clear and targeted strategies to bolster the competitiveness of firms in the e-commerce space. Regional cooperation on cross-border taxation and related customs challenges is just as crucial. Similarly, multilateral and regional trade cooperation can help harmonize policies and regulations across economies to promote e-commerce and facilitate digital trade more broadly. Finally, free trade zone strategies can be revisited to support e-commerce development while facilitating compliance to customs regulations.

1.5. Retail Fintech Payments: Facts, Benefits, Challenges, and Policies

Financial technology (fintech) is the use of technology to support and deliver financial services and payment. In 2019, digital payments accounted for 77% of the global fintech transaction value; in Asia, it accounted for even more at 86%.

In Chapter 5, Huang examines the current fintech landscape, benefits, and challenges brought by retail fintech payment systems, and discusses policy options. Five stylized facts characterize the current fintech payments system:

i. The relative importance—as measured by the average volume share—of card and e-money payments among cashless payment instruments is significant and rising in emerging economies.
ii. The average value per transaction through card and e-money is substantially smaller than other cashless payments instruments.
iii. Total mobile money transaction volume and value both increased substantially during 2011–2019.
iv. Mobile money transaction volume is the highest for airtime top-up in general and relatively high for merchant payment in East Asia and the Pacific.
v. The retail value of e-commerce is expanding exponentially, especially in Asia and the Pacific.

The study used the Alipay data in the PKU Digital Financial Inclusion Index of China data set covering 31 provinces from 2011 to 2018. Alipay, launched in 2004, is currently the dominant player in the payments space in the PRC. The econometric results show a strong relationship between e-commerce and fintech payments.

The study also provides evidence of the positive relationship between the adoption of fintech payments and transactions payment as well as remittances transfers. Fintech payments benefit from the unique characteristics of the platform economy in terms of big data, broad customer base, and multipurpose technology. They make retail payments more efficient, transparent, and inclusive, and act as an enabler for e-commerce, financial development, and financial inclusion.

As payment systems embrace new digital technologies and innovations to deliver more efficient and socially beneficial solutions, there is (need) to address associated risks and challenges such as the divide in access to digital payments, data security and privacy, and competition issues emerging from big-tech payment platforms.

Policies can be generally categorized in line with the following goals: (i) close existing loopholes in the regulatory system to reflect critical changes brought about by digitalization; (ii) expand access, particularly for socially disadvantaged groups; and (iii) promote regional cooperation on regulation, competition, and taxation.

1.6. Digital Divide and the Platform Economy: Looking for the Connection from the Asian Experience

The benefits of the platform economy are not equitably distributed within and across countries. Gaps exist based on levels of income, education, gender, and geographic location. There are four kinds of barriers—the so-called divides—that relate to access: motivational or mental, material, skills, and usage (van Dijk 2006). In Chapter 6, Quimba, Rosellon, and Calizo Jr. present a model to explain the relationship between the digital divide and the platform economy, taking off from van Dijk's (2006) cumulative and recursive model (Figure 1.4). This model extends the basic concept of access—understood as material access or the counting of people with computers or access to internet connections—to include motivational access, skills access, materials access, and usage access.

Using data from a number of Asian economies, Chapter 6 shows that people who live in urban or more affluent areas, who are neither too old nor too young, mostly male, more skilled/educated, and who have high levels of trust, have better access to computers and the internet. Interestingly, the chapter shows that digital platforms also create inequalities. For instance, accommodation platforms have created a wider income gap between the more commercialized and touristy areas and the periphery. Capital platforms tend to increase income inequality. To address these inequalities caused by digital platforms, policy interventions should address not only material access but also the other forms of disparity.

Figure 1.4: Cumulative and Recursive Model of Successive Kinds of Access to Digital Technologies

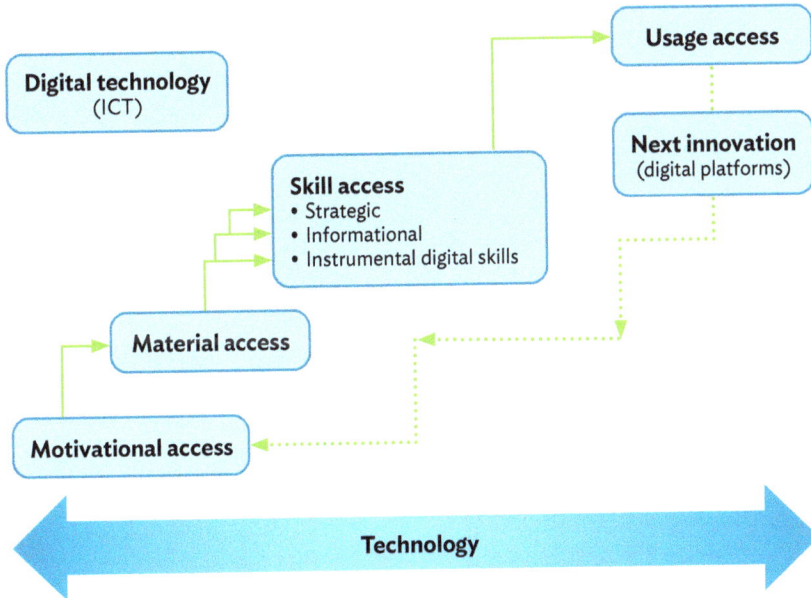

ICT = information and communication technology.
Note: The figure is a slightly modified version of Figure 1 in van Dijk (2006).
Source: Quimba, Rosellon, and Calizo Jr. (2021).

Given its findings, the chapter recommends the following policy reforms:

- Define and measure various indicators in the four areas of access and participation in digital platforms.
- Address barriers to access simultaneously to maximize and distribute the gains from digital platforms.
- Support projects that would provide at least material access to ICT in developing economies.
- Work with governments to develop plans for utilizing digitization, to facilitate innovation, and to support start-ups in developing platforms based on mobile applications.
- Facilitate among countries to ensure the regulatory convergence of ICT access and participation in the platform economy, and to safeguard data privacy and maintain trust in the digital economy.
- Support digital skills development for youth.

1.7. Promoting Competition in the Digital Platform Economy

High concentration and the presence of dominant digital platforms are common features across the globe given the network effects. A number of platforms, such as Alibaba, Amazon, Apple, Facebook, Google, and TikTok, have already become household names given the size of their markets. Of interest to competition policy is the manner by which market leaders are expanding their businesses. Leveraging their dominant position in one market to establish themselves in adjacent markets, sometimes to the detriment of competitors, is seemingly the trend. Markets in developing economies, such as those in Southeast Asia, exhibit this pattern of high concentration. Evidently, an assessment of Southeast Asia's e-commerce market in 2019 covering Indonesia, Malaysia, the Philippines, Singapore, and Viet Nam shows that Lazada and Shopee, which are the two leading firms, account for more than 55% of visits to the top 10 e-commerce websites (Iprice Group, App Annie, and SimilarWeb 2020).

Evans and Schmalensee (2007) posit that five factors exert strong influence market on the level of concentration in digital platform markets. These are congestion, network effects, platform differentiation, scale economies, and "multi-homing." Indirect network effects and scale economies are suggested to lead to higher concentration, whereas the other three are purported to have the opposite influence. The collection and use of big data is another prominent issue. Data can be utilized to ward off competitors. In some cases, data transferability is a material determinant of switching costs, stifling competition.

Figure 1.5 summarizes these factors in comparison with the ones considered by Libre, Jacildo, Diet, and Elvina in Chapter 7.

The chapter discusses the characteristics of digital platforms that significantly influence distribution of market power and identifies key areas for policy reforms.

- Instead of penalizing dominance and artificially creating a fragmented but inefficient market, *ex ante* policies that ensure contestability may be more appropriate.

Figure 1.5: Market Characteristics That Could Stifle Competition

Network effects: Value of the platform is positively correlated with the number of users.

Extreme returns to scale: Returns of producing digital goods and services are, in time, very large compared to its cost of production.

Data intensiveness: Perhaps the most important by-product of using digital platforms is the amount of data captured, e.g., targeted recommendations, behavioral nudges.

Switching costs: Real or perceived costs incurred by a consumer when changing suppliers for similar goods or services.

Source: Bernabe (2020).

- One way to ensure contestability is through "multi-homing" or by restricting exclusivity arrangements. Multi-homing means that users can join and use multiple platforms at minimal switching costs.
- Interoperability is a tool that can also promote and facilitate multi-homing. Interoperability pertains to the ease with which one system or platform integrates with another in access, exchange, and use of data.

In general, the growing market power of dominant digital platforms calls for more responsive rules on mergers and acquisitions, stronger *ex-ante* anti-trust regulations and mechanisms, and more vigorous cooperation between governments on cross-border issues to ensure that rules are complementary and consistent with each other.

1.8. Digitalization of Work and the Role of Universal Basic Income in Developing Asia

The emergence of labor platforms is changing the nature of work and employment enabled by these platforms. The jobs generated through digital service platforms are categorized into either cloud work or gig work, depending on whether the services and tasks are bound to a specific location or person. While many of these jobs are characterized by flexibility in terms of the number of work engagements and work schedule, income is sometimes not guaranteed and neither is social security.

The platform-based gig workers may be exposed to vulnerable labor conditions in the absence of legal protections such as a minimum wage, work safety, pension contribution, and health insurance. Many of them are considered self-employed or own-account workers as well, while work informality is highly present among the self-employed or own-account workers—86.2% of the region's self-employed are informal workers (ILO 2018).

These gig workers are similar to other informal workers in the sense that they usually lack coverage from social insurance or contributory schemes. Among other reasons are the exclusion from legal coverage, low and inconsistent earnings, and complicated administrative processes. They also tend to be excluded from social assistance or noncontributory schemes that are typically intended for the poor. Informal workers are often left without any social protection coverage, hence, the case of the "missing middle" exists (ILO 2017, 2019; Ulrichs 2016).

In this context, economies like the PRC and India have been examining the feasibility of a universal basic income (UBI). UBI is a social assistance mechanism that involves regular and unconditional transfer of uniform cash amounts to all individuals in a given country. This is particularly relevant to workers in the growing gig and platform economy. Although critics argue that UBI can disincentivize work, increase inflationary pressures, and add to the fiscal burden, it has potential to eliminate huge administrative costs and the inclusion or exclusion errors that are associated with targeted social assistance schemes.

In Chapter 8, Arbo and Kikkawa argue that UBI's potential impacts and feasibility depend on the program design, performance of existing social protection schemes, fiscal cost, and financing. A UBI can be considered to improve coverage and adequacy of social security benefits and broaden social protection systems subject to the assessments of the country-specific conditions. The following are identifiable trade-offs when comparing UBI with other social protection programs:

- When social assistance has substantial coverage and slight progressivity, barriers to access, eligibility and coverage, and delivery should be carefully studied and addressed. A UBI may be better motivated by various objectives under a comprehensive framework for social equity and social protection system than simply focusing on poverty reduction.
- When social assistance has high coverage but is not progressive, a UBI may be feasible, especially if it is difficult to improve progressivity within the existing programs; however, UBI should be combined with progressive financing.
- When social assistance has low coverage but is progressive, a UBI may extend coverage but also flatten the distribution, especially if budget-neutral. Hence, a more generous UBI design is preferable to ensure adequacy of benefits particularly at the bottom of the income distribution.

1.9. Digital Platforms and International Taxation in Asia

The emerging digital economy have new features that have implications for tax systems. These include (i) the mobility of intangibles and platform players, (ii) the increasing reliance on data and other intangible assets, (iii) the network effects, (iv) the spread of multisided business models, (v) the tendency toward monopoly or oligopoly in a digital economy, and (vi) the volatility that accompanies the low barriers to entry owing to technological advances (OECD 2015). In Chapter 9, Avendano and Rosenkranz argue that these features not only pose challenges to national tax systems but may also exacerbate concerns over Base Erosion and Profit Shifting (BEPS) practices.

The ongoing evolution of the digital economy presents challenges for tax systems, broadly in terms of the reduced need for physical presence (nexus), the growing utilization of data, and the uncertainties surrounding the accurate measurement of business income. The digital economy poses three main challenges: (i) the ability of digital businesses to operate in an area without a physical presence entails a review of the rules on physical presence (nexus rules), (ii) the extensive use and monetization of data requires examination of the economic value this generates and whether it is appropriately captured for tax purposes, and (iii) new business models such as cloud computing present difficulties in properly characterizing income for tax purposes (OECD 2015).

Meanwhile, the COVID-19 pandemic has substantially changed the digital economic landscape and has accelerated the adoption and use of digital technology and reorganization of business activities online and offline. Such changes complicate identification of taxable incomes and taxpayers creating possible tax leakages and loopholes. While several Asian economies have joined efforts to reach a global solution addressing BEPS and facilitating exchange of information, a strong and coordinated regional and international response is needed to ensure implementation of coordinated tax policies to stop tax evasion while avoiding costly unilateral measures. This will strengthen efforts to mobilize domestic resources to manage and control public debt in the aftermath of the COVID-19 pandemic.

References

Asian Development Bank (ADB). 2021. Asian Economic Integration Report 2021: *Making Digital Platforms Work for Asia and the Pacific*. Manila. http://dx.doi.org/10.22617/TCS210048-2.

Bukht, R. and R. Heeks. 2017. Defining, Conceptualising and Measuring the Digital Economy. *Development Informatics. Working Papers Series*. No. 68. Manchester: University of Manchester.

Evans, D. and R. Schmalensee. 2007. The Industrial Organization of Markets with Two-Sided Platforms. *Competition Policy International*. 3 (1). pp. 151–79.

Ianchovichina, E. and T. Walmsley, eds. 2012. *Dynamic Modeling and Applications for Global Economic Analysis*. Cambridge: Cambridge University Press.

International Labour Organization (ILO). 2017. *World Social Protection Report 2017–19: Universal Social Protection to Achieve the Sustainable Development Goals*. Geneva.

———. 2019. *Extending Social Security to Workers in the Informal Economy: Lessons from International Experience*. Geneva.

Iprice Group, App Annie, and SimilarWeb. 2020. *Year-End Report on Southeast Asia's Map of E-Commerce 2019*. https://backup.marketinginasia.com/wp-content/uploads/2020/03/2019-Year-End-Report-of-Map-of-E-commerce-iPrice-Group.pdf.

Kinda, T. 2019. E-commerce as a Potential New Engine for Growth in Asia. *IMF Working Paper*. WP/19/135. Washington, DC: International Monetary Fund.

Kramer, J., ed. 2020. *Digital Markets and Online Platforms: New Perspectives on Regulation and Competition Law*. Brussels: Centre on Regulation in Europe.

Moore, G. 2019. 3 ways to be a good leader in the Fourth Industrial Revolution. Geneva: World Economic Forum. https://www.weforum.org/agenda/2019/01/the-fourth-industrial-revolution-needs-new-forms-of-leadership/.

Organisation for Economic Co-operation and Development (OECD). 2015. Addressing the Tax Challenges of the Digital Economy, Action 1–2015 Final Report. OECD/G20 Base Erosion and Profit Shifting Project. https://doi.org/10.1787/9789264241046-en.

Otañez, A. 2017. Understanding the Impacts of the Fourth Industrial Revolution. *Shockoe: Mobile By Design.* https://shockoe.com/ideas/understanding-impacts-fourth-industrial-revolution/.

Ulrichs, M. 2016. Informality, Women and Social Protection: Identifying Barriers to Provide Effective Coverage. *ODI Working Paper.* No. 435. London: Overseas Development Institute.

United Nations Conference on Trade and Development (UNCTAD). 2020. UNCTAD Estimates of Global E-commerce in 2018. UNCTAD Technical Notes on ICT for Development. No. 15. Geneva.

van Dijk, J. 2006. Digital Divide Research, Achievements and Shortcomings. *Poetics.* 34 (4–5). pp. 221–235.

Measuring the Platform Economy: Concepts, Indicators, and Issues

Jose Ramon Albert[1]

2.1. Introduction

In recent decades, the rapid diffusion of digital technology into social and economic activities, known as "digitalization," has transformed national, regional, and global economies, including the nature of work.[2] Aside from the deluge of digital data, a major driver of digitalization is the increasing use of the internet. According to the International Telecommunications Union (ITU), as of the end of 2019, 53.6% of the global population, or 4.1 billion people, were using the internet, well up from 16.8% in 2005 (ITU 2019). However, past and current data also suggest a persisting digital divide that if unchecked can further exacerbate inequalities of opportunity and of outcome. The digital divide has undoubtedly contributed to the problems that arise from social and economic inequality and made managing the effects of the COVID-19 pandemic more challenging.

Alongside greater internet use and increased digitalization is the rise of the platform economy, i.e., a growing number of socioeconomic activities involving online intermediaries which provides a mechanism for customers and suppliers of goods and services to interact and transact (Kenney and Zysman 2016). Online platforms are becoming a primary mechanism in organizing a vast set of human activities. They may be viewed as online digital arrangements with algorithms organizing and structuring economic, sociocultural, and political activity.

---

[1] The author wishes to express his thanks to Jana Flor Vizmanos, research specialist at the Philippine Institute for Development Studies. Views expressed are those of the author and do not necessarily reflect the position of the Philippine Institute for Development Studies.

[2] This chapter was prepared as a background paper for ADB (2021) and draws from Albert (2020).

Platforms manifest in different forms, by purpose and size (OECD 2019). In the Philippines, where citizens are very active on social media, platforms such as Facebook, YouTube, Instagram, Google+, Twitter, Skype, Viber, LinkedIn, Pinterest, Snapchat, and WhatsApp are used by netizens to communicate with their social networks. Facebook, aside from enabling the sharing of digital media content, also offers a marketplace that competes with e-commerce platforms, of which, popular examples in the Philippines include Lazada, Shopee, and Zalora. Aside from these social media and e-commerce platforms, other popular online platforms in the Philippines include Google (search engine); Grab, Lalamove, and *Angkas* (for ride-sharing or logistics services); Netflix (for video streaming); Airbnb (accommodation services); CrowdFlowers and Microworkers (for crowdwork); and Zoom and Webex (for videoconferencing, online meetings, and group messaging).

The emergence of online or digital platforms is shifting competition toward platform-centric ecosystems in any economy. Platforms are providing new possibilities to consumers, businesses, and job seekers, enabling "innovative forms of production, consumption, collaboration and sharing through digital interactions" (OECD 2018,). The huge economic disruptions caused by the pandemic have spurred the use of these platforms. Some businesses also had an opportunity to get ahead of others that have not transformed digitally.

As of 2018, the total market size of companies in the global platform economy was estimated at $7.2 trillion (Dutch Transformation Forum 2018), up from an estimated $4.3 trillion 2 years earlier (Evans and Gawer 2016). About half (46%) of the platform companies with a value of at least $1 billion, are based in the United States (US), while a third (35%) are based in Asia—mostly in the People's Republic of China (PRC). These platform companies have a strong presence in four sectors: internet software and services, e-commerce and retail, social, and search. In recent years, however, platform companies have also shifted focus to a variety of other sectors. Platform companies are highly concentrated around seven superplatforms that each has a market value of over $250 billion: US-based Apple, Amazon, Microsoft, Google, Facebook, and PRC-based Alibaba and Tencent, which together have an aggregate market value of $4.9 trillion. This is 69% of the total market value of the 242 platform companies.

The importance of platforms in today's business environment is indicated by the fact that seven of the top eight companies across the world by market capitalization use platform-based business models (UNCTAD 2019).

The rise of platforms has brought about a host of positive economic outcomes. Platforms reduce inefficiencies in markets; create new markets; and bring more choice, products, and services to consumers (often at a lower cost), and flexible income to platform workers. Thus, platforms have driven up productivity through the highly efficient matching of buyers and sellers in e-commerce. Platforms also create a lot of social good. For example, eBay, Facebook, Instagram, and Google, together with leading animal welfare charities, have cooperated to reduce the black-market trade for prohibited products such as ivory and rhino horn (Bale 2018). Platforms are also causing major disruptions in doing business, however, profoundly changing all elements of the value chain, including product design, supply chain, manufacturing, and customer experience, while creating new business models. Meanwhile, during the pandemic, platforms such as Zoom, Webex, and Skype have provided venues for people to meet virtually. They have also become mechanisms for online learning.

But while these disruptions can lead to economic benefits, platforms can also raise concerns about fair competition, privacy issues, labor welfare, and taxation. Some platforms have also weakened social cohesion through social media "echo chambers" where fake news can spread easily. Thus, while creating new business models, platforms have also been disrupting the entire industries at scale, causing more vulnerability, uncertainty, complexity, and ambiguity (or collectively referred to as VUCA).[3]

This study aims to describe various concepts on the platform economy, based on an examination of past studies, and enriched by results of interviews with key informants. It proposes a framework toward measurement of the platform economy, describes key indicators from a household survey on internet use in the Philippines, and discusses policy implications. Research questions the study intends to answer include: (i) What exactly do we mean by the platform economy and related terminology, and what key indicators can be used to measure economic activities of online platforms? (ii) What are key drivers of value creation and capture in the platform economy? (iii) What policy responses can facilitate and stir value creation and capture, and ensure an inclusive transformation from the growth of the platform economy?

To answer these questions, the next section in this chapter depicts the context of the platform economy, i.e., digitalization. This section also discusses issues pertaining to measurements of the wider digital economy. The third

---

[3] See US Army Heritage and Education Center, http://usawc.libanswers.com/faq/84869.

section then describes challenges and solutions to measurements of the platform economy. The discussion also includes a definition and typology of platforms that identifies the main characteristics of digital platforms, a listing of requisite data and indicators for describing platforms, and possible data sources for the needed indicators. The fourth section provides a summary of key issues and policy implications.

2.2. Digitalization, the Digital Economy, and the Platform Economy

Undoubtedly, economies, nationally, regionally, and globally, are digitalizing: they are transforming under the influence of the internet and other information technologies (IMF 2018). The impact of this process depends on the speed of digitalization, while "megatrends" are evident in the growth of digital footprints that provide business intelligence and opportunities for addressing gaps in merely using traditional data sources (Albert and Martinez 2018, Martinez and Albert 2018). Further, internet use is growing over time and internet penetration varies across countries. In Asia and the Pacific, the ITU estimated the percentage of people using the internet in 2019 at slightly less than half (48.2%) of the region's population, a significant increase from about a tenth (9.7%) in 2015 (Figure 2.1). But this also reflects the digital divide: as half of people in the region are yet to use the internet. In the Philippines, ITU estimates internet penetration at 60.1%, as of 2017, even higher than the global and Asia and the Pacific averages, even though its internet penetration before 2011 was lower.

Global internet protocol traffic has also increased hugely, a proxy for data flows: from 100 gigabytes (GB) per second in 1992 to 46,600 GB per second in 2017. As reported by the United Nations Conference on Trade and Development (UNCTAD), global internet protocol traffic is projected to reach 150,700 GB per second by 2022 (UNCTAD 2019).

One of the main components of the platform economy is e-commerce. According to UNCTAD (2019), global e-commerce was valued at $29.4 trillion in 2017, with business-to-business (B2B) e-commerce representing 87% of the total. Of the $25.6 trillion B2B e-commerce in 2017, the US ($8.1 trillion) took the lion's share, followed by Japan ($2.8 trillion), Germany ($1.4 trillion), the Republic of Korea ($1.2 trillion), and the PRC ($0.9 trillion). In 2017, business-to-consumer (B2C) e-commerce sales that surpassed $100 billion were reported in

Figure 2.1: People Using the Internet, 2005–2018 (%)

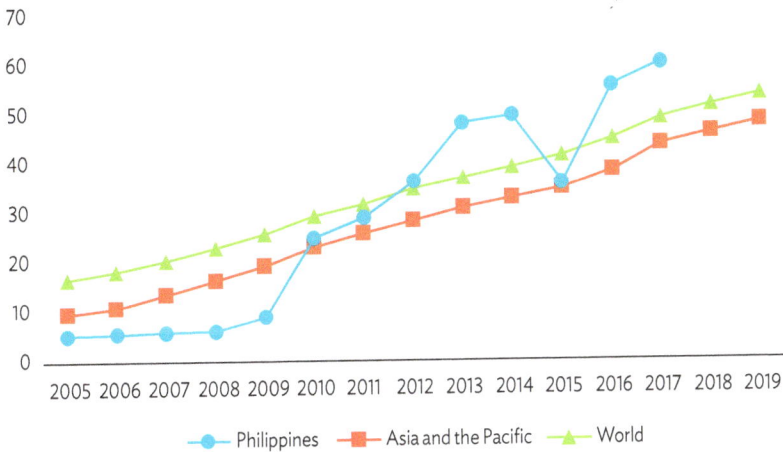

Note: Asia and the Pacific grouping is based on the definition of the source.
Source: International Telecommunications Union Statistics (accessed July 2020).

the PRC ($1.1 trillion), the US ($753 billion), the United Kingdom ($206 billion), and Japan ($147 billion). E-commerce also includes transactions through other platforms, such as those engaged in ride-hailing and accommodations-sharing.

UNCTAD also reports that a quarter of the global population aged 15 years and older, totaling about 1.3 billion people, shopped online in 2017, with the PRC having the largest number at 440 million (UNCTAD 2019). The growth of e-commerce and the platform economy is partly attributed to network effects, i.e., more users making the platform more valuable. Further, more users would mean more data: if the platform company knows how to leverage these data, it can improve its competitive advantage. Finally, given the traction, the platform can start offering different integrated services, making it more attractive to existing users and prospective customers. The WeChat platform and its payment solution WeChat Pay and Alipay of Alibaba, both based in the PRC, are excellent examples of the impact of network effects.

The e-commerce market, however, does not solely depend on the extent of internet users. There may be issues of trust about digital transactions in some societies, as suggested by the dominance of "cash is best" paradigms. In the Philippines, for instance, cash accounted for practically all local financial transactions as of 2018.[4] This may be why, before the pandemic, e-commerce had shallower roots in the country. According to Statista (2019), total digital revenues in the Philippines were $6.4 billion in 2019, but $4.5 billion was for online travel purchases. Across Asia, digital spending is 10.7% of per capita consumer expenditure, with the corresponding share in the Philippines at only 2.3%.

While the platform economy is growing fast, it is currently below the radar for most national statistics offices, including the Philippine Statistics Authority, because of the absence of a commonly accepted definition of the term "platform." Even the broader "digital economy" is not commonly measured by countries, likewise because definitions are lacking for "digital sector," also called the information technology or ICT sector.

According to UNCTAD, in its Digital Economy Report (UNCTAD 2019), the entire digital economy is less than 10% for most economies in recent years, whether measured by valued added or employment. The same report pointed out how definitions matter: estimates of the global digital economy can range from 4.5% of world GDP (using a narrow definition) to 15.5% of GDP (using a broad definition) based on 67 economies. Of these 67 economies, eight of the top 10 with the largest shares of ICT manufacturing gross value added as a percentage of GDP are in Asia and the Pacific, led by Taipei,China and followed by the Republic of Korea, Singapore, Malaysia, the Philippines, Thailand, the PRC, and Japan. From 2013 to 2015, ICT sector value added in the Philippines was estimated in the range of 3.2%–4.5% of GDP. Further, the ICT sector employment share was 1.0% as of 2015.

As of 2018, e-commerce was estimated in the Philippines at 9.5% of GDP (Digital Filipino and I-Metrics 2018). This figure is based on the e-Commerce Index, a supply-side estimation of e-commerce engagement of firms that participate in the Purchasing Managers Index, a composite of economic activities based on interviews of a randomly selected panel of supply chain executives from private sector companies.

The Hinrich Foundation (2019) estimates the value of digital trade-enabled benefits to the Philippines at ₱160 billion, or about $3.2 billion. Digital trade pertains to cross-border data flows, or the data exchange across

---

[4] Refer to Lucas (2018).

national jurisdictions that create economic value (Serafica and Albert 2018). While there is no universally accepted definition of digital trade, the concept of digital trade builds on the concept of e-commerce to include the latest digital innovations and a cross-border element. An emerging consensus on the scope of digital trade is that it includes all cross-border resident/nonresident transactions that are either digitally ordered, online platform enabled, and/or digitally delivered (Serafica and Albert 2018). If digital trade is fully leveraged in the Philippines, its value could grow by nearly 12 times to ₱1.9 trillion ($37 billion) by 2030. Further, digital exports are valued at ₱187 billion ($3.7 billion), representing 5.4% of the country's total export value, and are expected to grow to as much as ₱594 billion ($11.8 billion) by 2030. Currently, digital exports in the Philippines are largely driven by the Information Technology-Business Process Outsourcing (IT-BPO) firms.

In its latest e-conomy SEA 2019 report, Google, Temasek, and Bain & Company (2019) estimate that the internet economy, valued at $ 2.5 billion, contributes 2.1% of GDP in the Philippines, and has been growing between 20% and 30% annually since 2015. Compared to neighboring countries in the Association of Southeast Asian Nations (ASEAN), in the Philippines, the GDP penetration and growth of the internet economy during 2015–2019 was much lower (Figure 2.2), creating potential for higher impact.

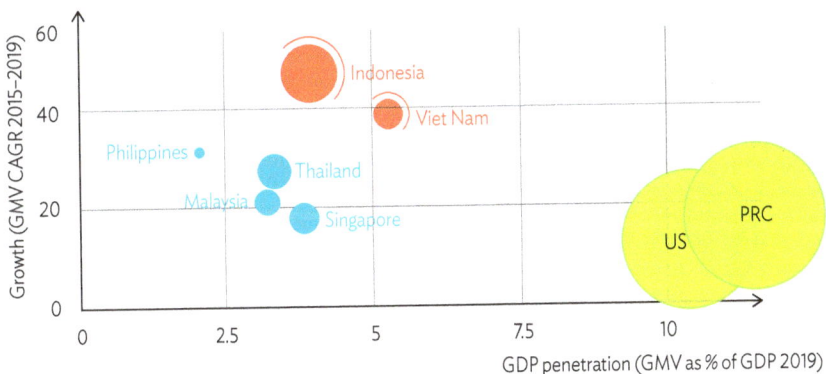

Figure 2.2: Growth in Internet Economy, 2015–2019 versus GDP Penetration (%), Select Southeast Asian Countries

CAGR = compounded annual growth rate, GDP = gross domestic product, GMV = gross merchandise value, PRC = People's Republic of China, US = United States.
Source: Google, Temasek and Bain & Company. (2019).

The Philippines' online media sector (advertising, gaming, subscription, music, and video on demand), grew a remarkable 42% per year from 2015 to 2019 (Google, Temasek, and Bain & Company 2019). Four other sectors—online travel (flights, hotels, vacation rentals); ride hailing (transport, food delivery); e-commerce; and digital financial services (payments, remittance, lending, investment, insurance)—comprise the internet economy in this report. Across Indonesia, Malaysia, the Philippines, Singapore, Thailand, and Viet Nam, the overall GDP penetration of the internet economy was 3.7%.

In all of Southeast Asia, the gross merchandise value of the internet economy was $100 billion in 2019, and was expected to triple by 2025 (Google, Temasek, and Bain & Company 2019). Half of Southeast Asia's 360 million internet users engage in the internet economy, which tripled from 1.3% of GDP in 2015 to 3.7% in 2019. Further, e-commerce and ride hailing across Southeast Asia have grown rapidly, with shifts in consumer behavior.

Varying estimates of the value of the internet economy (UNCTAD 2019; Hinrich Foundation 2019; Google, Temasek, and Bain & Company 2019; Digital Filipino and I-Metrics 2018) are due to differences in statistical frameworks, coverage, and data sources. The data ecosystem has expanded considerably beyond national statistical systems, especially in the wake of digital data (Albert et al. 2019). Data producers outside of government make use of various sources, from new surveys to *ad hoc* methods, such as web scraping of site usage to measure the economic performance of platforms, whether as part of the larger digital economy or a portion of the platform economy, such as the sharing economy. The direction and extent of bias in the use of these methods, however, is unknown and has not been specifically investigated.

The next section discusses how the platform economy can be measured comparably through a sound and robust statistical framework, especially as these measurements, when available, can help assess the impact that digitalization on countries and societies, and across countries. The chapter illustrates results in the Philippines using a household survey of internet use recently conducted by the Department of Information and Communications Technology, in cooperation with the Philippine Statistical Research and Training Institute.

2.3. Measuring the Platform Economy

The measurement of digital products and transactions, especially activities in platforms, should be tracked by governments to improve accuracy of economic and financial statistics, such as inflation, value added, employment, and productivity (IMF 2018). Measurements are helpful in designing policies and regulations to keep up with the rapid digitalization and its significant impact on wealth creation and inequality.

As noted, the platform economy is currently below the radar for most national statistics offices around the world. Again, this is primarily due to lacking definitions of "platform" or "digital economy." Further complications in the valuation of the platform economy include the wide variety of types of platforms, and the fact that many platforms offer parts of their services for free.

In 2016, the Organisation for Economic Co-operation and Development (OECD) surveyed national statistics offices about national accounts compilation practices; a year later, the International Monetary Fund (IMF) extended the OECD survey to national statistics offices of non-OECD countries. Results of both surveys suggested that the digital sector is hardly measured either because of data issues or the lack of resources to do so (IMF 2018). Malaysia's Department of Statistics was then considered an exception, as it was developing an ICT satellite account that included platforms. Last October 2019, the Philippines made public its plans to develop an ICT satellite account with the support of the World Bank (Ilarina, Polistico, and Pascacio 2019).

The digital economy can be viewed from three "scopes" (Figure 2.3). The core of the digital economy is the ICT sector, which produces foundational digital goods and services (e.g., IT and business process management services). Together with the ICT-producing sector, the emerging digital and platform services (e.g., Facebook and Google), constitute the digital economy in a narrow scope. The widest scope—use of ICT in all economic fields, such as automation, AI, and e-commerce as well as the sharing economy and the gig economy—is called the "digitalized economy" (ADB 2021).

Rather than defining the digital sector, an alternative approach is to examine digital transactions (Fortanier and Matei 2017). The OECD advisory expert groups on a digital economy satellite account in the national accounts and on digital trade in the balance of payments statistics take this approach. The conceptual framework identifies three mechanisms to classify digital

Figure 2.3: Three Scopes of Digital Economy

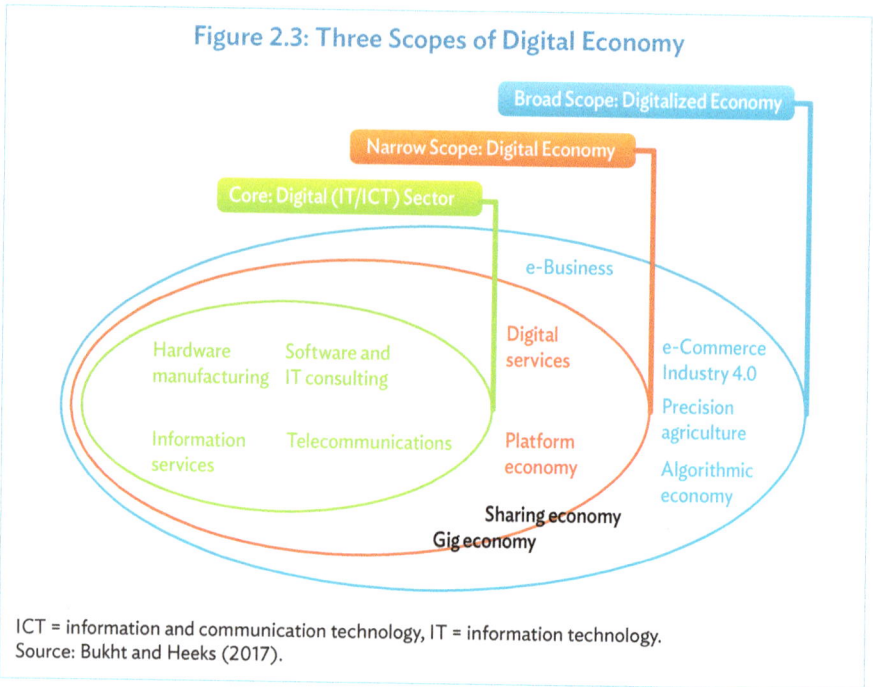

ICT = information and communication technology, IT = information technology.
Source: Bukht and Heeks (2017).

transactions: the nature of the transaction (how), the product (what), and the partners involved (who). Digital transactions can include those that are digitally ordered, digitally delivered, or platform-enabled, under one definition. This is related, though not equivalent, to the OECD (2011) definition of e-commerce, which emphasizes digitally ordered transactions. In this approach, a crucial issue is to obtain price data of digital products for estimating volume measures given the rapid quality changes of products.

UNCTAD (2019) estimates the digital economy using a definition suggested by Bukht and Heeks (2017), as the part of economic output derived from digital technologies with a business model based on digital goods and services. The same report points out that Hong Kong, China; Malaysia; and New Zealand are currently the only economies in Asia and the Pacific, and among 10 economies globally, that compile data on the digital sector through ICT satellite accounts or through aggregation of the appropriate International Standard Industrial Classification (ISIC) codes.

Frequently, the platform economy and the broader digitalized economy are not distinguishable, with the latter including the sharing and gig economies (Bukht and Heeks 2017). The sharing economy, which is a part of the platform economy, can have a narrow or a broad scope. By narrow, it refers only to the supply of underutilized assets; by broad, open labor and financial platforms are included (Figure 2.4). These terms can cover an entire spectrum, with varying degrees. Nonetheless, we can identify characteristics of platforms and, from which, define these terms as well as look into various typologies toward a measurement scheme.

Defining Platforms

In measuring the platform economy, the first step is to define platforms. The literature provides various, interrelated definitions of a platform (Box 2.1). This chapter defines a platform as a digital intermediary and infrastructure that brings together parties through the internet to interact, matching supply and demand in a multisided market. In short, platforms are digital matchmakers in the sense that they provide an avenue for consumers and

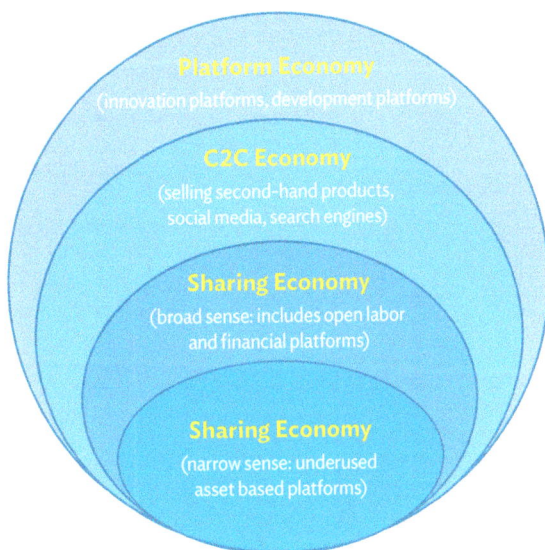

Figure 2.4: Senses of the Platform Economy

C2C = customer-to-customer.
Source: Heerschap, Pouw, and Atmé (2018).

Box 2.1: Definitions of Platform

Source	Definition
OECD 2019	Digital services that facilitate interactions between two or more distinct but interdependent sets of users (whether firms or individuals) who interact through the service via the internet
World Economic Forum (WEF 2017)	Technology-enabled business models that create value by facilitating exchanges and interactions.
Heerschap, Pouw, and Atmé 2018	A digital service based on technological, sociocultural, and economic infrastructure for facilitation and organization of online social (interactions) and economic (transactions) traffic between two or more distinct but interdependent groups of providers and users, with data as fuel (Van Dijck, Poell, and De Waal 2016, p. 11; OECD 2018, p. 13). Providers and users can be individuals and businesses as well as science organizations and government.
Langley and Leyshon 2017	A distinct mode of socio-technical intermediary and business arrangement that is incorporated into wider processes of capitalization.
	Intermediaries between two or more groups of participants with interdependent demands .. (with a) ... main market function .. typically described as the facilitation of interactions and transactions between producers of goods on one side and buyers or users on the other.
Tan et al. 2015	A commercial network of suppliers, producers, intermediaries, customers . . .and producers of complementary products and services termed "complementors" . . . that are held together through formal contracting and/or mutual dependency.
Kenney and Zysman 2016	A set of online digital arrangements whose algorithms serve to organize and structure economic and social activity; a set of shared techniques, technologies, and interfaces that are open to a broad set of users who can build what they want on a stable substrate; a set of digital frameworks for social and marketplace interactions.
	Catalyst that allows value to be created through interactions between various groups of market participants.
Koh and Fichman 2014	Two-sided networks . . . that facilitate interactions between distinct but interdependent groups of users, such as buyers and suppliers.
Pagani 2013	Multisided platform . . . exists wherever a company brings together two or more distinct groups of customers (sides) that need each other in some way, and where the company builds an infrastructure (platform) that creates value by reducing distribution, transaction, and search costs incurred when these groups interact with one another.

OECD = Organisation for Economic Co-operation and Development.
Source: Author.

suppliers of products and services to perform economic activities, including information exchange, demand matching, payment, and receipt and delivery of goods and services. Platforms not only match providers and users, but also facilitate likely transactions resulting from interactions; they differ in their role and the "products" they "exchange."

A platform has two functional layers: interactions and infrastructure. Platforms play a catalytic role for value creation in the interactions of various groups of market participants, leading to the exchange of information, trading, logistics, and other facilities to consumers from service providers. Two-sided platforms, such as ride-hailing platforms, enable two diverse types of participants to more readily engage in trade or some other interaction (Evans and Schmalensee 2007). Multisided platforms consist of more than two sets of participants (Evans 2018). Social media platforms such as Facebook, LinkedIn, and YouTube connect platform users to share various content (e.g., ideas, news, photos, and videos), as well as advertisers and content developers.

A platform essentially acts as a mediator of peer-to-peer services, empowering participants to transact goods, services, or even data. The kind of digital infrastructure in a platform increases the ease and speed of interactions of platform users, changes the scope of possible transactions from local to global, enlarges the choices of platform users, and lowers transaction costs for users to find each other and interact (Heerschap, Pouw, and Atmé 2018). While platform firms do not, by themselves, own the means of production, they establish a mechanism to connect suppliers and consumers of goods, services, and data (ADB 2021).

The platforms also proved beneficial to their respective users, enabling people, usually consumers, to become suppliers. With the rise of platforms, individuals have now become suppliers of services (as Grab drivers), food and accommodation industries (specifically in GrabFood and Airbnb, respectively), and culture and recreational industries (as individuals earning income from uploading vlogs and music or uploading content that influences other users onto social media platforms such as YouTube and Instagram) (ADB 2021).

Platforms have also managed to create jobs, such as drivers of ride-hailing platforms and riders of food delivery platforms, and cleaners. While these jobs may be new, matching workers to jobs on platforms is novel, including payment schemes (ADB 2021, Albert 2020). CrowdFlowers, Microworkers, and other digital labor or crowdwork platforms have facilitated the connection of employers with workers who may be spread across the world for the conduct of either microwork that requires low-level skills, or macrowork that involves complex tasks requiring particular skillsets (ILO 2018). These platforms may have helped people perform other kinds of jobs during the pandemic. Further, work engaged through platforms allows people to engage in gig work. Platform-mediated online jobs, however, may also just be retrofitting traditional issues of labor exploitation in a new form, and creating more precarious situations for workers (Chen 2019; Liu 2019). A report by JPMorgan Chase & Co. suggests that in the case of drivers for ride-sharing apps, driving is not a full-time job. Meanwhile, even if the number of drivers for platforms has risen rapidly, their average monthly earnings have also declined (Farrell, Greig, and Hamoudi 2018).

Value creation in platforms is driven by underlying technologies and infrastructure: cloud, social networks, and mobile. The cloud enables global infrastructure, allowing platforms to create content and applications for a global set of actors. Social networks connect people and allow them to maintain an online identity. Mobile allows interconnections anywhere, anytime.

Network effects distinguish platforms from other business models and are one of the main drivers of value creation in the platform economy (Evans 2016). The more people use a platform, the more attractive the platform becomes to potential new users, triggering a self-reinforcing feedback loop of growth for value creation. Network effects may either be direct or indirect (ADB 2021).

The market model behind platforms is not new. Even in ancient times, bazaars brought together retail merchants and buyers. In modern times, classified advertisements have linked advertisers to consumers. The difference of bazaars and classified ads from platforms is that the latter are (i) leveraging technology and interconnectivity, along with the power of digital data and data analytics; (ii) linking user groups; and (iii) allowing these groups to interact (Koskinen, Bonina, and Eaton 2019).

A key characteristic of the matching of supply and demand in platforms involves multisided relations built on trust. As Heerschap, Pouw, and Atmé (2018) point out, the relationships among actors in a platform can be identified as B2B, B2C, and customer-to-customer (C2C) (also called peer-to-peer), etc. (Table 2.1). But over time, the distinction between C2C and B2C transactions in platforms has become more and more vague. Booking, which was initially a B2C platform, has also been offering C2C accommodation services.

Table 2.1: Possible Relations between Actors in Platforms

Item		Buyer or Client			
		Consumer	Business	Government	Science
Seller or Provider	Consumer	C2C	C2B	C2G	C2S
	Business	B2C	B2B	B2G	B2S
	Government	G2C	G2B	G2G	G2S
	Science	S2C	S2B	S2G	S2S

B2B = business-to-business, B2C = business-to-customer, B2G = business-to-government,
B2S = business-to-science, C2C = customer-to-customer, C2B = customer-to-business,
C2G = customer-to-government, C2S = customer-to-science, G2B = government-to-business,
G2C = government-to-customer, G2G = government-to-government, G2S = government-to-science,
S2B = science-to-business, S2C = science-to-customer, S2G = science-to-government,
S2S = science-to-science.
Source: Author.

Multisided matching of supply and demand involves individual consumers and businesses, as well as governments and science. Each of these actors can be sellers (or providers of products or services) and buyers (or platform clients). In the strict sense of the word, a buyer in a platform need not always be a consumer. Consider a business, government agency, or person maintaining a profile on Facebook, Twitter, or another social media platform as a way to interact with the public. These platform actors are not necessarily buyers but merely users or clients of the platform.

The platform ecosystem always has at least three varied but interdependent actors: (i) sellers, (ii) buyers, and (iii) the platform itself. The platform sellers offer goods (e.g., Shopee and Lazada), services (e.g., MyKuya, Grab, YouTube, and Netflix) and/or information (e.g., Google and Facebook) to potential buyers. These products and services can be delivered either physically or digitally. Platform sellers receive data from the platform of their buyers. On the other hand, potential buyers search the platform for goods, services and/or information, and receive data from the platform about sellers. The platforms themselves are another actor in the ecosystem. The platform can have other roles, such as processing payments between buyers and sellers, and even taking charge of distribution of the product to the client. Advertisers constitute a fourth set of actors. On video-sharing platforms such as YouTube, advertisers subsidize the value of the attention provided by demand-side participants (viewers) for supply-side participants (uploaders).

The matching process can be transparent, e.g., initiated by the user, although it is often nontransparent (using algorithms involving governance rules for the matching). These algorithms are used for matching or ranking of search results, for setting prices, and for matching users with advertisements. Together with the ecosystems of participants, this distributed network of people is the social infrastructure of platforms.

Aside from the matching, transaction, and governance, other process elements of platforms include payment systems and ratings of users, as well as after-sales and support including complaints and their resolution (Figure 2.5). The matching and transaction processes in platforms are typically based on a user-driven trust mechanism that includes reviews and rating systems. Often, the providers are reviewed and evaluated, but sometimes users are as well.

Some platforms are characterized by switching costs. That is, users cannot easily transfer to other platforms. For instance, on Facebook, when users invest time and energy setting up their accounts; connecting with a community of friends and followers; and uploading content including posts, photos, and videos, this discourages them from switching to another platform, despite ethical scandals about Cambridge Analytica, or other social experiments on Facebook undertaken without their consent. When such are tied to an entire ecosystem of linked platforms, users may be even less willing to switch to another platform. Competition in platforms can be stifled when the market positions of platform giants are highly entrenched by positive network effects, economies of scale, and scope, especially switching costs (ADB 2021).

Figure 2.5: Process Elements of Platforms

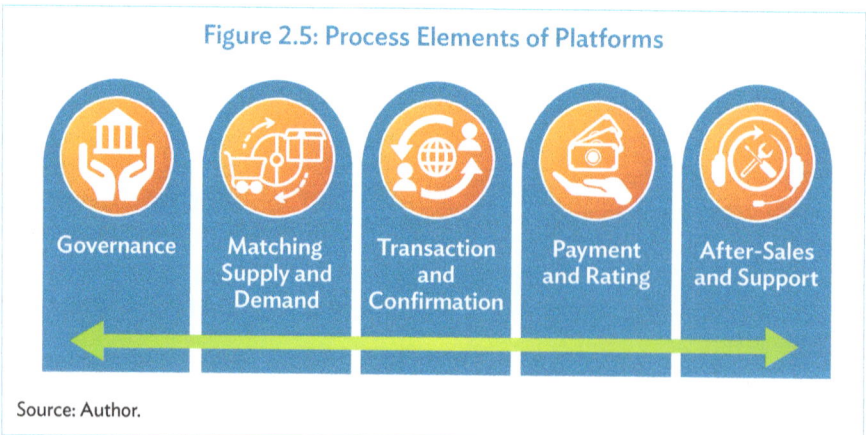

Governance | Matching Supply and Demand | Transaction and Confirmation | Payment and Rating | After-Sales and Support

Source: Author.

Relationships and transactions of platform users need not always be bi- or multidirectional. In the case of advertisers in a video-streaming platform, for instance, the interaction between the advertiser and users can occur in only one direction. Advertisers can reach users, but there is often no feedback from the user to the advertiser, and even when there is, it takes place outside the platform.

Sometimes the user turnover in the platform is generated by investors or the inclusion of extra services, such as insurance, logistic services, or cancellation fees. To attract more users, it is sometimes taken for granted that some platforms (e.g., Google and Facebook) provide free services. This kind of free use is an incentive to reinforce the participation of users and value creation within the platform.

Platforms can also have either a local or global reach. They can potentially reach clients from across the world, especially if the platforms offer goods or services that can be provided digitally, such as data, video, books, and music. Since it can scale without mass, a platform can grow quickly and efficiently to meet the demand that clients generate.

Platform-enabled companies, like other firms, generate data. The difference lies in the amount of digital data being collected from platform users, and the analytics that can be employed on these big data. Aside from the infrastructure of the platform and network effects, data is also another determinant of value creation. A platform utilizes user-generated data to match providers and clients (for example, by ranking providers or search results), set prices, and target users with advertisements. Platforms can use vast amounts of data, including user behavior data, to build detailed profiles of their providers and clients, and such processed data can even be sold as commodities. Classified ads can be customized with such data by inferring the moods, desires, and even fears of platform users through their app data, and even the rhythm of keyboard typing on the platform. While this can allow platforms to have better client relationship management, it can also intrude on privacy. Thus, the data collected on a platform are valuable.

Several platforms have also been disruptive, strongly challenging the traditional business models. Platform-enabled companies have significantly reduced the market shares of erstwhile dominant firms in some cases. Sharing platforms, in particular, leverage technology by matching excess capacity in private durable goods with demand, without transfer of ownership.

"Alibaba, the world's most valuable retailer, actually has no inventory. Uber, the world's largest taxi company, does not own any vehicle, while Airbnb, the world's largest accommodation provider, owns no real estate." (Goodwin 2015)

Since platforms do not incur costs of production, platform firms can scale faster and at much lower cost than traditional firms (World Bank 2019). Take, for example, Alibaba, the Chinese platform giant which specializes in e-commerce, retail, internet, and technology. This platform firm has gained 1 million users in merely 2 years and has more than 9 million online merchants and garnered annual sales of as much as $700 billion in 15 years. In contrast, IKEA, the Swedish multinational homewares firm, generated global annual sales of $42 billion in more than 7 decades of its existence (ADB 2021).

Platforms are either profit- or nonprofit-oriented. If access and use of the platform is not free-of-charge, providers and/or users pay commissions to the platform to be able to access and conduct transactions on the platform (Heerschap, Pouw, and Atmé 2018). Some video-streaming platforms may offer free access but provide top-up services for access to premium services. Finally, if a transaction between a provider and a client is completed on the platform, the buyer pays the seller if the transaction is not free. Platforms nearly always have electronic ordering, and usually the goods and services advertised on platforms can only be purchased digitally. Occasionally, the platform provides digital wallet and payment services to facilitate transactions. For instance, retail platform Shopee partnered with AirPay Technology, an electronic money issuer, and offers ShopeePay (in-app digital wallet) to clients for them to digitally pay for transactions.

Typology of Platforms

Platforms can be categorized either in specific or broad terms based on several criteria (OECD 2019; Heerschap, Pouw, and Atmé 2018). These typologies can help facilitate focused profiles that provide insights on the business environment. Typologies of platforms can also give policy makers an understanding of the traits of platforms, their similarities and differences, that can serve as inputs to policy formulation. A natural way to classify platforms is by functionality, i.e., according to what the platforms do or how they do it. Such an approach could involve a few broad categories or a large number of narrow categories.

The Center for Global Enterprise (Evans and Gawer 2016) groups platforms into four mutually exclusive types using a functional base. These groups include:

i. Transaction platforms which link parties (for example, drivers and passengers in Grab and Uber) more easily on the internet and through platform infrastructure, thus reducing costs and possible conflict in the transaction process. Nearly all platform companies (from social media platforms, to marketplaces, and those on media, music, money, financial technology, and gaming) are reported to fall into the transaction platform type. Further, most of the biggest digital platforms in the global "South" are transaction platforms, and this yields both positive and negative impacts on local institutional settings.

ii. Innovation platforms (such as Apple's iOS and Google's Android operating systems for mobile devices). These are technological building blocks, i.e., they supply technological infrastructure as the basis for third-party developers (Heerschap, Pouw, and Atmé 2018) to foster other services or products (such as apps for the iPhone and Android smartphones).

iii. Integration platforms which have characteristics of both transaction and innovation platforms. Further, they are more distinctive than the other platforms, because companies such as Google, Apple, Facebook, Alibaba, and Amazon have manufacturing supply chains.

iv. Investment platforms which includes companies that are not platforms per se (Heerschap, Pouw, and Atmé 2018). Instead they invest in platform companies or act as a holding company. These companies have clear investment approaches and provide investors "the back-end infrastructure and the front-end user experience." One example is Rocket Internet, which sets out to build a portfolio for companies in "undeserved" markets through regional domestic investment groups.

Platforms can also be divided broadly and functionally into

i. "those that are set up purely to act as intermediaries, matching buyers and sellers, where typically one or other pays an intermediation fee" (Ahmad and Ribarsky 2018); and

ii. those that are set up as electronic retailers, or e-tailers, who own the products being sold.

This distinction is important since, in national accounts, how transaction flows are recorded necessarily differs. In the case of e-tailers, products are sold through their platform, on which a distribution margin is applied and paid by the final buyer. For an accommodations or transportation platform in the sharing economy (such as Airbnb and Grab, respectively), the "platform does not take ownership of any of the goods or services, it merely provides a matching service charging commission fees" (Ahmad and Ribarsky 2018) that may be implicitly or explicitly stated on the invoice. Often, both the buyer and the seller pay these matching fees.

Typologies of platforms may also be based on the users that platforms have, the kinds of data they collect, and the strategies for platform participation. Another broad approach that uses a structural rather than functional base, but that does not suffer from problems of hybrids, is to separate platforms into three groups according to their overall scope and structure: (i) superplatforms, (ii) platform constellations, and (iii) stand-alone platforms (OECD 2019). The first group is a platform of platforms (such as WeChat and Facebook), with users entering through a single portal (either a website or an app); superplatforms contain many individual platforms. On the other hand, platform constellations (such as Google's main platforms) are collections of several platforms that are offered under one brand umbrella, co-existing in parallel and closely connected to one another. Unlike superplatforms, platform constellations can all be accessed separately without having to go through a single portal.

Platforms can also be classified by profit motive. In order "to attract more users, it is sometimes taken for granted that no profit is made" (Heerschap, Pouw, and Atmé 2018) for some platforms, especially at inception. Heerschap, Pouw, and Atmé (2018) add that "part of the use of the platform by users can be for free" and this is "an incentive to reinforce the participation and value creation of the platform." Sometimes the turnover is generated by investors or the inclusion of extra services, such as insurance, logistic services, or cancellation fees. According to Van Gorp and Batura (2015), for-profit platforms often use several revenue approaches:

i. subscriptions where end users pay for the provision of a service (like Netflix or Spotify);

ii. advertisements where end users access free services within the platform and this access is sustained by advertising revenue (examples include YouTube or Facebook); and

ii. an access model where content or app developers pay platforms to reach end users (such as iPhone or Android app stores).

Platforms, however, may derive revenues from multiple sources. Thus, this typology cannot also be expected to produce clear-cut mutually exclusive categories.

OECD (2019) provides another example of a broad functional typology of platforms that classifies platforms into

i. "capital platforms" (e.g., Airbnb which relies on matching capital owners with clients who rent the accommodations); and

ii. online labor platforms (such as CrowdFlowers and Microworkers that match workers with employers).

As in the case of the platform typology espoused by Gawer (2015), this typology has for its major limitation the existence of hybrid platforms. Transportation platforms such as Grab match drivers as well as cars with passengers, and thus fall into both capital platforms and online labor platforms.

OECD (2019) points out that broad functional typologies may not be useful on their own, but can be useful together with other approaches. The typology of Evans and Gawer (2016), which categorizes platforms into transaction, innovation, and investment, could, for instance, be seen as using criteria on product and services. Two other examples are the two sets of typologies (Codagnone et al. 2016), each involving two criteria. The first set uses profit orientation and interaction modality, while the second set is based on interaction modality and asset mix. "Profit orientation varies from not-for-profit to for-profit; interaction modality varies from organization-centered/led to peer-to-peer centered/led; and asset mix varies from capital to labor" (Heerschap, Pouw, and Atmé 2018). They provide examples to illustrate that platforms are in a continuum underlying the categories, rather than falling neatly into mutually exclusive types, and that some platforms are hybrids under both typologies.

A narrower functional typology could also be used to eliminate certain subcategories of platforms within broader groups in order to come up with a typology suitable for policy or business use. For instance, Platform Hunt (2016) suggests nine types of platforms: innovation platforms were broken down into (i) technology platforms and (ii) computing platforms; search engines were called (iii) utility platforms; social media platforms were categorized into (iv) interaction networks and (v) content crowdsourcing platforms; transaction platforms into (vi) marketplaces and (vii) on-demand service platforms; and other platforms were grouped into (viii) data-harvesting platforms and (ix) content distribution platforms.

Another example of narrow functional type of typologies is that given by OECD (2019), which groups platforms into: (i) ad-supported messaging platforms (WeChat, Facebook Messenger); (ii) app stores (Amazon Appstore for Android, Apple App Store, Google Play); (iii) C2Cs (MercadoLibre Marketplace, Taobao); (iv) labor freelancing/crowdsourcing (Freelancer, Mechanical Turk); (v) long-distance carpooling (BlaBlaCar); (vi) mobile payments (WeChat Pay, Alipay); (vii) search advertising (Baidu, Google); (viii) short-term accommodation (Airbnb); (ix) social media (Facebook, WeChat, YouTube); (x) superplatforms (WeChat, QQ); (xi) third-party B2Bs (e.g., Alibaba, Amazon Business); and (xii) third-party B2Cs (Amazon Marketplace, MercadoLibre Classifieds, Rakuten, Tmall).

Whether broad or narrow functional typologies are used, it will be challenging to have categories that do not overlap, since some platforms, especially superplatforms, have features across several categories. Functional typologies are also easily outdated as platforms evolve, thus requiring typologies to be regularly revisited for these to be relevant (ADB 2021).

Indicators and Measurements

In practice, the definition, features, and typologies of platforms entail a number of statistical challenges. Measurement of the platform economy in each country can be extremely challenging, beyond the absence of a common definition of what is meant by a platform. First, platforms may also not be physically located in a country concerned, thus their economic transactions are not actually directly part of national economic statistics. Given the possible cross-border scope of transactions in platforms, developing a complete list of platforms in a country can be challenging. Even if this could be done, gathering data from foreign-based platform companies may not be feasible, unless they are forced by laws in a country to set up a local branch or office.

Furthermore, "there is no specific economic activity code for platforms" (Heerschap, Pouw, and Atmé 2018). If platform companies are part of the business register or the census of business and industry in a country, Heerschap, Pouw, and Atmé (2018) note that "they will often not be included in the industry in which they are active, but rather in other industries." The authors also opine that "there is a growing tendency for horizontal and vertical integration of activities of platforms," which can be cross-sectoral, i.e., platforms could be active in several sectors. For example, Amazon, which used to sell only pre-owned music and books, now sells all kinds of products. The social media platform WeChat adds other services and functions to support its social media activities, including transportation services, marketplace activities, and payment options. "These types of combined [economic] activities of platforms usually do not fit well with the current classifications of official statistics" (Heerschap, Pouw, and Atmé 2018).

Platform companies are likely to be included in ICT or trade, but platforms are cross-sectoral and thus, they do not straightforwardly fit into official classification systems such as industrial classification codes. For instance, while the Philippine Standard Industrial Classification includes a sub-class class code [47913] for "retail sale via internet" within Wholesale and Retail Trade; Repair of Motor Vehicles and Motorcycles [Section G], there is no comparable sub-class code for platforms beneath specific services sectors (PSA n.d.). The classification is consistent with the ISIC of All Economic Activities Revision 4 (UN 2009), which recognizes e-commerce, i.e., "ownership of the goods or service through the Internet or by other electronic means," but not economic activities related to sharing of goods or services in ride-sharing or accommodations-sharing platforms.

Another measurement challenge is that transactions are not always financial. In social media platforms, for instance, transactions involve exchange of data and information, and thus, the valuation of such transactions can be quite challenging. Economic variables such as revenue and employment can also often be difficult to trace, since platforms spread supply across small-scale nonprofessional providers. Earnings and employment of these platforms may be underestimated in traditional business surveys and labor force surveys conducted by national statistics offices. Many digital platforms also do not publish their accounts or disaggregate these data across country boundaries.

Heerschap, Pouw, and Atmé (2018) posit that the "increase of international trade through platforms is difficult to visualize through traditional [economic] statistics, [especially] the national accounts [and] many platforms and providers are not [physically] located in the country concerned, therefore their economic transactions are not directly part of national statistics."

Despite all the challenges in measuring the platform economy, some national statistics offices, e.g., Statistics Canada (2017), the United Kingdom's Office for National Statistics (ONS 2017), and Eurostat (2018), have begun measurements given the growing importance of the platform economy. Many of these undertakings have focused on the sharing economy, which narrows platforms down to mostly C2C relations and transactions. Again as noted, in sharing platforms, transactions do not have transfer of ownership. Eurostat (2018) only considers sharing and lending of assets, such as homes, cars, etc., as part of the sharing economy. In other words, the gig economy, which provides supply of labor for small jobs, as well as crowdfunding platforms, are not part of the sharing economy in the Eurostat approach, but are separate categories of the C2C economy.

UNCTAD (2019) provides a conceptual framework for measuring the digital economy that uses national accounts prisms on products, production, and the nature of the transactions. This framework can also identify cases that need to be addressed for platform economy measurement within the scope of classification, output, and price measurement of services. As Barrera et al. (2018) point out, for the most part, the goods and services on platforms are not new but rather only transacted and delivered in new ways, and thus most of the relevant transactions in the digital economy, and the platform economy, in particular, are within the System of National Accounts production boundary (Table 2.2). That is, measuring the broader digital economy and the platform economy, in particular, through the national accounts is straightforward. Making use of a satellite account within the national accounts ensures that estimates of resulting indicators of the platform economy, when applied across countries, are comparable given the consistency in definitions, concepts, and classifications. This also recognizes conceptually the role of the enablers for the functioning of the platform economy, from technology to network effects to digital data.

Beyond a conceptual framework, a statistical framework requires "institutional arrangements—legislative, budgetary, organizational, collaborative and coordinative, managerial and customer relationship arrangements—to support the environment for integration of data compiled from various sources" (UN 2017). Further, the conceptual framework should be operationalized through "the statistical production process as an integrated production chain from the collection of basic data to the dissemination and communication of resulting statistics" (UN 2013). After identifying required data and their sources, the estimation would involve: (i) deciding on a conceptual definition of the platform economy; (ii) identifying the goods and services within the supply-use framework relevant for measuring the platform economy; (iii) identifying the industries responsible for producing these goods and services; and (iv) estimating the output, value added, employment, compensation, and other variables associated with socioeconomic activities of platforms (World Bank 2020).

The challenge in measurement is largely that the nature of digital goods and services are changing rapidly. New products such as digital intermediation services should be added to classification systems and properly recorded. An added complexity is the strong possibility that these transactions often include a cross-border component, and thus, such transactions should be unbundled into their separate flows (Loranger, Sinclair, and Tebrake 2018).

National statistics offices should revise their classification systems and update other statistical infrastructure more frequently to be able to adequately capture these rapid changes, otherwise key official economic statistics may not suitably describe the economy.

Further, despite the seeming suitability of using current conceptual frameworks on national accounts to estimate the platform economy, there is valid criticism that GDP does not properly account for the benefits obtained from free goods arising as a result of digitalization. Activities related to free data and knowledge are not in the production boundary of national accounts. Further, current increased production from households is not operationally accounted for, as households have always been considered only from the expenditure side. Yet, there is growing evidence that household production and income have been increasing recently on account of the platform economy.

Table 2.2: Platform Economy Cases by Type of Industry, Product, and Transaction

Case	Examples	SNA Production Boundary		Type of Industry			Transaction			Product		
		within	outside	non-digital	digital enabling platform	digital platform	digitally delivered	digitally ordered	platform enabled	non-digital services	digital services	digital information/data
1	**Non-digital services intermediated by platforms (C2C)**											
1.1	Sharing economy services (C2C transactions) intermediated via platforms	X		X				X	X	X		
1.2	Digital intermediation services for the sharing economy	X				X	X	X			X	
2	**Non-digital services intermediated by digital platforms (B2All*)**											
2.1.1	Non-digital service ordered online	X		X				X		X		

Table 2.2 continued

Case	Examples	SNA Production Boundary		Type of Industry			Transaction			Product		
		within	outside	non-digital	digital enabling	digital platform	digitally delivered	digitally ordered	platform enabled	non-digital services	digital services	digital information/data
2.1.2	Air transport/accommodation, ordered via intermediary platform	X		X				X	X	X		
2.2	Digital intermediation for corporate non-digital services	X				X	X	X			X	
	Booking, Hotels.com											
3	**Online product sales**											
3.1	Online retailers	X				X	(X)	X			X	
	Shopee, Lazada, Amazon											
3.2	Online sales by storefront retailers	X		X				X		X		
	Department stores selling a portion of their merchandise via own website											
4	**ICT Service Sector****											
4.1	ICT services: Data processing, hosting, and related activities; web portals	X			X		X			X		
	Data platforms: Google, Facebook											

continued on next page

Table 2.2 *continued*

Case	Examples	SNA Production Boundary		Type of Industry			Transaction			Product		
		within	outside	non-digital	digital enabling	digital platform	digitally delivered	digitally ordered	platform enabled	non-digital services	digital services	digital information/data
5	**Digitally delivered content and media**											
5.1	Paid	For a fee: Netflix, Spotify, eBooks	X				X	X	X			X	
5.2	Free	For free-collaborative: Wikipedia, Reddit		X		X		X	X			X	X

Note: row 5.1 "For a fee: Netflix, Spotify, eBooks" aligns as — within: X; digital platform: X; digitally delivered: X; digitally ordered: X; digital services: X.

Note: row 5.2 "For free-collaborative: Wikipedia, Reddit" aligns as — outside: X; digital enabling: X; digitally delivered: X; digitally ordered: X; digital services: X; digital information/data: X.

B2B = business-to-business, B2C = business-to-customer, B2G = business-to-government, B2S = business-to-science, C2C = customer-to-customer, ICT = information and communication technology, SNA = System of National Accounts.

* B2All includes B2B, B2C, B2G, and B2S.

** Other cases in the ICT service sector are part of the wider digital economy but not part of the platform economy.

Note: The framework is based on Barrera et al. (2018).

Source: Author and Barrera et al. (2018).

Although the economic activities of platforms are partly taken into account in the national accounts (Table 2.3), it is crucial to make a distinction between market and nonmarket transactions. In the latter, for example, trading of second-hand goods is not part of the valuation in national accounts (ADB 2021).

Working within the national accounts conceptual and statistical frameworks for measuring the platform economy can pose a limitation as traditional economic statistics from the national accounts do not always allow for gender, age, and other relevant disaggregated data to examine how various groups in society are affected by platforms and the emerging digitalization. Data constraints also limit the operationalization of a conceptual framework for any satellite account.

According to the Dutch Transformation Forum (2018), the total market size of companies in the global platform economy was $7.2 trillion in 2018, up from an estimated $4.3 trillion in 2016 (Evans and Gawer 2016). The 2018 estimate was based on a survey of 242 platform companies, while the 2016 estimate was based on 176 platform companies. The digital platform companies in 2018 were dominated by the US and the PRC: 72% of total market value were platforms based in the US, while 25% were from the PRC.

For a meaningful profile of platforms in a country, data from the actors on the platform are needed: providers, users, and the platforms themselves (Box 2.2). In other words, surveys have to be undertaken for these three different groups.

Table 2.3: Providers and Clients of Platforms

Case	Examples	Providers or Sellers/Producers (institutional sector)					Clients or Buyers/Users (institutional sector)				
		Corporations	Household	Government	NPISH*	RoW**	Corporations	Household	Government	NPISH	RoW
1	**Non-digital services intermediated by platforms (C2C)**										
1.1	Sharing economy services (C2C transactions) intermediated via platforms		X					X			
1.2	Digital intermediation services for the sharing economy	Food delivery and logistics services on GrabFood and Lalamove	X				X		X			
2	**Non-digital services intermediated by digital platforms (B2AII*)**										
2.1.1	Non-digital service ordered online	Air transport/ accommodation, ordered via airline/hotel own website	X					X		X	X	X
2.1.2		Air transport/ accommodation, ordered via intermediary platform	X					X		X	X	X
2.2	Digital intermediation for corporate non-digital services	Booking, Hotels.com	X					X	X	X	X	X

Table 2.3 *continued*

Case		Examples	Providers or Sellers/Producers (institutional sector)					Clients or Buyers/Users (institutional sector)				
			Corporations	Household	Government	NPISH*	RoW**	Corporations	Household	Government	NPISH	RoW
3	Online product sales											
3.1	Online retailers	Shopee, Lazada, Amazon	X					X	X	X	X	X
3.2	Online sales by storefront retailers	Department stores selling a portion of their sales via own website	X					X	X			
4	ICT service sector**											
4.1	ICT Services: Data processing, hosting, and related activities; web portals	Data platforms: Google, Facebook	X					X	X	X	X	X
5	Digitally delivered content and media											
5.1	Paid	For a fee: Netflix, Spotify, eBooks	X				X		X			X
5.2	Free	For free-collaborative: Wikipedia, Reddit	X	X	X	X	X	X	X	X	X	X

B2B = business-to-business, B2C = business-to-customer, B2G = business-to-government, B2S = business-to-science, C2C = customer-to-customer, ICT = information and communication technology, NPISH = nonprofit institutions serving households, RoW = rest of the world.

* B2All includes B2B, B2C, B2G, and B2S.

** Other cases in the ICT service sector are part of the wider digital economy but not part of the platform economy.

Note: The framework is based on Barrera et al. (2018).

Source: Author and Barrera et al. (2018).

Box 2.2: Data and Indicators Needed for Measuring the Platform Economy

Dimension	Data	Indicators
General Information on Platforms	■ Business name, registered name, and address of platform owner (including headquarters/main office and parent company, if any) ■ Website(s) of the platform(s) ■ Birth date/year that the platform(s) started operations ■ Geographic reach of the platform's operations (i.e., local, national, global) ■ Type of platform: (based on either general or specific functional base, or other typology) ■ Whether platform is part of C2C economy (yes/no) ■ Whether platform is part of sharing economy (broad and narrow definition) (yes/no) ■ Product(s) and service(s) exchanged between providers and users: asset and service mix (economic activity group) ■ Breakdown of providers by type (professional or nonprofessional) ■ Advertisement parties involved	■ Number of platforms by region ■ Proportion of platforms by age ■ Number of platforms by geographic reach ■ Proportion of platforms by type of platform ■ Number of platforms in the C2C economy; in the sharing economy ■ Number (and size) of platforms by economic activity group ■ Number of (and size) of platforms by type of provider ■ Number (and size) of platforms by advertisement parties involved
Economic Information on Platforms	■ Business model: profit orientation (profit, nonprofit, commission-based, advertisement-based or a combination); Other sources of income from other services or add-ons. Or more general: how the platform makes money ■ Employment: number of directly persons employed by platform (employers + employees, e.g., those maintaining tech infrastructure, administration, and marketing);	■ Number (and size) of platforms by business model ■ Number of employed (by sex) by type of platform (or economic group) ■ Number of employed by educational attainment and by type of platform (or economic group) ■ Hours worked by type of platform (or economic group) ■ Number of platforms by type of investors (or investments made) ■ Percentage of platforms that paid taxes

continued on next page

Box 2.2 *continued*

Dimension	Data	Indicators
	Characteristics of employed: breakdown by sex, breakdown by educational attainment; hours worked ■ Type of investors and investments made in the platform ■ Tax payment (and type, i.e., income tax, value-added tax, etc.) ■ Type of network effects: what drives the growth of the online platform (e.g., more participants, more transactions, more content, etc.) ■ Who sets the prices and circumstances of logistics (e.g., delivery of good or service) ■ Turnover, including source(s) of the turnover ■ Value added, i.e., turnover minus costs for intermediate goods and services ■ Investments made in the platform, including the type of partners ■ Type of providers: noncommercial and commercial	■ Number of platforms by type of network effects ■ Number of platforms by mechanism for setting prices and logistics ■ Average turnover, by source and by type of platform ■ Average value added, by type of platform (or economic activity group) ■ Average investments in platform, by type of platform (or economic activity group) ■ Number of platforms by type of providers
Social Information on Platforms	■ Verifying providers and their offers and checking for illegal content ■ Verifying clients ■ Advertisement parties involved ■ Collection of data of providers and clients and the uses of these data (e.g., algorithms and selling of data)	■ Number of platforms by type of verification process for providers ■ Percentage of platforms with verification process for clients by type of platform (or economic activity group) ■ Percentage of platforms with advertisement parties involved by type of platform (or economic activity group) ■ Number of platforms by type of platform and by type of data collection activities on platform users ■ Number of platforms by type of platform and by data collection use

continued on next page

Box 2.2 *continued*

Dimension	Data	Indicators
Basic Information on Platform Sellers	■ Name of individual/household respondent or Business ■ Background characteristics: location; year that the provider(s) started offering good or service in platform(s); individual/household or business ■ Reasons to use a platform ■ Type of goods or services offered (relative to some classification system); Part of sharing economy (i.e., offering use of idle asset, or not) ■ Number of transactions per year (including turnover)	■ Total number of unique sellers by type (individual/household vs business) ■ Total number of unique individual sellers (active or passive) by location (urban/rural, or region) ■ Growth rates in number of unique sellers (active or passive) ■ Total number of sellers by reasons to use a platform ■ Total number of sellers by type of goods or services offered ■ Percentage of sellers in sharing economy, by location
Economic Information on Platform Sellers	■ Number of transactions per year in past 2 years ■ Average prices per transaction ■ Average transaction costs made to use the platform (commission and/or access) ■ Investments and value added ■ Tax payment ■ International trade/cross-border transactions (percentage compared to all transactions) ■ Main source or supplementary source of income	■ Total number of transactions per year by location ■ Growth/decline of transactions per year, including total turnover. Estimate of total turnover: average price x number of transactions per year (minus transaction costs) ■ Total investments and value added ■ Percentage of sellers paying tax ■ Share of international trade/cross-border transactions (in percent) to total transactions ■ Percentage of sellers whose income from platforms is main source (or supplementary source) of income
Social Information on Platform Sellers	■ If the seller has a working relationship with the platform (relates mostly to indirect employment): hours worked and earnings (does this constitute the main income). Account should be taken of the fact that people can work for or be associated with more than one online platform ■ Total income ■ Social security ■ Legal contract ■ Training possibilities	■ Percentage of sellers with working relationship to the platform ■ Average hours worked by sex and by location ■ Average earnings by sex and by location (for those with platform incomes constituting the main source of income, and for others) ■ Average income by sex and by location ■ Percentage of sellers with social security ■ Percentage of sellers with training possibilities

continued on next page

Box 2.2 *continued*

Dimension	Data	Indicators
Basic Information on Platform Clients	▪ Name of platform client ▪ Background characteristics: Location; Year that the client(s) started purchasing good or service in platform(s); individual-household or business; number of visits to a platform per year; type of goods or services bought or shared, including prices; Reasons to use platform(s) ▪ Number of visits to an online platform per year (or month or week) ▪ Number of transactions per year (money spent, including the commission to the platform) ▪ Type of goods or services bought or shared ▪ Reasons to use online platform(s) ▪ Trust in platforms (e.g., role of reviews and rating systems) ▪ International trade/cross-border transactions (percentage compared to all transactions)	▪ Total number of unique clients by type (individual/household vs businesses) ▪ Total number of unique clients by sex and by location (and growth or decline) ▪ Average number of visits to a platform per year (or month or week) ▪ Total number of clients by type of goods or services bought or shared ▪ Average prices for major goods or services bought or shared ▪ Total number of clients by reason for using platform(s) ▪ Average share of cross-border transactions to total transactions
Economic Information on Platform Clients	▪ Average number of transactions per year (or month or week) ▪ Average expenditures on platforms, including the commission to the platform) ▪ International trade/cross-border transactions (to total transactions) in platform	▪ Number of transactions per year ▪ Growth/decline of transactions per year ▪ Average expenditures on platforms by type of platforms (including the commission to the platform) ▪ Share of cross-border transactions to total transactions in platform
Social Information on Platform Clients	▪ Trust in platforms (e.g., role of reviews and rating systems) ▪ Number of complaints on the platform (and of which, how much got sufficiently resolved)	▪ Average trust rating of platforms by type of platform ▪ Average number of complaints in platform(s) by type of platform

Note: Adapted from Heerschap, Pouw, and Atmé (2018).
Source: ADB (2021).

Key data and statistical indicators are needed to measure the platform economy. Heerschap, Pouw, and Atmé (2018) explain that "on the one hand, there is the need to separate platforms from the traditional economy. This means that specific indicators for platforms (and their operations), the providers (supply), the users (demand), and the advertisers, as well as the transactions, [are needed]. On the other hand, for comparison, [indicators of platforms need to be] linked with existing statistical indicators and domains."

A precondition for any new set of measurement processes is ensuring that the cost of collecting new data and the respondent burden has to be kept as low as possible. Descriptive indicators suggested below are restricted to basic characteristics of the platforms themselves, the providers of the platforms, and the users of the platforms.

Data Sources

The data for the proposed indicators listed can be collected from various sources. Regardless, it is initially important to have a sampling frame of platforms, which is unlikely to be available in many countries. National statistics offices could start with the most "important" platforms in terms of public visibility (ADB 2021).

Some data collection methods are better for platform firms. Since transactions on platforms concern cross-border digital trade, international cooperation is necessary. Possible options for data collection are (ADB 2021):

i. Setting up a new dedicated survey for measuring the platform economy. Survey questionnaires can be sent to providers and users, but especially to the platforms. Households are both consumers and producers; thus, the nature and extent of their consumption and productive activities needs a new survey that should also capture information on imports of goods and services directly undertaken by households. That households are now direct importers and exporters needs to be properly valued in national accounts. National statistics offices need to work with platform firms to obtain aggregate information on productive activities of households and cross-border flows. Since most platforms will not be very willing to share information, data sharing with national statistics offices needs to be mandatory by law, even when the headquarters of a platform company are outside the country (Scassa 2017), though there will be challenges in assuring cooperation.

ii. Alternatively, national statistics offices could make use of existing surveys (i.e., the Labor Force Survey, household surveys of ICT use, business surveys of ICT use) and add a module of questions on the platform economy. These surveys can target providers and users of platforms, but not the platforms themselves.

iii. The available digital footprints on platforms could be web-scraped. If there is already a list of platforms (with URLs) available in a country, national statistics offices can use web scraping and application programming interfaces to collect desired information from the websites of platforms (such as site visits of users, and possibly financial accounts) though this is not always an easy task. If a sampling frame of platforms is not available, an initial list could be created on the basis of a web search of the whole internet (focusing on a country domain) with a bot. With the aid of machine learning, a bot should be able to distinguish "normal" websites from websites with platforms.

The various typologies of platforms discussed in the previous section show the challenge in coming up with a single survey for all classifications of platforms, which can vary considerably in features from each other. For a sharing platform, the distinction can be blurry "between a natural person (peer) offering a service and a (micro) enterprise offering the same service" (Heerschap, Pouw, and Atmé 2018). Even in a gig or online labor platform, the difference between a natural person seeking a gig through a temporary employment agency or through a platform may not be straightforward. If all possible typologies of platforms and platform users are taken into account in a survey of platforms, providers, and clients, the survey questionnaires are likely to be long and complicated.

International organizations such as the UNCTAD, IMF, and OECD have set up work programs and international working groups to advance the statistical and conceptual frameworks that will help national statistics offices measure the digital economy and the platform economy in a consistent manner (European Commission et al. 2009). These international organizations have also conducted knowledge-sharing activities, bringing together experts and representatives of national statistics offices to look at measurement issues. Dedicated surveys could possibly be coordinated at regional levels by international organizations for developing economies that could target platforms especially, as well as platform users.

Some national statistics offices in advanced economies have been undertaking methodological work. The US Bureau of Economic Analysis is experimenting with approaches to look into transactions outside the production boundaries of national accounts to obtain a value of the consumption of "freely" available information, while the UK's Office of National Statistics has been re-examining its approach to accounts for quality change in the prices of digital products and services such as household broadband services (Loranger, Sinclair, and Tebrake 2018).

Developing countries should conduct household and business surveys on ICT use more regularly, harnessing administrative records and exploring data from innovative sources (such as web scraping) and integrating these with available data from traditional data to address data gaps. In the Philippines, the Department of Information and Communications Technology, in cooperation with the Philippine Statistical Research and Training Institute, in 2019 conducted the first ever National ICT Household Survey to gather baseline data on household access and use of ICT services and equipment. The survey provides measures of key indicators of household ICT use in support of national ICT development planning and policy making. The results suggested that among Filipinos aged 10 years and over, 43% use the internet, of which, more than half (53%) are in Metro Manila, i.e., the National Capital Region and its neighboring regions Calabarzon and Central Luzon (Figure 2.6). Since internet use of households is much lower outside of Metro Manila, much can be done to reduce the digital divide to ensure that digital dividends on platform use are made more inclusive.

Figure 2.7 shows that among Filipinos aged 10 years and above who go online, the bulk of internet activity for private or personal purposes is on social activities/communication (91%), access to information (41%), and leisure and/or lifestyle (34%). Around a tenth or less go online for creativity (12%), online transportation and/or navigation (8%), and professional life (6%) and online transactions (1%). These results validate information from We Are Social and Hootsuite (2020) that Filipinos connected to the internet are global leaders in the use of social media, and that the extent of e-commerce activities and online banking transactions are limited and thus should be an area of growth. There is evidence that in the COVID-19 pandemic,[5] Filipinos

---

[5] Refer to ABS-CBN (2020).

Figure 2.6: Distribution of Filipino Internet Users Aged 10 Years and Above by Region, 2019 (%)

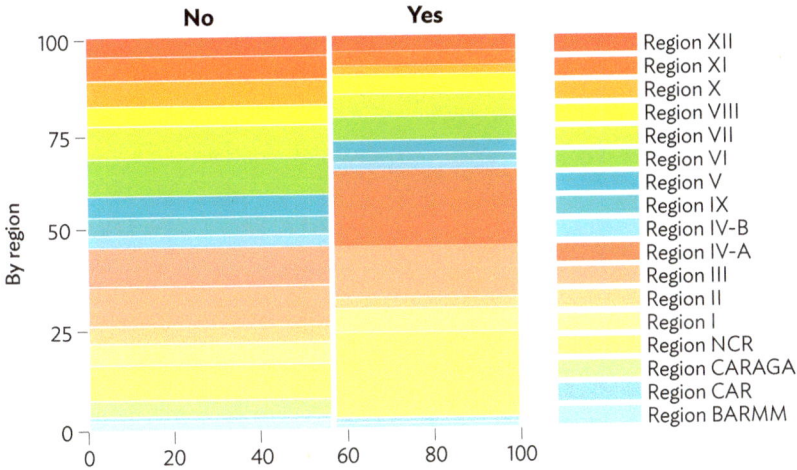

BARMM = Bangsamoro Autonomous Region in Muslim Mindanao, CAR = Cordillera Administrative Region, CARAGA = Caraga Administrative Region, NCR = National Capital Region.
Note: The question is: In the last 3 months, have you used the internet from any location?
Source: Author, based on Government of the Philippines, Department of Information and Communications Technology, 2019 National ICT Household Survey.

Figure 2.7: Private or Personal Internet Use among Filipinos Aged 10 Years and Above by Activity, 2019 (%)

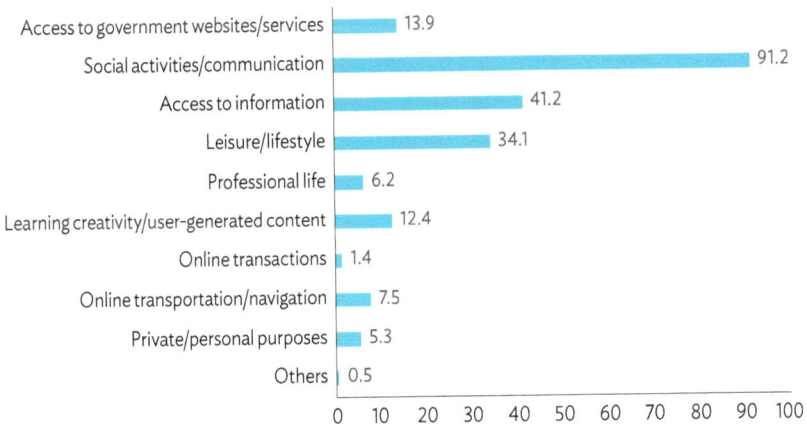

Activity	%
Access to government websites/services	13.9
Social activities/communication	91.2
Access to information	41.2
Leisure/lifestyle	34.1
Professional life	6.2
Learning creativity/user-generated content	12.4
Online transactions	1.4
Online transportation/navigation	7.5
Private/personal purposes	5.3
Others	0.5

Note: The question is: In the last 3 months, and from any location, for which of the following activities did you use the internet for private or personal purposes?
Source: Author, based on Government of the Philippines, Department of Information and Communications Technology, 2019 National ICT Household Survey.

have used platforms more to cope with restrictions on movement imposed by the government, and it is likely that such changes in consumption behavior will be sustained in a post-COVID-19 world.

A total of ₱15.5 billion was spent monthly on online purchases, led by Calabarzon, Metro Manila, and Central Luzon, which have a combined 70% share of total expenditures in the country. A third of total online spending was on clothing, while about a fifth was on household goods, with a tenth each on electronics and on cosmetics (Table 2.4).

Table 2.4: Total Monthly Expenditure from Online Purchases, by Type of Good/Service, 2019
(₱ hundred thousand)

Good/Service	Total Expenditure	Share to Total (%)
Creative content	105	0.1
Professional services	177	0.1
Financial products	303	0.2
Music downloads and music streaming subscriptions	752	0.5
Video downloads and video streaming subscriptions	884	0.6
Medicine	1,105	0.7
Books, magazines, or newspapers	1,288	0.8
Computer or video games	1,855	1.2
Tickets or bookings for entertainment events	1,863	1.2
Computer software	2,042	1.3
Food, groceries, alcohol, or tobacco	3,558	2.3
Travel products	4,494	2.9
Computer equipment or parts	7,429	4.8
Cosmetics and fragrances	14,910	9.6
Consumer electronics and accessories	16,100	10.4
Others	16,650	10.8
Household goods	28,100	18.2
Clothing, footwear, sporting goods, or accessories	53,080	34.3
TOTAL	**154,695**	**100.0**

Source: Author, based on Government of the Philippines, Department of Information and Communications Technology, 2019 National ICT Household Survey.

Table 2.5 shows that total monthly income from online selling across the country averaged ₱12.3 billion, with clothing garnering a fifth of online income, while a tenth each went to cosmetics (and fragrances), and another tenth came from income from food (including groceries, alcohol and tobacco).

Table 2.5: Total Monthly Income from Online Selling,
by Type of Good/Service, 2019
(₱ hundred thousand)

Good/Service	Total Monthly Income	Share to Total (%)
Books, magazines, or newspapers	38	0.0
Tickets or bookings for entertainment events	481	0.4
Computer software	1,123	0.9
Travel products	1,333	1.1
Medicine	1,869	1.5
Creative content	2,293	1.9
Computer equipment or parts	2,999	2.4
Household goods	5,273	4.3
Financial products	5,929	4.8
Computer or video games	7,413	6.0
Professional services	8,031	6.5
Consumer electronics and accessories	8,231	6.7
Food, groceries, alcohol, or tobacco	14,690	11.9
Cosmetics and fragrances	15,090	12.2
Clothing, footwear, sporting goods, or accessories	24,190	19.6
Others	24,330	19.7
TOTAL	123,313	100.0

Source: Author, based on Government of the Philippines, Department of Information and Communications Technology, 2019 National ICT Household Survey.

Average monthly income of Filipinos was estimated at around $175 (₱8,700) from online selling in the Philippines. Across regions, Davao and Eastern Visayas led in mean income from online selling, suggesting that while spending is skewed toward Metro Manila and surrounding districts, the income from online transactions tend to go outside of the urban area. The challenge here is for the Philippine Statistics Authority to integrate such information on household income (and production) into the production side of national accounts, as current accounting of household activities are treated more on the expenditure side. Further, the increasing production from households also has important implications on the measurement not only for economic, but also labor market performance. This chapter has hardly touched on issues about measuring the contribution of platforms to the labor market.

2.4. Conclusion

The emerging platform economy is a catalyst for wealth creation, social good, and innovation, providing groundbreaking benefits for producers and consumers. But the platform economy also brings many risks to fair competition; trustworthiness; and consumer rights, including data privacy and decent working conditions (Heerschap, Pouw, and Atmé 2018). This requires at least new regulatory frameworks that make socioeconomic growth inclusive, while exercising some restraint so as not to stifle digital innovations.

To get a good picture of the platform economy, new data and indicators are needed, and national statistics offices need to start work on measuring the platform economy, giving attention to national accounts compilation, as well as conduct of business surveys and new household surveys. Given the complex business processes of platforms, it is, however, a statistical challenge to obtain information from platforms, and even to make use of traditional data sources. Households are no longer just consumers but obtaining information on productive activities of households is challenging, so national statistics offices need to work with platforms to obtain this information.

Work has begun in the international statistical system on measuring the larger digital economy, and for some national statistics offices from more developed countries, work has also begun even on platform economy measurement, with a focus on the sharing economy. Measuring the platform economy and its impact can be challenging, however, because of the complexity, cross-sector and cross-border capacity, and rapid growth of platforms amid vastly changing goods and services. Usage data in platforms can proxy for economic value, thus web-scraping of platforms by national statistics offices can be a valuable tool for obtaining information on socioeconomic activities in platforms, aside from conducting new surveys of users of platforms as well as the platforms themselves.

Private organizations are also currently collecting various data, and generating information on the platform economy, but details on their methods and the extent of coverage of their work are unknown. National statistics offices can start working with these organizations, and re-engineer their existing surveys, e.g., labor force surveys, business surveys, household and business surveys on ICT usage, and supplement traditional data collection with alternative data sources.

National statistics offices need to develop mechanisms for integrating new data and new data sources into national accounts compilations. For instance, households have been typically viewed only from the expenditure side, but household production is increasing especially in the platform economy, and this has not been incorporated into national accounts estimation. Regional cooperation is required to address the cross-border nature of platforms, and how this affects economies. International cooperation is especially necessary for reaching out to platforms, which may not be physically present in countries. Further, guidance on statistical standards will need to be developed.

Measurements of the platform economy have wide policy implications for ensuring that a positive dynamic of social good from the platform economy continues while preventing possibilities for widening inequalities and power imbalances in society. Digital footprints left in platforms can expose platform users to misuse of personal data. Lack of trust, even by those connected to the internet on how personal data is kept and managed by platforms, can make platform users reluctant in engaging in electronic money transactions, and thus limit growth in electronic commerce, as has been in the case in the Philippines. While policies and laws have been in place in the Philippines to protect individuals from risks pertaining to privacy and cybersecurity, especially with the enactment of the Data Privacy Act of 2012 and the National Cybersecurity Plan 2022, these regulations must be regularly revisited in the wake of possible implementation deficits in these laws.

Governments should understand the dynamics in the platform economy given the many challenges in enforcing regulations on cross-border trade in digital services and products, as well as the current ambiguities in laws on digital taxation.[6] Even prior to the onset of the COVID-19 pandemic, several Asia and the Pacific economies, i.e., Australia, Bangladesh, Japan, New Zealand, the Republic of Korea, and Taipei,China, have had digital tax laws. In July 2020,

---

6   Refer to Quaderno (2020).

Indonesia introduced a 10% value-added tax (VAT) on all online transactions with no threshold, which means from the very first sale. Meanwhile, Malaysia introduced 6% VAT on digital services for foreign providers whose services rendered exceeds the threshold of RM500,000 (about $120,000) for a period of 12 months, while Singapore introduced a 7% VAT to foreign suppliers of digital services whose annual global turnover exceeded S$1,000,000 and whose sale of digital services to consumers in Singapore exceeded S$100,000. Given government need for other revenues in the wake of expected deficits for fighting the pandemic, increasing social protection coverage, and rebooting economies, the Philippines and several countries in the Asia and Pacific region, such as the PRC and Thailand, are also looking into digital taxation.

Policies need to be in place on the protection of consumer rights that can enhance trust toward platforms, specifically digital payments. Encouraging platforms, especially logistics and ride-sharing providers, to only use digital payment instruments will require a strong consumer protection policy framework, including a return-and-refund policy. Consumer confidence in the right to return a defective product and receive a refund can likely improve trust in digital payments. The difficulty is sometimes on the part of enforcement of laws. For instance, while the Consumer Act of the Philippines (or Republic Act 7394) provides for physically including price tags of goods and services, providers may not do so, and instead resort only to negotiations on private messages with platform clients.[7]

The pandemic has accelerated the shift toward online expenditure, boosting the growth of digital delivery models, including online banking, online learning, and online entertainment. This shift in consumer behavior may continue in the post-pandemic world as consumers increase their trust in platforms. Regulatory frameworks should address how to enhance safety and security, particularly how to observe data privacy for protecting the personal information of consumers in platforms. A key characteristic of platforms is that they are in winner-take-all situations and markets. Even when barriers to entry can be low, it is possible for first movers to have a huge advantage because of the high cost of switching platforms, and this can pose significant issues in fair competition.

---

[7]   Refer to Malasig (2020).

While a regular review of regulations especially about platforms is in order, regulators must also remember the need for an enabling environment that promotes wealth creation. Regulations should not easily stifle innovative activity but work toward ensuring that whatever benefits from platform use are ultimately shared within a country, so that prosperity can be more inclusive and sustainable especially in the new normal.

References

ABS-CBN. 2020. eCommerce Platform Lazada Shows Filipinos Spent Greater Time Online in Recent Months. 3 June. https://news.abs-cbn.com/advertorial/life/06/03/20/ecommerce-platform-lazada-shows-filipinos-spent-greater-time-online-in-recent-months.

Ahmad, N. and J. Ribarsky. 2018. Towards a Framework for Measuring the Digital Economy. *Paper prepared for the 16th Conference of the International Association for Official Statistics.* Paris: Organisation for Economic Co-operation and Development. https://www.oecd.org/iaos2018/programme/IAOS-OECD2018_Ahmad-Ribarsky.pdf.

Albert, J. R. 2020. Towards Measuring the Platform Economy: Concepts, Indicators, and Issues. *Philippine Institute for Development Studies Discussion Paper Series*, No. 2020-28. Manila. https://pidswebs.pids.gov.ph/CDN/PUBLICATIONS/pidsdps2028.pdf.

Albert, J. R. and A. Martinez, Jr. 2018. The Future of Data Today. Development Asia. 29 November. https://development.asia/explainer/future-data-today.

Albert, J. R., A. Martinez, Jr., K. Miradora, J. A. Lapuz, M. Martillan, C. de Dios, and I. Sebastian-Samaniego. 2019. Readiness of National Statistical Systems in Asia and the Pacific for Leveraging Big Data to Monitor the SDGs. *ADB Briefs*. Manila: Asian Development Bank. https://www.adb.org/sites/default/files/publication/491326/adb-brief-106-national-statistical-systems-big-data-sdgs.pdf.

Asian Development Bank (ADB). 2021. *Asian Economic Integration Report 2021: Making Digital Platforms Work for Asia and the Pacific.* Manila. http://dx.doi.org/10.22617/TCS210048-2.

Bale, R. 2018. National Geographic. Google, Facebook, and Other Tech Giants Unite to Fight Wildlife Crime Online. *National Geographic.* 7 March. https://www.nationalgeographic.com/news/2018/03/wildlife-watch-tech-companies-online-wildlife-crime-coalition/.

Barrera, E., R. Bravo, C. Cecconi, M. B. Garneau, and J. Murphy. 2018. Measurement Challenges of the Digital Economy. *Paper.* Rome: Voorburg Group. https://www.voorburggroup.org/Documents/2018%20Rome/Papers/2003.pdf.

Bukht, R. and R. Heeks. 2017. Defining, Conceptualising and Measuring the Digital Economy. *GDI Development Informatics Working Papers* no. 68., Manchester: University of Manchester. http://hummedia.manchester. ac.uk/institutes/gdi/publications/workingpapers/di/di_wp68.pdf.

Chen, J. Y. 2019. *Platform Economies the Boss's Old and New Clothes. Dog Days: Made in China Yearbook 2018*. Canberra: Australia National University Press. http://press-files.anu.edu.au/downloads/press/n5364/pdf/ article18.pdf.

Codagnone, C., F. Biagi, and F. Abadie. 2016. The Passions and the Interests: Unpacking the 'Sharing Economy'. JRC Science for Policy Report. Seville: Institute for Prospective Technological Studies. http://dx.doi. org/10.2791/474555.

Dutch Transformation Forum. 2018. Unlocking the Value of the Platform Economy: Mastering the Good, the Bad and the Ugly. https://dutchitchannel. nl/612528/dutch-transformation-platform-economy-paper-kpmg.pdf.

Evans, D. S. 2018. Essential Principles for the Design of Antitrust Analysis for Multisided Platforms. http://dx.doi.org/10.2139/ssrn.3261812.

Evans, D. and R. Schmalensee. 2007. The Industrial Organization of Markets with Two-Sided Platforms. Competition Policy International. 3 (1). pp. 151–179. https://papers.ssrn.com/sol3/Delivery.cfm/SSRN_ ID987341_code813174.pdf?abstractid=987341&mirid=1.

Evans, P. C. 2016. The Rise of Asian Platforms: A Regional Survey. The Emerging Platform Economy Series. 3. New York: The Centre for Global Enterprise. https://www.thecge.net/app/uploads/2016/11/ FINALAsianPlatformPaper.pdf.

Evans, P. C. and A. Gawer. 2016. The Rise of the Platform Enterprise: A Global Survey. *The Emerging Platform Economy*. Series No. 1 Report. New York: The Center for Global Enterprise. https://www.thecge.net/app/ uploads/2016/01/PDF-WEB-Platform-Survey_01_12.pdf.

European Commission, International Monetary Fund, Organisation for Economic Co-operation and Development, United Nations, and World Bank. 2009. *System of National Accounts 2008*. New York: United Nations. https://unstats.un.org/unsd/nationalaccount/docs/SNA2008.pdf .

Eurostat. 2018. *Measuring the Digital Collaborative Economy*. Luxembourg: European Commission.

Farrell, D., F. Greig, and A. Hamoudi. 2018. *The Online Platform Economy in 2018 Drivers, Workers, Sellers, and Lessors*. JPMorgan Chase Institute.

Fortanier, F. and S. Matei. 2017. Measuring Digital Trade: Results of the OECD-IMF Stocktaking Survey. Presented at 30th Meeting of the IMF Committee on Balance of Payments Statistics. www.imf.org/external/pubs/ft/bop/2017/pdf/17-07.pdf.

Gawer, A. 2015. Supplementary Written Evidence Accompanying Statements to the UK House of Lords in its Inquiry on Digital Platforms, UK House of Lords. http://data.parliament.uk/writtenevidence/committeeevidence.svc/evidencedocument/eu-internal-marketsubcommittee/online-platforms-and-the-eu-digital-single-market/written/23342.html.

Goodwin, T. 2015. The Battle Is For The Customer Interface. *TechCrunch*. 4 March. https://techcrunch.com/2015/03/03/in-the-age-of-disintermediation-the-battle-is-all-for-the-customer-interface/.

Google, Temasek and Bain & Company. 2019. e-Conomy SEA 2019. https://www.blog.google/documents/47/SEA_Internet_Economy_Report_2019.pdf.

Government of the Philippines, Department of Information and Communications Technology, 2019 National ICT Household Survey.

Heerschap, N., N. Pouw, and C. Atmé. 2018. Measuring Online Platforms. Centraal Bureau voor de Statistiek (CBS) Statistics Netherlands. https://www.cbs.nl/-/media/_pdf/2018/51/2018ep58-measuring-online-platforms.pdf.

Hinrich Foundation. 2019. *The Data Revolution: How the Philippines Can Capture the Digital Trade Opportunity at Home and Abroad*. Singapore: AlphaBeta. https://www.alphabeta.com/wp-content/uploads/2019/06/digitrade_philippines_1-pg-view.pdf.

Ilarina, V. R., F. S. Polistico, and M. C. Pascacio. 2019. Measuring the Digital Economy in the Philippines: Towards a Satellite Account. Fourteenth National Convention on Statistics, Crowne Plaza Manila Galleria, Manila. https://psa.gov.ph/sites/default/files/7.2.1%20Measuring%20the%20Digital%20Economy%20in%20the%20Philippines.pdf.

International Monetary Fund (IMF). 2018. Measuring the Digital Economy. IMF Policy Paper. Washington, DC. https://www.imf.org/en/Publications/Policy-Papers/Issues/2018/04/03/022818-measuring-the-digital-economy.

International Telecommunications Union (ITU). Statistics. https://www.itu.int/en/ITU-D/Statistics/Pages/stat/default.aspx (accessed July 2020).

Kenney, M. and J. Zysman 2016. The Rise of the Platform Economy. *Issues in Science and Technology*. XXXII (3). https://issues.org/the-rise-of-the-platform-economy/.

Koh, T. K. and M. Fichman. 2014. Multi-Homing Users' Preferences for Two-Sided Exchange Networks. *MIS Quarterly*. 38 (4). pp. 977–996. https://papers.ssrn.com/sol3/papers.cfm?abstract_id=1635615.

Koskinen, K., C. Bonina, and B. Eaton. 2019. *Digital Platforms in the Global South: Foundations and Research Agenda*. In P. Nielsen and H. C. Kimaro, eds. pp. 319–330. https://doi.org/10.1007/978-3-030-18400-1_26

Langley, P. and A. Leyshon. 2017. Platform Capitalism: The Intermediation and Capitalisation of Digital Economic Circulation. *Finance and Society*. 3 (1). https://doi.org/10.2218/finsoc.v3i1.1936.

Liu, H. Y. 2019. *Migrant Workers in the Digital Market: China's Platform Economy. The Asia Dialogue*. Nottingham: University of Nottingham's Asia Research Institute. https://theasiadialogue.com/2019/08/13/migrant-workers-in-the-digital-market-chinas-platform-economy/.

Loranger, A., A. Sinclair, and J. Tebrake. 2018. Measuring the Economy in an Increasingly Digitalized World: Are Statistics up to the Task? In Data Governance in the Digital Age. *Centre for International Governance Innovation (CIGI) Essay Series*. Waterloo. https://www.cigionline.org/sites/default/files/documents/Data%20Series%20Special%20Reportweb.pdf.

Lucas, D. L. 2018. BSP Goal: 20% of PH Transactions Digital by 2020. Inquirer. net. 18 January. https://business.inquirer.net/243515/bsp-goal-20-of-ph-transactions-digital-by-2020.

Malasig, J. 2020. PM is the Key? DTI Reminds Online Sellers to Display Prices on Online Platforms. Interaksyon. 1 June. https://www.interaksyon. com/trends-spotlights/2020/06/01/169660/pm-isthe-key-dti-reminds-online-sellers-to-display-prices-on-online-platforms/.

Martinez, A. and J. R. Albert. 2018. Big Data Can Transform SDG Performance. Here's How. *Asian Development Blog.* 22 June 2018. https://blogs.adb. org/blog/big-data-can-transform-sdg-performance-here-s-how.

Office for National Statistics (ONS). 2017. The Feasibility of Measuring the Sharing Economy: November 2017 Progress Update. Newport. https://www.ons.gov.uk/economy/economicoutputandproductivity/ output/articles/thefeasibilityofmeasuringthesharingeconomy/ november2017progressupdate.

Organisation for Economic Co-operation and Development (OECD). 2011. *OECD Guide to Measuring the Information Society, 2011.* Paris: OECD Publishing. https://doi.org/10.1787/9789264113541-en.

———. 2016. New Forms of Work in the Digital Economy. OECD Digital Economy Papers, No. 260. Paris: OECD Publishing. http://dx.doi.org/10.1787/5jlwnklt820x-en.

———. 2017. *OECD Digital Economy Outlook 2017.* Paris: OECD Publishing. https://doi.org/10.1787/9789264276284-en.

———. 2018. Online Platforms: A practical Approach to their Economic and Social Impacts. DSTI/CDEP(2018)5. Paris. https://one.oecd.org/ document/DSTI/CDEP(2018)5/en/pdf.

———. 2019. *An Introduction to Online Platforms and Their Role in the Digital Transformation.* Paris: OECD Publishing. https://doi.org/10.1787/53e5f593-en.

Pagani, M. 2013. Digital Business Strategy and Value Creation: Framing the Dynamic Cycle of Control Points, MIS Quarterly. 37(2). pp. 617–632. https://dl.acm.org/doi/10.25300/MISQ/2013/37.2.13.

Philippine Statistics Authority (PSA). n.d. Philippine Standard Industrial Classification. https://psa.gov.ph/classification/psic/.

Platform Hunt. 2016. The 9 Types of Software Platforms. Medium. 13 June 2016. https://medium.com/platform-hunt/the-8-types-of-software-platforms-473c74f4536a.

Quaderno. 2020. Digital Taxes around the World. 1 July. https://www.quaderno.io/blog/digital-taxes-around-world-know-new-tax-rules.

Scassa, T. 2017. Sharing Data in the Platform Economy: A Public Interest Argument for Access to Platform Data. *UBC Law Review*. 50(4). *Ottawa Faculty of Law Working Paper* No. 2018-08.

Schumpeter, J. A. 1942. *Capitalism, Socialism and Democracy. Third edition.* New York: Harper Perennial Modern Thought (2008).

Serafica, R. and J. R. Albert. 2018. Issues on Digital Trade. *PIDS Discussion Paper Series*. No. 2018-30. Manila: Philippine Institute for Development Studies. https://pidswebs.pids.gov.ph/CDN/PUBLICATIONS/pidsdps1830_rev.pdf.

Statista. 2019. Philippines Statista Country Report. April 2019.

Statistics Canada. 2017. Measuring the Sharing Economy in the Canadian Macroeconomic Accounts. *Latest Developments in the Canadian Economic Accounts*. Catalogue no. 13-605-X. Ottawa. https://www150.statcan.gc.ca/n1/en/catalogue/13-605-X.

Tan, B., S. L. Pan, X. Lu, and L. Huang. 2015. The Role of IS Capabilities in the Development of Multi-Sided Platforms: The Digital Ecosystem Strategy of Alibaba.com. *Journal of the Association for Information Systems*. 16 (4). pp. 248–280. https://aisel.aisnet.org/cgi/viewcontent.cgi?article=1706&context=jais.

United Nations (UN). 2009. International Standard Industrial Classification of All Economic Activities Revision 4. New York. https://unstats.un.org/unsd/publication/seriesM/seriesm_4rev4e.pdf.

———. 2013. *Guidelines on Integrated Economic Statistics.* Statistics Division. New York. https://unstats.un.org/unsd/publication/seriesf/Seriesf_108e.pdf.

———. 2017. *Implementation of SNA and SEEA at Global Level and Current Activities. Inter-regional Workshop on Strengthening Statistical Capacities for Building Macroeconomic and Sustainable Development Indicators in Latin America, the Caribbean and Asia-Pacific Countries.* Statistics Division. Santiago. https://www.cepal.org/sites/default/files/presentations/2017-07_6_3-unsd.pdf.

United Nations Conference on Trade and Development (UNCTAD). 2019. *Digital Economy Report 2019 – Value Creation and Capture: Implications for Developing Countries.* Geneva. https://unctad.org/en/PublicationsLibrary/der2019_en.pdf.

Van Gorp, N. and O. Batura. 2015. Challenges of Competition Policy in a Digitalised Economy. European Parliament. IP/A/ECON/2014-12. https://www.europarl.europa.eu/RegData/etudes/STUD/2015/542235/IPOL_STU(2015)542235_EN.pdf.

We Are Social and Hootsuite. 2020. Digital 2020 Philippines Report. https://datareportal.com/reports/digital-2020-philippines.

World Bank. 2019. *World Development Report 2019: The Changing Nature of Work.* Washington, DC. http://documents.worldbank.org/curated/en/816281518818814423/pdf/2019-WDR-Report.pdf.

———. 2020. A Better Normal Under COVID-19: Digitalizing the Philippine Economy. *Philippines Digital Economy Report 2020.* Washington DC. https://documents1.worldbank.org/curated/en/796871601650398190/pdf/Philippines-Digital-Economy-Report-2020-A-Better-Normal-Under-COVID-19-Digitalizing-the-Philippine-Economy-Now.pdf.

World Economic Forum (WEF). 2017. Digital Transformation Initiative: Unlocking B2B Platform Value. White Paper. Geneva. http://reports.weforum.org/digital-transformation/wp-content/blogs.dir/94/mp/files/pages/files/wef-platform-report-final-3-26-17.pdf.

Chapter 3

Digital Platforms, Technology, and Their Macroeconomic Impact

James Villafuerte, Badri Narayanan, and Thomas Abell

3.1. Overview of Digital Platforms

A digital platform is a digital marketplace that provides space for business and commerce between market players (Evans and Schmalensee 2007, Evans 2018).[1,2] Two-sided platforms link two different types of participants enabling them to gain through trade of goods and services or other forms of interaction (e.g., ride-hailing apps). Individually speaking, the two groups cannot capture the value created on their own. But as the number of people, participants, and transactions increases in the digital platform, the value of goods and services in these marketplaces rises, creating network externalities between the two types of participants. Multisided platforms involve more than two types of participants (e.g., content providers, search engines, and advertisers that connect users) and the network externalities are even larger.

As a business model, the mechanics of digital platforms are not new. Classified ads, for example, are an older, non-digital platform that uses printed information to advertise shopping malls, among other things, as a place for retail trade, leisure, and entertainment. Today, online platforms or digital marketplaces capture, transmit, and monetize digital information—including personal data—to support businesses and commerce (Evans and Gawer 2016).

---

[1]	No agreed definition or universal consensus exists on how to classify different types of digital platforms. The business models digital platforms create may be called the "platform economy," "collaborative economy," "sharing economy," "gig economy," "on-demand economy," and "peer economy." In contrast, Kenney and Zysman (2016) view a "platform economy" or "digital platform economy" as a more neutral term. The authors argue that it encompasses the increasing number of digital activities in business and social media. For the authors, "platform" is merely a set of online digital arrangements with algorithms organizing and structuring social and economic activities and transactions.

[2]	This chapter was prepared as a background paper for ADB (2021).

By and large, such marketplaces or platforms allow technologically mediated transactions, linking various groups and providing patrons a space to conduct activities or transactions (Koskinen, Bonina, and Eaton. 2019).

Chapter 3 of this book describes the scope, coverage, and comprehensive definition of the digital economy and platforms, and the difficulty in measuring their activities and contribution of the digital economy.

3.2. Key Technologies Driving the Growth of Digital Platforms

Digital platforms rely on a few enabling technologies that governments and development organizations should understand if they intend to provide appropriate support. Investments in these frontier and innovative technologies, alongside more advanced and effective design of policies and regulations, are crucial to successfully leveraging the digital economy for sustainable development (ADB 2021).

Five groups of key technologies drive digital platforms: (i) semiconductor technologies, (ii) infrastructure technologies, (iii) transactional technologies, (iv) integrating technologies, and (v) future technologies that will be important as future enablers of the digital economy (Figure 3.1). All these technologies are evolving rapidly, so development planning needs to be proactive. These categories, names, and definitions are not scientifically formulated and will vary depending on the relevant perspective. They can change.

The foundational nature of semiconductor technology is a useful starting point. Gordon Moore, former chief executive officer of Intel Corporation, observed in 1965 that semiconductors were doubling in complexity every 18–24 months. This exponential growth—Moore's Law—has improved semiconductor technology over 10 million-fold over the past 50-plus years (Figure 3.2). Improvement may be slowing, but it still represents the fundamental basis of most technological breakthroughs that underpin microprocessors, memory, communications, sensors, and imaging.

Figure 3.1: Technologies Shaping the Digital Platforms

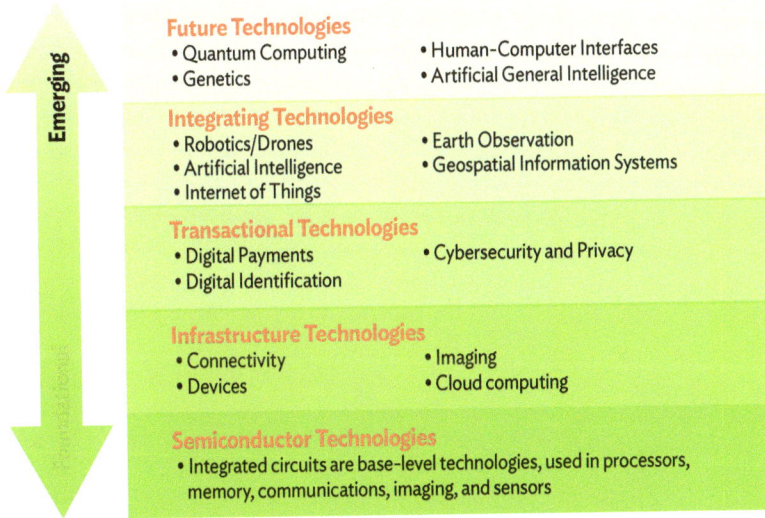

Emerging

Future Technologies
- Quantum Computing
- Genetics
- Human-Computer Interfaces
- Artificial General Intelligence

Integrating Technologies
- Robotics/Drones
- Artificial Intelligence
- Internet of Things
- Earth Observation
- Geospatial Information Systems

Transactional Technologies
- Digital Payments
- Digital Identification
- Cybersecurity and Privacy

Infrastructure Technologies
- Connectivity
- Devices
- Imaging
- Cloud computing

Semiconductor Technologies
- Integrated circuits are base-level technologies, used in processors, memory, communications, imaging, and sensors

Source: Abell (2020).

Infrastructure technologies, as the name would suggest, provide the basic building blocks for the platform economy (ADB 2021). These are:

- **Connectivity:** Digital connectivity enables people and services to communicate over wired, optical, and wireless networks. In 2019, internet connectivity reached 54% of the global population, driven mainly by expanding low-cost wireless networks. Reaching the remaining population is a key requirement for continued growth of the digital economy.

- **Devices:** People interact with the digital economy using a variety of devices, such as personal computers, smartphones, and wearables. Currently, the smartphone is the dominant device globally; and wearables, such as smart eyewear, earpieces, and watches, are poised to be the next trend.

- **Imaging:** Imaging technologies enable rapid progress in the use of photography and video.

Figure 3.2: Improvement in Semiconductor Technology

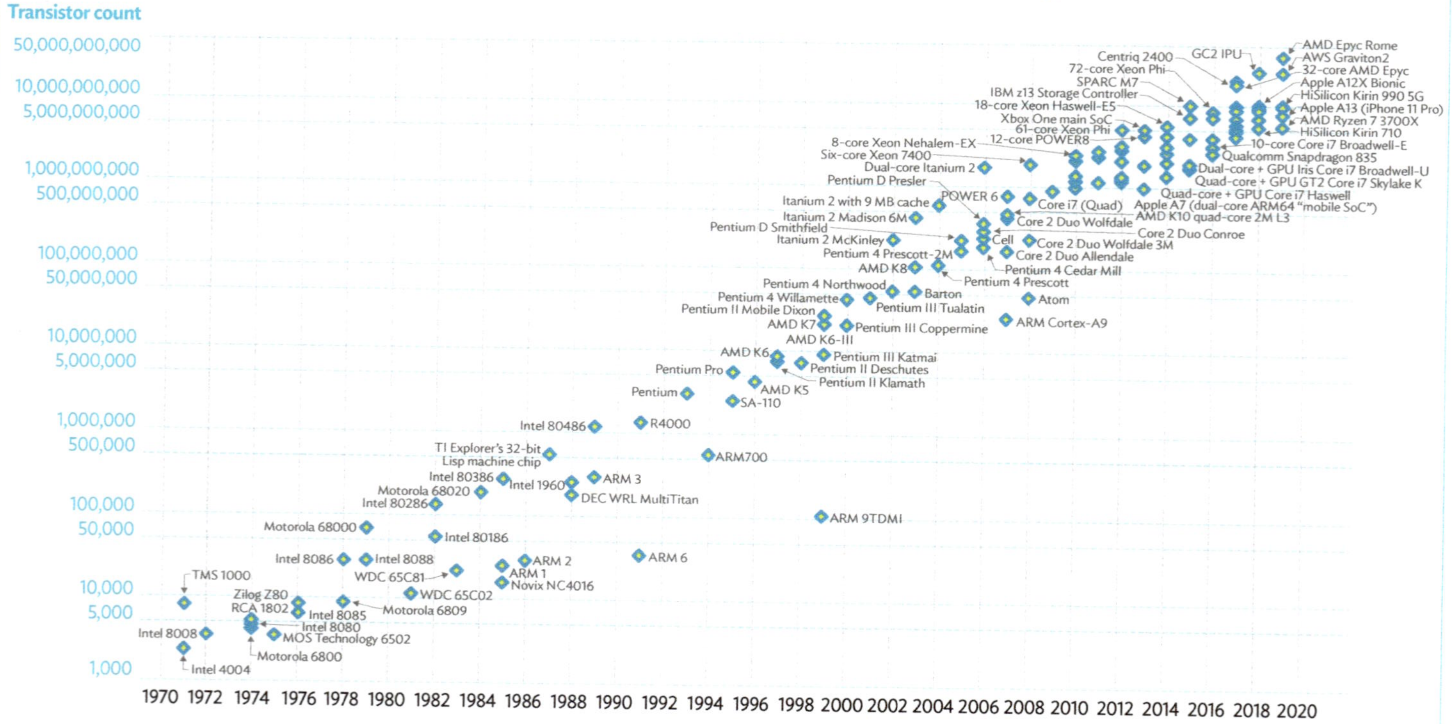

Sources: Roser and Ritchie (2013, 2020).

- **Cloud computing:** Cloud technology is on-demand scalable and cost-effective computing hardware that is cheaper and expandable compared to traditional computing equipment. This enables new services and technology start-ups.

The third group, transactional technologies, are the important enablers of digital commerce:

- **Digital payments:** Efficient, safe, and affordable digital payment tools for companies and individuals are crucial for allowing digital commerce to develop and thrive. Digital payments through online banking, mobile money accounts, or smartphone-based apps offer a relatively efficient and more secure payment model. This also allows users to create a digital footprint that builds up a credit history and keeps track of their economic activity.

- **Digital identity:** Secure, low-cost identity services are critical for the digital economy to enable citizens to access services, such as health, education, and bank accounts. In some instances, this has expanded to citizenship rights, such as the ability to receive social benefits or vote. In addition, emerging biometrics like facial recognition, fingerprinting, and iris scanning, are helping to leapfrog the paper-based approaches to build dependable and low-cost digital identification systems that can scale to national levels.

- **Cybersecurity and privacy:** Cybersecurity is crucial for keeping various types of data safe, enabling secure transactions, and managing devices. Cybersecurity tools are used to protect against unauthorized access to data centers and other similar systems. This is especially relevant for institutions related to banking, health, social protection, education, utilities, manufacturing, and communication.

Integrating technologies, meanwhile, enable digital platforms to combine multiple fundamental technologies to create new types of digital products and services (ADB 2021). These include:

- **Artificial intelligence:** Artifical intelligene (AI) defines a set of algorithms that tries to imitate a person's cognitive functions to identify and respond to increasingly complex real-world situations or challenges. AI also entails machine-learning languages that are capable of learning from training datasets, improving their problem–solving capability by applying their experience or intuition during the training stage, which is often supervised. The immense increase in computational power as well as the availability of big data have also supported recent AI advances. This is evident through AI applications in language translation, recognition of patterns and images, as well as medical diagnosis.

- **Robotics/drones:** The combination of AI, sensors, communications, and processing technologies underpin autonomous operation of vehicles, robots, and drones, delivering new products and services. Robotic technology has been extensively applied in the manufacturing sector for a few decades, and recent breakthroughs in computing have permitted wider and low-cost applications of robotics. Autonomous vehicles comprise one branch of robotics. Self-driving cars use a range of technologies, including machine vision systems with digital cameras, radar, light detection and ranging sensors, and advanced navigation platforms. Another branch of robotics is drones offering low-cost geo observation functions such as monitoring and mapping of physical infrastructure. They can also work with autonomous navigation systems to carry out more sophisticated instructions and tasks, such as search and rescue missions during disasters or package delivery.

- **Internet of Things:** Internet of Things (IoT) generally involves connecting sensors or devices directly to the internet through wireless networks or Bluetooth connections, and does not require a computer or mobile phone. IoT devices, which communicate and interact over the internet, can be remotely controlled. IoT devices in households are typically used for "smart home" solutions in order to control utilities and digital equipment, such as lighting, cameras, thermostats, and related systems (ADB 2021). IoT devices in commercial establishments commonly involve controlling sensors for temperature and humidity or to track movement using built-in cameras or sensors.

- **Earth observation:** Satellite technology, combined with sensors and communication capabilities, allow low-cost geo observation that can cover the entire world. This enables new products and services applicable for land management, agricultural production, and environment observation.

- *Geospatial information services:* Given their ability to accurately measure and measure physical locations, these systems can also assist key transactions and vital intermediary functions of digital marketplaces. In comparison to traditional paper-based maps, *geospatial information services* give users greater accuracy and capability in tracking and analyzing land, resources, infrastructure, and human activities. This will open new opportunities for designing and managing transportation systems.

The fifth group, future technologies, are under development and expected to emerge in the next few years as new drivers for digital platforms and the digital economy (ADB 2021). These technologies could disrupt current leading technologies and so should be closely monitored.

- *Genetics:* Genetic technologies, such as gene editing and gene sequencing, are one of the most noteworthy future technologies. Gene editing, using recently discovered clustered regularly interspaced short palindromic repeats (widely known as CRISPR), is rapidly developing into new solutions for treating diseases and improving agricultural performance. Meanwhile, gene sequencing has allowed examination and understanding of the early origins of our genetic composition that can be associated with many human diseases. It can also be used to analyze our evolution (ADB 2021).

- *Quantum computing:* Building on theoretical discoveries in quantum physics, quantum technologies are capable of outpacing digital computing and to further strengthen encryption systems. The current technologies may be mainly limited to research laboratories, but quantum is positioned to become a breakthrough disruptive technology.

- *Artificial general intelligence:* As AI becomes more powerful, on the back of big data, larger computing resources, and new modeling approaches, potential exists for the emergence of general intelligence that has the capability to perform human activities like writing, research, and art. This technology is highly controversial, with leading technology companies, academia, and governments prioritizing research in this area.

- ***Human–computer Interfaces:*** Current digital technologies are limited by the ability of people to speak or type into their devices. Communicating by typing or speech recognition are many times slower than digital communications, so new interface technologies are intended to enable humans to work more directly with digital solutions. Direct neural interfaces, for instance, are being designed to help people with speech or motor disabilities (ADB 2021).

Digital platforms and the digital economy are growing rapidly, driven by these key technologies. The companies and countries leading this growth are prioritizing their technology investments to maintain their leads.

3.3. Development Impacts of Digital Platforms

The internet and other digital technologies have contributed to the emergence of powerful online networks or digital marketplaces that can substantially reduce the cost of information, lowering information barriers, and cutting production and transaction costs. By reducing information and transaction costs, the internet helps promote commercial and social activities that can boost economic development in three major and interrelated ways (World Bank 2016, Figure 3.3):

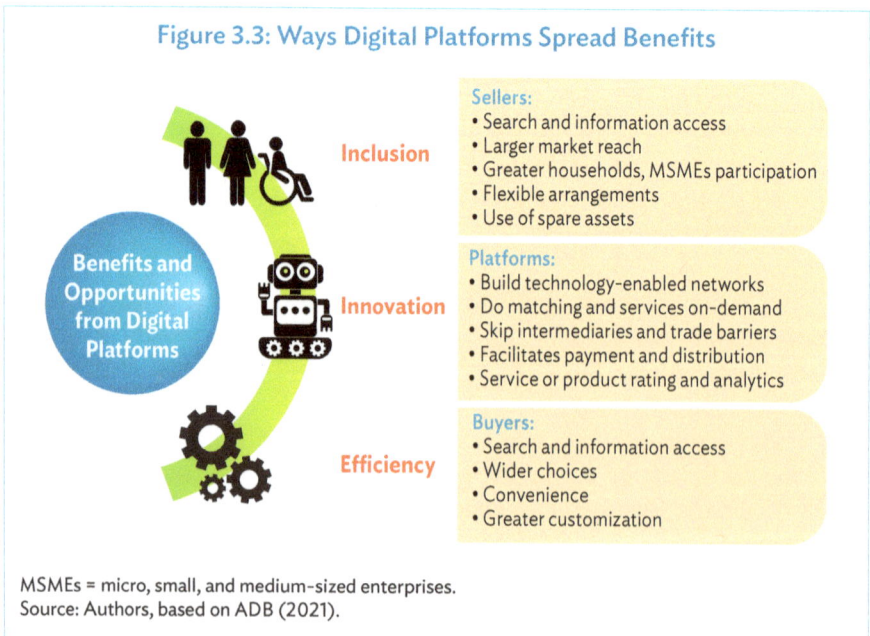

Figure 3.3: Ways Digital Platforms Spread Benefits

Benefits and Opportunities from Digital Platforms

Inclusion

Sellers:
- Search and information access
- Larger market reach
- Greater households, MSMEs participation
- Flexible arrangements
- Use of spare assets

Innovation

Platforms:
- Build technology-enabled networks
- Do matching and services on-demand
- Skip intermediaries and trade barriers
- Facilitates payment and distribution
- Service or product rating and analytics

Efficiency

Buyers:
- Search and information access
- Wider choices
- Convenience
- Greater customization

MSMEs = micro, small, and medium-sized enterprises.
Source: Authors, based on ADB (2021).

- *Inclusion* (search and information)—By enhancing the speed and reach of search algorithms, the internet can help meet data gaps and address information asymmetries more effectively. E-commerce platforms, for example, have enabled small producers or distributors to find and connect with consumers in real time, and to sell in both domestic and international markets. This has contributed to providing goods and services on demand, raising the quality of goods and services, as well as reducing prices.

- *Efficiency* (automation and coordination)—The internet, likewise, augments the production factors. It lowers the cost of performing certain functions such as inventory management and significantly improves efficiency by allowing companies to better allocate and use labor and capital, including spare assets. Enterprises, industries, households, as well as the public sector, can thus experience higher efficiency.

- *Innovation* (scale economies and platforms)—The internet enhances innovation by creating technology-enabled marketplaces that can bundle the ordering of goods and services, with their payment, as well as transportation and delivery. They have also allowed companies to take advantage of economies of scale through digital platforms and other online services that compete with traditional business models, such as Airbnb (lodging), Amazon and Alibaba (retail), Facebook (media), and Uber and Grab (transport). Through technology mediation, buyers and sellers also provide and receive feedback which helps the market expand and improve services.

UNCTAD (2019) notes that data and digital marketplaces are two key drivers of value in the digital era. Koskinen, Bonina, and Eaton (2019) argue that digital platforms hold promise in solving numerous developmental and societal challenges. The emerging digital platforms are particularly effective in addressing market frictions that exist in many developing economies due to absent or weak institutions, insufficient or huge information gaps, and hurdles arising from poor infrastructure. Nonetheless, the effectiveness of policy responses aimed at managing the impacts of digital platforms hinges on clear understanding of the interplay of these two factors and their implications for value creation and distribution of the gains.

Digital marketplace can also help attain the Sustainable Development Goals. Several notable examples have emerged during the pandemic, when the use of digital technology to access health and education services became a game changer. More so, apps contributed to new forms of employment generation through food delivery and ride hailing online, flexible work arrangements, and jobs for different skill levels; and generated additional income for individuals and households. Digital payment apps have also expanded access to financial services—which helped the unbanked receive payments, and crowdfund microenterprises, social projects, medical needs, and so forth.

3.4. Importance of Digital Platforms

According to the United Nations Conference on Trade and Development (UNCTAD 2019), the combined value of platform companies with a market capitalization of over $100 million in 2017 has exceeded $7 trillion, or roughly 20% of global gross domestic product (GDP). Digital platform use drives the growth of these companies. In 2019, seven of the eight largest companies in the world were platform companies—Alphabet, Alibaba, Amazon, Apple, Facebook, Microsoft, and Tencent.

Following Statista's data on six key sectors, including (i) e-commerce, (ii) transportation, (iii) online travel, (iv) e-services, (v) advertising technology (AdTech), and (vi) digital media, business-to-consumer digital platform revenues reached $3.8 trillion in 2019, roughly equivalent to 4.4% of global output (Figure 3.4). E-commerce accounted for more than half of global

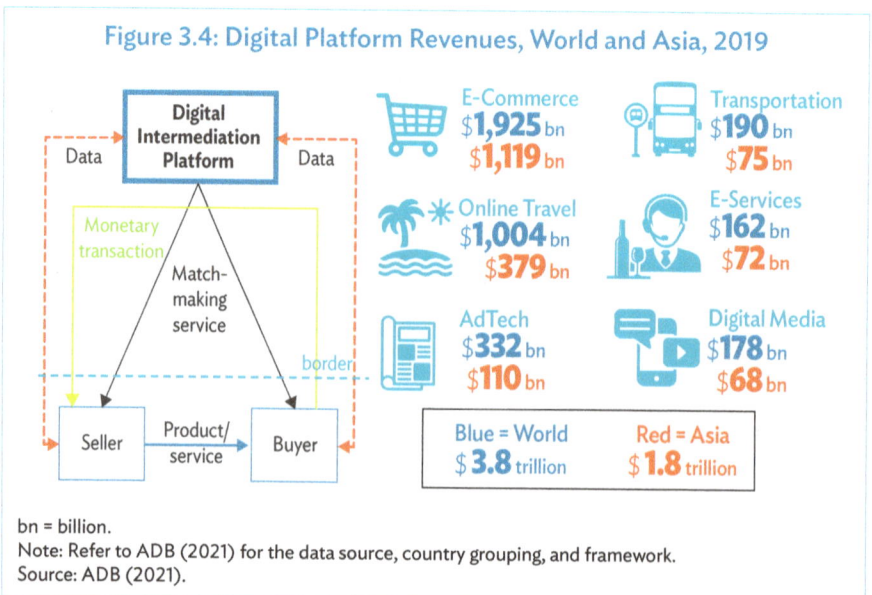

Figure 3.4: Digital Platform Revenues, World and Asia, 2019

Digital Intermediation Platform

Data — Data

Monetary transaction

Match-making service

border

Seller — Product/service — Buyer

E-Commerce $1,925 bn / $1,119 bn

Transportation $190 bn / $75 bn

Online Travel $1,004 bn / $379 bn

E-Services $162 bn / $72 bn

AdTech $332 bn / $110 bn

Digital Media $178 bn / $68 bn

Blue = World $3.8 trillion   Red = Asia $1.8 trillion

bn = billion.
Note: Refer to ADB (2021) for the data source, country grouping, and framework.
Source: ADB (2021).

revenues, yielding over $1.9 trillion (ADB 2021). Online travel follows with over $1 trillion in revenues, AdTech with $332 billion, and transport with $190 billion. In Asia, e-commerce generated the largest revenue, which amounted to $1.1 trillion, followed by online travel with $379 billion, AdTech with $110 billion, and transport with $75 billion.

Asia captured about 48% of total sales revenue in 2019, equivalent to $1.8 trillion or 6.1% of its regional GDP. Within Asia, 68% of total sales revenue or over $1.2 trillion was generated in the PRC, which represents about 8.8% of that country's GDP (ADB 2021). Globally, the US ranked third, generating $837 billion or 3.9% of its GDP. The euro area followed, with about $445 billion sales revenue equivalent to 3.3% of its GDP (Table 3.1).

Table 3.1: Digital Revenue by Region, 2019
($ billion)

Sector	World	Asia	Dev Asia (ex PRC)	PRC	ANZ + Japan	Euro area	US	RoW
Digital media	177.5	67.6	13.8	35.0	18.9	17.3	57.6	35.0
E-commerce	1,924.9	1,119.2	143.3	862.6	113.3	196.0	343.1	266.5
E-services	161.8	71.7	16.3	47.0	8.4	15.0	42.8	32.3
Online travel	1,003.8	379.5	127.8	179.8	71.9	173.5	199.1	251.8
AdTech	331.7	110.4	15.4	71.4	23.6	29.2	129.9	62.2
Transportation	190.3	75.4	19.8	48.8	6.8	14.2	64.2	36.5
Total	3,790.0	1,823.7	336.3	1,244.6	242.8	445.3	836.7	684.3
% of GDP	4.4	6.1	3.7	8.8	3.6	3.3	3.9	3.3
Per capita spend	513.9	432.3	121.1	863.6	1,547.6	1,308.2	2,542.5	275.1

ANZ+Japan = Australia, New Zealand, and Japan; GDP = gross domestic product; PRC = People's Republic of China; RoW = rest of the world; US = United States.
Notes: Refer to Table 8.3 of ADB (2021) for the list of economies. The raw data are taken from Statista.
Source: ADB (2021).

Per capita, however, the US leads other regions and countries in spending, recording $2,542 per capita spending on digital platforms. Australia, New Zealand, and Japan (as a group) follow, with $1,548 and the euro area with $1,308. The spending in Asia was way below, at only $432 per capita—lower than the average per capita spending worldwide.

Asia is also the growing in digital platform revenues based on most recent data available, recording double-digit growth in revenue in 2019 from 2018 (Table 3.2). The growth of digital platform revenue in Asia reached 16.1%, higher than the global growth rate, at 12.7%. The growth of digital platform

Table 3.2: Growth of Digital Revenue by Sector, 2019
(%)

Sector	World	Asia	Dev Asia (ex PRC)	PRC	ANZ + Japan	Euro area	US	RoW
Digital media	6.3	7.1	11.0	8.8	1.6	5.6	5.3	6.8
E-commerce	16.4	19.6	28.3	19.7	9.7	10.4	11.0	14.8
E-services	16.0	18.8	22.8	18.7	12.3	15.5	10.0	18.3
Online travel	7.2	9.1	10.2	10.7	3.3	5.6	6.0	6.6
AdTech	14.4	14.3	15.4	16.2	8.5	11.9	15.6	13.3
Transportation	8.0	12.4	12.4	13.6	4.7	6.9	4.3	6.6
Total	**12.7**	**16.1**	**18.3**	**17.5**	**6.9**	**8.4**	**9.5**	**10.8**

ANZ+Japan = Australia, New Zealand, and Japan; PRC = People's Republic of China; GDP = gross domestic product; RoW = rest of the world; US = United States.
Notes: Refer to Table 8.3 of ADB (2021) for the list of economies. The raw data are taken from Statista.
Source: ADB (2021).

revenues in developing Asia, excluding the PRC, is even faster, at 18.3%; while in the PRC the growth stands at 17.6%. In contrast, the growth of digital platform revenue in the US and euro area are only 9.5% and 8.4%, respectively. This suggests that Asia will be the center of global competition among the big digital platform companies in the world.

Looking at the composition of digital revenue by sector (Table 3.3), one sees Asia's dominant role in all sectors, except in AdTech, where the US dominates largely because of the role of Google and Facebook. In e-commerce, Asia captures over 58% of total sales revenue. In e-services, the region accounts for 44.3%, while its share is over 38% in both transportation and digital media, which is larger than the US (ADB 2021). The PRC remains the most active country in the region. For instance, it accounts for about 44.8% of the sales in e-commerce, 29.1% of the sales in e-services, and over 25% of sales in transportation (ADB 2021). While Australia, New Zealand, and Japan are advanced economies, their share in digital platform revenues are in single digits, except for digital media—which stands at 10.6%—where Japan plays an important role. The market in developing Asia (excluding the PRC) also plays a modest role, as it captures only from 10% to 13% of the revenues in online travel, transportation, and e-services; and only from 4% to 8% of the revenues in AdTech, e-commerce, and digital media.

Table 3.3: Digital Revenue, 2019
(% share of region in segment)

Sector	Asia	Dev Asia (ex PRC)	PRC	ANZ + Japan	Euro area	US	RoW
Digital media	38.1	7.8	19.7	10.6	9.7	32.4	19.7
E-commerce	58.1	7.4	44.8	5.9	10.2	17.8	13.8
E-services	44.3	10.1	29.1	5.2	9.3	26.5	20.0
Online travel	37.8	12.7	17.9	7.2	17.3	19.8	25.1
AdTech	33.3	4.6	21.5	7.1	8.8	39.2	18.7
Transportation	39.6	10.4	25.6	3.6	7.5	33.8	19.2
Total	**48.1**	**8.9**	**32.8**	**6.4**	**11.7**	**22.1**	**18.1**

ANZ+Japan = Australia, New Zealand and Japan; PRC = People's Republic of China; RoW = rest of the world; US = United States.
Notes: Refer to Table 8.5 of ADB (2021) for the list of economies. The raw data are taken from Statista.
Source: ADB (2021).

Another indicator of the importance of digital platforms is the growing number of users (Table 3.4). Among the digital platform sectors, AdTech—which includes social media apps such as Facebook and Google—ranks first in users, with over 4.1 billion, equivalent to more than half of the world population. E-commerce subscribers' accounts total close to 3.2 billion, about 60% of which are in Asia. Meanwhile, accounts in digital media that include e-services, Netflix, Spotify, and online travel and transport number over 1.4 billion, with 775 million in the region (ADB 2021).

Table 3.4: Total Users in 2019 and Growth Rate in 2018–2019

Segment	World		Asia	
	Number (million)	Growth Rate (%)	Number (million)	Growth Rate (%)
Digital media	1,438.3	6.1	774.8	6.5
E-commerce	3,170.8	15.4	1,876.4	17.9
E-services	815.4	12.1	463.6	13.6
Online travel	987.6	2.5	540.4	2.8
Transportation	632.6	2.8	403.9	3.2
AdTech-exposed internet users	4,119.5	9.2	2,338.0	11.9

Notes: Refer to Table 8.6 of ADB (2021) for the list of economies. The raw data are taken from Statista.
Source: ADB (2021).

3.5. Macroeconomic Impact of Digitalization

Historically, the rapid improvement in information and communications technology (ICT), which saw a significant drop in the price of broadband and smartphones and increased computing power, has unleashed the power of the internet economy. In the 3 years to 2018, the cost of international internet bandwidth for internet protocol transit dropped an average of 27% annually. This allowed businesses and people to increase data usage and expanded the availability and use of smartphones globally. The enhanced ability to process data created also a shift toward a data-centric business model and a new data value chain, where businesses now build comparative advantage based on their ability to collect, store, analyze, and monetize data. Similarly, the evolution of the various technologies will drive the growth of digital platforms.

In what follows, this chapter examines the macroeconomic benefits of increased usage of digital technology. This could be partly attributed to the transformation in work arrangement, education, acquiring goods and services, health provision, and entertainment that has occurred during the COVID-19 pandemic.

The size of the digital economy depends on the definition used. Presently, various studies estimate the size of the digital economy to be roughly between 4.5% and 15.5% of global GDP. The digital sector within the digital economy is even smaller. Its size is estimated to be somewhere between 1% and 6% of GDP (Villafuerte 2020). To estimate the macroeconomic benefits from the increased usage of digital technology, a scenario that leads to a 20% increase in the digital sector size from the baseline by 2025 is analyzed (Figure 3.5).

Scenario

The digital transformation scenario considers an increasing investment in the digital sector. This will directly impact the economy as output rises in sectors that use digital inputs more intensively. At the same time, aggregate productivity in the economy also goes up. Consequently, the size of the global digital sector is expected to rise an average of roughly $617 billion per year from baseline levels, or $3.1 trillion in total from 2021 to 2025. Similarly, the digital sector in Asia is expected to increase by about $184 billion per year from the baselines, or about $919 billion in 5 years.

Figure 3.5: Size of the Digital Sector, World and Asia ($ trillion)

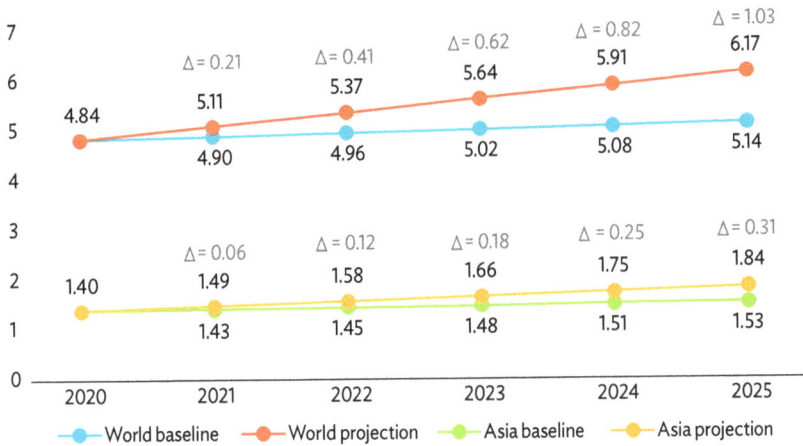

Notes: The calculations are based on the Global Trade Analysis Project (GTAP) database. Asia refers to Asia and the Pacific. In this case, economies that are not ADB members are included due to the aggregation of the Pacific subregion in GTAP. The numbers do not necessarily sum up due to rounding. Source: Authors.

This scenario tries to capture the digital transformation observed in 2020, when the COVID-19 pandemic led to online work from home, remote learning, telehealth, online purchases, and home deliveries for groceries, and the use of digital payments and e-wallets, to reliance on digital media and entertainment. It is expected that this trend will continue as social control measures remain in place because of the pandemic.

The expansion of investment was implemented by endogenizing productivity growth in the digital sector in line with the target 20% expansion in the output of the sector from 2020 to 2025. More importantly, it is also known that the expansion in the digital sector will boost total factor productivity in the economy. Based on a literature review, it is assumed that the total factor productivity across the world increases by 1% for every 10% of digital sector expansion. In other words, global total factor productivity also increases by 2% from 2020 to 2025 in the modeling scenario.

Model

The modeling exercise for this undertaking employs the recursive-dynamic GDyn developed by Ianchovichina and Walmsley (2012). The GDyn Model is the dynamic extension of the standard GTAP model, which is a multi-region multi-sector Computable General Equilibrium (CGE) model. This dynamic CGE model combines aspects of financial assets and associated income flows, capital accumulation, and investment theory. The model also takes a disequilibrium approach to account for capital mobility. It allows for short- and medium-term variances in the rates of return across regions that imply imperfect capital mobility. In the long run, these different rates can be eliminated to achieve perfect capital mobility across regions. Financial assets are also treated in a stylized way in this model to represent international capital mobility with no links to foreign accounts. In the real world there are many types of financial assets, but in the model there is only one financial asset—which is equity representing an indirect claim on a physical asset—but there is no financial sector. Adaptive expectations are also assumed in the model with the net rates of return, expected and actual, converging over time within and across regions.

Data

The simulation draws from Global Trade Analysis Project (GTAP) 10A database with a reference year of 2014 (Carrico, Corong, and van der Mensbrugghe 2020), which the authors updated to 2019 using World Bank macro data sets and the Asian Development Bank (ADB) Multi-Region Input–Output database. The results from the long containment scenario of a previous ADB study on the global economic impact of the pandemic were incorporated into the 2020 baseline. In addition, a number of the parameters used in this simulation exercise are based on Golub and McDougall (2006).

In order to extend the baseline for macro variables beyond 2020, particularly GDP and population projections by organizations such as the International Monetary Fund, Organisation for Economic Co-operation and Development, the United Nations (UN), and the World Bank were adopted. These are further revised and collated in the Shared Socioeconomic Pathways data set by the International Institute for Applied Systems Analysis (Riahi et al. 2017).[3] GDP projections are sourced from International Monetary Fund, the UN, and the World Bank, while the population and labor force growth projections are taken from the UN and the International Labour Organization. From the different scenarios in the Shared Socioeconomic Pathways data

---

[3] Refer to Moss et al. (2010); Arnell, van Vuuren, and Isaac (2011); van Vuuren et al. (2012); and Kriegler et al. (2012) for discussion on the methods.

set that represent different levels of interactions between sustainability and growth, a balanced projection was chosen for this exercise, which corresponds to the middle path of the Organisation for Economic Co-operation and Development methodology (ADB 2021).

After the baseline is developed, the policy simulation is implemented by expanding the size of digital sector in all economies covered incrementally by 20% from the baseline, to 2025. It is also assumed that use of greater digital inputs would increase total factor productivity growth by 2% in all sectors from 2020 to 2025, as previously noted. Note, however, that before the simulation exercise is carried out, the communication sector in GTAP is divided into the digital platform sector and other communication sector, using several global and national datasets, and literature as the basis.

Economic Impact

The simulation results show that broader digitalization will have a substantial impact on global economic growth, exports, and employment. The simulation exercise indicates an increase in global GDP by about $4.3 trillion per year, equivalent to 5.4% of the baseline 2020 GDP, and accumulates to about $21.4 trillion in 5 years. These are the same results shown in ADB (2021). Asia accounts for over 40% of the increase in global output, where output in the region is estimated to increase by about $1.7 trillion yearly, or about 6.1% of the baseline 2020 GDP. The total increase in output in Asia reaches more than $8.6 trillion over the 5-year period (Table 3.5). As mentioned, the output increase stems from larger investment and usage of the digital sector, which also generates improvement in total factor productivity. Roughly about a third of the GDP increase can be explained by the expansion of the digital sector while productivity improvement accounts for the rest.

The US and Europe—the Group of 2 (G2)—will also benefit significantly from this digital transformation capturing over 34% of the global increase in output equivalent to $7.2 trillion increase in GDP from 2021 to 2025.

Similarly, global trade is expected to increase by almost $2.4 trillion a year on average from 2021 to 2025 (Figure 3.6). This is commensurate to 5.5% increase in the 2020 baseline total trade. In total, this translates to over $11.8 trillion in additional trade value in 5 years. Asia will account for about 43% of this trade gain: with the region's cross-border trade value rising by over $1 trillion annually, or about 6.8% of their 2020 regional trade.

Table 3.5: GDP Impact of Digital Transformation, 2021–2025

Economy	Gains from same year baselines ($ billion)						
	2021	2022	2023	2024	2025	Total	Average
World	**1,532.6**	**2,950.4**	**4,311.0**	**5,646.0**	**6,974.4**	**21,414.4**	**4,282.9**
Asia	**606.5**	**1,180.2**	**1,738.0**	**2,287.6**	**2,832.9**	**8,645.0**	**1,729.0**
Australia and New Zealand	35.1	62.9	86.7	108.1	127.9	420.7	84.1
Central Asia	13.0	27.8	44.3	62.6	82.5	230.3	46.1
East Asia ex-PRC and Japan	50.5	95.4	137.0	176.5	214.7	674.0	134.8
PRC	183.2	338.8	470.6	580.2	667.9	2,240.7	448.1
Japan	137.1	268.8	398.9	529.5	662.1	1,996.4	399.3
Southeast Asia	88.9	181.8	280.2	385.1	496.9	1,432.9	286.6
South Asia	91.4	192.9	304.8	427.1	559.4	1,575.6	315.1
Pacific	7.2	11.8	15.4	18.6	21.5	74.4	14.9
G2	**565.5**	**1,048.3**	**1,479.1**	**1,875.7**	**2,249.4**	**7,217.9**	**1,443.6**
United States	232.1	422.5	586.1	730.8	862.0	2,833.5	566.7
EU-28	333.4	625.8	893.0	1,144.8	1,387.4	4,384.4	876.9
Rest of the World	**360.6**	**721.9**	**1,094.0**	**1,482.7**	**1,892.2**	**5,551.4**	**1,110.3**

Economy	Gains as proportion of 2020 baseline GDP (%)						
	2021	2022	2023	2024	2025	Total	Average
World	**1.9**	**3.7**	**5.5**	**7.2**	**8.8**	**27.1**	**5.4**
Asia	**2.1**	**4.1**	**6.1**	**8.0**	**9.9**	**30.3**	**6.1**
Australia and New Zealand	2.5	4.4	6.1	7.6	8.9	29.4	5.9
Central Asia	3.2	6.9	11.1	15.7	20.6	57.6	11.5
East Asia ex-PRC and Japan	2.2	4.2	6.0	7.7	9.4	29.4	5.9
PRC	1.5	2.9	4.0	4.9	5.6	18.9	3.8
Japan	2.7	5.3	7.9	10.5	13.1	39.5	7.9
Southeast Asia	2.6	5.4	8.3	11.3	14.6	42.2	8.4
South Asia	2.2	4.7	7.5	10.5	13.8	38.7	7.7
Pacific	13.0	21.2	27.8	33.5	38.7	134.2	26.8
G2	**1.7**	**3.2**	**4.5**	**5.7**	**6.8**	**21.9**	**4.4**
United States	1.4	2.5	3.5	4.3	5.1	16.7	3.3
EU-28	2.1	3.9	5.6	7.1	8.6	27.3	5.5
Rest of the World	**2.1**	**4.2**	**6.3**	**8.5**	**10.9**	**31.9**	**6.4**

EU = European Union, G2 = Group of 2, GDP = gross domestic product, PRC = People's Republic of China.
Notes: The calculations are based on the Global Trade Analysis Project (GTAP) database. Asia refers to Asia and the Pacific. In this case, economies that are not Asian Development Bank members are included due to the aggregation of the Pacific subregion in GTAP. The numbers do not necessarily sum up due to rounding.
Source: Authors.

Figure 3.6: Trade and Employment Impact from Digital Transformation, 2021–2025

a. Total Trade ($ trillion)

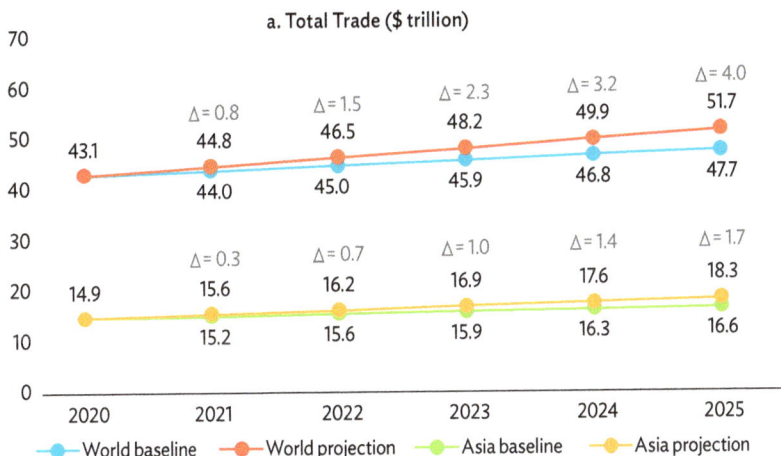

	2020	2021	2022	2023	2024	2025
World baseline	43.1	44.0	45.0	45.9	46.8	47.7
World projection	43.1	44.8 (Δ=0.8)	46.5 (Δ=1.5)	48.2 (Δ=2.3)	49.9 (Δ=3.2)	51.7 (Δ=4.0)
Asia baseline	14.9	15.2	15.6	15.9	16.3	16.6
Asia projection	14.9	15.6 (Δ=0.3)	16.2 (Δ=0.7)	16.9 (Δ=1.0)	17.6 (Δ=1.4)	18.3 (Δ=1.7)

— World baseline — World projection — Asia baseline — Asia projection

b. Total Employment (million)

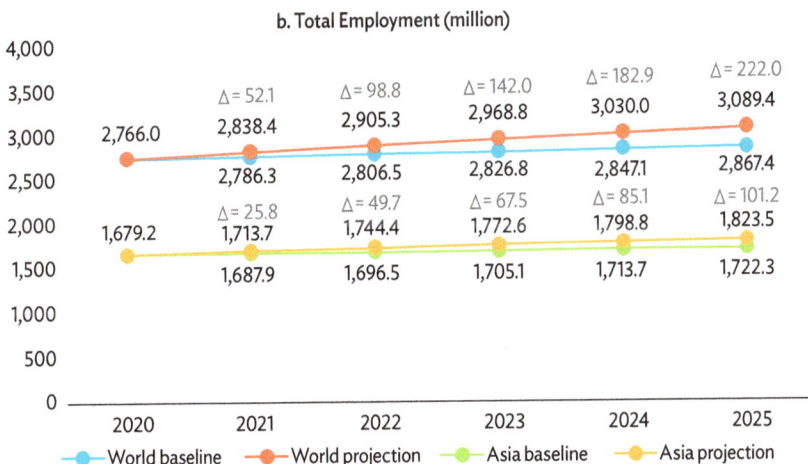

	2020	2021	2022	2023	2024	2025
World baseline	2,766.0	2,786.3	2,806.5	2,826.8	2,847.1	2,867.4
World projection	2,766.0	2,838.4 (Δ=52.1)	2,905.3 (Δ=98.8)	2,968.8 (Δ=142.0)	3,030.0 (Δ=182.9)	3,089.4 (Δ=222.0)
Asia baseline	1,679.2	1,687.9	1,696.5	1,705.1	1,713.7	1,722.3
Asia projection	1,679.2	1,713.7 (Δ=25.8)	1,744.4 (Δ=49.7)	1,772.6 (Δ=67.5)	1,798.8 (Δ=85.1)	1,823.5 (Δ=101.2)

— World baseline — World projection — Asia baseline — Asia projection

Notes: The calculations are based on the Global Trade Analysis Project (GTAP) database. Asia refers to Asia and the Pacific. In this case, economies that are not Asian Development Bank members are included due to the aggregation of the Pacific subregion in GTAP. The numbers do not necessarily sum up due to rounding.
Source: Authors.

In total, Asia will realize a $5 trillion gain in trade until 2025. The US and Europe are expected to capture 33% of the global increase in total trade equivalent to over $3.8 trillion in 2021–2025.

Global employment is estimated to increase by about 140 million jobs every year or equivalent to 5.0% of the 2020 baseline global employment. With this rate of expansion, total jobs generated will be about 698 million by the end of 2025. Similarly, employment in Asia is expected to expand more than 65 million a year from its baseline levels or equivalent to 3.9% of the 2020 baseline. In total, the region will create over 327 million jobs during the 5-year period. In contrast, the US and Europe will create an additional 57.8 million jobs during the same period.

The estimated impact of the digital sector expansion, however, is not the same across all subregions in Asia (Table 3.5). The Pacific subregion will realize the most notable gains, with GDP expected to increase by an average annual 26.8%, employment by 26.1%, and trade by 15.6%, from 2021 to 2025, compared to respective 2020 baseline levels. Next is Central Asia, where GDP is estimated to increase annually by an average of 11.5%, employment by 7.1%, and trade by 7.7% relative to the 2020 baseline levels, during the same period. It is followed by Southeast Asia with estimated average annual gains of 8.4% in GDP, 6.2% in employment, and 8.0% in trade, relative to the 2020 baseline, also for the same period.

The larger expansion in output, employment, and trade in these subregions demonstrate the critical role of digital connectivity in overcoming geographic challenges. It also indicates the important productivity contribution of higher level of investments in the digital sector, especially for economies with very little or emerging digital presence. Similarly, greater adoption and usage of digital technologies can bring about a stronger digitally enabled trade in services, which can boost growth in the internal and external flow of goods and services.

3.6. How These Benefits Are Realized

Where do these large macroeconomic benefits from digital transformation come from? Generally, the large output, trade, and employment responses in the models come from two channels. The first channel is the direct expansion of the digital sector, which also raises the outputs of sectors supplying inputs to the digital sector. For example, as the work-from-home arrangement becomes the norm, a significant increase is seen in the demand for electrical and electronics equipment, which has also supported jobs, manufacturing activities, and exports in Asia and the world. The demand for software development critical for many of these apps also supported the expansion of digital services. In digital payments, the need to avoid physical contact has seen greater use of online payment platforms and digital currency.

The second channel is the productivity spillover that higher usage of digital inputs brings to all sectors in the economy. For example, during the pandemic, the usage of digital technology has increased digital marketplaces, including telehealth, online education, e-commerce, and other digital platforms for the exchange of goods and services. These digital marketplaces generated high-quality goods and services and created new jobs and huge network externalities. In activities which require physical contact, many of the processes were also redesigned to automate and to shift to online some of the physical interactions. And they make the process faster and more efficient.

Digital technology can similarly enhance the delivery of essential public services. One example is public access to better and safer health services and education. Digital platforms can now deliver health services to remote communities using drones to deliver medical supplies. Artificial intelligence (AI) is used to recognize patterns in images or scans, increasing ability to customize and speed up responses to health emergencies. The pandemic also changed how and where we learn, and to learn new or more relevant skills. Presently, students of all ages are increasingly using smart devices to expand their knowledge.

Digital technology can also facilitate better design, targeting, and delivery of social assistance programs. In the Philippines, for example, *Bayan Bayanihan*, an emergency food program, used poverty maps made by innovative data analysis to identify vulnerable populations. More than a billion people can tap digital platforms across Asia and the Pacific, which give these technologies the power to help end poverty and promote social inclusion and equity.

On a wider scale, digital technology can help open and connect markets safely. However, this can only happen if underlying issues such as access to technology and digital connectivity have been addressed. These issues relate mainly to the phenomenon of the digital divide.

Improved logistics and delivery based on paperless and digital systems can ease trade flows, ensuring that critical supplies get where they are needed. Blockchain technology can help exploit the benefits of strong supply chains by streamlining border administration. And critically, developing systems and regulations that upgrade financial services and broaden digital payment options can deliver safe and secure payment and financial transactions that support market liquidity and reduce financial risk.

Digital technology can be an impetus for developing and strengthening new drivers of inclusive economic growth. As policies allow for the greater adoption and use of digital technology, micro, small, and medium-sized enterprises can boost productive scale and efficiency and expand markets. Supplemented by technical support, toolkits, and free advisory services, they can now join a range of new online business practices.

Human capital investment and developing digital skills is a lifelong process. Hence, the quality and relevance of digital education and training need to be boosted. In the workplace, AI can support career coaching, contributing to better job matching. Increasing access to smart devices and online training platforms will help re-educate, re-skill, and prepare workers for the future.

3.7. Policy Challenges of Digitalization

While digital marketplaces continue to develop rapidly, their success is not inevitable. How authorities in the region form policies and regulations to respond to opportunities and new challenges associated with technologies is important in maximizing the potential benefits and managing the risks associated with digital platforms. There are a few important priorities, as noted in ADB (2021).

First, investment in the digital sector needs to increase sharply across the region to support the projected expansion in the output of the digital sector. Globally, investment in the sector from 2020 to 2025 has to rise by an average of $701 billion annually or by $3.5 trillion in total, over the 5-year period (Figure 3.7). For Asia, investment in the digital sector should increase by about $182 billion annually or $910 billion over the 5-year span. These additional investments are needed to expand internet access and coverage and deliver affordable mobile and broadband services.

Figure 3.7: Investment Requirement, 2021–2025
($ trillion)

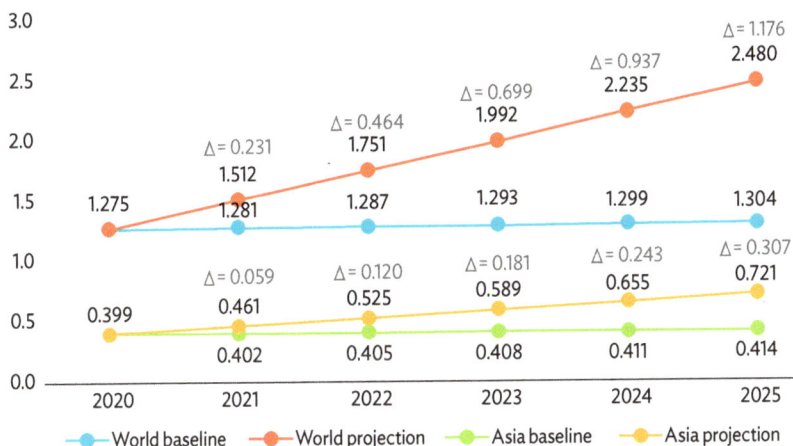

Notes: The calculations are based on the Global Trade Analysis Project (GTAP) database. Asia refers to Asia and the Pacific. In this case, economies that are not Asian Development Bank members are included due to the aggregation of the Pacific subregion in GTAP. The numbers do not necessarily sum up due to rounding.
Source: Authors.

Improving the trade and logistics processes and infrastructure is another key reform area to alleviate existing barriers to deliver the goods more efficiently. Evidently, the gap in the Logistics Performance Index between the best and worst-connected economies is wide. Increasing the application of digital technology to automate border procedures and customs clearance is vital. In addition, broadening the access to secure and safe digital financial services and payment systems can enable financial inclusion and inclusive growth. Consequently, investing in training to raise the level of digital skills and literacy by providing access to the necessary ICT devices and online teaching platforms is crucial. Moreover, a smart, transparent, effective, and robust regulatory system to protect personal data, prevent illegal activities, and strengthen cybersecurity will be useful.

Digital platforms will change markets, their participants, and the wider economy by reinventing market arrangements and creating new business models to generate and capture value. For instance, the growth of e-commerce in many economies has reduced retailers' profit margins and put enterprises out of business. The online platforms have also affected labor market arrangements through independent contracts, with little employment protection and social security (Villafuerte 2020). Hence, as Villafuerte (2020) explained, it is important to consider appropriate regulations to manage the unintended adverse effects attributed to the emergence of digital platforms, including:

- *Competition.* Digital platforms have a "double-edged" nature. Numerous micro-businesses around the world may gain from unprecedented opportunities provided by these platforms, but they can also give rise to one or very few "winners" due to strong network effects. Authorities ought to design policies that encourage more competition and ease barriers to entry, while maintaining the network effect benefits those large platforms can bring. Governments should also promote interoperability to help market players collaborate and innovate for the benefit of consumers.

- *Labor security and social protection.* Governments should consider rolling out emergency health and social services and increase the coverage of social protection systems to cover workers who may fall into poverty, regardless of their working arrangements. This would include workers who lose their jobs due to the closure of physical retail outlets as a result of competition from digital platforms.

- *Data access, privacy, and security.* Digital platforms should exercise caution and maintain transparency in using, sharing, and creating value from the intrinsic value of data. Policies and regulations should uphold individual privacy and ensure that access to data and information is secure and not used to discriminate against different groups. Authorities can also help build effective security policies, and regulations will ensure information bring more evenly distributed benefits. In addition, cybercrime must be addressed.

- *Taxation.* Among many other concerns, taxing digital platforms is challenging due to difficulties in classifying digital activities, regulatory issues, and lack of cross-border harmonization on tax matters. As digital-enabled transactions become increasingly cross-border, greater international cooperation and stronger dialogue on policy making related to taxation issues are crucial.

While digital platforms continue to emerge rapidly, success is not preordained, as there will be many challenges and disruptions. Although technology could bring adverse changes, it could also usher in positive and inclusive development impacts. For example, the diffusion and application of digital platforms that are already available have strong potential to significantly raise agricultural and rural productivity, increase access to health and education, and greatly improve standards of living. These new emerging technology platforms could also allow developing economies to pursue an innovation pathway different from what advanced economies have tracked. How Asian economies respond and manage this digital transformation will determine their economic fortune.

References

Abell, T. E. 2020. Key Technologies Critical to Growth of Digital Platforms and the Digital Economy. Unpublished Manuscript.

Arnell, N., D. van Vuuren, and M. Isaac. 2011. The Implications of Climate Policy for the Impacts of Climate Change on Global Water Resources. *Global Environmental Change*. 21 (2). pp. 592–603.

Asian Development Bank (ADB). 2021. *Asian Economic Integration Report 2021: Making Digital Platforms Work for Asia and the Pacific*. Manila. http://dx.doi.org/10.22617/TCS210048-2.

Carrico, C., E. Corong, and D. van der Mensbrugghe 2020. The GTAP version 10A Multi-Region Input Output (MRIO) Data Base. *GTAP Memorandum*. No. 34. Center for Global Trade Analysis, Purdue University.

Evans, D. and R. Schmalensee. 2007. The Industrial Organization of Markets with Two-Sided Platforms. *Competition Policy International*. 3 (1). pp. 151–179.

Evans, D. S. 2018. *Essential Principles for the Design of Antitrust Analysis for Multisided Platforms*. http://dx.doi.org/10.2139/ssrn.3261812.

Evans, P. 2016. The Rise of Asian Platforms: A Regional Survey. *The Emerging Platform Economy Series*. *3*. New York: The Centre for Global Enterprise.

Evans, P. and A. Gawer. 2016. The Rise of the Platform Enterprise: A Global Survey. *The Emerging Platform Economy Series, 1*. New York: The Centre for Global Enterprise.

Golub, A. and R. McDougall. 2006. New Household Saving Behavior in the Dynamic GTAP Model. 9th Annual Conference on Global Economic Analysis. Addis Ababa. https://www.gtap.agecon.purdue.edu/resources/download/2713.pdf.

Ianchovichina, E. and T. Walmsley, eds. 2013. *Dynamic Modeling and Applications for Global Economic Analysis*. Cambridge: Cambridge University Press.

Kenney, M. and J. Zysman. 2016. The Rise of the Platform Economy. *Issues in Science and Technology*. 32 (3). pp. 61–69.

Kriegler, E., B. O'Neill, S. Hallegatte, T. Kram, R. Lempert, R. Moss, and T. Wilbanks. 2012. The Need for and Use of Socio-economic Scenarios for Climate Change Analysis: A New Approach Based on Shared Socio-economic Pathways. *Global Environmental Change*. 22 (4). pp. 807–822.

Koskinen, K., C. Bonina, and B. Eaton. 2019. Digital Platforms in the Global South: Foundations and Research Agenda. In P. Nielsen and H. C. Kimaro, eds. *Information and Communication Technologies for Development. Strengthening Southern-Driven Cooperation as a Catalyst for ICT4D*. pp. 319–330, 2019. https://doi.org/10.1007/978-3-030-18400-1_26.

Moss, R. H., J. A. Edmonds, K. A. Hibbard, M. R. Manning, S. K. Rose, D. P. van Vuuren, T. R. Carter, S. Emori, M. Kainuma, T. Kram, G. A. Meehl, J. F. B. Mitchell, N. Nakicenovic, K. Riahi, S. J. Smith, R. J. Stouffer, A. M. Thomson, J. P. Weyant, and T. J. Wilbanks. 2010. The Next Generation of Scenarios for Climate Change Research and Assessment. *Nature*. 463 (7282). pp. 747–756.

Riahi, K., D. P. van Vuuren, E. Kriegler, J. Edmonds, B. C. O'Neill, S. Fujimori, N. Bauer, K. Calvin, R. Dellink, O. Fricko, W. Lutz, A. Popp, J. C. Cuaresma, S. Kc, M. Leimbach, L. Jiang, T. Kram, S. Rao, J. Emmerling, K. Ebi, T. Hasegawa, P. Havlik, F. Humpenöder, L. A. Da Silva, S. Smith, E. Stehfest, V. Bosettii, J. Eom, D. Gernaat, T. Masui, J. Rogelj, J. Strefler, L. Drouet, V. Krey, G. Luderer, M. Harmsen, K. Takahashi, L. Baumstark, J. C. Doelman, M. Kainuma. Z. Klimont, G. Marangoni, H. Lotze-Campen, M. Obersteiner, A. Tabeau, and M. Tavoniijo. 2017. The Shared Socioeconomic Pathways and their Energy, Land Use, and Greenhouse Gas Emissions Implications: An Overview. *Global Environmental Change*. 42. pp. 153–168. https://doi.org/10.1016/j.gloenvcha.2016.05.009.

Roser, M. and H. Ritchie 2013. Technological Progress. OurWorldInData.

———. 2020. Technological Progress. OurWorldInData. https://ourworldindata.org/technological-progress.

UNCTAD. 2018. *Fostering Development Gains from E-commerce and Digital Platforms*. Background note for the Intergovernmental Group of Experts on E-Commerce and the Digital Economy. Geneva.

———— . 2019. *Digital Economy Report 2019: Value Creation and Capture: Implications for Developing Countries*. New York: United Nations.

Van Gorp, N. and O. Batura. 2015. *Challenges for Competition Policy in a Digitalised Economy*. Study for the European Parliament's Committee on Economic and Monetary Affairs. http://www.europarl.europa.eu/RegData/etudes/STUD/2015/542235/IPOL_STU%282015%29542235_EN.pdf.

van Vuuren, D., M. Kok, B. Girod, P. Lucas, and B. de Vries. 2012. Scenarios in Global Environmental Assessments: Key Characteristics and Lessons for Future Use. *Global Environmental Change*. 22 (4). pp. 884–895.

Villafuerte, J. 2020. COVID 19: There's an App for That. In B. Susantono, Y. Sawada, and C.Y. Park, eds. *Navigating COVID-19 in Asia and the Pacific*. Manila: Asian Development Bank. https://www.adb.org/sites/default/files/publication/633861/navigating-covid-19-asia-pacific.pdf.

World Bank. 2016. *World Development Report 2016: Digital Dividends*. Washington, DC: World Bank.

Trade and E-Commerce in Asia: Policy Considerations

Ryan Jacildo[1]

4.1. Introduction

The continued rapid expansion of e-commerce globally presents growth opportunities for Asia and the Pacific economies.[2] To benefit, they have to navigate policy areas with a clear mindset and a forward-looking perspective. E-commerce transforms trade by making the flow of information more efficient throughout the transaction process, making the flow of funds faster and less costly through the ancillary e-payment services, and increasing the traffic of retail parcels across borders.

This chapter first seeks to establish empirically the extent to which e-commerce market development is influencing the bilateral flow of consumer goods trade in Asia and the Pacific. The proposition is that e-commerce activity of trading economies has a significant positive effect on the magnitude of their bilateral consumer goods trade. E-commerce development feeds into trade directly and indirectly. The direct channel pertains to transactions made online and the producer is based offshore. The indirect channel pertains to purchases that pass through traditional linkages but are distributed via the domestic e-commerce ecosystem.

[1] The author is grateful for the insightful comments and inputs from James Villafuerte, Ramonette Serafica, Mara Claire Tayag, Josef T. Yap, Paul Mariano, ADB Economics Research and Regional Cooperation Department colleagues, and participants of the workshop *Making Digital Economies Work for Asia* on 26 June 2020. The author also thanks Mara Claire Tayag and Paulo Rodelio Halili for the overall research and coordination support as well as Joshua Anthony Ortalla Gapay and Arjan Paulo Salvanera for their contribution to the database used in the study.
[2] This chapter was prepared as a background paper for ADB (2021).

The second objective of the chapter is to lay out the policy issues relevant to the linkage between e-commerce and trade. These issues include the competitiveness of local entrepreneurs in the digital space, the underlying support infrastructure, trade facilitation, and compliance to customs regulations.

In the subsequent discussion, Section 2 reviews the literature on the relationship between e-commerce and cross-border trade. Section 3 describes the framework of analysis, the characteristics of internet retailing and platform revenue data used in the analysis, and the details of the methodology. Section 4 lays out the results of the empirical exercise. Section 5 fleshes out the policy considerations given the empirical results. And Section 6 sums up key messages of the research.

4.2. Background

As it expands globally, e-commerce causes various industries to modify business models and amplifies "servicification." Enterprise participation in digital platforms is arguably underpinned by network effects (Kinda 2019). Global e-commerce sales are estimated to have exceeded $25 trillion in 2018, or about 30% of gross domestic product (GDP) of economies included in the assessment (UNCTAD 2020). The report indicates that the business-to-business segment accounts for about 83% of sales and the rest by business-to-consumer (B2C).[3]

The deepening penetration of e-commerce is particularly important in Asia and the Pacific. United Nations Conference on Trade and Development (UNCTAD 2020) data put the People's Republic of China (PRC), Japan, and the Republic of Korea in the top five economies for total e-commerce sales, led by the United States. A separate report shows that Asia and the Pacific accounted for an estimated 44% of global B2C e-commerce turnover in 2019 (Ecommerce Foundation 2019).

The growing clout of digital platforms in e-commerce cannot be overlooked. E-commerce transforms trade in at least three ways. First, internet-based marketplaces make the flow of information more cost-efficient. This includes finding markets or suppliers in another country, getting information about the products, and facilitating and monitoring orders.

---

[3] UNCTAD (2020) makes no mention of the business-to-government segment.

Second, the accompanying e-payment systems make the flow of funds faster and less costly, with built-in validation mechanisms. Finally, e-commerce increases the traffic of *parcelized* cross-border shipments.

Empirical literature examining the relationship between e-commerce development and trade has gained traction in recent years. The lack of official and publicly available comprehensive cross-border e-commerce transactions datasets, however, remains a considerable limitation. As a result, existing analyses use privately collected data that only provide glimpses of the dynamics, as ADB and the United Nations Economic and Social Commission for Asia and the Pacific (UNESCAP) (2018) point out. Nevertheless, consensus appears to be growing on the significant impact of e-commerce on trade. The empirical results of this chapter not only lend support to this view, but also provide information on the magnitude of association between e-commerce development and bilateral trade.

Lendle et al. (2016) look into e-commerce platform data and links the trends with international trade. Specifically, it examines the changes in the distance parameter between transactions done via eBay and offline traditional trade. Notably, in the mid-2000s, eBay was one of the largest global online marketplaces. The Lendle et al. (2016) dataset comprises 61 developing and developed economies from 2004 to 2007. The eBay product categories are matched with product descriptions from the six-digit level HS classification to make the basket of goods comparable. Using ordinary least squares (OLS) and poisson pseudo maximum likelihood (PPML) to estimate a gravity model, they find that the effect of distance is reduced by an average of 65% (across commodities) on eBay that is attributed to lower search cost. They argue that the reduction in distance effect rises when information frictions are higher (e.g., different languages between trading economies or when corruption is high).

Gomez-Herrera, Martens, and Turlea (2014), who analyze a cross-sectional dataset that compares the online and offline trade, also confirm the reduction in distance-induced trade costs in online trade compared to offline trade. The analysis draws from a commissioned survey that contained information on online domestic and cross-border B2C trade in goods between the European Union member states. OLS, PPML, and Heckman techniques were employed to estimate the specified gravity model.

Meanwhile, Kim, Dekker, and Heij (2017) postulate that distance remains a key dampener of cross-border trade. However, ancillary services, such as express delivery, reduce the distance effect for cross-border demand.

The study uses the data of the central distribution center in the Netherlands on cross-border e-commerce services to 721 regions in five European Union economies: Germany, Italy, Spain, Sweden, and the United Kingdom (then a member). The gravity model is estimated using OLS.

Incidentally, while the studies linking e-commerce and international trade are emerging, extensive literature has examined the relationship between information and communication technology (ICT) and trade. Xing (2017), who analyzes the role of ICT and e-commerce indices in the trading patterns of 51 developed and developing economies, concludes that access to advanced ICT and e-commerce applications stimulates bilateral trade flows. The study uses a cross-section dataset and estimates a gravity model by OLS. Freund and Weinhold (2002, 2004), Tang (2006), Clarke and Wallsten (2006), Vemuri and Siddiqi (2009), Choi (2010), Liu and Nath (2014), and Yushkova (2014) also provide empirical evidence of the significant positive contribution of ICT in facilitating cross-border flow of goods and services.

4.3. Research Objectives

The existing literature largely provides evidence of the relative ease of online goods transactions. An ample number of studies examine the value of ICT infrastructure in fostering e-commerce development as well. To add another dimension to the analysis, this study seeks to establish empirically the extent to which e-commerce market development is influencing the bilateral consumer goods trade in Asia and the Pacific.

The study posits that the level of joint e-commerce activity of trading economies has a significant positive effect on the magnitude of bilateral trade. Following the framework in Figure 4.1, e-commerce development feeds into trade directly and indirectly. The direct channel pertains to transactions done online wherein the producer is based offshore. The e-commerce integrated platforms are part of this process. The indirect channel pertains to purchases that pass through traditional linkages but are distributed via the domestic e-commerce ecosystem.

Moreover, this chapter lays out policy issues relevant to the linkage between e-commerce development and trade. Notwithstanding efforts to generate e-commerce official statistics, issues related to consumer and data protection, data localization, and digital infrastructure have been highlighted.

Figure 4.1: E-Commerce and Cross-Border Trade Linkages

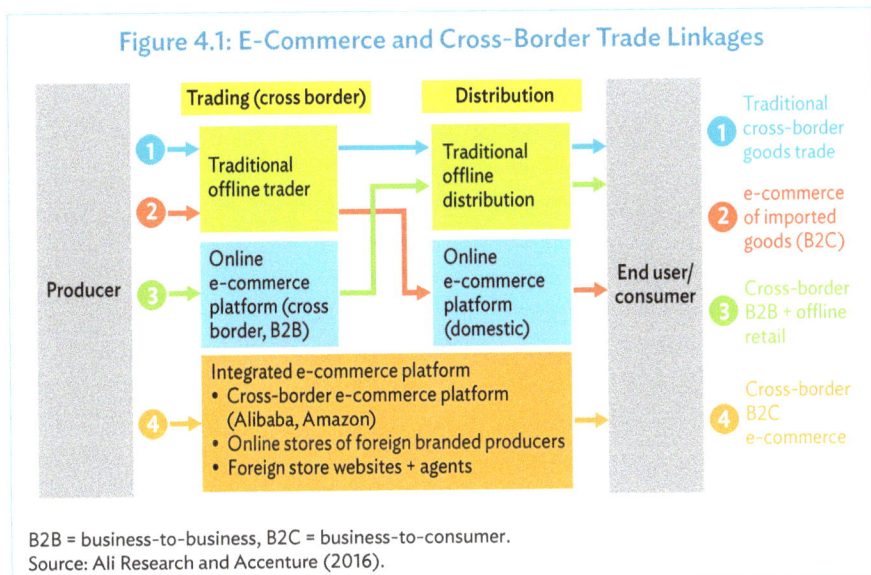

B2B = business-to-business, B2C = business-to-consumer.
Source: Ali Research and Accenture (2016).

Beyond these, concern exists about the ability of domestic firms to compete in e-commerce and for economies to maximize the value added of the local participation in e-commerce. Taxation, in particular the *de minimis* rule that can have domestic market competition implications, is another important issue. Finally, the evolving trade dynamics call into question the responsiveness of the trade agreements and free trade zone strategies to strengthen production bases and address related customs challenges.

4.4. Internet Retailing and Platform Revenues Data

The assessment takes advantage of e-commerce internet retailing data compiled by Euromonitor International at the country level and spanning 2006 to 2018, and platform revenues data in 2017 and 2018 from Statista. In this exercise, the internet retailing data serve as a proxy for the e-commerce market activity or e-commerce market development in each country. The e-commerce platform revenues data, on the other hand, proxy for e-commerce platform penetration.

Technically, internet e-commerce retailing is a subset of B2C e-commerce that excludes auctions or travel bookings (Francis and White 2004). However, it is arguably the biggest component of the B2C market. The internet retailing data of Euromonitor International is likewise one of the most comprehensive datasets available at present that is collected consistently over a considerable length of time.

Succinctly, the Euromonitor International internet retailing data refer to sales of consumer goods to the general public on the internet, including sales through mobile phones and tablets. The dataset is composed of sales from pure e-commerce websites and sites operated by traditional retail stores. The location of sales in the dataset refers to the consumer's country and the sources of information include public and private institutions. The dataset at hand covers 19 economies in Asia and the Pacific.[4] These economies each have data since 2006, except Azerbaijan (missing data in 2006), Pakistan (missing data in 2006 and 2007), and Viet Nam (missing data from 2006 to 2009).

Meanwhile, the platform revenues data are from Statista, compiled using primary survey, country-specific sources, industry associations, and third-party studies. E-commerce platform revenue comprises sales of physical goods via a digital channel to a private end user. In the dataset at hand, actual data are available for 2017–2018 covering 150 economies, of which 34 are from Asia and the Pacific.

4.5. General Trends and Preliminary Inspection

High-level inspection of the data show that the rate of expansion of internet retailing has been encouraging across Asian economies. Growth has gained some traction in recent years in Azerbaijan, Cambodia, the Lao People's Democratic Republic, Malaysia, Pakistan, the Republic of Korea, Singapore, Sri Lanka, Uzbekistan, and Viet Nam. Disaggregated data further reveal that the share of foreign retail sales grew faster across geographic clusters between 2011 and 2018 (Figure 4.2). This observation holds in 11 of 16 Asia and the Pacific economies, where disaggregation is available in our dataset. As a proportion of the countries' GDP, the range of ratios in 2018 is rather wide, i.e., between less than 0.02% and about 20%.

---

[4] The sample includes economies from Central Asia, East Asia, South Asia, and Southeast Asia.

Figure 4.2: Shares and Growth in Internet Retailing Sales by Segment

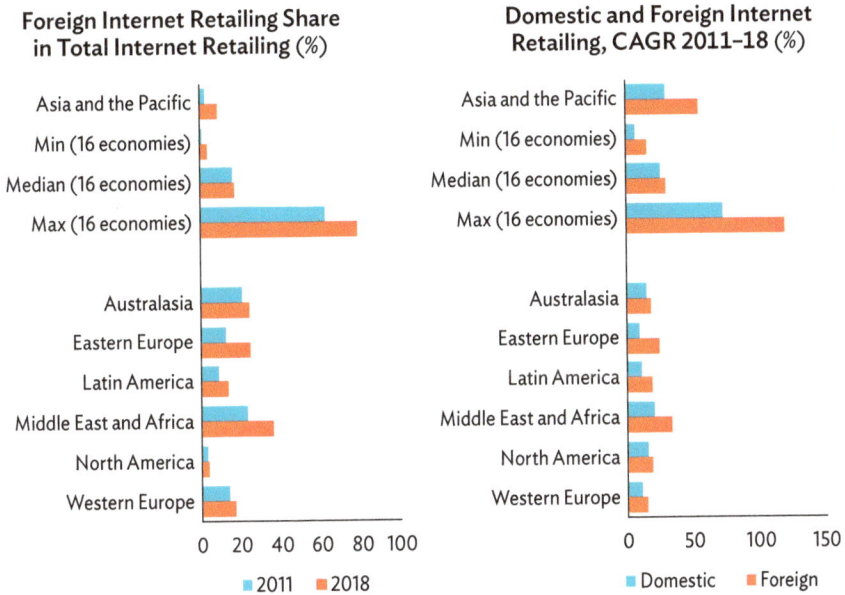

Foreign Internet Retailing Share in Total Internet Retailing (%)

(Categories: Asia and the Pacific, Min (16 economies), Median (16 economies), Max (16 economies), Australasia, Eastern Europe, Latin America, Middle East and Africa, North America, Western Europe; axis 0 20 40 60 80 100; legend: 2011, 2018)

Domestic and Foreign Internet Retailing, CAGR 2011–18 (%)

(Categories: Asia and the Pacific, Min (16 economies), Median (16 economies), Max (16 economies), Australasia, Eastern Europe, Latin America, Middle East and Africa, North America, Western Europe; axis 0 50 100 150; legend: Domestic, Foreign)

CAGR = compounded annual growth rate.
Note: Country groupings are based on the definitions of Euromonitor. Azerbaijan data start in 2007, Pakistan in 2008, and Viet Nam in 2010.
Source: Author, based on Euromonitor International Retailing industry edition 2019.

In cross-border transactions, the pair-wise, combined e-commerce internet retailing of the trading economies exhibits positive association with their bilateral trade (Figure 4.3), as expected. The association holds for both the full sample (2006–2018) and sub-sample (2012–2018). Similarly, digital e-commerce platforms are vital channels of digital retailing. Total e-commerce platform revenue in Asia and the Pacific 2017 and 2018 is about 3% of GDP in those 2 years (Figure 4.4). Among the subregions, East Asia has the highest ratio at almost 4%, then Oceania. Ratios are highly dispersed at the country level, i.e., between 5% and less than 0.04%. Overall, the combined e-commerce platform revenues of reporter and partner economies exhibit positive association with their bilateral consumer goods trade (Figure 4.5). The same can be observed if the sample is constrained to Asia and the Pacific reporting economies (Figure 4.6).

Figure 4.3: Combined Internet Retailing Sales and Bilateral Consumption Goods Trade, 2006–2018 and 2012–2018

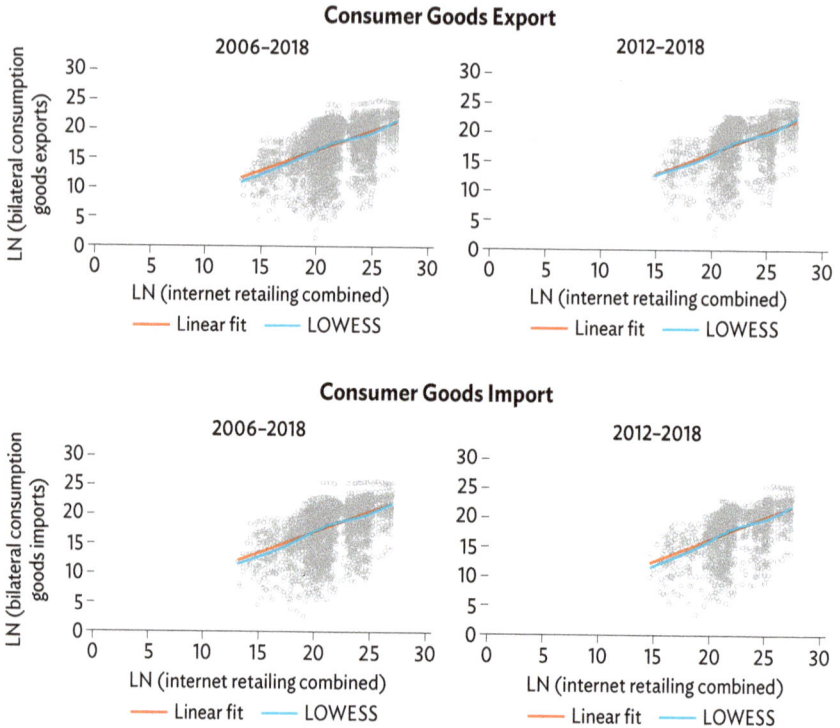

Consumer Goods Export

2006–2018

LN (bilateral consumption goods exports)

LN (internet retailing combined)

— Linear fit   — LOWESS

2012–2018

LN (internet retailing combined)

— Linear fit   — LOWESS

Consumer Goods Import

2006–2018

LN (bilateral consumption goods imports)

LN (internet retailing combined)

— Linear fit   — LOWESS

2012–2018

LN (internet retailing combined)

— Linear fit   — LOWESS

Note: LOWESS is a plot based on a locally weighted regression of the dependent and independent variables.
Sources: Author, based on Euromonitor International Retailing industry edition 2019 and UN Comtrade (accessed April 2020).

Figure 4.4: E-Commerce Platform Revenues, 2017–2018
(% of GDP)

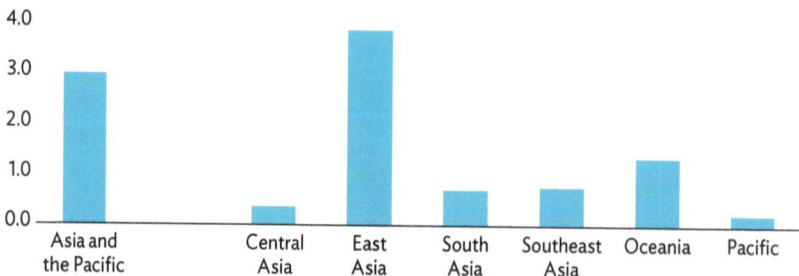

GDP = gross domestic product.
Source: ADB (2021).

Figure 4.5: Combined Platform Revenues and Bilateral Consumption Goods Trade, All Reporting Economies, 2017–2018

Consumer Goods Exports

Consumer Goods Imports

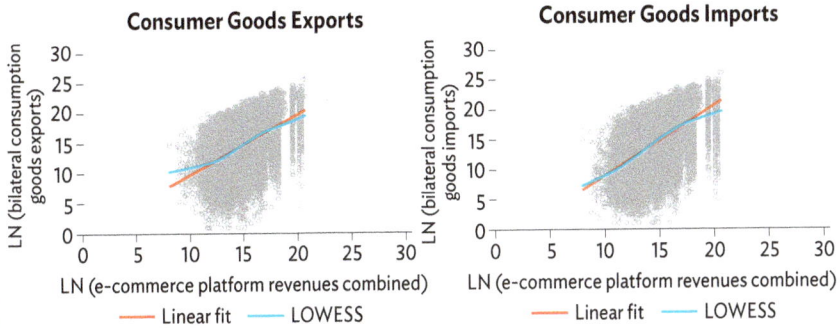

Note: LOWESS is a plot based on a locally weighted regression of the dependent and independent variables.
Sources: Author, based on Statista (2020a, 2020b) (accessed 15 July 2020) and UN Comtrade (accessed 15 April 2020).

Figure 4.6: Combined Platform Revenues and Bilateral Consumption Goods Trade, Reporting Asia and the Pacific Economies, 2017–2018

Consumer Goods Exports

Consumer Goods Imports

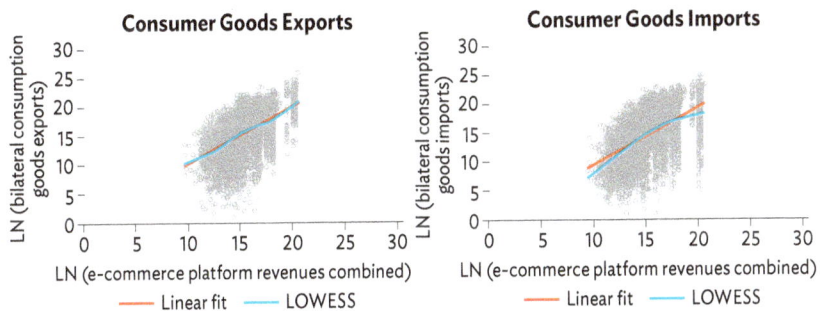

Note: LOWESS is a plot based on a locally weighted regression of the dependent and independent variables.
Sources: Author, based on Statista (2020a, 2020b) (accessed 15 July 2020) and UN Comtrade (accessed 15 April 2020).

4.6. The Gravity Model

To examine the relationship more rigorously, gravity model-based specifications are estimated. The analysis focuses on the sensitivity of consumer goods trade to the combined internet retailing activity and the penetration of e-commerce digital platforms in trading partner economies. The specification for the empirical exercise follows the theory-based gravity model of Anderson and van Wincoop (2003).[5] In this analysis, the baseline regression equation is given by equation 4.1, which is essentially split into fixed effects and trade cost variables and the combined e-commerce activity of the country pair. The extensive array of fixed effects control for the multilateral resistance.[6] These fixed effects also absorb the size variables and other observable and unobservable time-invariant characteristics of the economies (Yotov et al. 2016).

$$\text{Eq. 4.1.} \quad ln\, X_{ij,t} = c + \delta_{i,t} + \delta_{j,t} + \beta_1\, ln\, D_{ij} + \beta_2 Comcol_{ij} + \beta_3 Comlang_{ij} + \beta_4 Contig_{ij} + \beta_5 ln\, Eco_{ij,t} + \varepsilon_{ij,t}$$

D is the geographic distance. *Comcol, Comlang, Contig* are dummy variables indicating whether the partner economies have the same colonizer, a common official language, and common border, respectively. *Eco* is the combined internet e-commerce retailing sales (first set of estimates) and the e-commerce platform revenues in the two economies (second set of estimates). For this exercise, bilateral exports of consumption goods are used as the dependent variable. The betas are the parameters to be estimated and ε is the error term. Table 4.1 summarizes the data sources.

---

[5] Gomez-Herrera, Martens, and Turlea (2014) provide a detailed backstory of the use of the gravity model in analyzing trade flows. Lendle et al. (2016), Shepherd (2016), and Yotov et al. (2016) provide additional information on the derivation of the base equation.

[6] Following Anderson and van Wincoop (2003), the multilateral resistance captures the bilateral trade resistance between region i and region j with respect to region's i's resistance to trade with all regions, and region j's resistance to trade with all regions. The resulting panel is unbalanced. Fisher-type unit-root test was done to inspect the stationarity of the nominal variables.

Table 4.1: Primary Data and Data Sources

Data	Data Sources
Bilateral goods trade data	UN Comtrade database
Internet retailing e-commerce sales	Euromonitor International Retailing industry edition 2019
Platform revenues	Statista (2020a, 2020b)
Distance	CEPII
Contiguity	CEPII
Language	CEPII
Colonial history	CEPII
ICT indicators	World Bank, World Development Indicators

CEPII = Centre d'Etudes Prospectives et d'Informations Internationales, ICT = information and communication technology, UN = United Nations.
Note: All data in levels are in nominal terms.

Poisson pseudo maximum likelihood (PPML) is the primary estimation procedure employed, which, as proposed by Santos Silva and Tenreyro (2006), is advantageous in dealing with zero trade flows. The estimator is assessed to be well-behaved even if there are substantial numbers of zeros in the dataset (Santos Silva and Tenreyro 2011). More importantly, the PPML estimator is robust to heteroscedasticity. The PPML is also the suggested gravity model estimation technique in the manuals released by UNCTAD, World Trade Organization, and UNESCAP (Yotov et al. 2016; Shepherd 2016).

In estimating the PPML parameters, the codes put together by Correia, Guimarães, and Zylkin (2019) for *Stata* are utilized. This code set substantially increases the time efficiency in estimating the parameter values in the presence of multiple high-dimensional fixed effects. To ensure the existence of maximum likelihood estimates, the code identifies and does away with separated or problematic observations in the sample without losing relevant information.

For internet retailing sales, the panel dataset has an interval of 2 years, following Yotov et al. (2016). The rationale is that trade flows do not typically adjust within 1 year of changes in structural or policy variables. While it is desirable to have longer intervals akin to Trefler (2004) and Anderson and Yotov (2016), it will substantially reduce the observations. The Ramsey regression equation specification error test is used to assess the functional form of the PPML regression specifications. The baseline model is re-estimated using the gamma pseudo maximum likelihood (GPML), Heckman 2-stage sample selection, and OLS to check the robustness of the results.

To obtain information on parameter changes over time and across exported commodity types, variations of the baseline model have been estimated. Capital goods exports, intermediate goods exports, and total goods exports were also used as dependent variables. The idea is to examine potential spillovers into trade in other types of goods. The commodity compositions of consumer, intermediate, and capital goods follow the UN Comtrade Broad Economic Categories commodity classification and definitions. Technology access indicators such as internet and mobile phone usage have also been used in lieu of internet retailing e-commerce sales to extract information on their relative importance to consumer goods trade.

For the e-commerce platform revenues dataset, estimations are carried out in two ways due to the shortness of the time period, i.e., only 2 years. The dataset is first treated as a 2-year panel and then as a cross section (i.e., platform revenues and trade flows over the 2-year period are summed up) to verify if results hold or change. Estimations are also done across different regions, Asia and the Pacific, Europe, Africa, and the Americas, to draw information on variations in cross-regional dynamics. Consumer goods exports from UN Comtrade following the Broad Economic Categories classification are used as the dependent variable and PPML was the estimation technique employed in all platform-related estimations.

4.7. Results and Findings

The results of the estimations indicate that internet retailing e-commerce sales are seemingly positively driving the consumer goods trade. The corresponding parameter value using PPML estimation conveys a positive association between combined e-commerce sales of trading economies and their bilateral trade (Table 4.2, column 1). The positive association is supported by the results using the other three estimation techniques and is statistically significant in two, i.e., the OLS and Heckman (Table 4.2, columns 2–4). Separately, commonality in language and border are also associated with higher trade, while distance is a significant barrier to trade flows.[7]

---

[7] The beta parameters of the dummy variables give information on the semi-elasticities that can be calculated as $(e^{(beta)} - 1)*100$.

Table 4.2: E-Commerce and Consumption Goods Trade, 2006–2018

	Dependent Variable: Bilateral Consumption Goods Exports			
	PPML	**OLS**	**GPML**	**Heckman**[1]
Distance	−0.659***	−1.501***	−1.709***	−1.478***
	(0.1046)	(0.2166)	(0.2630)	(0.0764)
Common colony	−0.042	1.623***	1.749***	1.594***
	(0.1879)	(0.3885)	(0.2254)	(0.1211)
Common language	0.604***	−0.211	0.223	−0.194
	(0.1492)	(0.3185)	(0.2308)	(0.1505)
Contiguity	0.508***	0.433	0.655**	0.440***
	(0.1420)	(0.3200)	(0.2728)	(0.1352)
E-commerce	0.148**	0.156*	0.119	0.150***
	(0.0575)	(0.0940)	(0.1001)	(0.0402)
Constant	23.737***	16.548***	22.914***	16.824***
	(1.0406)	(2.8695)	(2.6022)	(1.0347)
Fixed effects:				
Exporter-year	Yes	Yes	Yes	Yes
Importer-year	Yes	Yes	Yes	Yes
Cluster exporter-importer	Yes	Yes	Yes	No
Total observations	1,977	1,935	1,977	2,229
Uncensored observations				1,935

CEPII = Centre d'Etudes Prospectives et d'Informations Internationales, GPML = gamma pseudo maximum likelihood, OLS = ordinary least squares, PPML = poisson pseudo maximum likelihood.
Notes: 1-FTA dummy variable sourced from the Asian Development Bank, Asia Regional Integration Center database was used as the auxiliary regression in the selection equation. The numbers in parentheses are the standard errors: *** p < 0.01, ** p < 0.05, * p < 0.10. The pseudo R-squared of the PPML is 0.9612. The Ramsey RESET Test was used to check the functional form.
Sources: Author, based on Euromonitor International Retailing industry edition 2019, UN Comtrade (accessed April 2020), and CEPII (accessed April 2020).

Interestingly, subsample inspection (2012–2018) supports the earlier finding on the relationship between internet retailing e-commerce sales and consumer goods cross-border trade and the parameter value has even risen using data in recent years (Table 4.3, column 1). The PPML internet retailing parameter, which indicates the elasticity of consumer goods exports to the combined internet retailing e-commerce activity (following Yotov et al. 2016), is positive, significant, and marginally higher than the full sample (i.e., from 0.148 to 0.165). The estimates using the other three methods indicate a similar story (Table 4.3, columns 2–4).

Table 4.3: E-Commerce and Consumption Goods Trade, 2012–2018

	Dependent Variable: Bilateral Consumption Goods Exports			
	PPML	OLS	GPML	Heckman[1]
Distance	-0.632 ***	-1.548 ***	-1.816 ***	-1.529 ***
	(0.1169)	(0.2317)	(0.2700)	(0.0995)
Common colony	-0.011	1.639 ***	1.635 ***	1.614 ***
	(0.1935)	(0.3962)	(0.2244)	(0.1554)
Common language	0.594 ***	-0.274	0.22	-0.251
	(0.1541)	(0.3377)	(0.2255)	(0.1995)
Contiguity	0.466 ***	0.367 ***	0.53 ***	0.374 **
	(0.1545)	(0.3385)	(0.2821)	(0.1754)
E-commerce	0.165 **	0.216 **	0.178 *	0.203 ***
	(0.0644)	(0.1003)	(0.1030)	(0.0536)
Constant	23.072 ***	16.552 ***	24.210 ***	16.643 ***
	(1.1354)	(3.0635)	(2.7920)	(1.2678)
Fixed effects:				
Exporter-year	Yes	Yes	Yes	Yes
Importer-year	Yes	Yes	Yes	Yes
Cluster exporter-importer	Yes	Yes	Yes	No
Total observations	1,239	1,219	1,239	1,352
Uncensored observations				1,219

GPML = gamma pseudo maximum likelihood, OLS = ordinary least squares, PPML = poisson pseudo maximum likelihood.
Notes: 1-FTA dummy variable sourced from the Asian Development Bank, Asia Regional Integration Center database was used as the auxiliary regression in the selection equation. The numbers in parentheses are the standard errors: *** $p < 0.01$, ** $p < 0.05$, * $p < 0.10$. The pseudo R-squared of the PPML is 0.9612. The Ramsey RESET Test was used to check the functional form.
Sources: Author, based on Euromonitor International Retailing industry edition 2019, UN Comtrade (accessed April 2020), and CEPII (accessed April 2020).

The parameter of distance in the PPML estimation, though still negative and significant, suggests that the variable is marginally less of an obstacle in the subsample.[8] In the same way, commonality in official language, albeit still significant in PPML, has a lower parameter value in the subsample and insignificant in other specifications. This could be explained by the greater availability of translation facilities, which bridges communication gaps across economies.

---

[8] In this setup, disentangling the determinants of the distance parameter is not straightforward. As Gomez-Herrera, Martens, and Turlea (2014) point out, it could include transport costs, import tariffs, costs due to regulatory differences between economies, financial transaction costs, and information costs to bring the trading partners together in a transaction, etc.

Estimations were also done across commodity types and the results indicate that the influence of internet retailing in commodities other than consumption goods is comparatively limited and statistically insignificant. Subsample estimations yield roughly similar results.

Moving to the platform penetration, PPML estimates using regional subsets purport that trade of Asia and the Pacific economies with regional partners is more sensitive to e-commerce platform development than trade with partners outside the region (Tables 4.4 and 4.5). This indicates the relative maturity of intra-regional e-commerce ties in Asia and the Pacific. It is seemingly the case in Europe (albeit statistically insignificant) but not in Africa and the Americas. Separate estimations treating the platform revenue dataset as a 2-year cross section (i.e., summing activities over a 2-year period) yield a picture consistent with these results.

Table 4.4: Platform Revenues and Consumption Goods Trade by Region with All Partners, 2017–2018

Reporters' Region	Asia and the Pacific	Europe	Africa	Americas
Partner: All reporting economies				
Dependent variable: Bilateral consumer goods exports				
Distance	-0.7373***	-0.5319***	-1.2789***	-0.4081***
	(0.1084)	(0.0833)	(0.1133)	(0.1138)
Common colonial ties	0.5431***	1.6975***	0.2464	0.4344
	(0.1806)	(0.3666)	(0.3471)	(0.6311)
Common language	-0.0732	0.2856*	0.8567***	0.3736***
	(0.1353)	(0.1602)	(0.1593)	(0.1161)
Contiguity	0.1615	0.6232***	1.0971***	1.5514***
	(0.1492)	(0.1135)	(0.2322)	(0.2183)
E-commerce platform	0.1467***	0.0177	0.3286***	0.0176
	(0.0513)	(0.0662)	(0.0983)	(0.0663)
Constant	24.9720***	24.8841***	21.0082***	24.3188***
	(1.2768)	(1.5809)	(2.4903)	(1.8346)
Fixed effects				
Exporter-year	Yes	Yes	Yes	Yes
Importer-year	Yes	Yes	Yes	Yes
Cluster exporter-importer	Yes	Yes	Yes	Yes
Number of observations	6,453	10,274	5,658	4,532
Pseudo R-squared	0.9540	0.9303	0.8382	0.9552

PPML = poisson pseudo maximum likelihood.
Note: PPML method is used. The numbers in parentheses are the standard errors: *** $p < 0.01$, ** $p < 0.05$, * $p < 0.10$.
Sources: Author, based on Statista (2020a, 2020b) and UN Comtrade (accessed April 2020).

Table 4.5: Platform Revenues and Consumption Goods Trade by Region with Regional Partners, 2017–2018

Reporters' Region	Asia and the Pacific	Europe	Africa	Americas
Partner: All reporting economies in the same region				
Dependent variable: Bilateral consumer goods exports				
Distance	-0.6392 ***	-0.5798 ***	-1.6511 ***	-1.0571 ***
	(0.0849)	(0.0814)	(0.1123)	(0.0866)
Common colonial ties	0.3689 **	1.5295 ***	-0.4239 *	3.7908 ***
	(0.1786)	(0.4247)	(0.2333)	(0.4022)
Common language	0.1941	0.3647 **	0.8673 ***	-0.461 ***
	(0.1568)	(0.1826)	(0.2281)	(0.1128)
Contiguity	0.381 ***	0.6263 ***	0.7895 ***	0.7225 ***
	(0.1395)	(0.0996)	(0.1994)	(0.1303)
E-commerce platform	0.2245 ***	0.0776	0.0508	-0.1074
	(0.0669)	(0.0755)	(0.1217)	(0.0668)
Constant	21.3234 ***	23.6575 ***	28.5839 ***	33.4504 ***
	(1.5092)	(1.6761)	(2.7275)	(1.9547)
Fixed effects				
Exporter-year	Yes	Yes	Yes	Yes
Importer-year	Yes	Yes	Yes	Yes
Cluster exporter-importer	Yes	Yes	Yes	Yes
Number of observations	1,515	2,659	1,682	921
Pseudo R-squared	0.9477	0.9314	0.8784	0.9852

PPML = poisson pseudo maximum likelihood.
Note: PPML method is used. The numbers in parentheses are the standard errors: *** $p < 0.01$, ** $p < 0.05$, * $p < 0.10$.
Source: Author, based on Statista (2020a, 2020b) and UN Comtrade (accessed April 2020).

Finally, the number of internet and mobile phone users of trading economies are found to be positively associated with consumer goods exports, with the former seemingly having broader impact than the latter (Table 4.6). Both metrics are significant components in e-commerce development. Despite the data limitations in capturing the quality dimension, the increase in parameter values between the full sample and subsubsample lends empirical support to the thesis that ICT tools help facilitate trade.

It cannot be ruled out that the elasticities could be higher if there were available data that adjusted the simple usage metrics for quality—a potential area of future research. Quality could be in terms of the improvement in speed and functionalities of the internet (e.g., cloud hosting) that are vital in e-commerce development. The same can be said of the capabilities of

Table 4.6: ICT Indicators and Consumption Goods Trade, 2006–2018 and 2012–2018

	Dependent Variable: Bilateral Consumption Goods Exports			
	PPML1 2006–18	PPML2 2006–18	PPML1 2012–18	PPML2 2012–18
Distance	-0.780***	-0.798***	-0.761***	-0.768***
	(0.0843)	(0.0849)	(0.0897)	(0.0891)
Common colony	0.246	0.276	0.288	0.328*
	(0.1921)	(0.1840)	(0.1974)	(0.1870)
Common language	0.143	0.133	0.125	0.121
	(0.1084)	(0.1096)	(0.1146)	(0.1155)
Contiguity	0.469***	0.46***	0.401***	0.391***
	(0.1221)	(0.1227)	(0.1294)	(0.1293)
Internet		0.175***		0.19***
		(0.0628)		(0.0706)
Mobile telephone	0.145*		0.151*	
	(0.0754)		(0.0814)	
Constant	26.114***	25.736***	25.884***	25.225***
	(1.5513)	(1.1643)	(1.7287)	(1.3615)
Fixed effects:				
Exporter-year	Yes	Yes	Yes	Yes
Importer-year	Yes	Yes	Yes	Yes
Cluster exporter-importer	Yes	Yes	Yes	Yes
Total observations	27,675	24,943	16,000	13,379
Pseudo R-squared	0.9604	0.9604	0.9599	0.9598

CEPII = Centre d'Etudes Prospectives et d'Informations Internationales, ICT = information and communication technology, PPML = poisson pseudo maximum likelihood.
Notes: PPML method is used. The numbers in parentheses are the standard errors: *** $p < 0.01$, ** $p < 0.05$, * $p < 0.10$.
Sources: Author, based on UN Comtrade; World Bank, World Development Indicators Database; and CEPII (accessed April 2020).

the current generation of mobile phones in the applications that they can accommodate—a digital tool, together with websites, that is exploited heavily by e-commerce enterprises and platforms to expand their reach.

For instance, Abeliansky and Hilbert (2016) suggest that data speed quality matters most for developing economies' exports, whereas the subscription quantity is more relevant for developed economies. The reason for this is that data speed in developing economies is deemed generally far from the "frontier," thus, incremental improvement can be material in facilitating trade, while the increase in high-speed subscriptions in developed economies are argued to result in the opening of new markets.

4.8. National Policy and Regional Cooperation Implications

The growing role of e-commerce in trade facilitation could lead to significant adjustments in the supply and value chain in coming years. Digital platforms, therefore, with their ancillary tucked-in services will arguably play an even more pronounced role moving forward. As Fine (1998) and Weil (2013) aptly posit, integrated value chains are "unbundled, attacked, and commoditized" in the short run, before a new wave of innovations will drive the re-bundling and de-commoditization.

The prevailing circumstances are both an opportune time to further the development of the inclusiveness agenda and to review trade and related policies. ADB and UNESCAP (2018) highlight a number of crucial policy issues to help economies foster e-commerce. These are largely issues that pertain to digitalization as a whole, including e-commerce induced trade. For governments, the report underlined the importance of official statistics for monitoring and analysis. It stressed the need to work on harmonizing applicable laws and regulations, including taxation, and improve the access to and quality of ICT infrastructure such as e-payments systems. It also underscored the need to attract foreign players to reap potential gains from technology transfer, facilitate development of the ICT skills of the locals, and enact the requisite regulations on intellectual property, cybersecurity, consumer protection, and data protection, among other things.

Beyond the cross cutting digitalization policy concerns, there are three important policy areas that are specifically relevant to cross-border e-commerce transactions (ADB 2021). These are:

- competition, customs administration, and trade taxation;

- the role of multilateral initiatives and trade agreements in resolving policy disconnects; and

- the responsiveness of free trade zone or economic processing zone strategies in light of the increasing role of platforms and other digital media in trade.

Taxation, Competition, and Customs Administration Issues

Trade taxation is one contentious topic, as ADB and UNESCAP (2018) note. Parcelization of transactions has allowed overseas e-commerce players to benefit from a certain degree of customs duties exemptions subject to the countries' *de minimis* rules. The principle behind this practice is to avert spending more on tax administration than the amount that can be collected.

De minimis regimes that apply to e-commerce tend to vary across economies. In a meeting of the Asia-Pacific Economic Cooperation in 2011, a *de minimis* threshold of $100 was endorsed (APEC 2011). However, this direction of policy cooperation has not gained much traction since. In comparison, the customs duties on digital trade, which are also under intense scrutiny of late, are subject to a long-standing World Trade Organization (WTO) agreement.[9] After the WTO formally adopted its Work Programme on Electronic Commerce in 1998 (WTO 1998a, 1998b), the moratorium on imposing customs duties on electronic transmissions has been extended a number of times and remains in place as of this writing. The discussions on these extensions are not straightforward as some WTO members have raised concerns on the implications for government revenue.

Terzi (2011) notes that digital innovations such as the internet have opened markets that were previously relatively difficult to penetrate, which makes it akin to trade liberalization. Against this characterization, keeping, if not raising, the *de minimis* thresholds enables trade flows and is deemed to generate substantial net economic benefits (Holloway and Rae 2012; International Chamber of Commerce 2015).

---

[9] In digital trade, a multilateral agreement on customs duties exists on electronic transmissions, which can be traced back to 1998 under WTO auspices (International Chamber of Commerce 2019). The moratorium is reviewed every 2 years and the governments agree on its extension at the biennial WTO Ministerial Conference. The moratorium remains in place as of this writing. In their decision in December 2019, the WTO members agreed to maintain the practice of not imposing customs duties on electronic transmissions until the 12th Ministerial Conference (WTO 2019), which scheduled in late 2021. Nevertheless, the loss in potential revenue as transactions volume has increased several fold is becoming an issue in many economies, notwithstanding efficiency gains from free-flowing data. For instance, Bangga (2019) estimates that because of the moratorium, the WTO developing member economies, as a group, incur tariff revenue loss of about $10 billion annually, using average bound duties, and $5.1 billion, using average most favored nation (MFN) applied rate.

On the other hand, the thresholds have become somewhat a regulatory gateway for the relatively cheaper products from offshore producers to access the domestic markets and compete with domestic firms. In this sense, e-commerce does tend to magnify comparative advantages of some economies in international trade of certain goods.

Enabling local entrepreneurs and enterprises to participate in e-commerce is one thing; making them more competitive in the e-commerce environment is another matter. In the absence of appropriate policies, economies unable to produce goods that can compete well in the e-commerce space may confine local platform participants largely to the distribution aspect of the cross-border supply chain. Thus, the interventions ought to go beyond training local players with the digital aspects of e-commerce and providing infrastructure support. Economies need to have a clear idea about the business activities that can be feasibly pursued in the e-commerce space and how these will be supported.

As also noted by ADB (2021), the World Customs Organization sorts cross-border e-commerce customs administration into three clusters: (i) trade facilitation and security, (ii) fairness and efficiency in tax collection, and (iii) protection against criminal exploitation of e-commerce (Table 4.7). The first cluster deals with policy adjustments to the emerging trade environment to ensure efficiency, timely transmission of information, and credibility of data. The second cluster is about recognizing mechanisms that misapply the systems' rules on parcelized goods and ensuring compliance with other rules (e.g., rules of origin classification and valuation rules). The third cluster concerns possible ways to prevent, detect, and pursue customs-related legal offenses in the digital space.

Multilateral Initiatives and Trade Agreements

Multilateral initiatives and trade agreements are a crucial tool in facilitating regulatory catch-up, especially in less developed economies. Apart from taxation, these initiatives and agreements can address the ease of information exchange between all the parties in e-commerce transactions. This mainly involves linkages between customs offices, which is judged to be not yet well-developed (WCO 2017).

Table 4.7: Customs Administration Challenges Related to Cross-Border E-Commerce

Trade Facilitation and Security	Fair and Efficient Collection of Duties and Taxes	Protection of Society— Criminal Exploitation of E-Commerce
Ensuring speed and efficiency in the clearance process for an increasing volume of transactions	Identifying abuse or misuse of *de minimis* for illicit trade purposes (splitting of consignments/ undervaluation)	Setting up a specialized unit to trawl the internet for information which might be of use in preventing, detecting, investigating, and prosecuting a customs-related offense (drug trafficking/counterfeited and pirated goods/illicit financial flows/ money laundering)
Managing change from a few large/bulk shipments into a large number of low-value and small shipments	Ensuring compliance with classification and origin rules	Enhancing international cooperation and ensuring that agreements on mutual legal assistance are in place to allow for investigations or prosecutions when websites are hosted outside a national territory
Managing risks posed by limited knowledge on importers and the e-commerce supply chain (new class of sellers and buyers/occasional shippers and buyers)	Integration of e-commerce versus traditional trade	Making the most of existing technologies, especially those related to data analysis
Ensuring data quality (accuracy and adequacy of the data received)		
Defining the role and responsibility (liability) of e-commerce operators to assist governments (e-vendors/intermediaries)		

Note: The entries in the table were directly lifted from the source.
Sources: ADB (2021) and World Customs Organization, http://www.wcoomd.org/en/topics/facilitation/ activities-and-programmes/ecommerce.aspx?p=1 (accessed August 2020).

At the global level, the WTO leads the policy dialogues and the framing of multilateral accords to coordinate and harmonize the policy actions of different countries and forge plurilateral agreements based on existing WTO agreements and frameworks. The WTO Work Programme on Electronic Commerce sets to *"to examine all trade-related issues relating to global electronic commerce"* (WTO 1998a). In line with this, a number of WTO members endorsed the Joint Statement Initiative on e-commerce in 2017 and negotiated trade-related aspects of e-commerce thereafter (Ismael 2020).[10]

---

[10] Ismael (2020) lays out a succinct timeline of key actions regarding the work program.

The World Customs Organization (WCO) created the Working Group on E-Commerce to lay out the framework of standards on cross-border e-commerce and their implementation based on an in-depth look at issues and multi-stakeholder collaboration and as a follow-up to the WCO Luxor Resolution on Cross-Border E-Commerce in 2017 (WCO 2018a). The framework aims to create a robust and transparently governed e-commerce global supply chain. It specifically targets the harmonization of risk assessment procedures, revenue collection, and border cooperation.

The WCO has also released a set of guidelines in 2018 pertaining to customs and trade rules on the clearance of low-value and small e-commerce shipments and parcels (WCO 2018b). What these frameworks need are implementing rules and regulations in every jurisdiction to strengthen cross-border governance. The broadening automation in customs procedures through national single windows and the progress in creating integrated national single windows (e.g., the Association of Southeast Asian Nations single window) can be leveraged to pursue the objectives in these frameworks.

Lopez-Gonzalez and Ferencz (2018) likewise highlight the increasing importance and usage of regional trade agreements (RTAs), considering the complexity of trade rules and the rapidly evolving business models and landscape (including digital platforms).

E-commerce-related RTA provisions typically cover promotion of e-commerce activity; cross-border cooperation; and moratoriums on customs duties and domestic legal frameworks including electronic authentication, consumer protection, personal information protection, and paperless trading. Monteiro and Teh (2017) cite examples of agreements that contain e-commerce development provisions and involve Asia and the Pacific. These include RTAs between the PRC and the Republic of Korea; Hong Kong, China and New Zealand; the Republic of Korea and Singapore; Japan and Australia; Thailand and New Zealand; and Japan and Mongolia, among others.

One key challenge is to ensure that overlapping RTAs do not exacerbate the "spaghetti" or "noodle bowl effect" resulting in unintended friction—such as conflicting rules of origin—that affect the cost of trading. As Monteiro and Teh (2017) note: "even in RTAs negotiated by the same country, e-commerce provisions vary significantly."

Free Trade Zone Strategies

Free trade zone or economic processing zone strategies are also crucial in promoting e-commerce. They help facilitate compliance with trade rules and assist customs authorities in their work. In many economies in Asia and the Pacific, these strategies need to reviewed and revised. The PRC has taken the lead in this area by establishing cross-border e-commerce comprehensive pilot zones. A total of 105 zones are spread over four regions in the country (Zhang 2020).

The objectives stipulated by the Government of the PRC State Council (2020) include building brands, developing cross-border e-commerce, stabilizing foreign capital flows related to trade, raising the quality of trade, and addressing pertinent transaction security concerns. Preferential tax treatment, such as value-added tax exemptions, consumption tax on retail exports exemptions, and corporate income tax reductions, are offered in the pilot zones.

Malaysia is another early mover in the region and it could serve as a good benchmark for the other economies once performance indicators are released. The Government of Malaysia launched a digital free trade zone in 2017 in order to strengthen the participation of local enterprises in cross-border, e-commerce activities (METDC n.d.).

The Alibaba Group-led electronic World Trade Platform (eWTP) is a notable recent initiative of the digital free trade zone (Yean 2018). The hub in Malaysia is incidentally the first eWTP pilot project outside of the PRC (eWTP n.d.[a]). eWTP is deemed a step toward establishing the digital version of the Silk Road, designed to complement the Belt and Road Initiative.[11] The initiative was likewise part of the core policy recommendations of the *Business 20* (the private sector caucus within the G20) and cited in the G20 communiqué in 2016 (International Trade Centre and Ali Research 2018).

---

[11]   As of this writing, the eWTP has at least six partner economies on at least three continents (eWTP, n.d.[b]).

4.9. Conclusion

E-commerce influences trade flows directly through online purchases from an offshore producer and indirectly through traditional channels but distributed via domestic e-commerce facilities. Taking advantage of the internet retailing sales data and the e-commerce platform revenues data that are available for many economies, the study analyzed the extent to which the joint e-commerce market development in trading economies is affecting the magnitude of bilateral trade of consumer goods.

Utilizing the PPML estimation technique, the results show that bilateral consumer goods trade flow is positively associated with the combined e-commerce development of the trading economies. The linkage is statistically robust and appears to be gaining traction in recent years. Estimations using platform revenues data further reveal that platform development or penetration helps significantly bolster consumer goods trade in Asia and the Pacific economies. It is also shown that intra-regional consumer goods trade in the region is relatively more sensitive to e-commerce platform penetration than trade with economies outside the region. Separately, internet and mobile phone usage, which is an enabler of e-commerce, are found to be positive drivers of trade of consumer goods as well. Distance is still a significant barrier, although it is seemingly becoming less of a constraint over time. Difference in languages is also becoming less important.

As e-commerce deepens its trade penetration, a number of policy issues stand out that are important to maximizing welfare gains. The value of rolling out of official statistics on e-commerce trade flows cannot be overstated. At the operations level, the underpinning digital infrastructure needs to be strengthened. Meanwhile, enacting the requisite regulations on intellectual property, consumer protection, data protection, and cybersecurity will establish a trustworthy e-commerce market.

Beyond the general enabling policies, a clear approach to bolster the competitiveness of domestic enterprises in the digital space is also necessary. This includes taxation issues that are tied with cross-border transactions, such as the *de minimis* rule, that ought to have consensus, at least at the regional level.

Another area pertains to trade agreements. Multilateral agreements and initiatives play an important role in harmonizing the policy approaches. Since multi-country negotiations can be quite tedious, regional trade agreements can be valuable in this regard. One key challenge concerning RTAs is to contain the noodle bowl effect resulting from overlapping agreements.

Finally, it is an opportune time for many economies in the region to review and revise decades-long free trade zone or economic processing zone strategies to make them more responsive to developments in digitally driven cross-border trade. More than supporting e-commerce development, these strategies are valuable in facilitating compliance to the trade rules and in helping customs authorities address the challenges they face related to e-commerce trade flows.

References

Abeliansky, A. L., and M. Hilbert. 2016. Digital Technology and International Trade: Is it the Quantity of Subscriptions or the Quality of Data Speed that Matters? *Telecommunications Policy*. 41 (1). pp. 35–48. https://doi.org/10.1016/j.telpol.2016.11.001.

Ali Research and Accenture. 2016. *Global Cross Border B2C e-Commerce Market 2020: Report highlights & Methodology Sharing*. Presentation. United Nations Conference on Trade and Development, Geneva. https://unctad.org/system/files/non-official-document/dtl_eweek2016_AlibabaResearch_en.pdf.

Anderson, J. E. and E. van Wincoop. 2003. Gravity with Gravitas: A Solution to the Border Puzzle. *The American Economic Review*. 93 (1). pp. 170–192. https://doi.org/10.1257/000282803321455214.

Anderson, J. E. and Y. V. Yotov. 2016. Terms of Trade and Global Efficiency Effects of Free Trade Agreements, 1990–2002. *Journal of International Economics* 99. pp. 279–298. https://doi.org/10.1016/j.jinteco.2015.10.006.

Asia-Pacific Economic Cooperation (APEC). 2011. *Annex A - Pathfinder to Enhance Supply Chain Connectivity by Establishing a Baseline De Minimis Value*. Honolulu. https://www.apec.org/Meeting-Papers/Annual-Ministerial-Meetings/2011/2011_amm/annex-a.

Asian Development Bank (ADB). 2021. *Asian Economic Integration Report 2021: Making Digital Platforms Work for Asia and the Pacific*. ADB: Manila. http://dx.doi.org/10.22617/TCS210048-2.

Asian Development Bank and United Nations Economic and Social Commission for Asia and the Pacific (ADB and UNESCAP). 2018. *Embracing the E-commerce Revolution in Asia and the Pacific*. Manila.

Bangga, R. 2019. Global Trade of Electronic Transmissions: Implications for the South. *UNCTAD Research Paper*, No. 29. Geneva. https://unctad.org/en/PublicationsLibrary/ser-rp-2019d1_en.pdf.

Centre d'Etudes Prospectives et d'Informations Internationales (CEPII). *Geography Database*. Paris. http://www.cepii.fr/CEPII/en/bdd_modele/bdd_modele.asp (accessed April 2020).

Choi, C. 2010. The Effect of the Internet on Services Trade. *Economics Letters.* 109 (2). pp. 102–104. https://doi.org/10.1016/j.econlet.2010.08.005.

Clarke, G. R. G. and S. J. Wallsten. 2006. Has the Internet Increased Trade? Developed and Developing Country Evidence. *Economic Inquiry.* 44 (3). pp. 465–484. https://doi.org/10.1093/ei/cbj026.

Correia, S., P. Guimarães, and T. Zylkin. 2019. PPMLHDFE: Fast Poisson Estimation with High-Dimensional Fixed Effects. *The Stata Journal: Promoting Communications on Statistics and Stata.* 20 (1). pp. 95–115. https://doi.org/10.1177/1536867X20909691.

Ecommerce Foundation. *2019. Global B2C E-commerce Report: Global 2019.* Light Report Edition. Amsterdam. https://embed.ecommercewiki.org/reports/807/ecommerce-report-global-2019.

Electronic World Trade Platform (eWTP). n.d.(a). *Milestones.* https://www.ewtp.org/milestones.html (accessed May 2020).

_____. n.d. (b). Public Service Platform. https://www.ewtp.org/psp.html (accessed May 2020).

Euromonitor International. Retailing Industry edition 2019.

Fine, C. H. 1998. *Clockspeed: Winning Industry Control in the Age of Temporary Advantage.* New York: Perseus Books.

Francis, J. E. and L. White. 2004. Internet Retailing: Back to the Future. In *Proceedings of the Australian and New Zealand Marketing Academy Conference.* Wellington: Australian and New Zealand Marketing Academy. https://ro.uow.edu.au/cgi/viewcontent.cgi?article=1838&context=commpapers.

Freund, C. and D. Weinhold. 2002. The Internet and International Trade in Services. *American Economic Review.* 92 (2). pp. 236–240. https://doi.org/10.1257/000282802320189320.

_____. 2004. The Effect of the Internet on International Trade. *Journal of International Economics.* 62 (1). pp. 171–189. https://doi.org/10.1016/S0022-1996(03)00059-X.

Gomez-Herrera, E., B. Martens, and G. Turlea. 2014. The Drivers and Impediments for Cross-border e-Commerce in the EU. *Information Economics and Policy*. 28. pp. 83–96. Seville: Institute for Prospective Technological Studies, Joint Research Centre, European Commission. https://doi.org/10.1016/j.infoecopol.2014.05.002.

Government of the People's Republic of China, State Council. 2020. Reply of the State Council on Agreeing to Establish Comprehensive Pilot Zones for Cross-Border E-Commerce in 46 Cities and Regions Including Xiongan New District. *National Letter*, (2020) No. 47 (in Mandarin). Beijing. http://www.gov.cn/zhengce/content/2020–05/06/content_5509163.htm.

Holloway, S. and J. Rae. 2012. De Minimis Thresholds in APEC. *World Customs Journal*. 1 (6). pp. 31–62. http://worldcustomsjournal.org/Archives/Volume%206%2C%20Number%201%20(Mar%202012)/04%20Holloway_Rae.pdf.

International Chamber of Commerce. 2015. ICC Policy Statement on Global Baseline De Minimis Value Thresholds (2015). Policy statement. Paris. https://iccwbo.org/publication/icc-policy-statement-on-global-baseline-de-minimis-value-thresholds-2015/.

———. 2019. *WTO Moratorium on Customs Duties on Electronic Transmissions–A Primer for Business*. Paris. https://iccwbo.org/content/uploads/sites/3/2019/11/2019-icc-wto-moratorium-custom-duties.pdf.

International Trade Centre and Ali Research. 2018. *What Sells in e-Commerce: New Evidence from Asian LDCs*. Geneva. http://www.intracen.org/uploadedFiles/intracenorg/Content/Publications/AssetImages/What%20sells%20in%20ecommerce_final_%20Hi-res.pdf.

Ismael, Y. 2020. *E-commerce in the World Trade Organization: History and Latest Developments in the Negotiations under the Joint Statement*. Geneva: International Institute for Sustainable Development and CUTS International.

Kim, T. Y., R. Dekker, and C. Heij. 2017. Cross-Border Electronic Commerce: Distance Effects and Express Delivery in European Union Markets. *International Journal of Electronic Commerce*. 21 (2). pp. 184–218. https://doi.org/10.1080/10864415.2016.1234283.

Kinda, T. 2019. E-Commerce as a Potential New Engine for Growth in Asia. *IMF Working Paper*, WP/19/135. https://www.imf.org/~/media/Files/Publications/WP/2019/WPIEA2019135.ashx.

Lendle, A., M. Olarreaga, S. Schropp, and P.L. Vezina. 2016. *There Goes Gravity: eBay and the Death of Distance. Economic Journal*.126 (591). pp. 406–41. Oxford: Oxford University Press. https://doi.org/10.1111/ecoj.12286.

Liu, L. and H. K. Nath. 2014. Information and Communications Technology and Trade in Emerging Market Economies. *Emerging Markets Finance and Trade*. 49 (6). pp. 67–87. https://doi.org/10.2753/REE1540–496X490605.

Lopez-Gonzalez, J. and J. Ferencz. 2018. Digital Trade and Market Openness. *OECD Trade Policy Papers*, No. 217. https://doi.org/10.1787/1bd89c9a-en.

Malaysia External Trade Development Corporation (METDC). n.d. *Digital Free Trade Zone (DFTZ)*. Kuala Lumpur.

Monteiro, J. A. and R. Teh. 2017. Provisions on Electronic Commerce in Regional Trade Agreements. *WTO Working Paper*, ERSD-2017–11. Geneva. https://www.wto.org/english/res_e/reser_e/ersd201711_e.pdf.

Santos Silva, J. M. C. and S. Tenreyro. 2006. The Log of Gravity. *The Review of Economics and Statistics*. 88 (4). pp. 641–658. https://www.mitpressjournals.org/doi/pdf/10.1162/rest.88.4.641.

_____. 2011. Further Simulation Evidence on the Performance of the Poisson Pseudo Maximum Likelihood Estimator. *Economics Letters*. 112 (2). pp. 220–222. https://doi.org/10.1016/j.econlet.2011.05.008.

Shepherd, B. 2016. *The Gravity Model of International Trade: A User Guide (An updated version)*. Bangkok: United Nations Economic and Social Commission for Asia and the Pacific and Asia-Pacific Research and Training Network on Trade (UNESCAP and ARTNet). https://www.unescap.org/resources/gravity-model-international-trade-user-guide-updated-version.

Statista. 2020a. Statista Digital Market Outlook. https://www.statista.com/outlook/digital-markets (accessed July 2020).

————. 2020b. Mobility Market Outlook. https://www.statista.com/outlook/mobility-markets (accessed July 2020).

Tang, L. 2006. Communication Costs and Trade of Differentiated Goods. *Review of International Economics*. 14 (1). pp. 54–68, https://doi.org/10.1111/j.1467–9396.2006.00560.x.

Terzi, N. 2011. The Impact of E-Commerce on International Trade and Employment. *Procedia–Social and Behavioral Sciences*. 24. pp. 745–753. https://doi.org/10.1016/j.sbspro.2011.09.010.

Trefler, D. 2004. The Long and the Short of the Canada-U.S. Free Trade Agreement. *American Economic Review*. 94 (4). pp. 870–895. https://doi.org/10.1257/0002828042002633.

United Nations Conference on Trade and Development (UNCTAD). 2020. UNCTAD Estimates of Global E-commerce in 2018. *UNCTAD Technical Notes on ICT for Development No 15*. Geneva: United Nations Conference on Trade and Development. https://unctad.org/en/PublicationsLibrary/tn_unctad_ict4d15_en.pdf.

United Nations Statistics Division. UN Comtrade Database. https://comtrade.un.org/ (accessed March 2020).

Vemuri, V. K., and S. Siddiqi. 2009. Impact of Commercialization of the Internet on International Trade: A Panel Study Using the Extended Gravity Model. *The International Trade Journal*. 23 (4). pp. 458–484. https://doi.org/10.1080/08853900903223792.

Weil, H. 2013. The Dynamics of Global Supply Chains: The Imperatives for Success in a New Market Ecology. In *Global Value Chains in a Changing World*. Edited by D. Elms and P. Low. Geneva: World Trade Organization. https://www.wto.org/english/res_e/booksp_e/aid4tradeglobalvalue13_e.pdf.

World Bank. *World Development Indicators*. https://databank.worldbank.org/source/world-development-indicators (accessed March 2020).

World Customs Organization (WCO). 2017. *WCO Study Report on Cross-Border E-Commerce*. Brussels. http://www.wcoomd.org/-/media/wco/public/global/pdf/topics/facilitation/activities-and-programmes/ecommerce/wco-study-report-on-e_commerce.pdf?la=en.

_____. 2018a. *Cross-Border E-Commerce Framework of Standards*. Brussels. http://www.wcoomd.org/-/media/wco/public/global/pdf/topics/facilitation/activities-and-programmes/ecommerce/wco-framework-of-standards-on-crossborder-ecommerce_en.pdf?db=web.

_____. 2018b. *Immediate Release Guidelines*. Brussels. http://www.wcoomd.org/-/media/wco/public/global/pdf/topics/facilitation/instruments-and-tools/tools/immediate-release-guidelines/immediate-release-guidelines.pdf?db=web.

_____. n.d. *Cross-Border e-Commerce*. Brussels. http://www.wcoomd.org/en/topics/facilitation/activities-and-programmes/ecommerce.aspx?p=1.

World Trade Organization (WTO). 1998a. *Work Programme on Electronic Commerce*. Geneva. https://www.wto.org/english/tratop_e/ecom_e/wkprog_e.htm.

_____. 1998b. *Declaration on Global Electronic Commerce*. Geneva.

_____. 2019. Work Programme on Electronic Commerce. *General Council Decision*. 10 December. Geneva. https://docs.wto.org/dol2fe/Pages/FE_Search/FE_S_S009-DP.aspx?language=E&CatalogueIdList=259703,259704,259705,259706,259710,259651,259652,259663,259304,259264&CurrentCatalogueIdIndex=5&FullTextHash=&HasEnglishRecord=True&HasFrenchRecord=True&HasSpanishRecord=True.

Xing, Z. 2017. The Impacts of Information and Communications Technology (ICT) and E-Commerce on Bilateral Trade Flows. *International Economics & Economic Policy*. 15 (3). pp. 565–586. https://doi.org/10.1007/s10368–017–0375–5.

Yean, T. S. 2018. The Digital Free Trade Zone (DFTZ): Putting Malaysia's SMEs onto the Digital Silk Road. *Perspective*. 2018 (17). Singapore: Yusof Ishak Institute. https://www.iseas.edu.sg/images/pdf/ISEAS_Perspective_2018_17@50.pdf.

Yotov, Y. V., R. Piermartini, J.A. Monteiro, and M. Larch. 2016. *An Advanced Guide to Trade Policy Analysis: The Structural Gravity Model.* United Nations and World Trade Organization. Geneva: WTO Publications. https://vi.unctad.org/tpa/web/docs/vol2/book.pdf.

Yushkova, E. 2014. Impact of ICT on Trade in Different Technology Groups: Analysis and Implications. *International Economics and Economic Policy.* 11. pp. 165–77. https://doi.org/10.1007/s10368–013–0264–5.

Zhang, Z. 2020. 46 New Cross-Border E-Commerce Zones Unveiled by China. *China Briefing.* 15 May. https://www.china-briefing.com/news/china-unveils-46-new-cross-border-e-commerce-zones-incentives-foreign-investors-faqs/.

Retail Fintech Payments: Facts, Benefits, Challenges, and Policies

Yueling Huang

5.1. Introduction

Digital technology is reshaping many aspects of personal lives and business practices, and payment systems are no exception.[1] In fact, payment is the most important business area in financial technology (fintech), comprising 77% of transaction value worldwide in 2019. This number is even higher in Asia (85%), compared with 9% in alternative lending and 5% in personal finance. Up to 92% of fintech users worldwide are in digital payments (Statista 2020). Fintech presents a unique opportunity for emerging economies to leapfrog, in that renovation of traditional financial systems in these countries is not costly. Given such importance and relevance of fintech payments for Asia and emerging economies, this chapter comprehensively and empirically assesses the growing penetration of fintech payment systems, evaluates their impacts and challenges, and reflects on ways to improve.

What is a fintech payment system? Figure 5.1 lists different types of payment systems and classifies them based on the level of digitization. Most payment systems (except for physical cash) require both financial intermediary efforts to connect the senders and recipients of transactions as well as technological infrastructure to securely and accurately clear and settle these transactions. Traditional payment methods (leftmost in Figure 5.1) such as bank drafts, checks, and letters of credit involve more formal financial institutions, typically banks, but a limited role for digital technologies. Digital payment systems gradually took over with the emergence of debit cards, credit cards, and electronic fund transfers. Cash can also be more easily withdrawn

---

[1] This chapter was prepared as a background paper for ADB (2021).

anytime from ATMs, reducing the need to visit banks physically. In addition to the adoption of cards and cashless payments, digitally enabled clearing and settlement facilities such as an automated clearing houses and real-time gross settlement have also greatly ensured cheaper, faster, and safer transactions. Since smaller payments can now be better implemented electronically, reliance on cash has been reduced, which also facilitates record-keeping and increases transparency.

This chapter defines fintech payments (rightmost in Figure 5.1), as those that leverage the latest advances in digital technology. Fintech payments reinforce the benefits of earlier digital payment solutions (middle, Figure 1) in efficiency, convenience, and transparency. Fintech payments also foster financial inclusion, as a substantial part of fintech firms' customers were previously unbanked or underbanked. In the economies of the Association of Southeast Asian Nations (ASEAN), 41% of users of fintech payments were unbanked or underbanked in 2018 (CCAF, ADB Institute, and FinTechSpace 2019). Previous digital payment solutions, such as debit or credit cards, did not impart this benefit, as these payment methods typically require access to

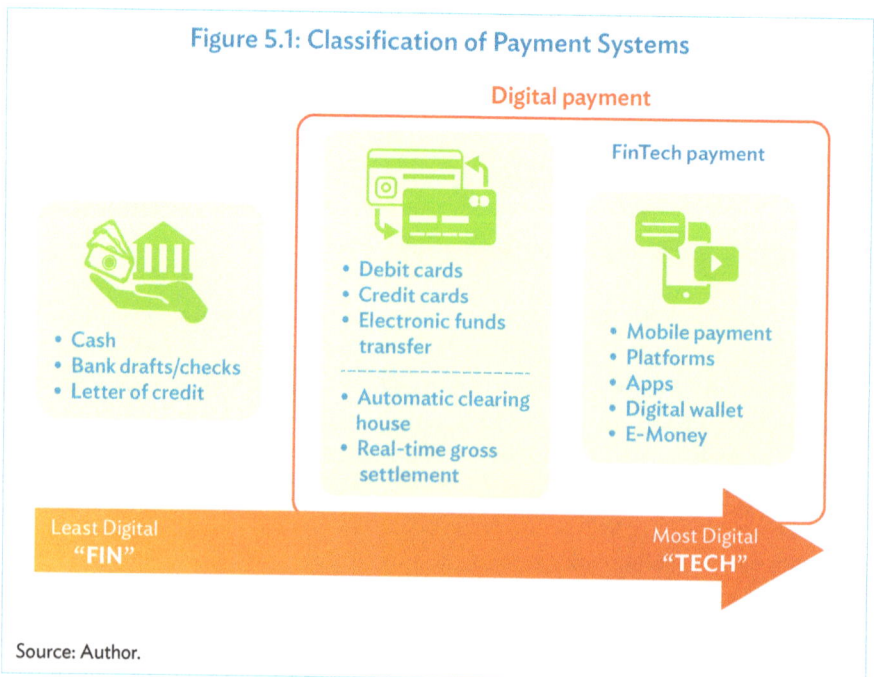

Figure 5.1: Classification of Payment Systems

Digital payment

FinTech payment

- Cash
- Bank drafts/checks
- Letter of credit

- Debit cards
- Credit cards
- Electronic funds transfer
- - - - - - - - - - - - - - - -
- Automatic clearing house
- Real-time gross settlement

- Mobile payment
- Platforms
- Apps
- Digital wallet
- E-Money

Least Digital
"FIN"

Most Digital
"TECH"

Source: Author.

a financial account. This chapter will deal with three other aspects to which fintech payments have brought convenience: e-commerce, spillover effect on the development of other fintech products, and remittance transfers.

This chapter focuses on retail payment systems, i.e., payment systems that transfer large volumes of funds of relatively small value.[2] Two main segments of retail payment systems are consumer-to-consumer (C2C) and consumer-to-business (C2B) (see Table A5.1 for examples). The focus is on retail payments because individuals and small and medium-sized enterprises are the two largest customer segments of fintech payments—52% and 26% of fintech payment users on average in ASEAN in 2018, respectively (CCAF, ADB Institute, and FinTechSpace 2019).

The chapter mainly examines the current fintech payments landscape and its impacts, both within the context of the People's Republic of China (PRC) and across countries. It uses aggregate and cross-country data to highlight five stylized facts on payment systems, some unique to Asia. Exploiting province-level variation of Alipay from the PKU Digital Financial Inclusion Index of China (PKU-DFIIC), the chapter uses the PRC as a country case study to empirically evaluate the benefits of fintech payment systems on e-commerce and fintech development, in general. The analysis also extends to the cross-country level in terms of e-commerce and remittances transfers using primarily data from the World Bank's Global Findex Database. Finally, the chapter outlines several challenges faced by fintech payments and offers policy recommendations.

CCAF, ADB Institute, and FinTechSpace (2019) provide a comprehensive overview of the fintech ecosystem in the ASEAN region. A recent report by the Bank of International Settlements (2020) discusses the relationships between fintech payments and efficiency, inclusion, competition as well as central banking. Aron and Muellbauer (2019) focus on the economics of mobile money and revisit the empirical evidence from the micro literature, especially in terms of financial inclusion. Agarwal et al. (2020) exploit the introduction of QR-code payment technology in 2017 by DBS, the largest bank in Singapore. They show that due to reduction in frictions and transaction/cash-handling costs, mobile payments stimulate small business creation, especially in poorer communities. Fintech payments also enable more efficient distribution of government transfers, which is particularly relevant during crisis times such as the current

---

2   This is as opposed to wholesale payments, which involve transactions of large value. Therefore, certain commercial transactions, if of low value (e.g., purchase of grocery items from a supermarket), are also considered retail payments.

pandemic. Bangura (2016) estimates that the costs saved by Sierra Leone's shift to mobile wallets to distribute payments to frontline workers during the Ebola crisis was more than $10 million. During the COVID-19 pandemic, many national governments are also encouraging the distribution of cash assistance digitally. Prominent examples include the distribution of consumption coupons via Alipay and WeChat Pay in PRC (Agur Peria, and Rochon 2020), the PromptPay system in Thailand (Rutkowski et al., 2020), and "Bono COVID-19" in Chile (Prady, 2020). Compared to the more traditional payment methods, digital G2P (government-to-person)/G2B (government-to-business) payments have the advantages of being more transparent, timelier, less costly, better at identifying intended beneficiaries through digital ID, and targeting the most deserving recipients more accurately (Agur Peria, and Rochon 2020; Auer, Cornelli, and Frost, 2020; Una et al., 2020). This chapter differs from the literature in terms of its data-driven approach and comprehensiveness of the empirical assessment of the benefits of fintech payments.

The rest of the chapter is organized as follows: Section 2 reviews the related literature on fintech and its implications. Section 3 documents five stylized facts on the current payment systems landscape. Section 4 empirically evaluates the role of fintech payments within the context of the PRC. Section 5 extends the empirical analysis to a cross-country framework. Section 6 discusses the potential challenges of fintech payments systems and offers policy recommendations. Section 7 concludes.

5.2. Literature Review

Klein (2020) describes the current digital payments landscape in the PRC. Shen, Hueng and Hu (2020) show that promoting financial literacy and digital financial products are essential for advancing financial inclusion. Using data on the province-level variation in Alipay penetration in the PRC, this chapter highlights the positive relationship between fintech payments and e-commerce and the spillover effect on development in other fintech products.

Furthermore, using data from Alibaba, Fan et al. (2018) show that e-commerce increases aggregate domestic trade and results in 1.6% welfare gains on average and even higher in smaller and more remote cities. E-commerce thus enhances financial inclusion. In a recent paper, Kang, Wang, and Ramizo (2021) assess the role of technology in business-to-consumer (B2C) e-commerce in Asia, but they mainly focus on ICT.

5.3. The Fintech Payments Landscape

This section presents five stylized facts about the current fintech payments landscape.

1. *The relative importance (as measured by the average volume share) of card and e-money payments among cashless payment instruments is significant and rising in emerging economies. Among card and e-money payment instruments, the relative importance of e-money is rising, whereas that of credit cards is declining in emerging economies. Such trend is also present in developed economies, albeit at a much smaller magnitude (Figure 5.2).*

    Panel (a) of Figure 5.2 plots the average volume share by cashless payments instruments in emerging economies versus developed economies from 2014 to 2018. Card and e-money is the dominant cashless payment instrument in both emerging and developed economies, taking up around 70% and 60%, respectively, of the total cashless payment volume. Use of cards and e-money is also on a clear upward trend, while checks are moving in the opposite direction in emerging and developed economies. The average share of direct debit is also declining, more so in developed economies.

    Panel (b) deals only with card/e-money payment instruments. The average volume share of e-money increases from approximately 20% in 2014 to nearly 30% in 2018 in emerging economies. This increase is mainly at the expense credit cards, which declined from 40% to 30%. The trends are much more stable in developed economies. Similar to emerging economies, credit cards are in decline and e-money is on the rise, but only slightly. Debit cards are the most prevalent instrument in emerging and developed economies, although they capture around 70% of the share in developed economies, compared to only 40% in emerging economies.

    These trends suggest that e-money, which corresponds to our definition of fintech payments, is relevant for emerging economies. Their relatively underdeveloped traditional payment systems may in fact provide natural comparative advantage for emerging economies in the adoption of fintech payments.

Figure 5.2: Relative Importance of Payment Instruments by Volume

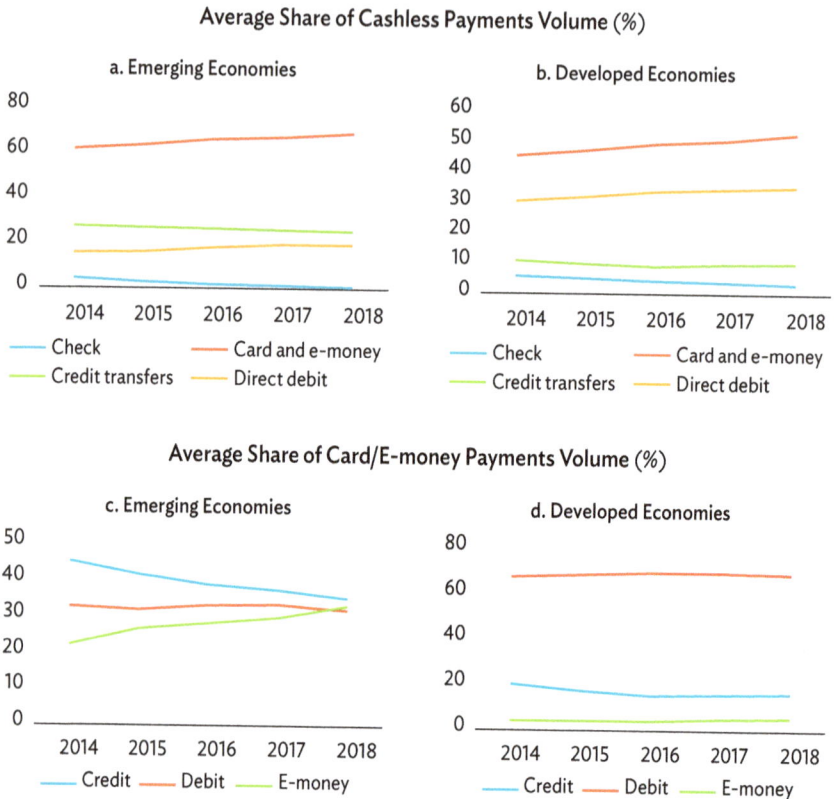

Average Share of Cashless Payments Volume (%)

a. Emerging Economies

b. Developed Economies

Check — Card and e-money
Credit transfers — Direct debit

Average Share of Card/E-money Payments Volume (%)

c. Emerging Economies

d. Developed Economies

— Credit — Debit — E-money

Note: Emerging economies include Indonesia, the Republic of Korea, Singapore, and others. Developed economies include Belgium, France, Germany, Italy, and the United States.
Source: Author, based on BIS (2020).

2. *Average value per transaction through cards and e-money is substantially smaller than other cashless payment instruments. Average value per transaction through e-money is the smallest among all card and e-money payment instruments in emerging and developed economies, and smaller in emerging markets than in developed economies (Figure 5.3).*

The left panel of Figure 5.3 clearly shows that the average value per transaction of card and e-money is substantially smaller than other cashless payments instruments. Cards represent the wave of digital payment innovations preceding fintech payments, whereas e-money is the closest to our definition of fintech payments. The right panel of Figure 5.3 indicates that fintech payments (in this case e-money) can accommodate even smaller payment values than credit and debit cards. As a result, fintech payments reinforce the existing benefits that debit and credit cards provide for retail payments. Table A5.2 in Appendix 1 compares cash, debit card, credit card, and fintech payments in terms of cost, speed, security, transparency, and inclusion.

Figure 5.3: Average Value per Transaction by Payment Instrument ($)

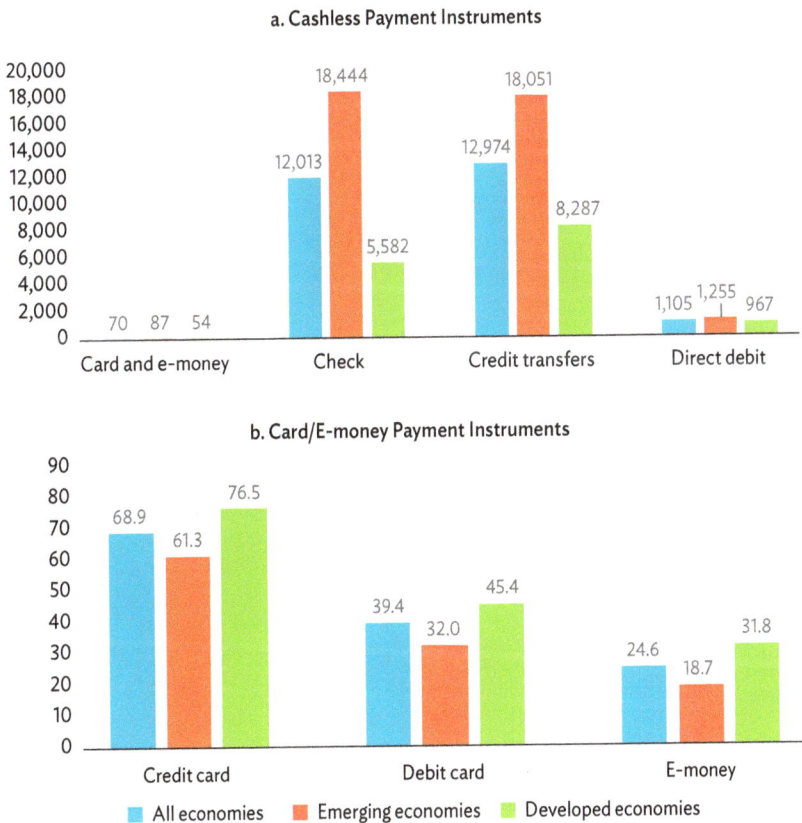

a. Cashless Payment Instruments

b. Card/E-money Payment Instruments

Note: Emerging economies include Indonesia, the Republic of Korea, Singapore, and others. Developed economies include Belgium, France, Germany, Italy, and the United States.
Source: Author, based on BIS (2018).

3. *Total mobile money transaction volume and value increased substantially during 2011–2019. Mobile money is most widely used in sub-Saharan Africa, followed by East Asia and the Pacific and South Asia (Figure 5.4).*

Figure 5.4: Trends in Mobile Money Transaction Volume and Value

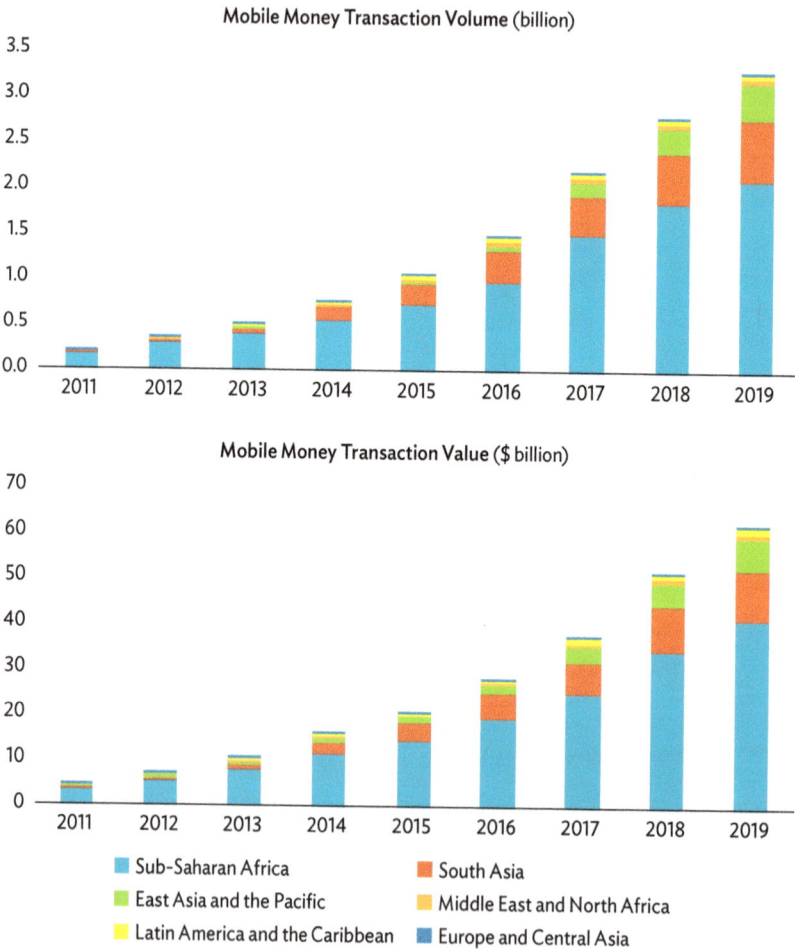

Mobile Money Transaction Volume (billion)

Mobile Money Transaction Value ($ billion)

Legend:
- Sub-Saharan Africa
- South Asia
- East Asia and the Pacific
- Middle East and North Africa
- Latin America and the Caribbean
- Europe and Central Asia

Note: The Global System for Mobile Communications Association (GSMA) database only considers mobile money services that are "available to the unbanked, e.g., people who do not have access to a formal account at a financial institution." Therefore, fintech payment systems that need to be linked to a financial account or credit card (e.g., Alipay, WeChat Pay, Apple Pay, Google Pay) do not qualify as mobile money. Regional groupings follow the definitions of the source.
Source: GSMA (2020).

According to the definition by the Global System for Mobile Communications Association, a mobile money service "must be available to the unbanked, e.g., people who do not have access to a formal account at a financial institution [...and...] must offer a network of physical transactional points ... that make the service widely accessible to everyone". Therefore, many fintech payment systems that need to be linked to a financial account or credit card (e.g., Alipay, WeChat Pay, Apple Pay, Google Pay) do not qualify as mobile money according to their definition. The fact that mobile money has to be available to the unbanked implies it contributes to financial inclusion.

4. *Mobile money transaction volume is the highest for airtime top-up[3] globally and relatively high for merchant payment in East Asia and the Pacific, followed by peer to peer (P2P) and cash-in/cash-out. Mobile money transaction value is the highest for P2P, followed by cash-in/cash-out (Figure 5.5).*

Notably, mobile money is used frequently in merchant payments in East Asia and the Pacific and South Asia. The high transaction volume but low average value per transaction suggests that mobile money is widely adopted when transacting with smaller merchants. Compared to debit and credit cards, the lack of fees associated with fintech payments is particularly attractive to small merchants. The engagement of smaller merchants in adopting more digital payment methods (rather than cash) increases transparency and facilitates the inclusion of the potentially large informal economy in these countries, as electronic transactions can be more accurately recorded.

---

[3] Airtime top-up refers to adding credit to a mobile phone to connect to the telecom's network.

Figure 5.5: Mobile Money by Usage

a. Transaction Volume in December 2019 (%)

World

East Asia and the Pacific

South Asia

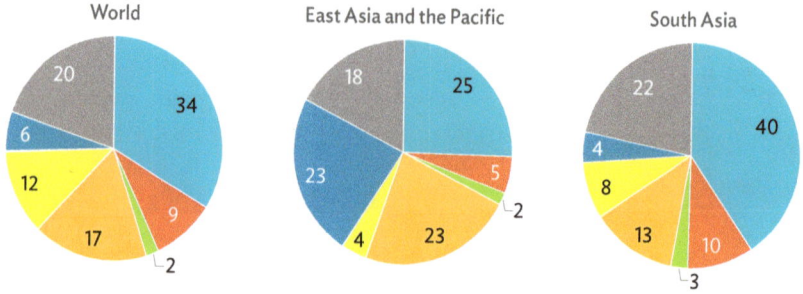

b. Transaction Value in December 2019 (%)

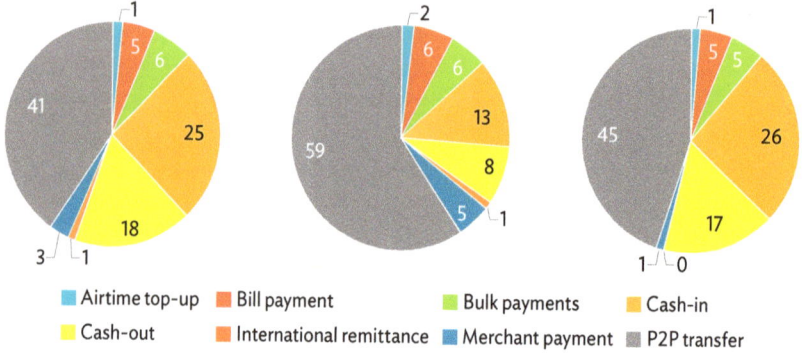

- ■ Airtime top-up
- ■ Bill payment
- ■ Bulk payments
- ■ Cash-in
- ■ Cash-out
- ■ International remittance
- ■ Merchant payment
- ■ P2P transfer

c. Average Value per Transaction in December 2019 ($)

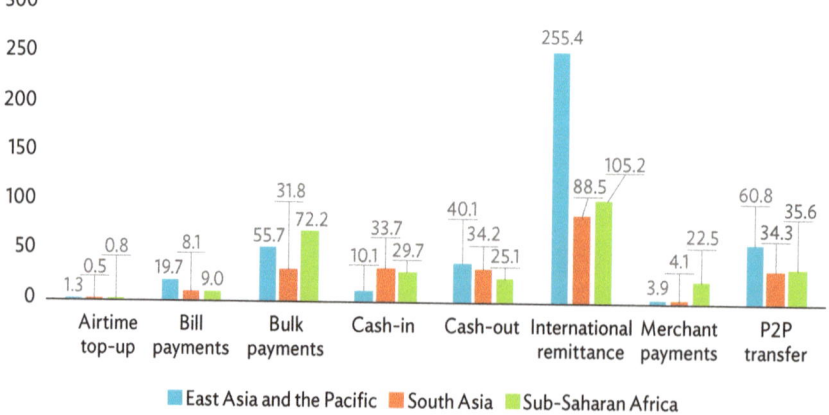

- ■ East Asia and the Pacific
- ■ South Asia
- ■ Sub-Saharan Africa

P2P = peer to peer.
Note: The country groupings are based on the definitions of the source.
Source: Author, based on GSMA (2020).

5. *The retail value of e-commerce is expanding exponentially, especially in Asia and the Pacific. E-commerce payment methods vary substantially across countries in Asia, with the PRC paying predominantly online while countries such as Malaysia and Viet Nam pay predominantly in cash in person (Figure 5.6).*

To sum up, fact 1 reveals the growing importance of digital payments (card and e-money). A finer breakdown suggests that the driving force behind this trend is fintech payments, as measured by the average share of e-money transaction volume, especially in emerging economies. Fact 2 shows how fintech payments are revolutionizing retail payments by accommodating even smaller payment values, which reinforces the benefits of previous types of digital payments (e.g., credit or debit cards). Facts 3 and 4 are related to mobile money,

Figure 5.6: E-Commerce Payment Methods by Selected Asian Economies in 2017

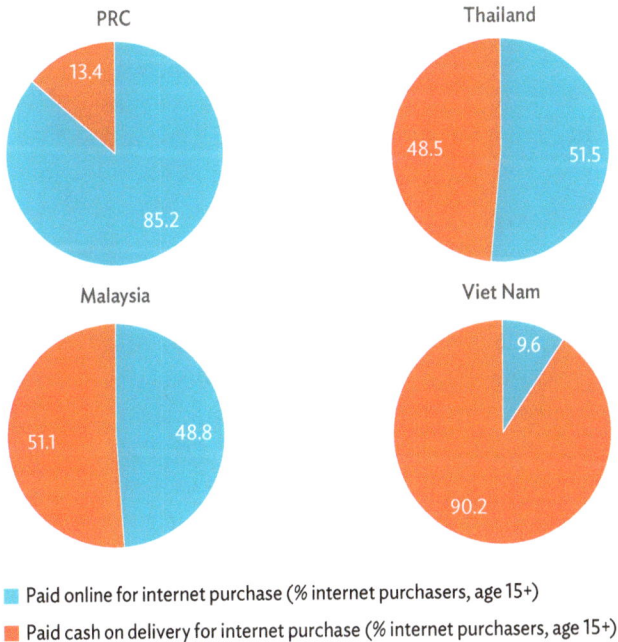

PRC

13.4

85.2

Thailand

48.5   51.5

Malaysia

51.1   48.8

Viet Nam

9.6

90.2

■ Paid online for internet purchase (% internet purchasers, age 15+)

■ Paid cash on delivery for internet purchase (% internet purchasers, age 15+)

PRC = People's Republic of China.
Source: Author, based on Global Findex Database (2017).

a prominent type of fintech payment. P2P and cash-in/cash-out seem to play the most significant roles in mobile money usage. Mobile money is also used frequently for merchant payment in East Asia and the Pacific and South Asia, particularly small merchants. Fact 5 is related to e-commerce and e-commerce payments.

These facts imply several key benefits of fintech payments in convenience (facts 1, 2, and 4); access and transparency of small value transactions (facts 2 and 4); financial inclusion of the unbanked (fact 3); and small merchants (fact 4). They also imply a potential relationship with e-commerce (fact 5) and remittances transfers (fact 4). In sections 5.4 and 5.5, this chapter details the impacts of fintech payments on e-commerce, general fintech development, and remittances transfers.

5.4. Country Case Study: People's Republic of China

This chapter chooses the PRC as a case study as it is leading the global fintech payments market. The dominant player is Ant Financial (the provider of Alipay), an affiliate company of the tech giant Alibaba Group, specializing in fintech. As of the first quarter of 2020, Alipay captured 55.4% of market share in the PRC, followed by Tencent's WeChat Pay and QQ Wallet (38.8%) (iResearch 2020). The number of active Alipay users reached 1.2 billion in 2019 (Klein 2020).

Specifically, we exploit province-level variation of Alipay from the PKU Digital Financial Inclusion Index of China (PKU-DFIIC) to study the role of fintech payments on e-commerce and the spillover effect on other fintech products, two important areas for economic development and inclusion. Fan et al. (2018) show that e-commerce increases aggregate domestic trade and results in 1.6% welfare gains on average. The welfare gain is even higher in smaller and more remote cities. Fintech services have expanded the set of financial services available to the public, particularly those who had lacked engagement with the traditional financial system. Therefore, in addition to the direct impact on the unbanked and smaller merchants suggested in Section 3, fintech payments can also lead to inclusive development indirectly, through e-commerce and development in other fintech products.

Fintech payments, e-commerce, and the development of other fintech products (e.g., e-saving, P2P lending, online wealth management) are strongly intertwined and difficult to disentangle. The underdeveloped traditional electronic payment systems in the PRC (i.e., debit or credit cards) and its e-commerce platform Taobao incentivized Alibaba to develop Alipay back in 2004, which in turn expanded its e-commerce business due to the convenience of transactions (Chorzempa 2018). Similarly, following the success of Alipay, a variety of fintech services have been integrated with the e-wallet function (e.g., Yu'e Bao for savings and investment, Huabei/Ant Check for credit payment, Ant Fortune for wealth management, Zhima Credit for credit scoring). All these services complement each other, thereby broadening the consumer base, and generate a rich amount of data. Ant Financial, as an aggregator of big data, can leverage the data created and further target their service requirements. Given this complicated relationship, the methodology controls for multiple factors and exploits the panel structure to alleviate as much endogeneity as possible.

The main variable of interest is fintech payment penetration, which is measured using the digital payment index for 31 provinces in the PRC from the PKU-DFIIC data from 2011–2018. PKU-DFIIC is an index on fintech inclusion compiled based on Ant Financial's massive dataset. The raw data provide 31 "specific indicators" on digital financial inclusion. Using both the coefficient of variation weighing method (objective weighing) and analytical hierarchy process (subjective weighing), these "specific indicators" are then combined into a comprehensive set of "level 2 dimension indicators." These include account coverage rate, payment, money funds, credit, insurance, investment, credit investigation, etc., which are used as the main measures of fintech penetration and fintech development. These "level 2 dimension indicators" are then consolidated into three "level 1 dimension indicators": breadth of coverage, depth of usage, and level of digitalization, which are then consolidated into the PKU-DFIIC. Figure A5.1 in the Appendix provides an illustration of the index system. A more detailed description of the specific indicators used can also be found in Table 5.2 of Institute of Digital Finance, Peking University (2019).

The payment index is a composite of three elements: number of payments per capita, amount of payments per capita, and proportion of the number of high-frequency active users (50 times or more each year) to number of users with at least one frequency each year (Institute of Digital Finance, PKU 2019). The Eastern Coastal Area, where Shanghai and Alibaba's headquarters Zhejiang are located, is the leader in fintech payments. The Big Northwest PRC, which includes the more remote and less developed provinces such as Xinjiang, Gansu, Qinghai, and Ningxia (Figure 5.7, panel a), is also the region with the lowest average payment index. However, regions lagging behind are rapidly converging (Figure 5.7, panels a and b). Panels c and d of Figure 5.7 further confirm the positive relationship between fintech payment and GDP per capita and negative relationship between fintech payment growth and GDP per capita in the cross-section. Figure A5.2 in the Appendix shows that the GDP-weighted averages also yield similar patterns.

E-commerce

The PRC is among the leading countries in e-commerce, with particularly robust growth in recent years, driven by a confluence of factors. The subsequent exercise empirically examines the effect of fintech payments on e-commerce. The results are shown in Table 5.1, whereby the dependent variable, the log of e-commerce sales value, is regressed on the log of payment index and a set of controls: log GDP per capita, share of rural population, share of population aged 65 and above, log of broadband subscribers, and log of average persons served by every postal office. The effect of payment is positive and statistically significant across different specifications, which include various fixed effects such as time fixed effects, region fixed effects and time-region fixed effects. Column (1) is the baseline pooled ordinary least squares (OLS) results without fixed effects. A 1% increase in the payment index is associated with 0.586% increase in e-commerce sales value.[4] After taking out time fixed effects, the coefficient increases to 2.012% (Column [2]). Column (3) removes regional fixed effects and the coefficient is 0.449, hence it is robust at around 0.5%. Log GDP per capita, log of broadband subscribers, and log of average persons served by postal office (which measures the level of postal services) are, as expected, positively related to e-commerce and are all statistically significant. Meanwhile, the share of rural population is negatively associated with e-commerce and is also statistically significant.

---

[4] To make sense of the magnitude of a 1% increase in payment index, note that the cross-sectional average of payment index increases from 46.54 in 2011 to 260.86 in 2018, or almost 460%.

Figure 5.7: The PKU-DFIIC Payment Index by Economic Region

a. Payment Index in Eight Economic Regions

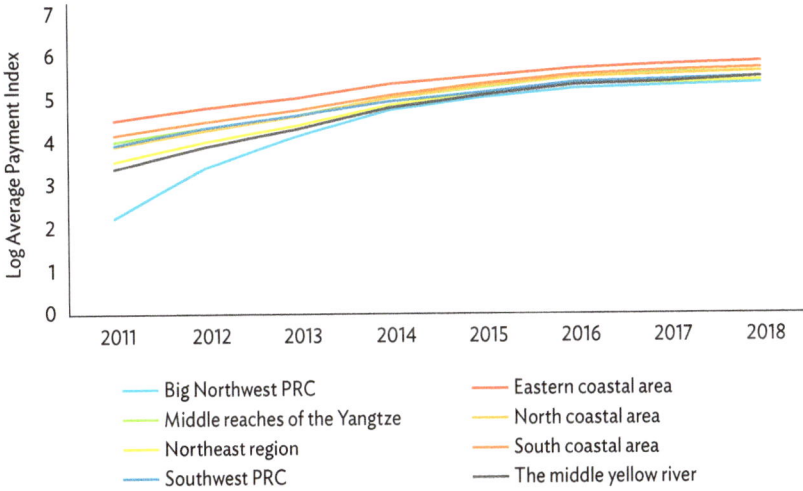

Legend:
- Big Northwest PRC
- Middle reaches of the Yangtze
- Northeast region
- Southwest PRC
- Eastern coastal area
- North coastal area
- South coastal area
- The middle yellow river

b. Convergence in Fintech Payments

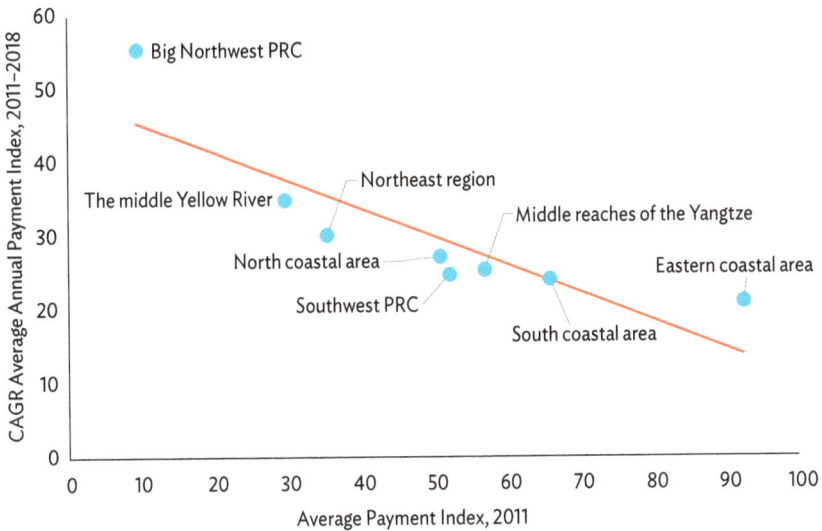

continued on next page

Figure 5.7 *continued*

c. Fintech Payment vs. GDP per Capita

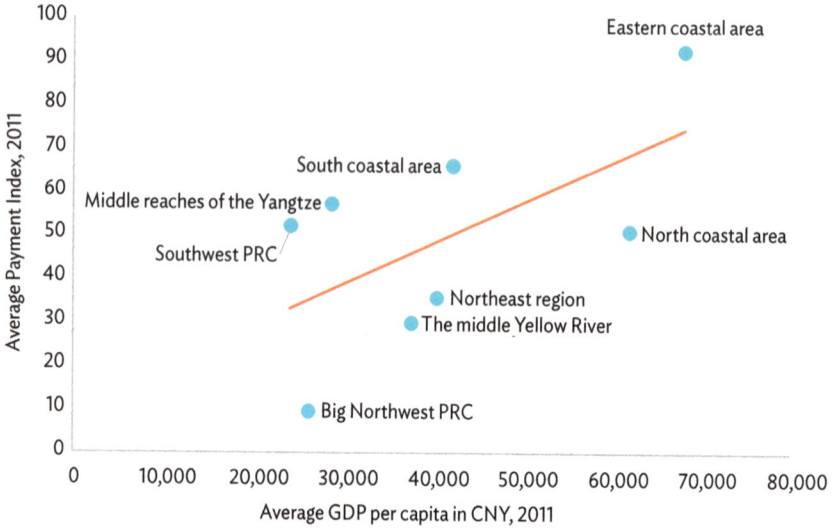

d. Fintech Payment Growth vs. GDP per Capita

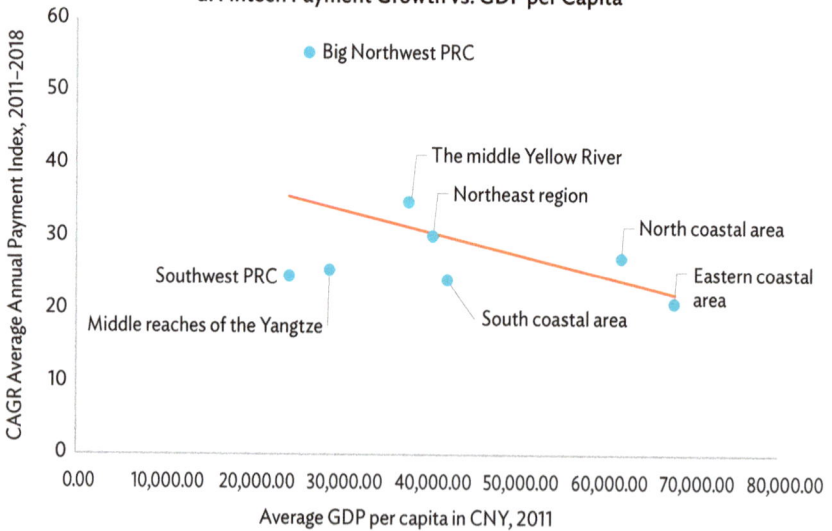

CAGR = compounded annual growth rate, PRC = People's Republic of China.
Sources: Author, based on Institute of Digital Finance, Peking University (2019) and the National Bureau of Statistics (2019).

Table 5.1: Fintech Payment and E-Commerce in the People's Republic of China
(pooled OLS)

	(1)	(2)	(3)	(4)
Log of payment index	0.586 ***	2.012 ***	0.449 **	0.990 *
	(0.193)	(0.344)	(0.182)	(0.579)
Log of GDP per capita	0.571 *	0.430 *	0.410	0.587 **
	(0.290)	(0.259)	(0.253)	(0.285)
Share of rural population	–3.126 ***	–2.340 ***	–3.434 ***	–2.893 ***
	(0.859)	(0.751)	(0.716)	(0.808)
Share of population 65 and over	–0.867	0.431	–2.498	–2.530
	(2.558)	(2.490)	(2.933)	(3.354)
Log of broadband subscribers	0.835 ***	0.762 ***	0.722 ***	0.771 ***
	(0.0581)	(0.0600)	(0.0669)	(0.0782)
Log of average persons served by postal office	0.325 **	0.290 **	0.191	0.0950
	(0.134)	(0.139)	(0.135)	(0.192)
Constant	9.639 **	4.073	14.32 ***	9.894 **
	(3.795)	(3.787)	(3.446)	(5.001)
Time fixed effects (FE)	No	Yes	No	No
Region FE	No	No	Yes	No
Region-time FE	No	No	No	Yes
Observations	186	186	186	186
R-squared	0.822	0.852	0.879	0.893

GDP = gross domestic product, OLS = ordinary least squares, PKU-DFIIC = Peking University-Digital Financial Inclusion Index of China.
Notes: Robust standard errors in parentheses, *** $p<0.01$, ** $p<0.05$, * $p<0.1$. Regions are defined as the eight economic regions by the National Bureau of Statistics.
Sources: Author's estimates, based on PKU-DFIIC (2019) and the National Bureau of Statistics (2019) data.

Determining the effect of fintech payment is challenging because of endogeneity. Fintech payments and e-commerce are jointly determined, and causality may run in both directions. Therefore, the baseline results are verified in two ways. The first method implements the pooled OLS regression but with the log of payment index in previous period as the main regressor (Table 5.2). The second method uses the fixed effects estimator with the log of payment index and log of lagged payment index as the main regressor, respectively (Table 5.3). The results confirm that the positive association between e-commerce and fintech payment, although the lagged payment index typically yields a smaller coefficient estimate than the payment index in current period.

Table 5.2: Fintech Payment and E-Commerce in the People's Republic of China
(pooled OLS, lagged payment index)

	(1)	(2)	(3)	(4)
Log of lagged payment index	0.350**	1.173***	0.274*	0.570
	(0.148)	(0.281)	(0.140)	(0.509)
Log of GDP per capita	0.644**	0.658**	0.451*	0.648**
	(0.289)	(0.279)	(0.254)	(0.295)
Share of rural population	−3.003***	−2.045***	−3.331***	−2.769***
	(0.871)	(0.783)	(0.731)	(0.811)
Share of population 65 and over	−0.713	0.603	−2.274	−2.456
	(2.591)	(2.552)	(2.950)	(3.305)
Log of broadband subscribers	0.842***	0.785***	0.724***	0.772***
	(0.0584)	(0.0587)	(0.0688)	(0.0738)
Log of average persons served by postal office	0.275**	0.159	0.153	0.0396
	(0.138)	(0.138)	(0.142)	(0.179)
Constant	10.49***	7.114**	15.10***	11.98***
	(3.798)	(3.546)	(3.454)	(4.447)
Time fixed effects (FE)	No	Yes	No	No
Region FE	No	No	Yes	No
Region-time FE	No	No	No	Yes
Observations	186	186	186	186
R-squared	0.819	0.846	0.877	0.893

GDP = gross domestic product, OLS = ordinary least squares, PKU-DFIIC = Peking University-Digital Financial Inclusion Index of China.
Robust standard errors in parentheses, *** $p<0.01$, ** $p<0.05$, * $p<0.1$.
Source: Author's estimates, based on PKU-DFIIC (2019) and the National Bureau of Statistics (2019) data.

Table 5.3: Fintech Payment and E-Commerce in the People's Republic of China
(fixed effects estimator)

	(1)	(2)	(3)	(4)
Log of payment index	0.888***	0.926***		
	(0.213)	(0.223)		
Log of lagged payment index			0.712***	0.734***
			(0.183)	(0.176)
Log of GDP per capita	0.189	0.193	0.354	0.362
	(0.296)	(0.295)	(0.282)	(0.282)
Share of rural population	4.963	4.396	3.523	2.932
	(3.727)	(3.588)	(3.225)	(3.183)
Share of population 65 and over	−0.225	0.566	0.0363	0.797

continued on next page

Table 5.3 *continued*

	(1)	(2)	(3)	(4)
	(3.721)	(3.471)	(3.591)	(3.593)
Log of broadband subscribers	0.434**	0.486**	0.131	0.17
	(0.210)	(0.227)	(0.230)	(0.236)
Log of average persons served by postal office		0.164		0.145
		(0.149)		(0.131)
Constant	14.15***	12.28**	15.99***	14.42***
	(4.175)	(4.752)	−3.825	−4.074
Observations	186	186	186	186
R-squared	0.606	0.612	0.611	0.615
Number of provinces	31	31	31	31

GDP = gross domestic product, PKU-DFIIC = Peking University–Digital Financial Inclusion Index of China.
Note: Robust standard errors in parentheses, *** $p<0.01$, ** $p<0.05$, * $p<0.1$.
Sources: Author's estimates, based on PKU-DFIIC (2019) and the National Bureau of Statistics (2019) data.

As a robustness check, the same specification in Table 5.1 is estimated without the log of average persons served by postal office as control. Results are robust and reported in Table A5.5 in the Appendix. The log of e-commerce purchase value is also used as the alternative measure of e-commerce. In principle, the sales value and purchase value should be fairly similar, and may differ slightly due to factors such as transportation costs and local taxes. The elasticity of e-commerce to payment index is generally higher for sales than purchases but remains robust (Appendix Tables A5.6 to A5.8).

Fintech Development

The multiple functions of technology, availability of big data, and broad customer base of digital platforms are factors that generate complementarity among fintech products. Five types of fintech products[5] other than payments are regressed to gauge the spillover effect of fintech payments on fintech development in general using pooled OLS with region-year fixed effects and the fixed effects estimator (Table 5.4 and Table 5.5, respectively). To reduce endogeneity, the log of lagged payment index is used as the main regressor. Similar to the regressions on e-commerce, control variables are the log of GDP per capita, share of rural population, and population aged 65 and above, as well as the log of broadband subscribers. The outcome variables are the log of the index of five main fintech products: insurance, money funds, credit, investment

---

[5]   The five are insurance, monetary fund, credit, investment, and credit investigation.

and credit investigation from PKU-DFIIC. Tables 5.4 and 5.5[6] present a consistently strong relationship between fintech payment and the development of other fintech products. Credit investigations, investment, and money funds show the largest response to fintech payments. A 1% increase in payment index increases credit investigation index by more than 5%, investment index by almost 3%, and money funds index by more than 2%. This is consistent with Ant Financial's success in its saving/investment/money funds service Yu'e bao, and credit investigation service Zhima Credit. The coefficient of log GDP per capita is negative and statistically significant for these three fintech products. One possible explanation could be that these fintech services are replacing traditional financial institutions in more impoverished areas, where the provision of such services by formal financial institutions is rather limited.

Table 5.4: Fintech Payment and Fintech Development in the People's Republic of China
(region-year fixed effects)

	Insurance	Monetary Fund	Credit	Investment	Credit Investigation
Log of lagged payment index	0.483***	1.343***	0.402***	1.934***	3.994***
	(0.034)	(0.089)	(0.034)	(0.089)	(0.250)
Log of GDP per capita	0.265***	−0.0115	−0.0104	−0.168	−0.948***
	(0.059)	(0.157)	(0.096)	(0.137)	(0.221)
Share of rural population	0.628***	0.225	−0.705**	−0.187	−0.725
	(0.141)	(0.452)	(0.280)	(0.348)	(0.610)
Share of population 65 and over	1.105	−2.092*	−0.936	−0.153	0.226
	(0.703)	(1.084)	(0.766)	(1.620)	(1.888)
Log of broadband subscribers	−0.0691***	−0.0164	0.147***	−0.0633*	−0.109**
	(0.013)	(0.035)	(0.017)	(0.034)	(0.054)
Constant	0.956	−1.417	2.426**	−2.670*	−4.745*
	(0.661)	(1.699)	(1.124)	(1.520)	(2.441)
Observations	215	185	215	155	123
Number of provinces	31	31	31	31	31

GDP = gross domestic product, PKU-DFIIC = Peking University–Digital Financial Inclusion Index of China. PRC = People's Republic of China, FE = fixed effects.
Note: Robust standard errors in parentheses, *** p<0.01, ** p<0.05, * p<0.1.
Sources: Author's estimates, based on PKU-DFIIC (2019) and the National Bureau of Statistics (2019) data.

---

[6] The number of observations varies across fintech products because some products were introduced later than 2011, the starting year of the PKU-DFIIC.

Table 5.5: Fintech Payment and Fintech Development in the People's Republic of China
(fixed effects estimator)

	Insurance	Monetary Fund	Credit	Investment	Credit Investigation
Log of lagged payment index	0.483***	1.343***	0.402***	1.934***	3.994***
	(0.034)	(0.089)	(0.034)	(0.089)	(0.250)
Log of GDP per capita	0.265***	–0.0115	–0.0104	–0.168	–0.948***
	(0.059)	(0.157)	(0.096)	(0.137)	(0.221)
Share of rural population	0.628***	0.225	–0.705**	–0.187	–0.725
	(0.141)	(0.452)	(0.280)	(0.348)	(0.610)
Share of population 65 and over	1.105	–2.092*	–0.936	–0.153	0.226
	(0.703)	(1.084)	(0.766)	(1.620)	(1.888)
Log of broadband subscribers	–0.0691***	–0.0164	0.147***	–0.0633*	–0.109**
	(0.013)	(0.035)	(0.017)	(0.034)	(0.054)
Constant	0.956	–1.417	2.426**	–2.670*	–4.745*
	(0.661)	(1.699)	(1.124)	(1.520)	(2.441)
Observations	215	185	215	155	123
Number of provinces	31	31	31	31	31

GDP = gross domestic product, PKU–DFIIC = Peking University-Digital Financial Inclusion Index of China.
Note: Robust standard errors in parentheses, *** $p<0.01$, ** $p<0.05$, * $p<0.1$.
Sources: Author's estimates, based on PKU–DFIIC (2019) and the National Bureau of Statistics (2019) data.

To summarize, through the lens of the PRC's Alipay, this analysis shows that fintech payment penetration is higher for regions with higher GDP per capita, but the less-penetrated regions are catching up. Using regression analyses, it highlights how fintech payments act as an enabler for e-commerce and general fintech development, with far-reaching implications for financial development and inclusion.

5.5. Cross-Country Study

This section examines the implications of fintech payment systems at the cross-country level. The share of population over the age of 15 that has made or received a digital payment in the past year from World Bank's Global Findex Database is used to capture digital payment penetration. This share increased from 41% in 2014 to 52% in 2017 worldwide. Note that the definition of digital payments does not exclude more traditional digital payment methods such as debit and credit cards. Of interest is the relationship of digital payments with e-commerce and remittances transfer.

E-commerce

Table 5.6 presents estimation results for the effect of digital payment penetration on e-commerce. The analysis obtains the retail value of e-commerce ($ million) from the Euromonitor International Retailing industry edition 2019. It converts all the values to US dollars since they are reported in domestic currency. The coefficient of digital payment penetration is positive and statistically significant at the 1% level. Moreover, broadband access seems to contribute positively to e-commerce. The pooled OLS estimate suggests that a 10-percentage-point increase in digital payment penetration is related to a 0.39% increase in the retail value of e-commerce. The estimate is slightly higher once time effects and/or region fixed effects are extracted. Appendix Table A5.9 resents similar regressions using log retail value of mobile e-commerce ($ million) as the dependent variable.

Table 5.6: Digital Payments and E-commerce
(cross-country)

	(1)	(2)	(3)	(4)
Digital	0.0394 ***	0.0402 ***	0.0540 ***	0.0573 ***
	(0.013)	(0.014)	(0.015)	(0.019)
Log of GDP per capita	0.599	0.575	0.698	0.622
	(0.401)	(0.421)	(0.427)	(0.526)
Share of rural population	-0.00176	-0.00205	0.0291	0.029
	(0.017)	(0.017)	(0.019)	(0.023)
Share of population 65 and over	2.189	2.086	4.725	4.651
	(7.318)	(7.373)	(10.300)	(7.140)
Log of broadband subscribers per 100 people	0.615 *	0.622 *	0.496	0.503 *
	(0.323)	(0.327)	(0.353)	(0.303)
Constant	-20.58 ***	-20.40 ***	-23.31 ***	-22.80 ***
	(3.411)	(3.505)	(3.892)	(4.613)
Time fixed effects	No	Yes	No	Yes
Region fixed effects	No	No	Yes	Yes
Observations	153	153	153	153
R-squared	0.516	0.516	0.547	0.548

GDP = gross domestic product.
Notes: Robust standard errors in parentheses, *** p<0.01, ** p<0.05, * p<0.1. Regions follow the World Bank definition, which are High Income, East Asia and the Pacific, Europe and Central Asia, Latin America and the Caribbean, Middle East and North Africa, South Asia, and sub-Saharan Africa.
Sources: Author's estimates, based on Global Findex Databases 2014 and 2017, Euromonitor International Retailing industry edition 2019, and the World Development Indicators database (accessed 19 August 2020).

Remittances Transfer

The three broad categories with the greatest level of mobile phone penetration are account access, followed by domestic remittances transfer and utility bills payment. In 2017, nearly 40% of those with an account[7] accessed it through a mobile phone, and about a third with a *financial* account accessed it through a mobile phone. Meanwhile, in 2014, only an average of 10% of senders or recipients of domestic remittances do so through a mobile phone. This number increased to one-quarter in 2017. This analysis explores the relationship between payment methods and domestic remittances transfer as an example of how digital payments add convenience to personal lives. Since remittances are particularly relevant for developing countries due to regional and urban–rural disparities, the convenience brought by fintech payments may encourage labor mobility and increase the welfare of migrant workers and their families, making development more inclusive.

Among senders and recipients of domestic remittances, cash/in-person transfer dropped from a cross-country average of 50% in 2014 to 30% in 2017. Roughly half of the decrease is met by the increase in payments through financial accounts, and the remaining by the increase in mobile payments (Figure 5.8).

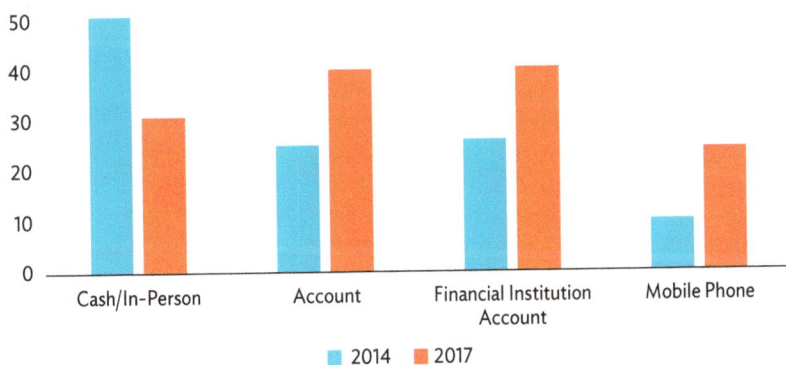

Figure 5.8: Payment Methods for Domestic Remittance Transfers

Note: Total countries is 120, with 110 in 2014 and 109 in 2017.
Source: Author, based on Global Findex Databases (2014, 2017).

---

[7]   An account is either an account at a bank or other financial institution ("financial account") or account for mobile money service ("mobile money account").

Due to data limitations, most of the evidence related to remittances is descriptive and suggestive. More reliable cross-country data on fintech payments penetration will enable us to better assess the effects of fintech payments on various economic outcomes.

5.6. Challenges and Policy Recommendations

As payment systems embrace cutting-edge digital technologies, boosting efficiency and achieving socially beneficial solutions, reflecting on the challenges ahead and coping policies can help sustain progress.[8]

The discussion here looked at how fintech payments make retail payments more efficient, transparent, and inclusive. The chapter has presented empirical evidence of fintech payments in areas such as e-commerce, fintech development, and domestic remittances transfers, and has argued that fintech payments leverage the platform nature of their providers in terms of big data, broad customer base, and multi-purpose technology; and enable e-commerce and fintech development.

The analysis considered four additional benefits and their corresponding risks for efficiency/convenience, transparency, security, and network effects.

1) *Efficiency/convenience*

With fintech payments, carrying and transaction costs fall and real-time settlement increases efficiency, particularly for liquidity-constrained firms and households. The benefits of lower costs and greater efficiency and convenience extend to unbanked individuals, due to the availability of mobile accounts for this group.

However, a digital divide exists among the less tech-savvy (e.g., the elderly or less educated who lack knowledge of digital products) and those without access to smartphones, internet, or computers (such as lower-income or rural households), and thus unable to take advantage of the efficiency and convenience of fintech payments. Lack of financial literacy may also put some consumers and businesses at more risk due to the complexity and newness of fintech payment

---

[8]   ADB (2021) also discuss these points.

systems relative to more traditional payment methods. Since most of these groups are also more socially deprived, the digital divide in payments can exacerbate existing social disparities.

Another caveat is the tendency of overreliance on fintech payments. Leveraging the benefits of fintech payments should not preclude other means of payments, especially acceptance of cash. Rather, cash and fintech payments should be treated as complements, and the transition to a more digitalized system should be gradual. In Section 3, fact 4 indicates that a large percentage of mobile money transactions are for cash-in/cash-out purposes. Auer, Cornelli, and Frost (2020) call for the defense of cash and promotion of contactless payments and digital currencies at the same time during the pandemic. Fintech payments are still at a relatively early stage in the diffusion process. Alvarez and Argente (2020) show that a complete ban of cash for payment for Uber rides can induce an average loss of about 50% of expenditures on trips for riders who used to paid in cash before the ban. This outcome disproportionately burdens low-income households.

2) **Transparency**

Fintech payments expand the set of transactions made digitally, enhancing electronic recordkeeping. With the advent of blockchain technologies, the irrevocability of electronic records is strengthened. This enhanced transparency can contribute to collection of taxes; reduction of the informal economy; and detection of illegal activities such as fraud, money laundering, and corruption.

Fintech payments generate a huge amount of data, ranging from personal information, transaction history, credit history, financial situation, social networks, and consumption behavior. To this end, digital technologies create too much transparency. Fintech payment providers can exploit this data advantage with machine-learning algorithms to study and predict behavior, so that businesses can better match customers with product offerings and reap higher profits. Governments can leverage these data and better identify the most vulnerable individuals subject to cash assistance in crises, including people in the informal economy. Unbanked individuals can have access to credit as their transaction and credit histories are now verifiable. This increase in transparency arising from big data can also assist in crime detection. However, the downside is obvious: unrestricted use of personal data may lead to consumer privacy violation and discriminatory business practices.

3) *Security*

Electronic recordkeeping protects consumers and fosters trust. The complexity of fintech payment systems provides additional layers of safety in the prevention of cyberattacks, but such complexity also renders the system harder to recover if cyberattacks actually take place.

Since traditional payment options have subjected consumers to possible infection during the COVID-19 pandemic, fintech payment systems have been advantageous. However, they may be more vulnerable in other scenarios, such as network disruptions or cyberattacks. The availability of a diversified set of payment methods can increase resilience, as payment methods can back up each other in case of temporary disruption.

New forms of illegal activities may arise as the digital economy expands. There may be less risk of physical wallet theft, but criminals can steal smartphones, identity, information, and assets in e-wallets. Although greater transparency improves the detection of fraud, money laundering, and corruption, increased cost-effectiveness and convenience of cross-border transactions may facilitate cross-border crimes and money laundering.

4) *Network effects*

Fintech payment platforms embody the main characteristics of traditional networks in terms of network externalities, economies of scale, high fixed costs, and low marginal costs. They also incorporate features such as big data usage, broad user base, and multi-purposefulness (BIS 2020). Hence, fintech payment systems can leverage customer data and networks to encourage the adoption of other fintech services such as e-saving, credit payment, credit scoring, P2P lending, and wealth management. Nevertheless, these unique characteristics will be more prone to create excessive market power. Competition policies should therefore be re-considered to address potential problems.

Policy makers and fintech payment providers can work together to tackle these challenges. Policies can be broadly categorized as fulfilling the following goals: (i) fill existing loopholes of the regulatory system to reflect key changes resulting from digitalization such as privacy breach and excessive market power; (ii) expand access, particularly to the more socially disadvantaged groups; and (iii) promote regional cooperation. Governments and central banks are also encouraged to utilize digital technology in their own business practices.

More specifically:

1) *Bridging existing regulatory gaps to reflect emerging legal issues arising from fintech payments.*

   Fintech payments, and the rise of the digital economy in general, introduce unprecedented risks, including but not limited to data privacy breaches, violation of consumer rights, cybersecurity, identity theft, and anti-competitive practices. Regulatory systems should keep up with recent developments in the fintech industry and bridge existing gaps.

2) *Encouraging interoperability between platforms.*

   Since technology can be widely applicable, many fintech payment providers (e.g., GrabPay, Alipay, WeChat Pay) mix a variety of services, ranging from e-saving, wealth management, P2P lending to online shopping, ride hailing, social networks, and food delivery. These "super apps" greatly increase convenience, but without regulation, may create excessive market power and eventually harm consumer welfare and innovation. Encouraging interoperability between platforms is a way to reduce switching costs and maintain sufficient competition between platforms. This is essential to maintain fair opportunities for small fintech providers, incentivize long-run innovation, improve convenience of services to customers, and build a healthy digital ecosystem.

3) *Providing relevant devices, connectivity, digital ID/know-your-customer and digital/financial literacy, especially to more socially disadvantaged groups.*

To mitigate the digital divide in payments, governments should address potential obstacles among people with difficulty adopting new technology. These may include individuals who lack mobile phones, internet, or computers; valid documentation for identity verification; or technical knowledge for operation.

4) *Maintaining the provision of alternative payment options, especially the availability of cash.*

As fintech payments are still at a relatively early stage in the diffusion process, availability to more socially disadvantaged groups remains limited. While promoting fintech payments, the government should not abolish more traditional payment options, especially cash, but rather treat them as complementary. Mobile money providers should continue to provide and improve cash-in/cash-out services.

5) *Promoting regional cooperation in the standardization of industry practices, addressing cross-border crimes, and payment systems integration.*

Fintech payment systems greatly facilitate cross-border transactions through lower transaction costs, faster settlement, and increased convenience. As the world becomes more interconnected, governments should collaborate regionally and promote payment system integration, for which standardization of industry practices is a crucial first step.

A more integrated system can help deal with cross-border crimes, reduce transaction costs, improve accessibility and reach, and encourage resource and skill/capabilities sharing. During the pandemic, many countries have recognized the importance of cross-border payments, particularly for remittances for less developed countries. In February 2020, the G20 recognized the importance of enhancing cross-border payments and planned a three-stage process to address this pressing need.

However, payment integration is challenging, as multiple stakeholders are involved and countries can differ in their existing systems. For instance, countries may differ in sophistication of digital financial infrastructure and regulation intensity. Moreover, some countries may be generally more decentralized than others, which raises the question of the extent of government intervention. Lastly, countries may simply differ in preferences of payment instruments, with some preferring QR payments (e.g., the PRC, Thailand) and others preferring credit card (e.g., the United States, Japan).

The focus of policy efforts thus depends on the level of digital financial infrastructure development. Table 5.7 suggests key policy focus areas for countries at the initial, developing, and advanced stages of digital financial infrastructure development.

Table 5.7: Policy Focus Areas by Digital Financial Infrastructure Development

Stage	Policy Focus Areas
Initial	■ Establish basic telecommunication infrastructure (e.g., broadband, mobile) ■ Digitalize administrative network such as national ID and know your customer ■ Improve digital and financial literacy
Developing	■ Enhance interoperability between financial infrastructure ■ Consumer incentive policies such as tax exemption for diffusion
Advanced	■ Policies and regulations for effective management and financial market stability (e.g., competition policies, data privacy protection) ■ Cross-border cooperation and standardization

Source: Author.

5.7. Conclusion

As the financial industry is transformed, traditional financial services are giving way to frontier digital technologies. This fintech revolution is affecting payments most among business areas. This chapter has evaluated the state and impact of fintech payments using a data-driven approach, focusing on retail payments.

It documents five stylized facts regarding fintech payment systems. Using province-level data on Alipay's penetration in the PRC, it shows the positive impact of fintech payments on e-commerce and the spillover effect on the development of other fintech products. The cross-country analyses highlight the importance of fintech in e-commerce and remittances transfers. Fintech payments benefit from the unique characteristics of the platform economy, including in big data, broad customer bases, and multi-purpose technology. These make retail payments more efficient, transparent, and inclusive and enable e-commerce, general fintech/financial development, and financial inclusion. With more data available, future research can exploit the impact of fintech more thoroughly.

Fintech payments are still at early stage of adoption in most emerging economies and a digital divide can exacerbate income inequality. Governments should therefore address the potential obstacles among people at a technical or knowledge disadvatage. To advance Asia's payment systems through fintech, policies should also aim to bridge existing regulatory gaps to reflect key changes spawned by digitalization such as data privacy, identity theft, cybersecurity, and anti-competitive practices. Enhancing interoperability, standardization, and cross-border payments should also get attention.

Appendix

Table A5.1: Examples of Consumer-to-Consumer and Consumer-to-Business Fintech Payment Systems

Segment	Example
C2C	▪ Venmo, Xoom
	▪ Remittances: Ria, Transferwise
C2B	▪ US: Apple Pay, Google Pay
	▪ China: Alipay, WeChat Pay
	▪ Southeast Asia: GrabPay, GCash
	▪ Digital wallet: Starbucks, Uber

C2B = consumer-to-business, C2C = consumer-to-consumer.
Note: Examples of payment systems for each segment may not be the only segment
the system serves to.
Source: Author.

Table A5.2: Characteristics by Payment Methods

	Cash	Debit Card	Credit Card	Fintech Payments
Carrying cost	High	Medium	Medium	Low
Processing cost	Medium	High	High	Low
Speed	Low	Medium/high	Medium/high	High
Security	Theft, robbery	Theft, robbery	Theft, robbery	Identity theft
Transparency	Low	High	High	High
Inclusion	High	Medium	Low	High

Source: Author.

Table A5.3: Key Variables and Data Sources

Data Source	Definition/Variable
Bank for International Settlements, Red Book Statistics for CPMI Countries, 2014–2018	■ Relative importance of cashless payment instrument = transaction volume of payment instrument/total transaction volume of cashless payments ■ Value per transaction = transaction value/transaction volume
GSMA, Global Mobile Money Dataset, 2020	■ Mobile money service must meet the following criteria: (i) include transferring money and making and receiving payments using the mobile phone; (ii) be available to the unbanked; (iii) offer a network of physical transaction points which can include agents, outside of bank branches and ATMs, that make the service widely accessible to everyone; (iv) mobile banking or payment services (e.g., Apple Pay and Google Wallet) that offer the mobile phone as just another channel to access a traditional banking product are not included; and (v) payment services linked to a traditional banking product or credit card (e.g., Apple Pay and Google Wallet) are not included (GSMA, 2020). ■ See Appendix B of GSMA (2020) for more definitions of airtime top-up; bill payment; bulk disbursement; cash-in, cash-out; and international remittance enabled by mobile money. ■ Transaction value or volume of mobile money by region ■ Transaction value/volume/average value per transaction by usage
PKU Digital Financial Inclusion Index of China (PKU-DFIIC), 2011–2018	■ Log of payment index ■ Log of insurance index ■ Log of money fund index ■ Log of credit index ■ Log of investment index ■ Log of credit investigation index
National Bureau of Statistics of China, 2011–2018	■ Log of e-commerce sales (purchase) value (million CNY) ■ Log of primary insurance payment value (100 million CNY) ■ Log of gross domestic product per capita ■ Share of rural population = rural population (10,000 persons)/total population (10,000 persons) ■ Share of population aged 65 and above = population aged 65 and above in sample survey/total population in sample survey ■ Log of broadband subscribers

continued on next page

Table A5.3 *continued*

Data Source	Definition/Variable
World Bank, Global Findex Survey, 2011, 2014, 2017	■ Share of people aged 15+ who made or received a digital payment in the past year ■ Share of internet purchases aged 15+ who pay by cash/online ■ Share of senders/recipients of domestic remittances aged 15+ through a mobile phone ■ Share of payers of utility bills aged 15+ through a mobile phone ■ Share of those with (financial) accounts aged 15+ who access through a mobile phone ■ Share of recipients of agricultural products payments aged 15+ through a mobile phone ■ Share of recipients of self-employment payments aged 15+ through a mobile phone ■ Share of recipients of agricultural products payments aged 15+ through a mobile phone ■ Share of wage recipients aged 15+ through a mobile phone ■ Share of recipients of government payments aged 15+ through a mobile phone ■ Share of senders/recipients of domestic remittances aged 15+ in cash/person ■ Share of senders/recipients of domestic remittances aged 15+ through (financial) accounts
World Bank, World Development Index, 2011, 2014, 2017	■ Log GDP per capita ■ Rural population (% of total population) ■ Share of population aged 65 and above = Total population aged 65 and above/Total population ■ Log of broadband per 100 people ■ Official exchange rate (LCU per $, period average) ■ Real effective exchange rate index (2010 = 100)
Euromonitor International Retailing industry edition 2019	■ Log of e-commerce retail value (excluding sales tax, in LCU) ■ Log of mobile e-commerce retail value (excluding sales tax, in LCU)

CPMI = Committee on Payments and Market Infrastructures, GDP = gross domestic product GSMA = Global System for Mobile Communications Association, LCU = local currency unit, PKU = Peking University.
Source: Author.

Figure A5.1: Index System of PKU-DFIIC

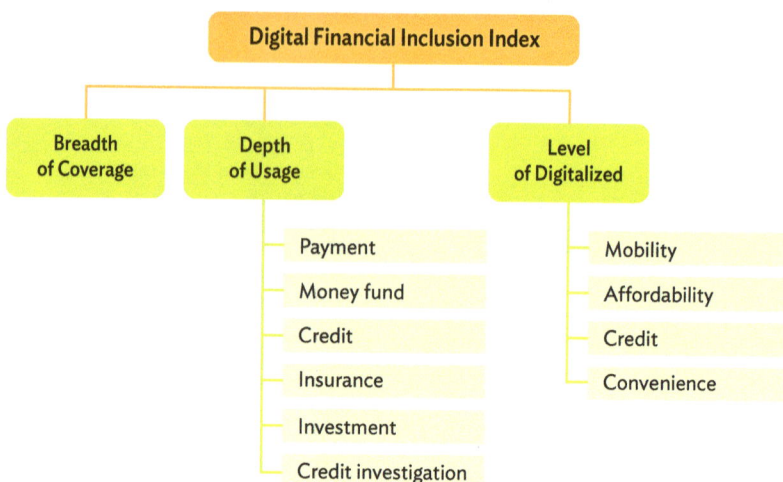

PKU-DFIIC = Peking University – Digital Digital Financial Inclusion Index of China.
Source: Institute of Digital Finance, Peking University (2019).

Table A5.4: Emerging versus Developed Economies in BIS CPMI Countries Data

Emerging Economies	Developed Economies
Argentina, Brazil, China (People's Republic of), Indonesia, Korea (Republic of), Mexico, the Russian Federation, Saudi Arabia, Singapore, South Africa, Turkey, and other economies	Australia, Belgium, Canada, France, Germany, Italy, Japan, the Netherlands, Spain, Sweden, Switzerland, the United Kingdom, the United States

BIS = Bank for International Settlements, CPMI = Committee on Payments and Market Infrastructures.
Source: BIS, 2018.

Figure A5.2: PKU-DFIIC Payment Index (GDP-weighted average)

a. Payment Index in Eight Economic Regions

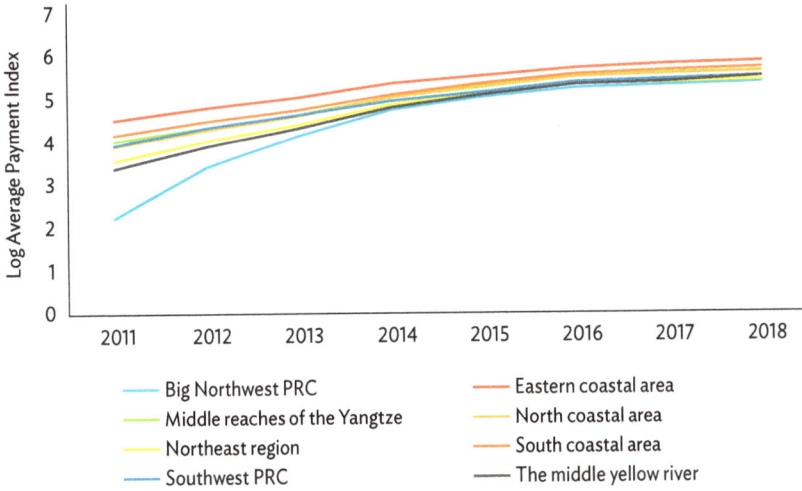

Legend:
- Big Northwest PRC
- Middle reaches of the Yangtze
- Northeast region
- Southwest PRC
- Eastern coastal area
- North coastal area
- South coastal area
- The middle yellow river

b. Convergence in Fintech Payments

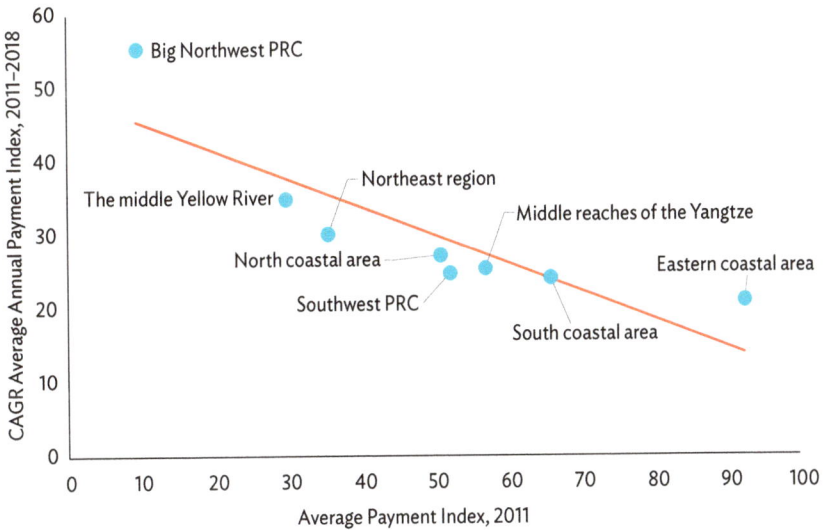

continued on next page

Figure A5.2 *continued*

c. Fintech Payment vs. GDP per Capita

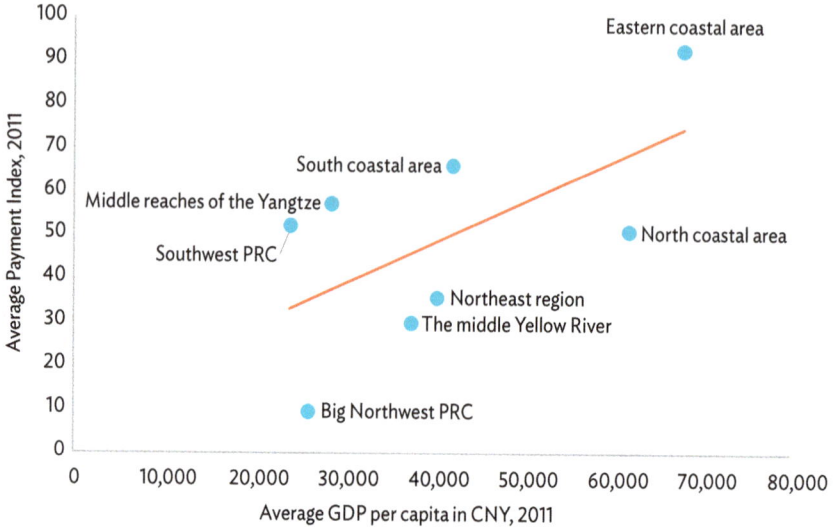

x-axis: Average GDP per capita in CNY, 2011
y-axis: Average Payment Index, 2011

- Eastern coastal area
- South coastal area
- Middle reaches of the Yangtze
- Southwest PRC
- North coastal area
- Northeast region
- The middle Yellow River
- Big Northwest PRC

d. Fintech Payment Growth vs. GDP per Capita

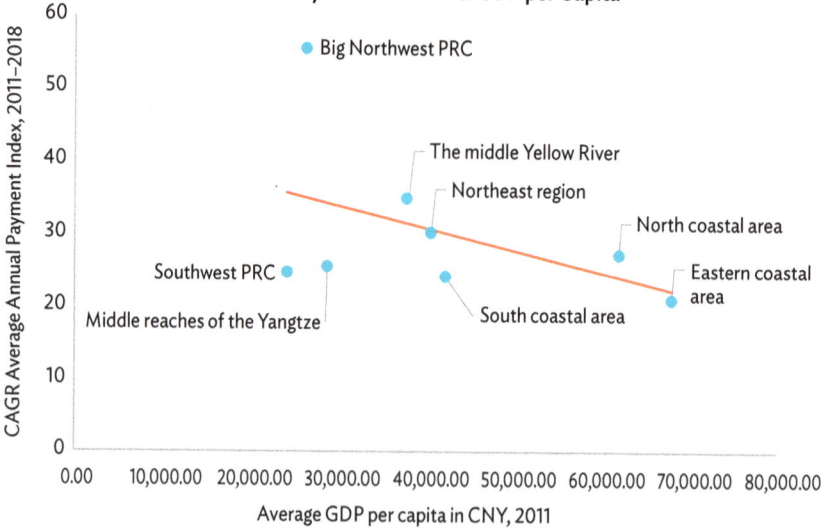

x-axis: Average GDP per capita in CNY, 2011
y-axis: CAGR Average Annual Payment Index, 2011–2018

- Big Northwest PRC
- The middle Yellow River
- Northeast region
- North coastal area
- Southwest PRC
- Middle reaches of the Yangtze
- South coastal area
- Eastern coastal area

CAGR = compounded annual growth rate, GDP = gross domestic product, PKU-DFIIC = Peking University-Digital Financial Inclusion Index of China, PRC = People's Republic of China.
Sources: Author, based on PKU-DFIIC (2019) and National Bureau of Statistics (2019).

Table A5.5: Fintech Payment and E-Commerce
(pooled OLS, no postal service control)

	(1)	(2)	(3)
Log of payment index	1.756**	0.316**	0.900*
	(0.300)	(0.141)	(0.522)
Log of GDP per capita	0.350	0.336	0.560
	(0.265)	(0.251)	(0.279)
Share of rural population	−2.489***	−3.464***	−2.901***
	(0.746)	(0.695)	(0.798)
Share of population 65 and above	0.883	−2.511	−2.404
	(2.396)	(2.885)	(3.297)
Log of broadband subscribers	0.799***	0.738***	0.781***
	(0.0558)	(0.0647)	(0.0749)
Constant	5.189	3.598	−2.393
	(3.055)	(2.658)	(3.580)
Time fixed effects (FE)	Yes	No	No
Region FE	No	Yes	No
Region-time FE	No	No	Yes
Observations	186	186	186
R-squared	0.848	0.878	0.893

GDP = gross domestic product, OLS = ordinary least squares, PKU-DFIIC = Peking University-Digital Financial Inclusion Index of China.
Note: Robust standard errors in parentheses,*** p<0.01, ** p<0.05, * p<0.1.
Sources: Author's estimates, based on PKU-DFIIC (2019) and the National Bureau of Statistics (2019) data.

Table A5.6: Fintech Payment versus E-Commerce Purchase
(pooled OLS)

	(1)	(2)	(3)	(4)
Log of payment index	0.396**	0.868**	0.233	0.344
	(0.198)	(0.372)	(0.190)	(0.637)
Log of GDP per capita	0.180	0.118	−0.206	−0.195
	(0.344)	(0.334)	(0.318)	(0.360)
Share of rural population	−4.871***	−4.591***	−5.873***	−5.762***
	(1.102)	(1.100)	(1.085)	(1.174)
Share of population 65 and above	−2.975	−2.293	−1.680	−0.799
	(2.736)	(2.763)	(3.140)	(3.487)
Log of broadband subscribers	0.892***	0.876***	0.920***	0.953***
	(0.0671)	(0.0747)	(0.0778)	(0.0882)

continued on next page

Table A5.6 *continued*

	(1)	(2)	(3)	(4)
Log of average persons served by postal office	0.410***	0.337**	0.274*	0.161
	(0.149)	(0.163)	(0.165)	(0.227)
Constant	14.13***	12.91***	20.48***	20.44***
	(4.448)	(4.823)	(4.104)	(6.045)
Time fixed effects (FE)	No	Yes	No	No
Region FE	No	No	Yes	No
Region–time FE	No	No	No	Yes
Observations	186	186	186	186
R–squared	0.820	0.826	0.863	0.877

GDP = gross domestic product, OLS = ordinary least squares, PKU-DFIIC = Peking University-Digital Financial Inclusion Index of China.
Note: Robust standard errors in parentheses, *** p<0.01, ** p<0.05, * p<0.1.
Sources: Author's estimates, based on PKU-DFIIC (2019) and the National Bureau of Statistics (2019) data.

Table A5.7: Fintech Payment versus E-Commerce Purchase
(lagged payment index)

	(1)	(2)	(3)	(4)
Log of lagged payment index	0.189	0.405	0.0831	0.144
	(0.154)	(0.292)	(0.152)	(0.499)
Log of GDP per capita	0.233	0.218	–0.176	–0.168
	(0.344)	(0.345)	(0.319)	(0.372)
Share of rural population	–4.792***	–4.538***	–5.825***	–5.740***
	(1.110)	(1.124)	(1.094)	(1.172)
Share of population 65 and above	–2.698	–2.170	–1.321	–0.794
	(2.741)	(2.755)	(3.160)	(3.462)
Log of broadband subscribers	0.905***	0.897***	0.932***	0.955***
	(0.0685)	(0.0726)	(0.0788)	(0.0845)
Log of average persons served by postal office	0.341**	0.261	0.209	0.136
	(0.155)	(0.160)	(0.172)	(0.220)
Constant	15.13***	14.82***	21.39***	21.41***
	(4.499)	(4.610)	(4.149)	(5.269)
Time fixed effects (FE)	No	Yes	No	No
Region FE	No	No	Yes	No
Region–time FE	No	No	No	Yes
Observations	186	186	186	186
R–squared	0.817	0.823	0.862	0.877

GDP = gross domestic product, OLS = ordinary least squares, PKU-DFIIC = Peking University-Digital Financial Inclusion Index of China.
Note: Robust standard errors in parentheses, *** p<0.01, ** p<0.05, * p<0.1.
Sources: Author's estimates, based on PKU-DFIIC (2019) and the National Bureau of Statistics (2019) data.

Table A5.8: Fintech Payment versus E-Commerce Purchase
(fixed effects estimator)

	(1)	(2)	(3)	(4)
Log of payment index	0.730***	0.618**		
	(0.229)	(0.303)		
Log of lagged payment index			0.447*	0.478**
			(0.233)	(0.222)
Log of GDP per capita	0.0868	0.0516	0.189	0.200
	(0.411)	(0.408)	(0.403)	(0.397)
Share of rural population	−0.389	0.938	−1.390	−2.218
	(4.249)	(4.090)	(4.163)	(4.384)
Share of population 65 and above	−2.027	−4.792	−1.910	−0.844
	(4.866)	(5.499)	(6.139)	(5.833)
Log of broadband subscribers	0.429	0.302	0.203	0.257
	(0.261)	(0.336)	(0.171)	(0.180)
Log of average persons served by postal office	0.234			0.203
	(0.203)			(0.186)
Constant	15.92**	18.66***	20.34***	18.15***
	(5.811)	(5.342)	(5.562)	(5.819)
Observations	186	186	186	186
R-squared	0.456	0.447	0.430	0.437
Number of provinces	31	31	31	31

GDP = gross domestic product, OLS = ordinary least squares, PKU–DFIIC = Peking University–Digital Financial Inclusion Index of China.
Note: Robust standard errors in parentheses, *** p<0.01, ** p<0.05, * p<0.1.
Sources: Autho's estimates, based on PKU–DFIIC (2019) and the National Bureau of Statistics (2019) data.

Table A5.9: Digital Payments and Mobile E-Commerce
(cross-country)

	(1)	(2)	(3)	(4)
Digital	0.0408***	0.0304*	0.0663***	0.0599**
	(0.0152)	(0.0156)	(0.0187)	(0.0234)
Log of GDP per capita	1.565***	1.866***	0.821	0.999
	(0.509)	(0.529)	(0.602)	(0.649)
Share of rural population	0.00340	0.00965	0.0261	0.0278
	(0.0252)	(0.0253)	(0.0249)	(0.0293)

continued on next page

Table A5.9 *continued*

	(1)	(2)	(3)	(4)
Share of population aged 65 and above	6.504	6.797	−3.354	−3.065
	(5.542)	(5.537)	(10.91)	(7.696)
Log of mobile per 100 people	0.270	0.208	0.939***	0.907**
	(1.274)	(1.272)	(0.317)	(0.450)
Constant	−32.28***	−34.41***	−27.40***	−28.69***
	(8.504)	(8.640)	(5.738)	(5.797)
Time fixed effects	No	Yes	No	Yes
Region fixed effects	No	No	Yes	Yes
Observations	120	120	119	119
R-squared	0.545	0.554	0.605	0.607

GDP = gross domestic product, OLS = ordinary least squares, PKU-DFIIC = Peking University-Digital Financial Inclusion Index of China.
Note: Robust standard errors in parentheses, *** $p<0.01$, ** $p<0.05$, * $p<0.1$.
Sources: Author's estimates, based on Global Findex Databases 2014 and 2017, Euromonitor International Retailing industry edition 2019, and the World Development Indicators database.

References

Agarwal, S., W. Qian, Y. Ren, H. Tsai and B. Yeung. 2020. The Real Impact of FinTech: Evidence from Mobile Payment Technology. *NUS Business School Working Paper*.

Agur, I., S. M. Peria, and C. Rochon. 2020. Digital Financial Services and the Pandemic: Opportunities and Risks for Emerging and Developing Economies. *IMF Fiscal Affairs: Special Series on COVID-19*. Washington DC: International Monetary Fund.

Alvarez, F. and D. Argente. 2020. Consumer Surplus of Alternative Payment Methods: Paying Uber with Cash. *Working Paper*.

Aron, J. and J. Muellbauer. 2019. The Economics of Mobile Money: Harnessing the Transformative Power of Technology to Benefit the Global Poor. *Oxford Martin School Working Paper*. Oxford.

Asian Development Bank (ADB). 2021. Asian Economic Integration Report 2021: Making Digital Platforms Work for Asia and the Pacific. Manila. http://dx.doi.org/10.22617/TCS210048-2.

Auer, R., G. Cornelli, and J. Frost. 2020. Covid-19, Cash, and the Future of Payments. *BIS Bulletin 2020 No. 3*. Basel: Bank of International Settlements.

Bangura, J. A. 2016. Saving Money, Saving Lives: A Case Study on the Benefits of Digitizing Payments to Ebola Response to Workers in Sierra Leone.

Bank for International Settlements (BIS). 2020. *BIS Annual Economic Report 2020*. Basel, Switzerland.

CCAF, ADBI, and FinTechSpace. 2019. *ASEAN FinTech Ecosystem Benchmarking Study*. Cambridge, United Kingdom.

Chorzempa, M. 2018. How China Leapfrogged Ahead of the United States in the FinTech Race. Washington DC: Peterson Institute for International Economics. https://www.piie.com/blogs/china-economic-watch/how-china-leapfrogged-ahead-united-states-fintech-race.

Euromonitor International. Retailing industry edition 2019.

Fan, J., L. Tang, W. Zhu, and B. Zou. 2018. The Alibaba Effect: Spatial Consumption Inequality and the Welfare Gains from E-Commerce. *Journal of International Economics*. 114. pp. 203–220.

GSMA. 2020. *2019 State of the Industry Report on Mobile Money*. London, United Kingdom.

iResearch. 2020. *2020 Q1 Chinese Third-Party Mobile Payments Market Report*. https://www.iresearch.com.cn/Detail/report?id=3601&isfree=0.

Institute of Digital Finance, Peking University (PKU). 2019. *The Peking University Digital Financial Inclusion Index of China (2011-2018)*. Beijing.

Klein, A. 2020. China's Digital Payments Revolution. *Brookings Institution Report*. https://www.brookings.edu/wp-content/uploads/2020/04/FP_20200427_china_digital_payments_klein.pdf.

Prady, D. 2020. Reaching Households in Emerging and Developing Economies: Citizen ID, Socioeconomic Data, and Digital Delivery. *IMF Fiscal Affairs: Special Series on COVID-19*. Washington DC: International Monetary Fund.

Rutkowski, M., A. Garcia Mora, G. L. Bull, B. Guermazi, and C. Grown. 2020. Responding to Crisis with Digital Payments for Social Protection: Short-Term Measures with Long-Term Benefits. *World Bank Blogs*. 31 March. https://blogs.worldbank.org/voices/responding-crisis-digital-payments-social-protection-short-term-measures-long-term-benefits.

Sender, H. 2020. China's New Digital Currency Takes Aim at Alibaba and Tencent. *Financial Times*. https://www.ft.com/content/fec06de9-ac43-4ab8-81f3-577638bd3c16?accessToken=zwAAAXO5zrrAkdP-wG3prENKuNOB81d2OL08Fg.MEUCIClZUceuOZplO5tjtius9kuo9zmXDvql_741rEaSqGPlAiEA59iUtL53pH4llqrG_iixJdC4n4O-vQ9kQ5wYLeq7XZc&sharetype=gift?token=325a4af8-c1db-43d5-946b-95de026308db (accessed August 2020).

Shen, Y., C. J. Hueng, and W. Hu. 2020. Using Digital Technology to Improve Financial Inclusion in China. *Applied Economics Letters*. 27 (1). pp. 30–34.

Statista. 2020. *Statista Digital Market Outlook*. Hamburg.

Una, G., R. Allen, S. Pattanayak, and G. Suc. 2020. Digital Solutions for Direct Cash Transfers in Emergencies. *IMF Fiscal Affairs: Special Series on COVID-19*. Washington DC: International Monetary Fund.

Digital Divide and the Platform Economy: Looking for the Connection from the Asian Experience

Francis Mark Quimba, Maureen Ane Rosellon, and Sylwyn Calizo Jr.[1]

6.1. Introduction

In 2019, 5.2 billion people (62.0% of the global population) subscribed to mobile services (UNCTAD 2019).[2] Mobile technologies and services, including digital platforms, generated about $4.1 trillion of economic value added or about 4.7% of global gross domestic product (GDP), and countries continue to reap the benefits resulting from the greater productivity and efficiency of mobile services. Indeed, the GSM Association (GSMA)—an organization that represents the interests of mobile operators worldwide—projected that the economic value of mobile services will increase to 4.9% of world GDP by 2024 (GSMA 2020), suggesting the foundation for the platform economy is strengthening.

However, large segments of the population are unable to benefit from the platform economy, partly because of the digital divide, thus creating a *platform divide*. The digital divide is defined as "the gap between individuals, households, businesses, and geographic areas at different socio-economic levels with regard to both their opportunities to access information and communication technologies (ICT) and to their use of the internet for a wide variety of activities" (OECD 2001).

---

[1]   Senior research fellow, supervising research specialist, and research specialist, respectively, from the Philippine Institute for Development Studies.

[2]   This chapter was prepared as a background paper for ADB (2021) and draws from Quimba, Rosellon, and Calizo (2020).

The rapid growth and value of digital platforms has been observed in Asia (Google, Temasek, and Bain 2019), with the United States (US) hosting the majority of the 70 highest-valued digital platforms. However, benefits may not be uniformly distributed across and within countries in the region. A number of studies (Fraiberger and Sundararajan 2015; CUTS International 2018a and 2019; Quimba and Calizo 2018) show that digital platforms reduce inequality by spreading opportunity and providing income to people at the bottom of the income distribution. Meanwhile, other studies reveal that digital platforms, as part of the sharing economy,[3] may be contributing to the increase in inequality (Schneider 2014; Schor 2014). This prompted the Asia-Pacific Economic Cooperation (APEC) in 2017 to launch its Internet and Digital Economy Road Map (APEC 2017, 6) for APEC economies to "bridge the digital divides between and within economies, regions, and groups," and in particular to "ensure that digital strategies incorporate a gender perspective that addresses women's needs and circumstances" to "bridge the digital gender divide."

This chapter looks at the pattern of digital divides in Asia and relates this to participation in digital platforms, seeking answers to the following research questions:

i.   How does the digital divide affect the platform economy?
ii. How can the platform economy affect existing divides
     (not necessarily digital)?

The chapter describes Asia's experience to try to understand how the digital divide is affecting the various cultures and economies in the region and vice versa. It attempts to explain the link between the level of digital access and the participation in the platform economy, hopefully providing sufficient bases for policy reforms to narrow the digital and platform divides. The chapter begins with an extensive look at the platform economy and the digital divide, its important concepts and case examples from Asian economies. The chapter concludes with policy recommendations.

---

[3]   The sharing economy refers to businesses that focus on the sharing of underutilized assets, monetized or not, in ways that improve efficiency, sustainability, and community (Rinne 2017). Examples are the popular accommodations giant Airbnb and the multimodal transport platform Grab.

6.2. Platform Economy and Digital Divide

The definition of digital platform used here follows UN Conference on Trade and Development (UNCTAD) (2019) description of the digital platform landscape to cover as many types as possible, including both nonprofit-oriented and profit-oriented digital platforms.[4] The discussion will include examples (Box 6.1) from various subcategories of profit-oriented digital platforms such as electronic payments, e-commerce platforms, and services e-commerce platforms (e-health, tourism, digital labor). This allows the chapter to use as case examples the performance of specific platforms in certain countries.

Box 6.1: Examples of Digital Platforms

Accommodation platforms operate an online community marketplace for suppliers to list, and users to discover, and book accommodations whether online or through a mobile phone. Airbnb is such a platform and provides the means of communication and mediates interaction and sometimes payment between the supplier landlord and the user guest. Airbnb is an accommodation platform that provides users lower search costs, access to alternative modes of accommodation, and additional benefits such as sustainable and conscious consumption and even sources of travel information (Pins n.d.).

Remote work platforms provide a venue for freelancers to gather and cater to a broad range of clients (e.g., business owners, start-ups, and entrepreneurs, among others). An example of such work platforms would be Upwork (Fulltime Nomad 2017) which posts jobs under 12 major sections: (i) web, mobile, and software development; (ii) IT and networking; (iii) data science and analytics; (iv) engineering and architecture; (v) design and creative; (vi) writing; (vii) translation; (viii) legal; (ix) administrative support; (x) customer service; (xi) sales and marketing; and (xii) accounting and consulting.

Digital finance refers to "financial services delivered through mobile phones, personal computers, and the internet or cards linked to a reliable digital payment system" (Ozili 2018, 330). Examples would be Alipay and GCash.

Digital health platforms were brought about by the "disruptive technologies that provide digital and objective data accessible to both caregivers and patients leading to an equal level of doctor-patient relationship with shared decision-making" (Mesko et al. 2017). Related to digital health is mobile health (mHealth), which is the use of mobile devices, such as mobile phones, patient monitoring devices, personal digital assistants and wireless devices, for medical and public health practice.

E-learning refers to the use of information and communication technology to support learning and/or deliver education, either in a synchronous (when the lessons are carried out in real-time) or asynchronous format (pre-recorded and the learners progress at their own pace.) Virtual classrooms are examples of synchronous e-learning while

continued on next page

---

[4] A more extensive discussion on the definition of digital platforms is found in Chapter 2 of this volume.

A platform mapping by UNCTAD (2019) indicates that the top global digital platforms are highly concentrated geographically, particularly in the US and the People's Republic of China (PRC) (Figure 6.1). GSMA (2020) data for Asia and the Pacific show that while mobile broadband coverage is already at 94.0% on average, half of those covered choose not to use the internet. As noted, the benefits of the platform economy are not equitably distributed within and across countries, owing to differences in levels of income, education, gender, and geographical location.

Figure 6.1: Distribution of Main Global Platforms by Region, 2018

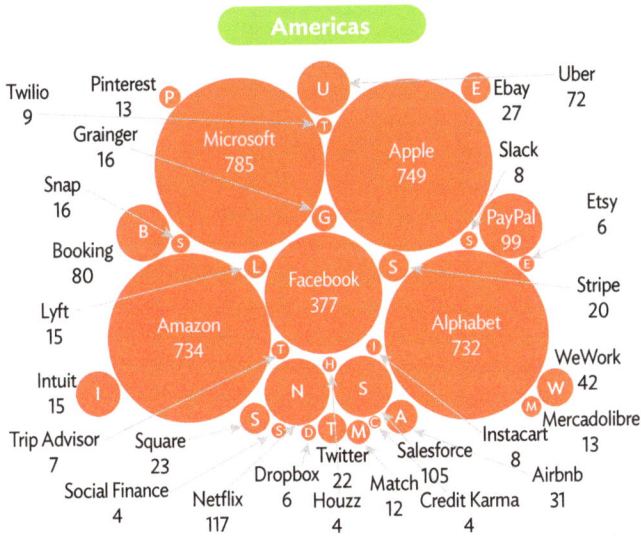

continued on next page

Figure 6.1 *continued*

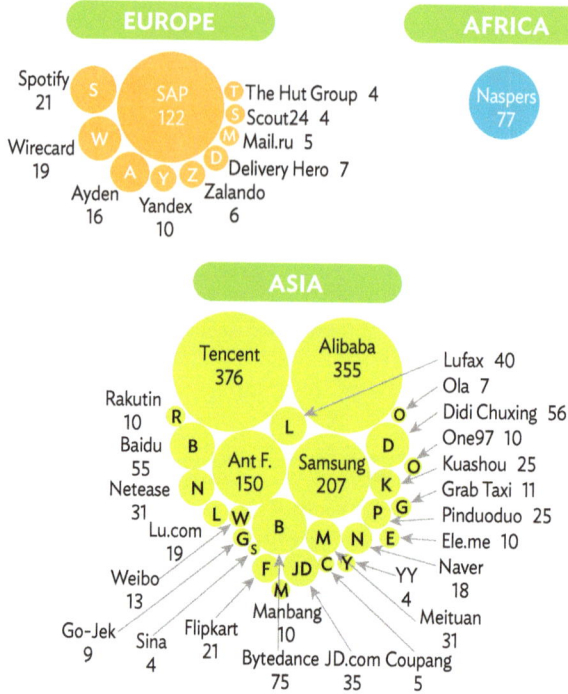

EUROPE

Spotify 21
SAP 122
S
T The Hut Group 4
S Scout24 4
M Mail.ru 5
Wirecard 19
W
D Delivery Hero 7
A Y Z Zalando 6
Ayden 16
Yandex 10

AFRICA

Naspers 77

ASIA

Tencent 376
Alibaba 355
Lufax 40
Ola 7
Didi Chuxing 56
One97 10
Kuashou 25
Grab Taxi 11
Pinduoduo 25
Ele.me 10
Naver 18
Meituan 31

Rakutin 10
R
L
O
Baidu 55
B
D
Netease 31
N
Ant F. 150
Samsung 207
O
K
Lu.com 19
L W
G S
B
P G
M N E
Weibo 13
F JD C Y
YY 4
Go-Jek 9
Sina 4
Flipkart 21
Manbang 10
M
Bytedance 75
JD.com 35
Coupang 5

Source: UN Conference on Trade and Development (2019).

Cumulative and Recursive Model of Digital Divide

As a means of explaining the relationship between digital divide and the platform economy, this chapter slightly modified van Dijk's (2006) cumulative and recursive model (Figure 6.2). This model extends the basic concept of access—understood as *material access* or the counting of people with computers or access to internet connections—to include *motivational access*, *skills access*, and *usage access*.

Figure 6.2: Cumulative and Recursive Model of Successive Kinds of Access to Digital Technologies

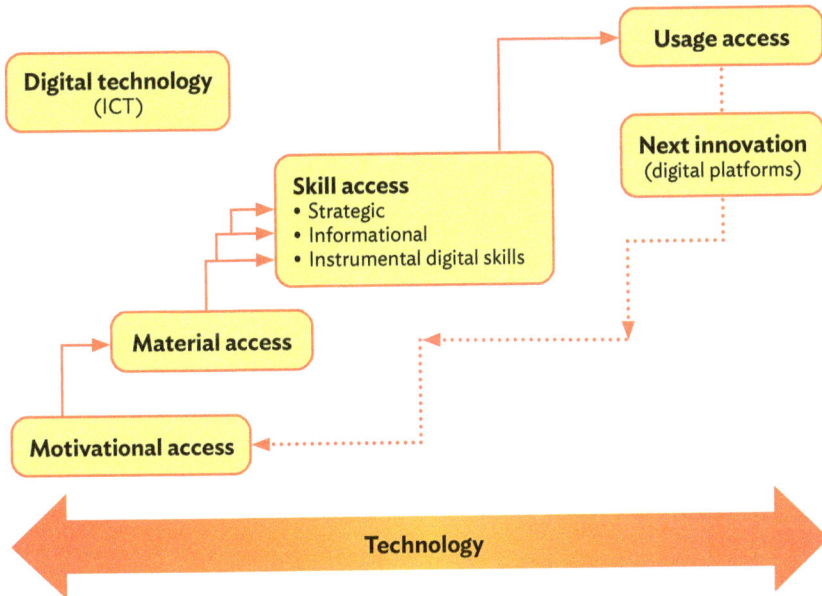

ICT = information and communication technology.
Note: The figure is a slightly modified version of Figure 1 in van Dijk (2006).
Source: Authors, based on van Dijk (2006).

Van Dijk (2006) distinguishes four kinds of barriers to access (divides), corresponding to each of the four types of access. One, the *motivational or mental access divide* is pushed by the lack of elementary digital experience, fear of technology, and a perceived intimidation from new technology.

Two, the *material access divide* includes barriers that limit physical access to a computer or a mobile phone, and network connection. This would also include the cost of internet subscriptions and mobile phone accounts.

Three, the *skills access divide* is related to the user's capability to maximize benefits from ICT. Skills access involves three types of skills: operational skills or knowing how to operate hardware and software; informational skills necessary to navigate and process information; and strategic skills (van Deursen and van Dijk 2011; Ghobadi and Ghobadi 2013) or how to use ICT for personal and societal development. Skills access can be constrained by insufficient digital skills caused by unfamiliarity with technologies, inadequate education, or lack of social support. Ghobadi and Ghobadi (2013) point out that low income and education and lack of time to learn new things are critical factors in all three types of skills.

Four, *usage access divide* is about how individuals actually utilize ICT which is affected by their demographic characteristics (e.g., social class, education, age, gender, and ethnicity) and the quality of their digital infrastructure (e.g., reliability of internet connection). Usage access divide is also manifested in users' active and passive use of ICT—the former is about publication of creative content in various platforms, whereas the latter refers to the consumption of creative content.

The first three types of access follow a relatively linear order of precedence—the skills needed to participate in the platform economy are dependent on the motivation to learn and the physical access to basic technology. It is only when people have acquired the necessary skills can they participate in the platform economy.

Van Dijk's (2006) model suggests that when a technology is fully appropriated, a new innovation arises and the entire process repeats. Usage access enables people to maximize the use of the technology which may lead to innovations. Usage opportunities are enhanced in the discovery and use of more complex applications and innovations, such as the platform economy.

Digital platforms, for example, are a value addition to access to computers, internet, and digital technology. In reality, it would be nearly impossible to discuss digital platforms separately from ICT and the ICT sector. The digital sector, as the core of the digital economy, is consistent with the representation of the digital economy used by Bukht and Heeks (2017) and cited by UNCTAD (2017).

Underpinning the platform economy are the IT/ICT sectors or the foundation of the digital economy. Thus, the digital divide can be seen as a determinant of the use of digital platforms, as material and skills access affects how digital platforms will be used and maximized. Moreover, the inherent nature of some digital platforms inadvertently creates or exacerbates digital divides, as active involvement is preconditioned on the presence of the motivation, materials, and skills, precluding participation of those who lack these.

Figure 6.2 also depicts that any new product or innovation faces the same types of access and limitations. As a new product or service, a platform would have to break the motivational barriers preventing access. Some factors would be specific to the platform itself, such as trust in the platform, perception of the ease of use, room for personal innovation, and task characteristics. The limited availability of certain applications on specific mobile operating systems can hinder material access. For instance, if the platform is only accessible through Apple's iOS, then those using Android mobile phones would automatically be excluded.[5]

Knowledge of mobile applications or digital platforms also affects their use. For some individuals and businesses, learning to use the platform may be too costly in time and money, among other things. Effective usage of platforms would also be affected by policy and infrastructure.

Certain segments of the population have better access to computers and the internet.

The following indicators portray the existing digital divide in Asia. This could be manifested in a global divide (across countries) or in a social divide (within countries).

Motivational access

Motivational access refers to the desire to have a computer or a mobile phone and to be connected to the internet. This desire is affected by social, cultural, or psychological factors.

Trust and perception of the internet

One of the main barriers to access is the lack of knowledge about the internet. In a survey of selected economies from 2014 to 2015 as examined by Wu et al. (2016), it is found that over two-thirds of those currently offline did not know what the internet is (Figure 6.3). Only 13% of the offline population in Thailand and 11% in Indonesia knew what the internet is.

---

5   Android and Apple's iOS are mobile operating systems widely used in the industry. However, iOS is used exclusively by Apple while Android is developed and used by multiple parties, such as Google and the Open Handset Alliance.

Figure 6.3: Awareness and Understanding of the Internet Among Non-Users, 2014–2015
(% of non-internet users)

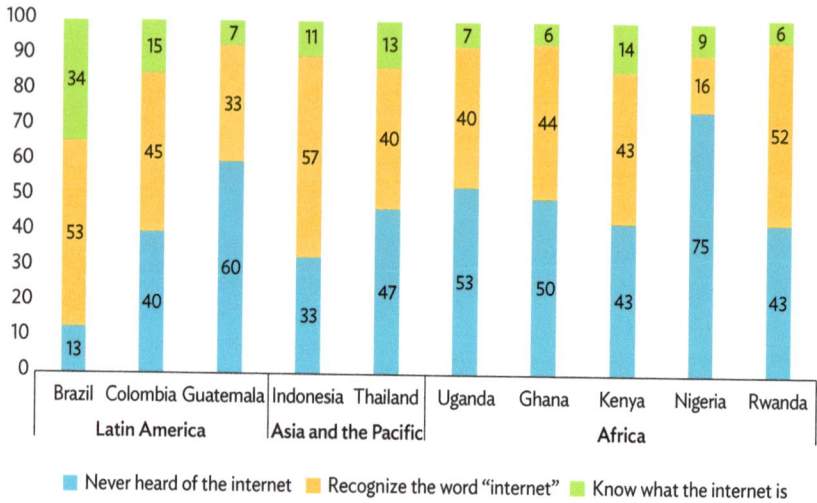

	Brazil	Colombia	Guatemala	Indonesia	Thailand	Uganda	Ghana	Kenya	Nigeria	Rwanda
Know what the internet is	34	15	7	11	13	7	6	14	9	6
Recognize the word "internet"	53	45	33	57	40	40	44	43	16	52
Never heard of the internet	13	40	60	33	47	53	50	43	75	43

Latin America | Asia and the Pacific | Africa

Legend: ■ Never heard of the internet ■ Recognize the word "internet" ■ Know what the internet is

Source: Wu et al. (2016).

Perception and trust affect the motivation to use digital technology and participate in the platform economy. The presence or perception of corruption in the business environment tends to breed distrust in policy governance and e-commerce transactions. As the platform economy is largely associated with digital transactions and e-commerce, high levels of corruption would dissuade participation in the platform economy.

Countries with low incidence of corruption (e.g., Israel, Japan, Singapore, and Switzerland) are associated with higher rates of e-commerce, while countries that rank lowest in e-commerce index also have high incidence of corruption (Figure 6.4). Similarly, UNCTAD (2017) posits that low propensity for online shopping among developing countries may reflect lack of trust in the online environment, limited awareness of e-commerce, and cultural preferences.

Figure 6.4: Corruption and E-Commerce, 2017

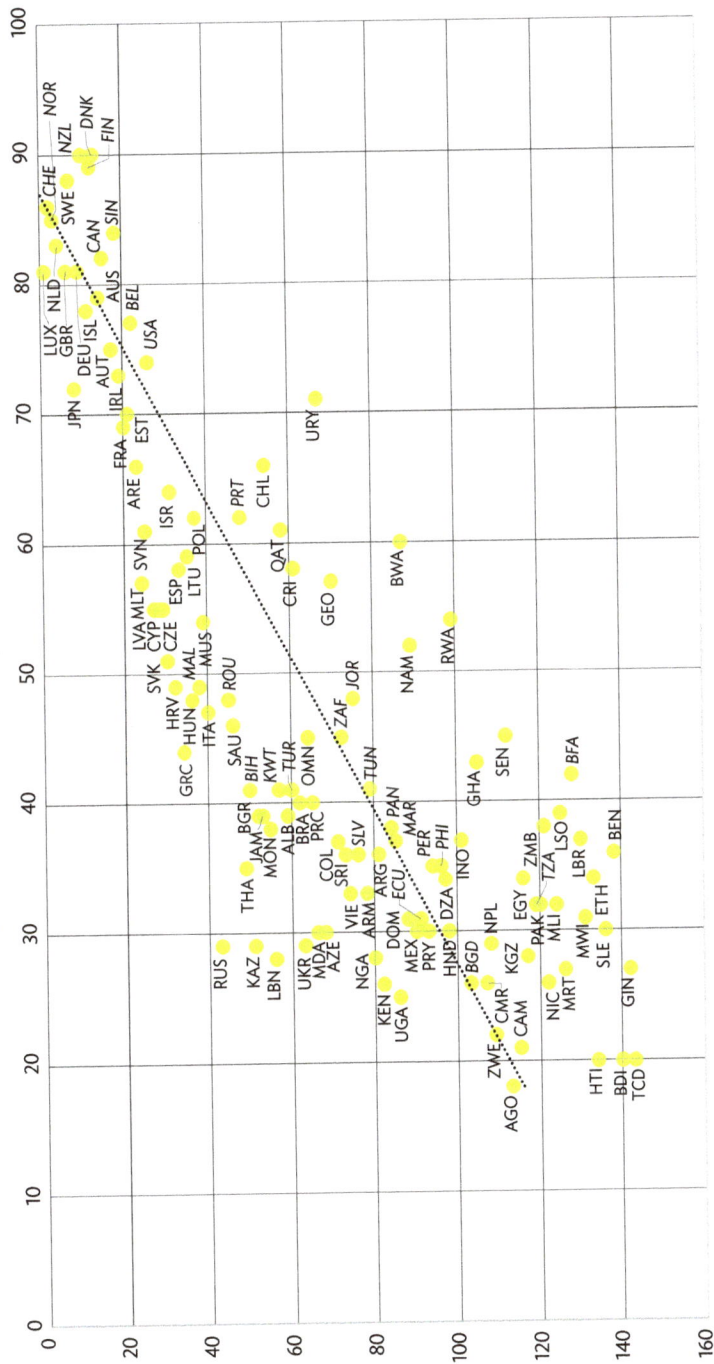

Note: Country labels are placed to the left of their data point, but some country labels (italicized) are placed to the right of their data point to improve chart readability.
Source: Authors' calculations, based on World Bank TCdata360 (accessed July 2020).

Gender Divide

UNCTAD (2019) reports that in about two-thirds of countries worldwide, there are more male internet users than females (Figure 6.5). It is only in the Americas that the proportion of women using the internet is higher than of men.

The gap between male and female internet user penetration rates is on average about 22.8% in developing countries and 2.3% in developed countries. The bigger gaps are observed in least developed countries, at 42.8%, and Africa, at 33.0%. The gap widened from 2013 to 2019. Noticeably, a large increase in the global gender gap occurred in just 2 years, from 11.6% in 2017 to 17.0% in 2019.

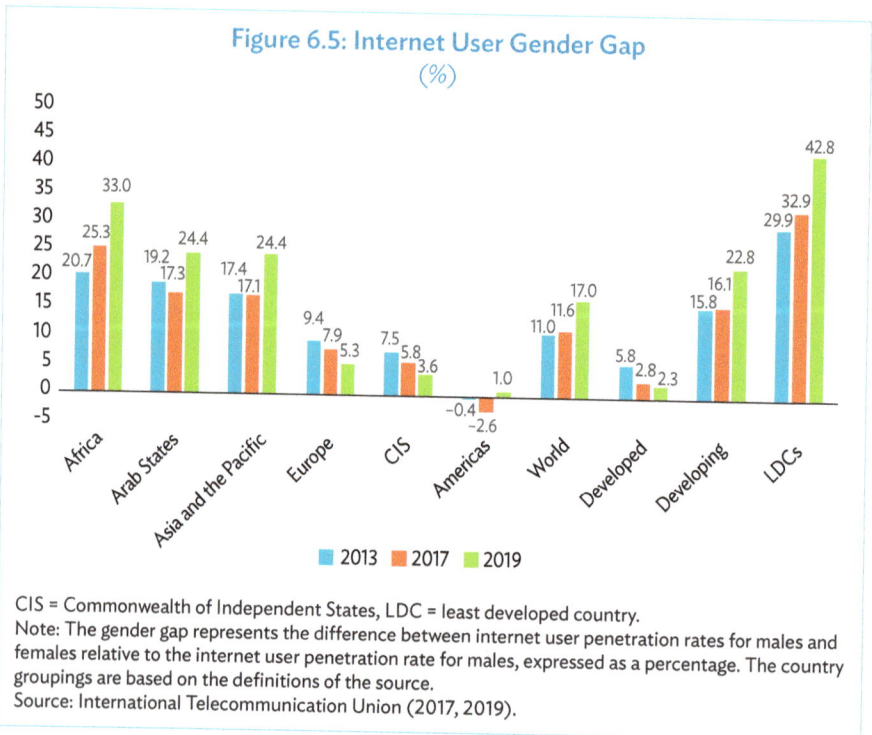

Figure 6.5: Internet User Gender Gap (%)

CIS = Commonwealth of Independent States, LDC = least developed country.
Note: The gender gap represents the difference between internet user penetration rates for males and females relative to the internet user penetration rate for males, expressed as a percentage. The country groupings are based on the definitions of the source.
Source: International Telecommunication Union (2017, 2019).

Data for a number of economies also show that males have better ICT access than females (Figure 6.6). Moreover, data for Sri Lanka show that females have lower computer and digital literacy than males. In Viet Nam, the proportion of males (82.0%) using the internet for personal use is significantly

Figure 6.6: Indicators of ICT Access in Selected Asian Economies by Gender

a. Computer Literacy and Digital Literacy Rates in Sri Lanka by Gender, 2018 (%)

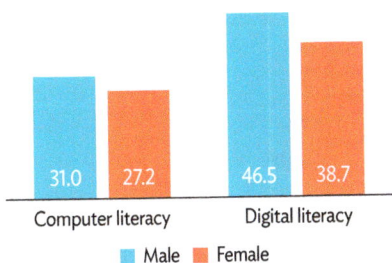

	Male	Female
Computer literacy	31.0	27.2
Digital literacy	46.5	38.7

■ Male ■ Female

b. Internet users in India by Gender, 2019 (%)

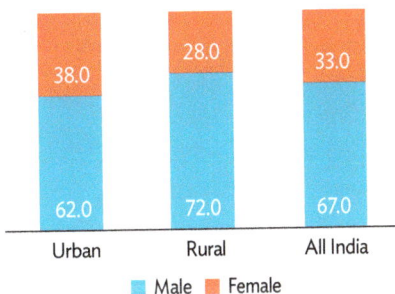

	Male	Female
Urban	62.0	38.0
Rural	72.0	28.0
All India	67.0	33.0

■ Male ■ Female

c. Gender Distribution of Internet Users in the PRC by Gender, 2014–2020 (%)

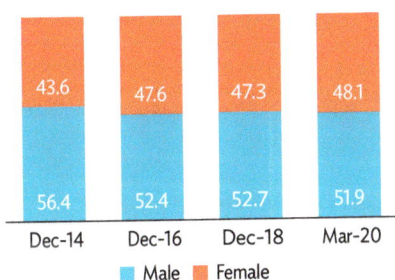

	Male	Female
Dec-14	56.4	43.6
Dec-16	52.4	47.6
Dec-18	52.7	47.3
Mar-20	51.9	48.1

■ Male ■ Female

d. Monthly Internet Penetration Rate in the Philippines, 2006–2019 (%)

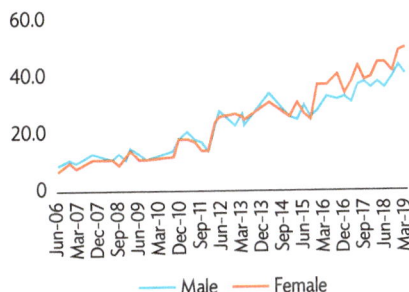

60.0
40.0
20.0
0

Jun-06, Mar-07, Dec-07, Sep-08, Jun-09, Mar-10, Dec-10, Sep-11, Jun-12, Mar-13, Dec-13, Sep-14, Jun-15, Mar-16, Dec-16, Sep-17, Jun-18, Mar-19

— Male — Female

e. Vietnamese Who Use the Internet for Personal Purposes, 2017 (% of population)

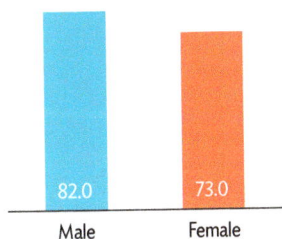

Male	82.0
Female	73.0

f. Methods by which Households in Taipei,China Access the Internet, August 2019 (%)

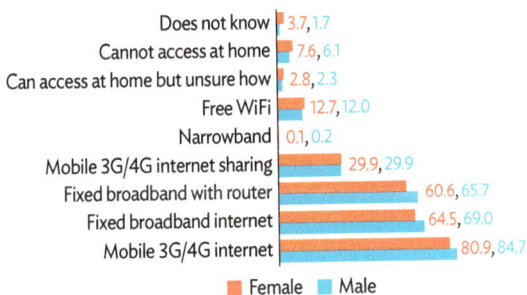

	Female	Male
Does not know	3.7	1.7
Cannot access at home	7.6	6.1
Can access at home but unsure how	2.8	2.3
Free WiFi	12.7	12.0
Narrowband	0.1	0.2
Mobile 3G/4G internet sharing	29.9	29.9
Fixed broadband with router	60.6	65.7
Fixed broadband internet	64.5	69.0
Mobile 3G/4G internet	80.9	84.7

■ Female ■ Male

ICT = information and communication technology, PRC = People's Republic of China.
Note: The data for the PRC; the Philippines; and Taipei,China are obtained from Statista (accessed July 2020). The ultimate data sources are indicated below.
Sources: Ecomobi (2017); Government of the People's Republic of China, China Internet Information Center (2020a); Government of Sri Lanka, Department of Census and Statistics (2018); and Government of Taipei,China, National Development Council (2019).

higher than of females (73.0%). In Taipei,China, access to internet at home via paid services (e.g., mobile 3G or 4G internet, fixed broadband internet, and fixed broadband with router) is lower for females. It is only in the Philippines where the data shows that females have better access to the internet. Junio (2019) finds that there is a gender divide in digital financial services. In Japan, males tend to participate more in online shopping than females (Figure 6.7).

Various reasons for the gender disparity in access to the internet and participation in the digital economy include physical access and socio-cultural characteristics of women, interest, and ability. Sey, Kang, and Junio (2019) explain how culture, interest, and ability affect women's access to the internet and participation in the digital economy. Lack of useful content for women also affects their use.

In a survey done by Gillwald, Galpaya, and Aguero (2019), they find that despite internet services being relatively affordable in Bangladesh and Pakistan, women could not afford to be connected due to their low income and lack of skills. For women online, this lack of skills leaves them vulnerable to privacy and safety threats, while social and cultural norms and attitudes prevent them from maximizing their use of the internet.

However, economy-level data also show breakthroughs in the participation of women in digital technology. In Taipei,China, more women use online banking and mobile payments than men. In the PRC, e-commerce activity is higher for women than men. Females have better access to e-learning than males in the Philippines and in Viet Nam. This is consistent with the findings of the United Nations University (Junio 2019) that there were breakthroughs in access of females to digital technology.

Figure 6.7: Gender Divide in ICT Use by Selected Asian Economies

a. Online Shopping Users in Japan, April–July 2017 (%)

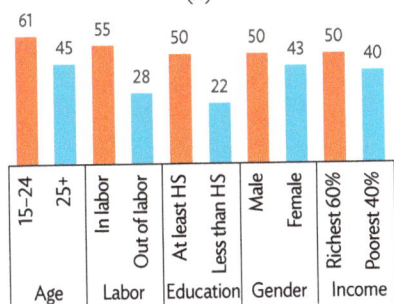

b. Most Well-Known Ride Hailing Apps in the ROK by Gender, March 2019 (%)

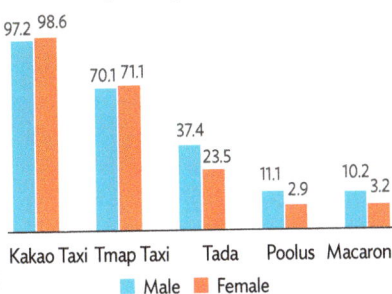

■ Male ■ Female

c. E-commerce Type Preference in the PRC by Gender, 2017Q2 (%)

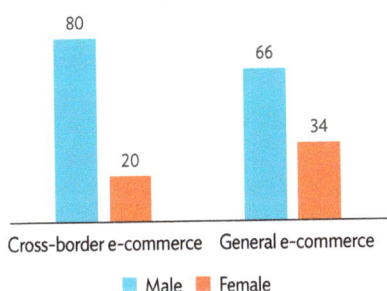

■ Male ■ Female

d. E-learning in the Philippines and Viet Nam by Gender, 2018 (%)

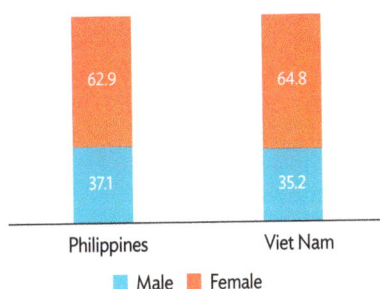

■ Male ■ Female

e. E-money Usage for Shopping Online in Indonesia by Age Group and Gender, 2017 (%)

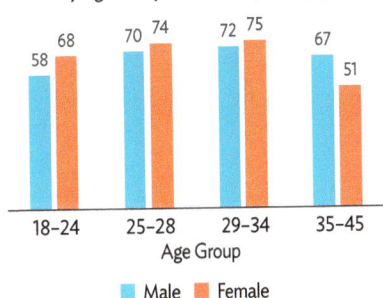

■ Male ■ Female

f. Mobile Payment and Online Banking in Taipei,China by Gender (%)

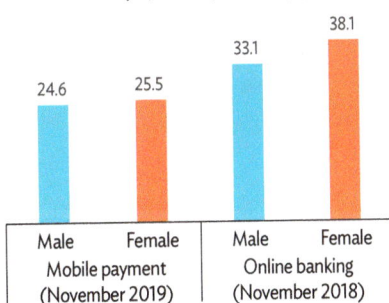

HS = high school, PRC = People's Republic of China, ROK = Republic of Korea.
Note: The data for Indonesia; Japan; (the) PRC; ROK; and Taipei,China are obtained from Statista (accessed July 2020). The ultimate data sources are indicated below.
Sources: Analysys (2017); Cabauatan et al. (2018); CUTS International (2018a); Google and GfK (2018a); Google and GfK (2018b); Opensurvey (2019); and World Bank (2017).

Age Divide

Internet access and participation in digital platforms are more common in the not so young or not so old (Figure 6.8). In the Philippines, while the 18–24 year olds are the most active internet users, the 25–34 year cohort does the most online shopping since this is the income-earning group. In Japan, the younger generations are more active in digital platform activities such as video sharing and uploading, but those that involve monetary transactions attract those already earning incomes.

In Singapore, 96.0% of those who were 15–34 years old in 2018 had individual access to a computer, while only 33.0% of those aged 60 years old and over did (Figure 6.9). In the Republic of Korea, the pattern for mobile internet usage is similar, although the peak is wider at 20–49 years old. The 60–69 cohort has high mobile internet use but significantly lower for the older ages.

The discrepancy in access by age groups is not only in material access but also in skills. In Sri Lanka, for example, computer or digital literacy is highest among 15–24 years old. These are similar to the patterns displayed in the Republic of Korea and Singapore. In the PRC, internet users are mostly 20–39 years old.

One reason the older age group ranks last in usage of technology and participation in the digital economy is that the generation did not grow up with the rapidly evolving digital technology unlike those who are younger (Viens 2019). Another possible reason would be the lack of a need to form personal and social identities over social media, as these would have been well established by the time social media platforms like Facebook launched. Motivational barriers, such as lack of interest and security issues, also explain the limited use of internet for the older generation, as they see no good reason to go online. The older generations are the least confident about protection for a range of security threats (Murnane 2016).

Figure 6.8: Participation in the Digital Economy in Selected Economies by Age Group

a. E-commerce App Users in the PRC by Age Group, February 2018 (%)

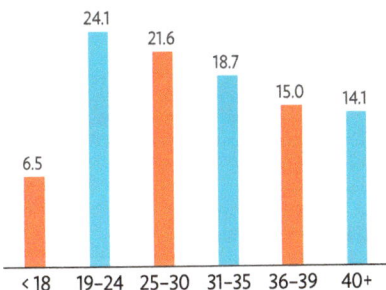

< 18	19–24	25–30	31–35	36–39	40+
6.5	24.1	21.6	18.7	15.0	14.1

b. Use of Internet in Japan by Age Group, 2018 (%)

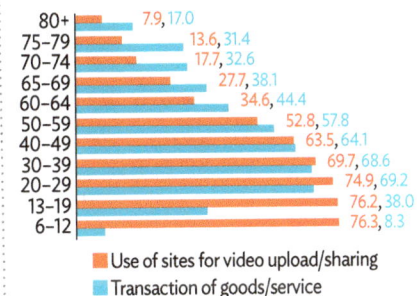

Age group	Use of sites for video upload/sharing	Transaction of goods/service
80+	7.9	17.0
75–79	13.6	31.4
70–74	17.7	32.6
65–69	27.7	38.1
60–64	34.6	44.4
50–59	52.8	57.8
40–49	63.5	64.1
30–39	69.7	68.6
20–29	74.9	69.2
13–19	76.2	38.0
6–12	76.3	8.3

■ Use of sites for video upload/sharing
■ Transaction of goods/service

c. Share of Online Consumers in India, 2016 (%)

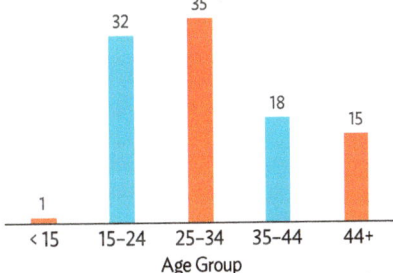

< 15	15–24	25–34	35–44	44+
1	32	35	18	15

Age Group

d. Share of Online Shoppers in Canada by Age Group, April 2019 (%)

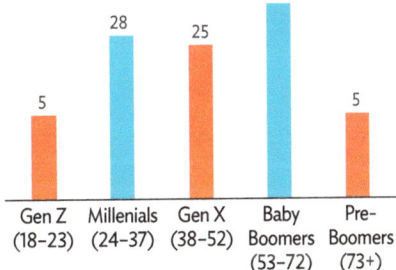

Gen Z (18–23)	Millenials (24–37)	Gen X (38–52)	Baby Boomers (53–72)	Pre-Boomers (73+)
5	28	25	37	5

e. Online Shoppers and Internet Users in the Philippines by Age Group (%)

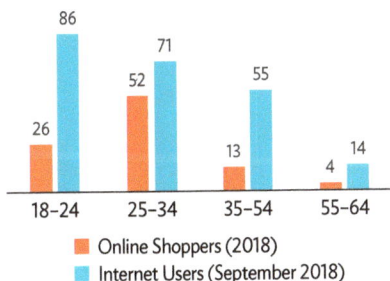

Age group	Online Shoppers (2018)	Internet Users (September 2018)
18–24	26	86
25–34	52	71
35–54	13	55
55–64	4	14

■ Online Shoppers (2018)
■ Internet Users (September 2018)

f. Mobile Payment Usage in Taipei,China by Age Group, September–November 2019 (%)

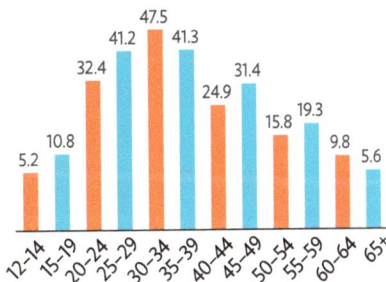

12–14	15–19	20–24	25–29	30–34	35–39	40–44	45–49	50–54	55–59	60–64	65+
5.2	10.8	32.4	41.2	47.5	41.3	24.9	31.4	15.8	19.3	9.8	5.6

PRC = People's Republic of China.
Notes: The data for Canada; the PRC; the Philippines; and Taipei,China are obtained from Statista (accessed July 2020). The ultimate data sources are indicated below.
Sources: Canada Post (2020); Government of Japan, Ministry of Internal Affairs and Communications (2020); iResearch (2018); Picodi and Esquiremag.ph (2019); Quartz and Flipkart (2016); and Social Weather Stations (2018).

Figure 6.9: Access to the Internet in Selected Economies by Age Group

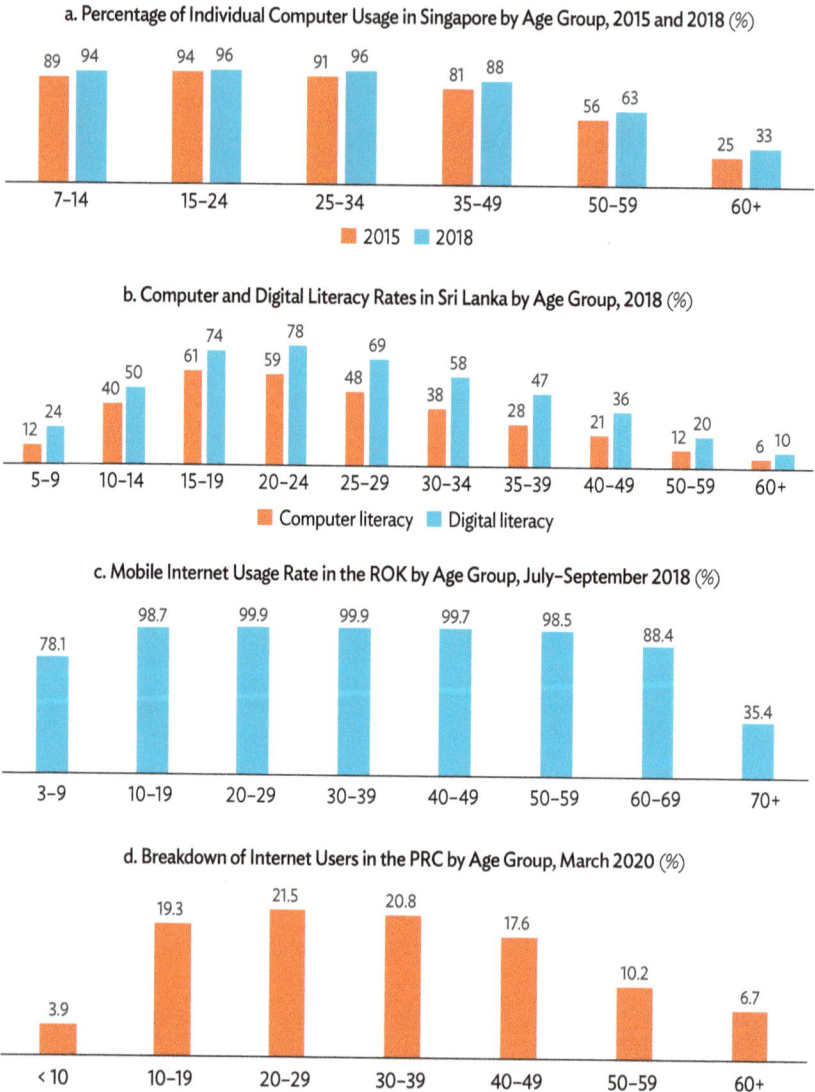

a. Percentage of Individual Computer Usage in Singapore by Age Group, 2015 and 2018 (%)

b. Computer and Digital Literacy Rates in Sri Lanka by Age Group, 2018 (%)

c. Mobile Internet Usage Rate in the ROK by Age Group, July–September 2018 (%)

d. Breakdown of Internet Users in the PRC by Age Group, March 2020 (%)

PRC = People's Republic of China, ROK = Republic of Korea.
Note: The data for the PRC and ROK are obtained from Statista (accessed July 2020). The ultimate sources are indicated below.
Sources: Government of the Republic of Korea, Ministry of Science and ICT, Korea Internet and Security Agency and Market Metrix (2019); Government of the People's Republic of China, China Internet Information Center. (2020b); Government of Sri Lanka, Department of Census and Statistics (2018), and Government of Singapore, Infocomm Media Development Authority (2019a).

Material Access

The material access divide is manifested in the gap in physical access to computers, network, and platforms among developed, developing, and least developed countries. The ratio of internet users to total population illustrates the differences in access among countries especially since the internet can be accessed via a number of devices (e.g., computer, mobile phone, personal digital assistant, video game consoles, or digital television). Figure 6.10a shows that more than 85.0% of the population in developed countries in 2019 used the internet, while it is 53.6% in developing countries and just 16.1% in least developed countries.

Figure 6.10: Selected Material Access Indicators by Income Groups

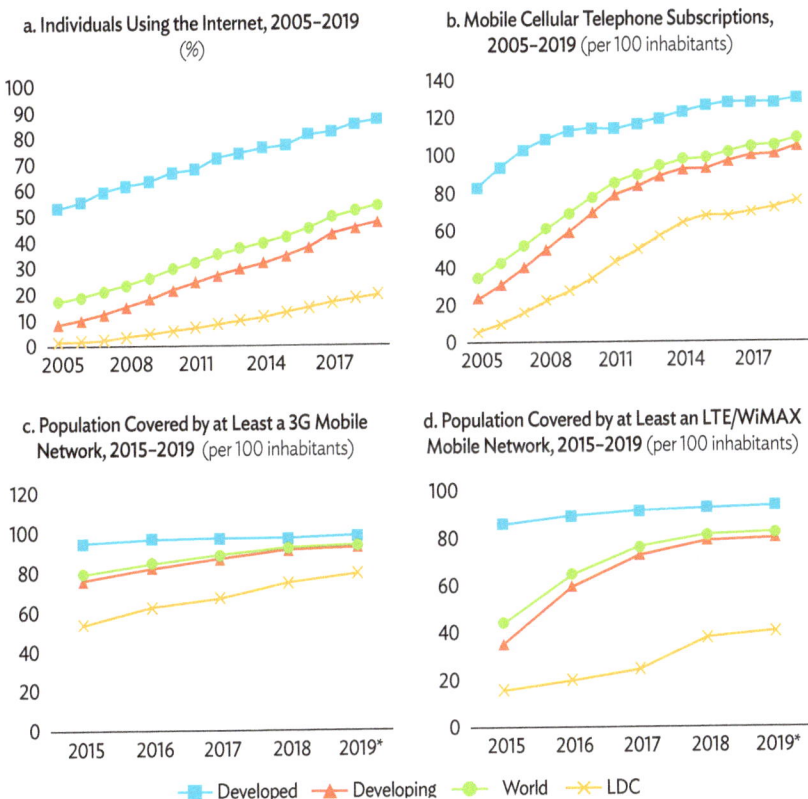

a. Individuals Using the Internet, 2005–2019 (%)

b. Mobile Cellular Telephone Subscriptions, 2005–2019 (per 100 inhabitants)

c. Population Covered by at Least a 3G Mobile Network, 2015–2019 (per 100 inhabitants)

d. Population Covered by at Least an LTE/WiMAX Mobile Network, 2015–2019 (per 100 inhabitants)

Developed — Developing — World — LDC

LDC = least developed countries, LTE = Long Term Evolution, WiMAX = Worldwide Interoperability for Microwave Access.
Note: 2019 data are estimates. The country groupings are based on the definitions of the source.
Source: Authors, based on International Telecommunication Union Indicators Database (accessed July 2020).

The Asia and Pacific region has the second-lowest proportion of people having used the internet in the past 3 months in 2019, while Europe, Americas, and the Commonwealth of Independent States (CIS) countries have the highest proportion in the same time period (Figure 6.11).[6]

Figure 6.11: Selected Material Access Indicators by Region

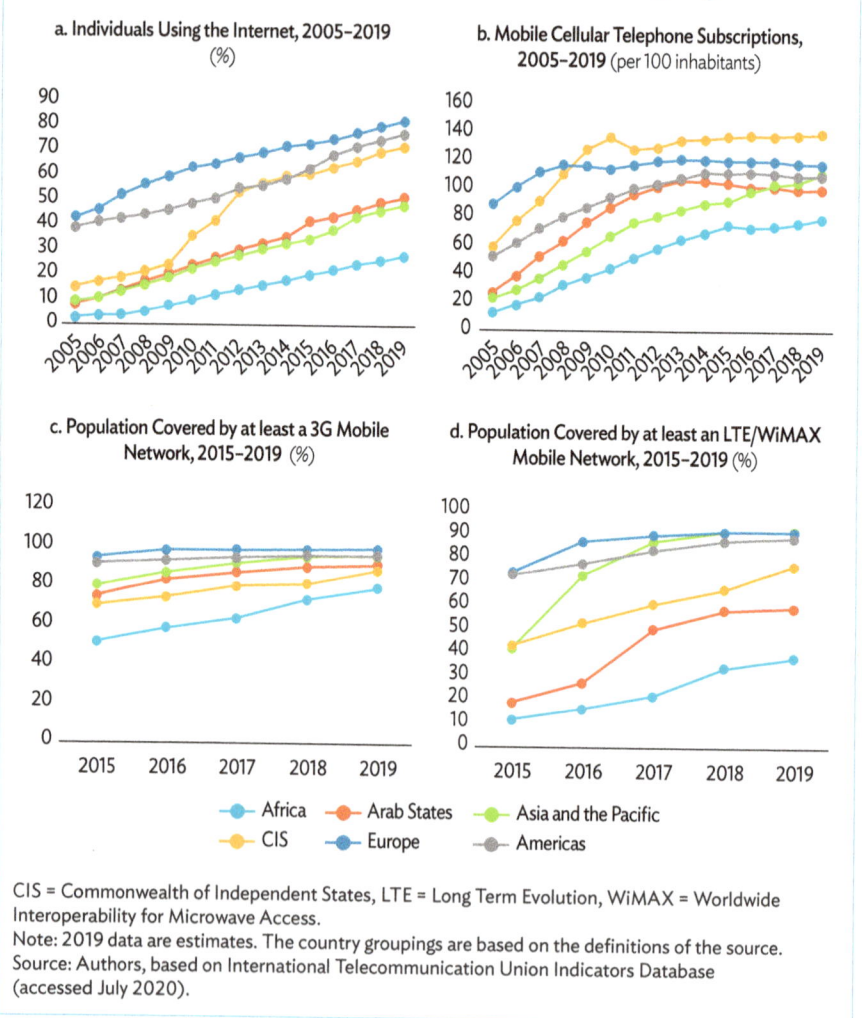

a. Individuals Using the Internet, 2005–2019 (%)

b. Mobile Cellular Telephone Subscriptions, 2005–2019 (per 100 inhabitants)

c. Population Covered by at least a 3G Mobile Network, 2015–2019 (%)

d. Population Covered by at least an LTE/WiMAX Mobile Network, 2015–2019 (%)

Africa — Arab States — Asia and the Pacific — CIS — Europe — Americas

CIS = Commonwealth of Independent States, LTE = Long Term Evolution, WiMAX = Worldwide Interoperability for Microwave Access.
Note: 2019 data are estimates. The country groupings are based on the definitions of the source.
Source: Authors, based on International Telecommunication Union Indicators Database (accessed July 2020).

---

[6] The CIS was founded in 1991 after the dissolution of the Union of Soviet Socialist Republics. The CIS refers to Armenia, Azerbaijan, Belarus, Georgia, Kazakhstan, the Kyrgyz Republic, Moldova, the Russian Federation, Tajikistan, Turkmenistan, Ukraine, and Uzbekistan.

The number of mobile cellular telephone subscriptions in the population is an indication of the potential access to the internet. Figure 6.10 shows that developed countries have significantly outpaced developing countries and least developed countries in mobile cellular telephone subscriptions. By region, the CIS has the highest mobile phone subscriptions since 2009, overtaking Europe (Figure 6.11). Asia and the Pacific subscriptions have risen steadily since 2005, closing the gap with Europe and the Americas. This is consistent with the trend in Asia's performance on the digital economy (Google, Temasek, and Bain 2019).

Mobile coverage of at least a 3G network indicates the availability of internet or mobile connection that can be used to participate in the digital technology, and Figure 6.10c shows that developed countries still outpace both developing countries and least developed countries in providing this service. The divide is more prominent for Long Term Evolution (LTE) and Worldwide Interoperability for Microwave Access (WiMAX) as shown in Figure 6.10d. The availability of a more advanced mobile network is necessary for new innovations in the digital economy (Docebo 2018; GSMA 2020), and with developing countries and least developed countries falling behind, this will surely lead to a gap in the usage of new applications. The Asia and Pacific region seems to be at par with the front-runner in this field as it has seen significant increases of this service from 2015, thus, overtaking the Americas (Figure 6.11d).

Data from GSMA's (2020) Consumer Insights Survey 2019[7] shows that while developing Asia has a high usage rate of smartphones for communication, it is lagging behind in terms of the use of smartphones for information, entertainment, and financial/digital commerce (Table 6.1).

North America, Western Europe, and Asia have the largest share of revenue in e-learning (Figure 6.12). Further, North American vendors are already exploring more advanced e-learning technologies such as artificial intelligence, virtual assistants, augmented reality, and virtual reality in e-learning solutions. So while other countries are still exploring currently available technologies in e-learning, such as the development of massive open online courses, more advanced regions are now pushing boundaries, expanding the divide.

---

[7] This survey covers seven country groupings: developed Asia; developing Asia; Europe and the Commonwealth of Independent States; Latin America; Middle East and North Africa; North America; and sub-Saharan Africa.

Table 6.1: Smartphone Users Engaging in Activity At Least Once Per Week, 2019
(%)

Region	Communication	Information	Entertainment	Financial/Digital Commerce
Developed Asia	58	34	31	28
Developing Asia	68	18	25	12
Europe and CIS	63	36	30	26
Latin America	79	42	40	22
MENA	78	49	43	32
North America	60	35	38	28
Sub-Saharan Africa	67	19	22	17

CIS = Commonwealth of Independent States, MENA = Middle East and North America.
Note: The country groupings are based on the definitions of the source.
Source: GSM Association (2020).

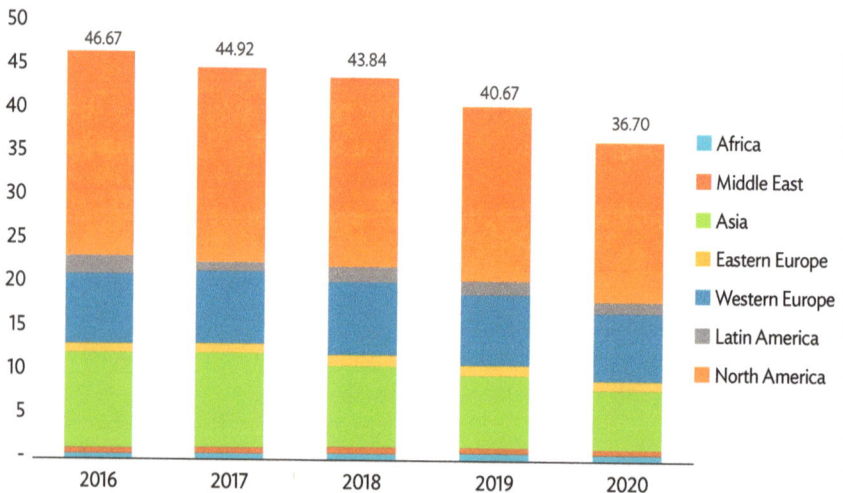

Figure 6.12: Worldwide Revenue Forecasts for Self-Paced Global E-learning Market Size by Region, 2016–2020, ($ billion)

Note: The country groupings are based on the definitions of the source.
Source: Docebo (2018).

According to UNCTAD's (2019) Digital Economy Report, the digital divide exists within countries based on income, education, gender, ethnicity, and geographical location, regardless of the country's level of development. Even developed countries see some material access divide among its population. For instance, computer ownership is 97.0% for those living in private housing and around 86.0% for those in public housing in Singapore (Figure 6.13).

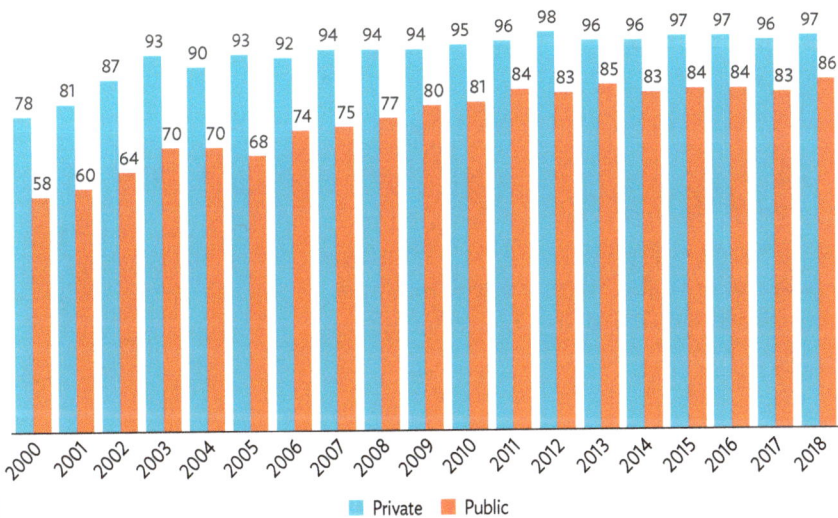

Figure 6.13: Computer Ownership in Singapore by Housing Type, 2000–2018 (% of population)

Source: Government of Singapore, Infocomm Media Development Authority (2019b).

In Sri Lanka, computer and digital literacies are significantly higher for those living in urban areas (Figure 6.14). In 2018, 40.4% of those living in urban areas are considered computer literate, only 27.5% in rural areas, and just 10.8% among those living in estate areas. [8]

---

[8] In Sri Lanka, estate areas refer to "all plantations which are 20 acres or more in extent and with 10 or more resident laborers." These areas are characterized by low living standards and widespread poverty. Also, the estate sector has traditionally been behind both the urban and rural sectors. For a background on Sri Lanka's poverty and welfare, see Newhouse, Suarez-Becerra, and Doan (2016).

Figure 6.14: Computer and Digital Literacy in Sri Lanka by Area, 2016–2018
(% of population)

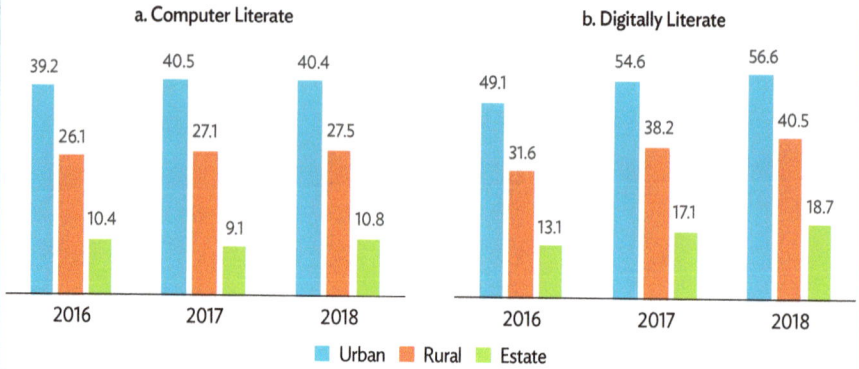

a. Computer Literate

Year	Urban	Rural	Estate
2016	39.2	26.1	10.4
2017	40.5	27.1	9.1
2018	40.4	27.5	10.8

b. Digitally Literate

Year	Urban	Rural	Estate
2016	49.1	31.6	13.1
2017	54.6	38.2	17.1
2018	56.6	40.5	18.7

■ Urban ■ Rural ■ Estate

Source: Government of Sri Lanka, Department of Census and Statistics (2018).

High-income countries have more mobile health programs than low-income countries (Figure 6.15). For instance, from among all countries that accessed or provided health services, high-income countries had a 37.0% share, more than double that of low-income countries.

Figure 6.15: Distribution of Mobile Health Programs by Income Group
(% share of total)

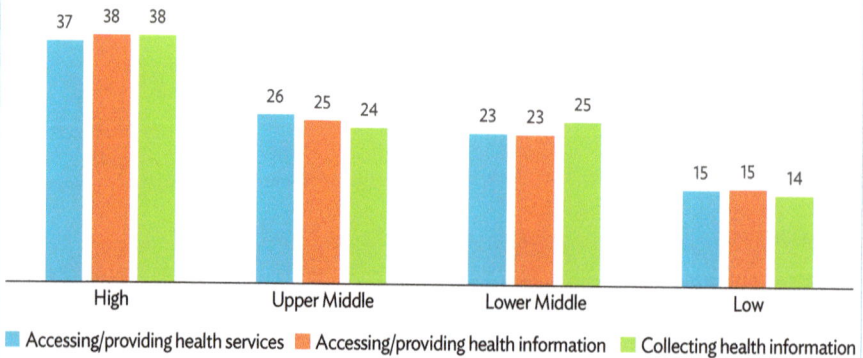

Income Group	Accessing/providing health services	Accessing/providing health information	Collecting health information
High	37	38	38
Upper Middle	26	25	24
Lower Middle	23	23	25
Low	15	15	14

■ Accessing/providing health services ■ Accessing/providing health information ■ Collecting health information

Note: Accessing/providing health services include health call centers, toll-free emergency calls; treatment adherence; appointment reminders; mobile telehealth; and emergencies, while accessing/providing health information includes community mobilization; access to information, resources, databases, and tools; decision support systems; electronic patient information/records; and mLearning. Meanwhile, collecting health information refers to health surveys, surveillance, and patient monitoring. The country groupings are based on the World Health Organization (WHO) definitions (2016).
Source: Authors, based on WHO (2016).

Skills Access

Countries with higher income tend to have more people with digital skills (Table 6.2). As these countries gain more from the digital and platform economy, the low-income and lower middle-income countries will fall further behind in digital access and development.

Table 6.2: Digital Skills by Region and Income Group, 2017 and 2019
(score)

Region and Income Group	2017	2019
East Asia and the Pacific	4.7	4.6
High income	5.1	5.0
Upper middle income	4.8	4.8
Lower middle income	4.1	4.1
Europe and Central Asia	4.7	4.6
High income	4.9	4.9
Upper middle income	4.3	4.3
Lower middle income	4.4	4.3
Low income	no data	4.4
South Asia	3.8	4.0
Upper middle income	3.9	4.2
Lower middle income	3.9	4.0
Low income	3.7	3.7

Note: Extent to which population possesses sufficient digital skills (e.g., computer skills, basic coding, and digital reading). 1 = not all; 7 = to a great extent. Data are based on the World Economic Forum's Global Competitiveness Index 4.0: Digital Skills Among Population indicator. A change in methodology occurred in 2018, so 2017 data have been backcast. The technical note on "backcasting" in the 2017 edition of the GCI 4.0 describes the use of "the GCI 4.0 methodology, the weighted averages of the 2016 and 2017 editions of the Executive Opinion Survey (in most cases) and the values for all the other indicators from one period earlier than the period used in the 2018 edition of the GCI 4.0" (e.g., for the latter, if an indicator for 2018 GCI 4.0 uses 2016 data, the backcast 2017 edition uses 2015 data). Further description can be found here: https://reports.weforum.org/global-competitiveness-report-2018/appendix-c-the-global-competitiveness-index-4-0-methodology-and-technical-notes/. The country groupings are based on the definitions of the data source.
Sources: Authors, based on World Bank TCdata360 (accessed May 2020) and Schwab (2017, 2019).

Figure 6.16 shows a positive correlation between having digital technological skill and use of advanced data analytics and data analysis. There is also a positive correlation between digital and technological skills availability and digital readiness of companies. Without digital and technological skills, people would tend to use ICT for less productive purposes.

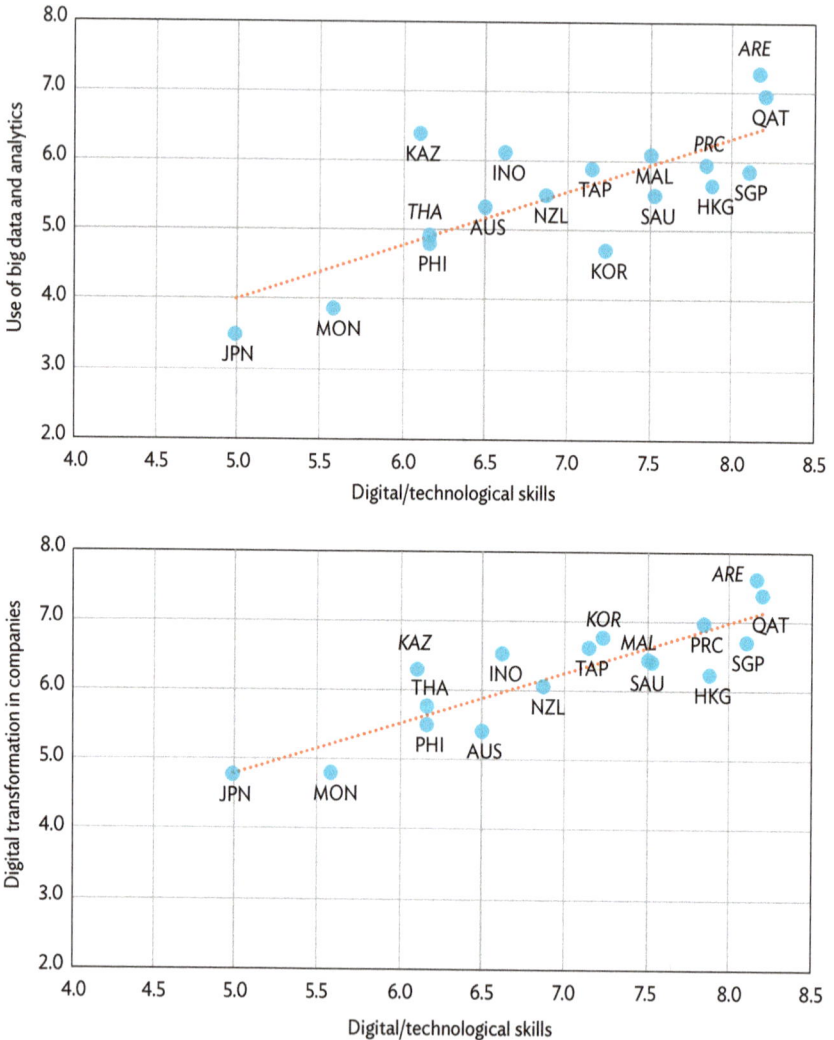

Figure 6.16: Digital and Technological Skill and Use of Advanced Technologies in Selected Asian Economies, 2019

AUS = Australia; ARE = United Arab Emirates; HKG = Hong Kong, China; INO = Indonesia; JPN = Japan; KAZ = Kazakhstan; KOR = Republic of Korea; MAL = Malaysia; MON= Mongolia; NZL = New Zealand; PHI = Philippines; PRC = People's Republic of China; QAT = Qatar; SAU = Saudi Arabia; SIN = Singapore; TAP = Taipei,China; THA = Thailand.

Notes: Use of big data analytics is based on the assessment of the respondents to the Executive Opinion Survey on whether companies are very good at using big data and analytics to support decision-making. They score from 1 (lowest) to 10 (highest). Digital transformation in companies is based on whether digital transformation in companies is generally well implemented. Respondents score 1 (lowest) to 10 (highest). Economy labels are placed below their data point but some economy labels (italicized) are placed above their data point to improve chart readability.

Source: Authors, based on IMD World Competitiveness Online (accessed July 2020)

Figure 6.17 shows that the better-skilled have better digital access. Usually, in the Philippines, college undergraduates and college graduates would register to the Technical Education and Skills Development Authority (TESDA) Online Program.[9] It is also those who have higher education who use mobile banking in the PRC.

Figure 6.17: Selected Cases and Educational Attainment (%)

a. Distribution of Mobile Banking Users in the PRC by Level of Education (2015)

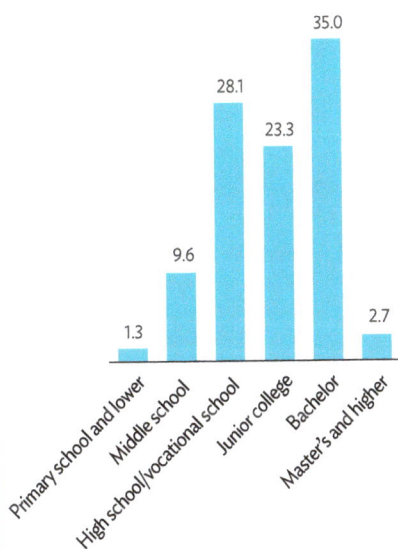

Level of Education	%
Primary school and lower	1.3
Middle school	9.6
High school/vocational school	28.1
Junior college	23.3
Bachelor	35.0
Master's and higher	2.7

b. Registered to TOP in the Philippines by Level of Education (January–February 2018)

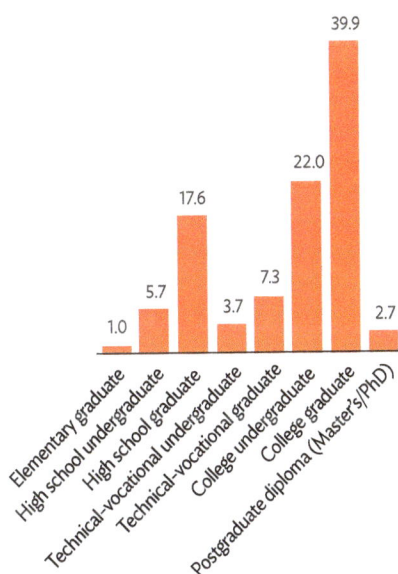

Level of Education	%
Elementary graduate	1.0
High school undergraduate	5.7
High school graduate	17.6
Technical-vocational undergraduate	3.7
Technical-vocational graduate	7.3
College undergraduate	22.0
College graduate	39.9
Postgraduate diploma (Master's/PhD)	2.7

PRC = People's Republic of China, TOP = TESDA Online Program.
Note: The data for the PRC are obtained from Statista (accessed July 2020). The ultimate source is indicated below.
Sources: Analysis (2016) and Cabauatan et al. (2018).

Analysis of unpublished data from the Philippines' 2019 National ICT Household Survey results shows that people who have access to computers make use of the technology mostly for basic communication and for entertainment

---

9 In the Philippines, TESDA is a government agency that provides technical and vocational education and training. One of their programs to expand reach is the TESDA Online Program. For more on the TESDA Online Program, see: https://www.e-tesda.gov.ph/.

and gaming. A smaller number use it to send e-mails, encode data, use word processing software, and transfer files between a computer and other devices, and even for distance/online/computer-aided learning. The more advanced tasks—such as running a software program, data management and analysis, using modeling, simulation, and rendering software—are performed by the least number of computer users. Those with higher education tend to use the internet for more advanced tasks, such as using the internet for learning (e.g., online courses, academic research, e-books, and dictionaries); production of creative or user-generated content (e.g., managing a personal homepage, blogging, and vlogging); and online transactions (e.g., online banking, online booking/reservation, and online shopping).

Digital platforms also face (or cause) their own usage divide.

As platforms continue to be embraced, new manifestations of divides stemming from the use of the platform may be observed. As early as 2011, van Deursen, van Dijk, and Peters (2011) foresaw the appearance of a usage gap between those who systematically use and benefit from advanced digital technology and the more difficult applications for work and school, and those using basic digital technologies for simple tasks and mostly for entertainment.

Platforms may disproportionately benefit those who are already better off.

Accommodation platforms

Airbnb is one of the successful start-ups that benefited from the sharing economy. Airbnb defines itself as "a social website that connects people who have space to spare with those who are looking for a place to stay" (Quattrone et al. 2016). Since the company's establishment in 2008, it has grown to more than 1.5 million properties and a global presence in over 190 countries.

Using data from Inside Airbnb,[10] Tom Slee,[11] and unofficial maps available online at the Database of Global Administrative Areas (GADM),[12] Quimba, Rosellon, and Calizo (2020) observed Airbnb postings in four areas: Hong Kong, China; Seoul, Republic of Korea; Singapore; and Sri Lanka.

---

[10] Inside Airbnb is a website maintaining open data of public Airbnb listings across 25 countries. For more on Inside Airbnb, see http://insideairbnb.com/.
[11] Tom Slee has collected Airbnb listings from cities around the world. He provides open access data through his blog: https://tomslee.net/category/airbnb-data.
[12] GADM is a project hosted by the Center for Spatial Sciences at the University of California, Davis that provides shape files of administrative areas in all countries at all levels of subdivision.

The maps show that there is a concentration of Airbnb postings in the central districts and busy areas. Areas in the periphery, while having some Airbnb postings, do not enjoy the scale that is observed in the central districts.

Airbnb listings proliferating in areas with high levels of commercialization and near areas of interest were also observed in European countries, such as Bulgaria (Roelofsen 2018), Switzerland (Larpin et al. 2019), and Spain (Adamiak et al. 2019). Furthermore, studies have shown that the patterns of participation in Airbnb (proxied by the distribution of Airbnb listings) are closely related to the distribution of tourism demand and accommodation capacity (Adamiak et al. 2019; Domenech et al. 2019; Strommen-Bakhtiar and Vinogradov 2019). The use of the platform may exacerbate the highly unequal distribution of income and development between rural and urban areas.

Case of crowdwork/gig economy[13]

Crowdworkers are well educated, as shown by data in 2017. Close to one-fourth of the workers have a technical certificate or have some university education, 37.0% have a bachelor's degree, while 20.0% have a postgraduate degree or higher education. Those who have only a high school diploma make up barely 18.0% of crowdworkers (Figure 6.18).

In addition, "Upwork" jobs remain limited by freelancers' skills and capabilities. For instance, data from Upwork shows that most of the jobs available to freelancers require advanced knowledge in computer programming. A quick scan of the top 30 trending jobs posted in the past 12 hours[14] requires technical skills that can be divided into three major groups: (i) creative (photo editing, creative writing, copywriting, animation, landscaping, graphic design); (ii) technical (technical writing, HTML or website development, programming (Python), data extraction, and language translation); and (iii) administrative support, which had only two job posts (6.7%).

Earning from platforms is affected by ownership of capital.

---

[13] The gig economy is being referred to jobs or "gigs" that are short term or intermittent and temporary, wherein work can be transacted online using digital platforms (web-based or location-based applications) and delivered online or offline (bound to a specific location). Crowdwork refers to work where *"tasks are assigned to a specific individual or given to an undefined group of people online (crowd)"* and are transacted and delivered online (Bayudan-Dacuycuy et al. 2020, 4). Examples of crowdsourcing platforms are Amazon Mechanical Turk (AMT), Clickworker, CrowdFlower, Microworkers, Prolific, Upwork.

[14] Top 30 trending jobs in Upwork as of 19 May 2020, 1:48 PM (Philippine Standard Time). Upwork's freelance jobs by category can be accessed here: https://www.upwork.com/freelance-jobs/.

Figure 6.18: Educational Level of Crowdworkers by Platform (%)

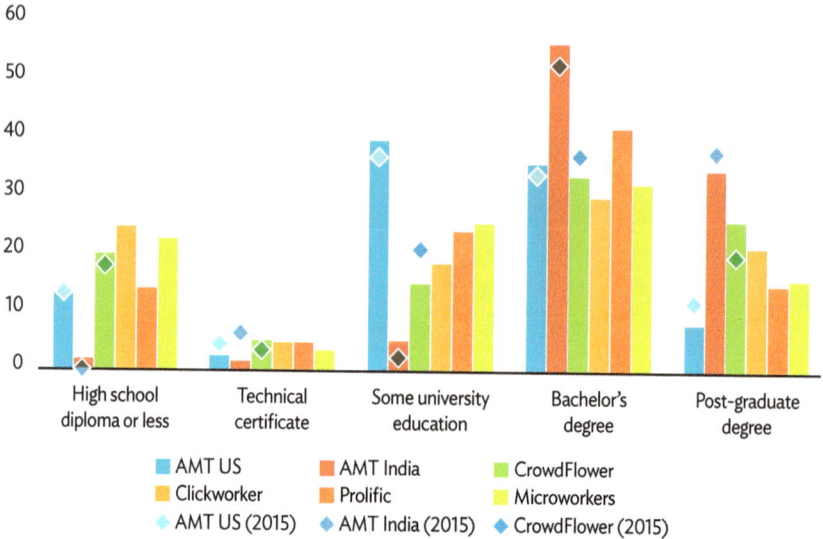

Note: The International Labour Organization conducted two surveys of "crowdworkers": one in 2015 (diamonds) and another in 2017 (bars). The 2015 survey's sample consisted of workers who had completed at least 500 tasks, and had achieved a 95.0% or greater task acceptance rate from the platform Amazon Mechanical Turk (AMT). Apart from AMT, the 2015 survey also included quality workers from CrowdFlower. In 2017, the survey's sample was expanded to include other quality workers from other crowdsourcing platforms, such as Clickworker, Microworkers, and Prolific.
Source: Berg et al. (2018).

The study by Farrel and Greig (2016) shows that those who have assets which can be leased earn more from digital platforms (Figure 6.19) than those who participate only in labor platforms.

There are indirect users of digital platforms.

Certain segments of the population make use of platforms through proxies. Llanto, Rosellon, and Ortiz (2018) analyze the case of Konek2Kard[15] in the Philippines and find that clients experienced an easier, faster, and more convenient service, which includes the ability to transact in real time throughout the day—an important feature considering that these clients are either working or busy with household chores—with the use of digital platforms. Proxy users, such as older clients who let their grandchildren or

---

[15] "Konek2Kard" or "k2c" is a mobile banking application introduced by CARD Bank, a microfinance-oriented rural bank in the Philippines (Llanto, Rosellon, and Ortiz 2018).

Figure 6.19: Earnings in Months with and without Platform Earnings in the United States ($)

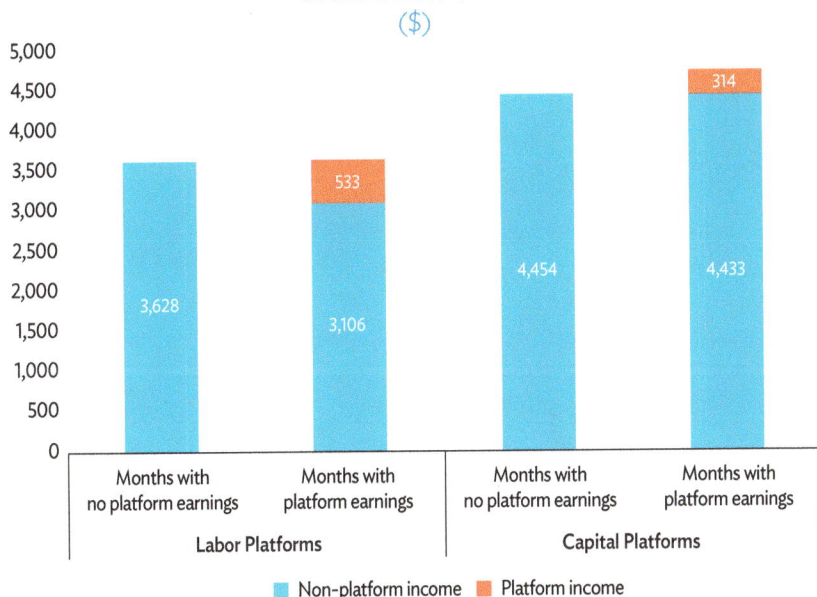

Source: Farrel and Greig (2016).

younger kin perform their online activities, were also observed implying a skills gap between using a mobile phone and doing transactions on digital platforms.

Trusting and comfortably using ICT does not translate to trusting digital platforms.

Many studies have raised a number of challenges to achieving effective e-learning, which are strongly related to digital divide.[16] The most obvious barrier is lack of material access. These same studies have raised the importance of having access to stable and reliable internet in order for e-learning to be successful. But as demonstrated by van Dijk's (2006) model, the platform technology will face its own set of barriers to access. For instance, the motivation and perception of teachers and students of the benefits of digital platforms in learning have to be considered. In Viet Nam, teachers and students doubt the effectiveness of internet learning, remarking that

---

[16] See Kovachev et al. 2011; Rogers 2011; Handal, MacNish, and Petocz 2013; Sarrab, Al-Shihi, and Rehman 2013; Kim, Lee, and Kim 2014; Rius, Masip, and Clariso 2014; Cabauatan et al. 2018; CUTS International 2018a.

e-learning is inferior to face-to-face learning (MacCallum and Jeffrey 2009; CUTS International 2018a). Others cite privacy concerns (Cummings, Merrill, and Borrelli 2010; Binsaleh and Binsaleh 2013; Popescu and Ghita 2013) and distractions (Handal, MacNish, and Petocz 2013; Morales 2013) as factors affecting motivation to use e-learning platforms. Segments of the population that face this motivational divide would not even consider using e-learning.

6.3. Conclusions and Policy Recommendations

This chapter presents the manifestations of digital divides in Asia in terms of ICT indicators and factors related to access, such as culture, trust, and skills. These are demonstrated as differences in access of certain groups, by geographic location, age, gender, and adequate skills. The more educated and wealthier are seen to benefit more from the digital economy as they are able to participate more in online shopping, produce more content online, and use e-learning and e-health platforms.

As noted by van Dijk's (2006) model, the digital platforms also create their own divides. The case of accommodation platforms shows that the more commercialized, well-off, and touristy areas will benefit more from digital accommodation platforms thus further intensifying the income and development inequality between these areas and the periphery. Some platforms also face trust and security issues while other platforms will tend to increase the income inequality among individuals as documented by the study of JP Morgan (Farrell and Greig 2016) on ownership of assets for use in platforms.

Given the findings of this chapter, the following are recommendations for policy reforms as also laid out in ADB (2021) and Quimba, Rosellon, and Calizo (2020):

   i. Define and measure various indicators in the four areas of access and participation in digital platforms. There were scarce data from Oceania and other island countries in the Pacific. It is crucial to have complete data on standard indicators to fully understand the complete picture of digital divides in Asia.

   ii. Address various barriers simultaneously to maximize and distribute the gains from digital platforms. Ensuring material access and the requisite infrastructure to support internet access are necessary conditions for participation in digital platforms, but these are not sufficient. There is also a need to address cultural barriers and skills inadequacy.

iii. Support projects that would provide at least material access to ICT in least developed countries. Data show that least developed countries fall behind other economies in ICT access and participation in the platform economy. With ICT infrastructure remaining inadequate, it would be difficult for least developed countries to catch up with the developed economies. Governments need to recognize the impact of disparities in digital access and participation in the platform economy on income inequality.

iv. Work with governments to develop plans for utilizing digitization, to facilitate innovation, and to support start-ups in developing platforms which are based on mobile applications. Use of mobile phone and digital technology must be pushed beyond communication and entertainment and into higher-value products and services like e-learning, e-health, creatives, and artificial intelligence protocols.

v. Cooperation among countries must be facilitated to ensure, over time, the convergence of ICT access and participation in the platform economy, likewise to safeguard data privacy and maintain trust in the digital economy.

vi. Support greater digital skills development for the youth. The data from Upwork reveals that most of the tasks involved are computer-related and require familiarity with the internet. There is a need to reskill and retool adults to allow and expand their participation in the digital economy. There is also a need to educate people on the functions of and benefits from using digital technology.

References

Adamiak, C., B. Szyda, A. Dubownik, and D. Garcia-Alvarez. 2019. Airbnb Offer in Spain: Spatial Analysis of the Pattern and Determinants of its Distribution. *International Journal of Geo-Information*. 8 (3). p. 155.

Analysis. 2016. Distribution of Mobile Banking Users in China in 2015, by level of education. In *Statista*. https://www.statista.com/statistics/646164/china-mobile-banking-users-by-level-of-education/ (accesssed July 2020).

————. 2017. Preferred E-commerce Types in China as of 2nd quarter 2017, by gender. In *Statista*. https://www.statista.com/statistics/856357/china-preferred-e-commerce-types-by-gender/ (accesssed July 2020).

Asian Development Bank (ADB). 2021. *Asian Economic Integration Report 2021: Making Digital Platforms Work for Asia and the Pacific*. Manila.

Asia-Pacific Economic Cooperation (APEC). 2017. APEC Internet and Digital Economy Roadmap. Considerations from Senior Officials' Meeting Da Nang, Viet Nam. 6–7 November. http://mddb.apec.org/Documents/2017/SOM/CSOM/17_csom_006.pdf.

Bayudan-Dacuycuy, C., A. Orbeta Jr., R. Serafica, and L. K. Baje. 2020. Online Work in the Philippines: Some Lessons in the Asian Context. *PIDS Discussion Paper Series*. 2020–29. https://www.pids.gov.ph/publications/7154.

Berg, J., M. Furrer, E. Harmon, U. Rani, and M. Silberman. 2018. *Digital Labour Platforms and the Future of Work: Towards Decent Work in the Online World*. International Labour Organization: Geneva. https://www.ilo.org/wcmsp5/groups/public/---dgreports/---dcomm/---publ/documents/publication/wcms_645337.pdf.

Binsaleh, S. and M. Binsaleh. 2013. Mobile Learning: What Guidelines Should We Produce in the Context of Mobile Learning Implementation in the Conflict Area of the Four Southernmost Provinces of Thailand. *Asian Social Science*. 9 (13). pp. 270–281. https://www.ccsenet.org/journal/index.php/ass/article/view/30824.

Bukht, R. and R. Heeks. 2017. Defining, Conceptualising and Measuring the Digital Economy. *Development Informatics Working Paper.* 68. https://diodeweb.files.wordpress.com/2017/08/diwkppr68-diode.pdf.

Cabauatan, M., S., Jr. Calizo, F. Quimba, and L. Pacio. 2018. E-Education in the Philippines: The Case of Technical Education and Skills Development Authority Online Program. *PIDS Discussion Paper Series.* 2018–08. https://www.pids.gov.ph/publications/6102.

Canada Post. 2020. Distribution of Online Shoppers in Canada as of April 2019, by age group. 2020 Canadian E-commerce Benchmark Report. In *Statista.* https://www.statista.com/statistics/1044434/canada-online-shoppers-by-age-group/ (accesssed July 2020).

Consumer Unity & Trust Society (CUTS) International. 2018a. *Going Digital: From Innovation to Inclusive Growth in Vietnam.* https://cuts-ccier.org/pdf/going-digital-from-innovation-to-inclusive-growth-in-vietnam.pdf.

Cummings, J., A. Merrill, and S. Borrelli. 2010. The Use of Handheld Mobile Devices: Their Impact and Implications for Library Services. *Library Hi Tech.* 28 (1). pp. 22–40. https://www.emerald.com/insight/content/doi/10.1108/07378831011026670/full/html.

Docebo. 2018. E-Learning Trends 2019. https://kometa.edu.pl/uploads/publication/634/550a_A_Docebo-E-Learning-Trends-2019.pdf?v2.8.

Domenech, A., B. Larpin, R. Schegg, and M. Scaglione. 2019. Disentangling the Geographic Logic of Airbnb in Switzerland. *Erdkunde.* 73 (4). pp. 245–258. https://www.erdkunde.uni-bonn.de/archive/2019/disentangling-the-geographical-logic-of-airbnb-in-switzerland.

Ecomobi. 2017. Vietnam Digital Landscape 2017. https://www.vietnambusiness.tv/market-research/marketing-media/628/vietnam-digital-landscape-2017.

Eng, T. 1978. Residential choice in public and private housing in Singapore. *Ekistics.* 45 (270). pp. 246–249. https://www.jstor.org/stable/43619004?seq=1 (accessed 3 July 2020).

Farrell, D. and F. Greig. 2016. *Paychecks, Paydays, and the Online Platform Economy: Big Data on Income Volatility*. JP Morgan Chase Institute. https://institute.jpmorganchase.com/content/dam/jpmc/jpmorgan-chase-and-co/institute/pdf/jpmc-institute-volatility-2-report.pdf.

Fraiberger, S. and A. Sundararajan. 2015. Peer-to-Peer Rental Markets in the Sharing Economy. *NET Institute Working Paper*. 15–19.

Fulltime Nomad. 2017. What is Upwork & How to Make Money with It? 20 March. https://www.fulltimenomad.com/what-is-upwork/.

Ghobadi, S. and Z. Ghobadi. 2013. How Access Gaps Interact and Shape Digital Divide: A Cognitive Investigation. *Journal of Behaviour & Information Technology*. 34 (4). pp. 330–340. https://www.tandfonline.com/doi/abs/10.1080/0144929X.2013.833650#preview.

Gillwald, A., H. Galpaya, and A. Aguero. Towards understanding the digital gender gap in the Global South. In *Taking Stock: Data and Evidence on Gender Equality in Digital Access, Skills, and Leadership*. United Nations University and EQUALS. https://www.itu.int/en/action/gender-equality/Documents/EQUALS%20Research%20Report%202019.pdf.

Global Generations Policy Institute and the Harvard Generations Policy Program. 2006. The Age of Explosion: Baby Boomers and Beyond. Harvard Generations Policy Journal. Cambridge, MA. https://www.belfercenter.org/sites/default/files/files/publication/internet.pdf.

Google and GfK. 2018a. Distribution of Men Using E-money for Online Shopping in Indonesia as of November 2017, by age group. In *Statista*. https://www.statista.com/statistics/959528/indonesia-male-e-money-usage-for-buying-food-online-by-age/ (accessed July 2020).

———. 2018b. Distribution of Women Using E-money for Online Shopping in Indonesia as of November 2017, by age group. In *Statista*. https://www.statista.com/statistics/959528/indonesia-female-e-money-usage-for-buying-food-online-by-age/ (accessed July 2020).

Google, Temasek, and Bain. 2019. e-Conomy SEA 2019. https://www.temasek. com.sg/en/news-and-views/subscribe/google-temasek-e-conomy-sea-2019.

Government of Japan, Ministry of Internal Affairs and Communications. 2020. Internet Usage Rate by Age Group. Japan Statistical Yearbook 2020. https://www.stat.go.jp/english/data/nenkan/69nenkan/1431-12.html (accessed July 2020).

Government of the People's Republic of China, China Internet Information Center. 2020a. Distribution of Internet Users in China from December 2017 to December 2020, by gender. 45th Statistical Report on Internet Development in China. In *Statista*.

_____. 2020b. Breakdown of Internet Users in China from December 2016 to March 2020, by age. 45th Statistical Report on Internet Development in China. In *Statista*. https://www.statista.com/statistics/265150/internet-users-in-china-by-age/ (accessed July 2020).

Government of the Republic of Korea, Ministry of Science and ICT, Korea Internet and Security Agency; and Market Metrix 2019. Mobile Internet Usage Rate in South Korea in 2018, by age group. 2018 Survey on Internet Usage. In *Statista*. https://www.statista.com/statistics/1012884/south-korea-mobile-internet-usage-rate-by-age-group/ (accessed July 2020).

Government of Singapore, Infocomm Media Development Authority. 2019a. Individual Computer Usage by Age. https://data.gov.sg/dataset/individual-computer-usage (accessed July 2020).

_____. 2019b. Computer Ownership by Housing Type. https://data.gov.sg/dataset/computer-ownership-by-housing-type (accessed July 2020).

Government of Sri Lanka, Department of Census and Statistics. 2018. Computer Literacy Statistics—2018. Battaramulla. http://www.statistics.gov.lk/ComputerLiteracy/StaticalInformation/Bulletins/2018-Annual.

Government of Taipei,China, National Development Council. 2019. In *Statista*.

GSM Association (GSMA). 2020. *The Mobile Economy 2020*. https://www.gsma.com/mobileeconomy/wp-content/uploads/2020/03/GSMA_MobileEconomy2020_Global.pdf.

Handal, B., J. MacNish, and P. Petocz. 2013. Adopting Mobile Learning in Tertiary Environments: Instructional, Curricular and Organizational Matters. *Education Sciences*. 3 (4). pp. 359–374.

Institute for Management Development (IMD). World Competitiveness Online. https://worldcompetitiveness.imd.org/ (accessed July 2020).

International Telecommunication Union (ITU). 2017. *ICT Facts and Figures 2017*.

——— . 2019. *Measuring Digital Development: Facts and Figures 2019*. https://www.itu.int/en/ITU-D/Statistics/Documents/facts/FactsFigures2019.pdf.

———. *Indicators Database*. https://www.itu.int/en/ITU-D/Statistics/Pages/publications/wtid.aspx (accessed July 2020).

iResearch. 2018. Age Distribution of E-commerce App users in China as of February 2018. In *Statista*. https://www.statista.com/statistics/871581/china-age-distribution-of-e-commerce-app-users/ (accessed July 2020).

Junio, D. 2019. Gender Equality in ICT Access. In *Taking Stock: Data and Evidence on Gender Equality in Digital Access, Skills, and Leadership*. Tokyo: United Nations University and EQUALS. https://www.itu.int/en/action/gender-equality/Documents/EQUALS%20Research%20Report%202019.pdf.

Kim, H., M. Lee, and M. Kim. 2014. Effects of Mobile Instant Messaging on Collaborative Learning Processes and Outcomes: The Case of South Korea. *Journal of Educational Technology & Society*. 17 (2). pp. 31–42. https://www.jstor.org/stable/jeductechsoci.17.2.31?seq=1.

Ko, E., D. Chiu, P. Lo, and K. Ho. 2015. *The Journal of Academic Librarianship*. 41 (5). pp. 567–577. https://www.sciencedirect.com/science/article/abs/pii/S0099133315001536.

Kovachev, D., Y. Cao, R. Klamma, and M. Jarke. 2011. Learn-As-You-Go: New Ways of Cloud-Based Learning for the Mobile Web. In H. Leung, E. Popescu, Y. Cao, R. W. H. Lau, and W. Nejdl, eds. *Advances in Web-Based Learning*.

Larpin, B., J. Mabillard, M. Scaglione, P. Favre, and R. Schegg. 2019. An Analysis of Regional Developments of Airbnb in Switzerland: Insights into Growth Patterns of a P2P Platform. In *Information and Communication Technologies in Tourism*. Cham: Springer.

Llanto, G., M. Rosellon, and M. Ortiz. 2018. E-finance in the Philippines: Status and Prospects for Digital Financial Inclusion. *PIDS Discussion Paper Series*. 2018–22. https://www.pids.gov.ph/publications/6722.

MacCallum, K. and L. Jeffrey. 2009. Identifying Discriminating Variables that Determine Mobile Learning Adoption by Educators: An Initial Study. Paper, Ascilite Auckland 2009. https://www.ascilite.org/conferences/auckland09/procs/maccallum.pdf.

Mesko, B., Z. Drobni, E. Benyei, B. Gergely, and Z. Gyorffy. 2017. Digital Health is a Cultural Transformation of Traditional Healthcare. *mHealth*. 3 (38). pp. 1–8. https://www.ncbi.nlm.nih.gov/pmc/articles/PMC5682364/.

Morales, L. 2013. What is mLearning and How Can It Be Used to Support Learning and Teaching in Econometrics? *Higher Learning Research Communications*. 3 (1). pp. 18–37. https://scholarworks.waldenu.edu/hlrc/vol3/iss1/2/.

Murnane, K. 2016. How the Boomers Differ from Everybody in Their Approach to Online Privacy and Security. *Forbes*. https://www.forbes.com/sites/kevinmurnane/2016/04/18/how-the-boomers-differ-from-everybody-in-their-approach-to-online-privacy-and-security/#46f45ede254d.

Newhouse, D., P. Suarez-Becerra, and D. Doan. 2016. *Sri Lanka Poverty and Welfare: Recent Progress and Remaining Challenges.* World Bank. http://documents1.worldbank.org/curated/en/996911467995898452/pdf/103281-WP-P132922-Box394864B-PUBLIC-poverty-and-welfare-021216-final.pdf.

OpenSurvey. 2018. Most Well-known Ride hailing Apps in South Korea as of March 2019, by gender. Mobiliy Trend Report 2018. In *Statista.* https://www.statista.com/statistics/1013472/south-korea-wellknown-ride-hailing-mobile-apps/ (accessed July 2020).

Organisation for Economic Co-operation and Development (OECD). 2001. Understanding the Digital Divide. https://www.oecd.org/digital/ieconomy/1888451.pdf.

Ozili, P. 2018. Impact of Digital Finance on Financial Inclusion and Stability. *Borsa Istanbul Review.* 18 (4). pp. 329–340. https://www.sciencedirect.com/science/article/pii/S2214845017301503?via%3Dihub.

Phang, S. and M. Helble. 2016. Housing Policies in Singapore. *ADBI Working Paper.* 559. Tokyo. https://papers.ssrn.com/sol3/papers.cfm?abstract_id=2753487.

Picodi and Esquiremag.ph. 2019. Distribution of Online Shoppers in the Philippines in 2018, by age group. In *Statista.* https://www.statista.com/statistics/1032036/age-group-distribution-online-shoppers-philippines/ (accessed July 2020).

Pins, D. n.d. Accommodation Platforms in Germany and Their Usability. Sharing & Caring. http://sharingandcaring.eu/node/454.

Popescu, E. and D. Ghita. 2013. Using Social Networking Services to Support Learning. In H. Leung, E. Popescu, Y. Cao, R.W.H. Lau, and W. Nejdl, eds. *Advances in Web-Based Learning.*

Quartz and Flipkart. 2016. Distribution of Online Consumers across India in 2016, by age group. In *Statista.* https://www.statista.com/statistics/759142/india-distribution-online-consumers-by-age-group/ (accessed July 2020).

Quattrone, G., D. Proserpio, D. Quercia, L. Capra, and M. Musolesi. 2016. Who Benefits from the "Sharing" Economy of Airbnb? https://dl.acm.org/doi/pdf/10.1145/2872427.2874815.

Quimba, F. and S., Jr. Calizo. 2018. Going Digital: From Innovation to Inclusive Growth in the Philippines. *PIDS Discussion Paper Series.* 2018–19. https://www.pids.gov.ph/publications/6678.

Quimba, F., M. Rosellon, and S., Jr. Calizo. 2020. Digital Divide and the Platform Economy: Looking for the Connection from the Asian Experience. *PIDS Discussion Paper Series.* 2020–30. Philippine Institute for Development Studies. https://www.pids.gov.ph/publications/7155.

Rinne, A. 2017. What Exactly is the Sharing Economy? World Economic Forum, Geneva. https://www.weforum.org/agenda/2017/12/when-is-sharing-not-really-sharing/.

Rius, A., D. Masip, and R. Clariso. 2014. Student Projects Empowering Mobile Learning in Higher Education. *International Journal of Educational Technology in Higher Education.* 11 (1). pp. 192–207. https://link.springer.com/article/10.7238/rusc.v11i1.1901.

Roelofsen, M. 2018. Exploring the Socio-Spatial Inequalities of Airbnb in Sofia, Bulgaria. *Erdkunde.* 72 (4). pp. 313–327. https://www.erdkunde.uni-bonn.de/archive/2018/exploring-the-socio-spatial-inequalities-of-airbnb-in-sofia-bulgaria.

Rogers, K. 2011. *Mobile Learning Devices.* Bloomington, IN: Solution Tree Press.

Sarrab, M., H. Al-Shihi, and O. Rehman. 2013. Exploring Major Challenges and Benefits of M-Learning Adoption. *British Journal of Applied Sciences & Technology.* 3 (4). pp. 826–839. http://www.sciencedomain.org/abstract/1418.

Schneider, N. 2014. Owning is the New Sharing. *Shareable.* https://www.shareable.net/owning-is-the-new-sharing/.

Schor, J. 2014. Debating the Sharing Economy. Great Transition Initiative. https://greattransition.org/publication/debating-the-sharing-economy.

Schwab, K, ed. 2017. The Global Competitiveness Report 2017-2018. Geneva: World Economic Forum http://reports.weforum.org/global-competitiveness-index-2017-2018/?doing_wp_cron=1634094540.55982 39898681640625000#topic=data.

———. 2019. The Global Competitiveness Report 2019. Geneva: World Economic Forum.

Sey, A., J. Kang, and D. Junio. 2018. *Taking Stock: Data and Evidence on Gender Equality in Digital Access, Skills and Leadership*. United Nations University Institute on Computing and Society.

Social Weather Stations. 2018. Share of Internet Users in the Philippines as of September 2018, by age group. In *Statista*. https://www.statista.com/statistics/998362/share-internet-users-philippines-age-group/ (accessed July 2020).

———. 2019. Monthly Internet User Penetration Rate in the Philippines from June 2006 to March 2019, by gender. In *Statista*. https://www.statista.com/statistics/1104737/philippines-monthly-internet-user-penetration-rate-by-gender/ (accesssed July 2020).

Strommen-Bakhtiar, A. and E. Vinogradov. 2019. The Adoption and Development of Airbnb Services in Norway: A Regional Perspective. *International Journal of Innovation in the Digital Economy*. 10 (2). pp. 28–39. https://www.igi-global.com/gateway/article/223434#pnlRecommendationForm.

United Nations Conference on Trade and Development (UNCTAD). 2017. *Information Economy Report 2017: Digitalization, Trade and Development*. https://unctad.org/en/PublicationsLibrary/ier2017_en.pdf.

———. 2019. *Digital Economy Report 2019: Value Creation and Capture: Implications for Developing Countries*. https://unctad.org/en/PublicationsLibrary/der2019_en.pdf.

van Deursen, A. and J. van Dijk. 2011. Internet Skills and the Digital Divide. *New Media & Society*. 13 (6). pp. 893–911. https://journals.sagepub.com/doi/abs/10.1177/1461444810386774?journalCode=nmsa.

van Deursen, A., J. van Dijk, and O. Peters. 2011. Rethinking Internet Skills: The Contribution of Gender, Age, Education, Internet Experience, and Hours Online to Medium- and Content-Related Internet Skills. *Poetics*. 39 (2). pp. 125–144. https://www.sciencedirect.com/science/article/abs/pii/S0304422X11000106?via%3Dihub.

van Dijk, J. 2006. Digital Divide Research, Achievements and Shortcomings. *Poetics*. 34 (4–5). pp. 221–235. https://www.sciencedirect.com/science/article/pii/S0304422X06000167.

Viens, A. 2019. This Graph Tells Us Who's Using Social Media the Most. World Economic Forum (WEF). https://www.weforum.org/agenda/2019/10/social-media-use-by-generation/.

World Bank. 2017. Share of People Using the Internet to buy Something Online in Japan in 2017, by type of population. The Global Findex Database 2017. In *Statista*. https://www.statista.com/statistics/942094/japan-online-shopping-user-share-by-population-type (accessed July 2020).

_____ . TCdata360. https://tcdata360.worldbank.org/ (accessed May and July 2020).

World Health Organization (WHO). 2016. *Global Diffusion of eHealth: Making Universal Health Coverage Achievable*. https://apps.who.int/iris/bitstream/handle/10665/252529/9789241511780-eng.pdf?sequence=1.

Wu, P., M. Jackman, D. Abecassis, R. Morgan, H. de Villiers, and D. Clancy. 2016. *State of Connectivity 2015: A Report on Global Internet Access*.

Promoting Competition in the Digital Platform Economy

Philip Libre, Ryan Jacildo, Kimberly Diet, and Jessmond Elvina[1]

7.1. Introduction

As digital platforms emerge as powerful engines of innovation, their role in our daily lives is increasing.[2] New markets are delivering services that greatly improve convenience and quality of life for many.

These new markets and business models also create new challenges for regulators and government agencies. One major concern is the "winners-take-most" dynamics of many digital platform markets as a few large firms become dominant. Digital companies are now able to combine several factors and strategies to gain greater understanding of consumer psychology to influence behavior and to crowd out new potential competitors and thus shape the competitive landscape of the digital economy. Such factors include strong network effects, "multisidedness,"[3] massive data capture, increased computational power, and use of new technologies. Given the pervasiveness of the digital economy in many aspects of our economic lives, its developments impact consumer welfare, competition policy, and the growth trajectories of countries.

---

[1] This chapter benefited from the comments and review of Johannes Benjamin Bernabe, commissioner at the Philippine Competition Commission; James Villafuerte, senior economist at the Asian Development Bank (ADB); and Josef T. Yap, consultant at ADB.

[2] This chapter was prepared as a background paper for ADB (2021).

[3] Multisidedness in a platform means it accommodates more than one distinct group or type of users. The various groups are the "sides," and the platform functions by facilitating the interaction of these different sides. For example, the entertainment platform YouTube facilitates interaction among viewers, content creators, and advertisers. The term is further elaborated in a succeeding section on multisidedness and network effects.

By and large, competition is considered welfare-enhancing for consumers in a market as it engenders lower prices, higher quality, and more choices; incentivizes innovation; and encourages productivity. In this context, several factors have shed light on the function of competition law and policy in the digital platforms market. Specifically, competition authorities are looking into the indirect network effects in multisided markets such as when the value of a platform increases as the number of users grow. Consumers may gain from the presence of a few dominant platforms instead of having several, fragmented platforms where the indirect network effects are not fully realized. These dominant platforms tend to create an integrated network of related services and conducting transactions using a single account is more convenient than having multiple accounts on different platforms. Nevertheless, standard economic doctrine suggests that highly concentrated markets with less competition often result in suboptimal outcomes.

The dominance of a few large companies in digital platform markets is evident. Globally, the "big four" (Google, Apple, Facebook, and Amazon) are household names, and in some instances have become synonymous with the services they offer, such as the case of "googling" when searching on the internet or "friending" (from Facebook) when connecting with someone on social media. In Southeast Asia, the market research firm Iprice (Iprice Group n.d.) finds that the e-commerce platforms Lazada and Shopee account for more than 55% of total visits to the top 10 e-commerce websites in the countries covered by the study (Indonesia, Malaysia, the Philippines, Singapore, and Viet Nam). In the Philippines, these two account for more than 90% of total visits to the top 10 e-commerce websites.

Recently, market leaders have started to leverage their positions in one market to penetrate adjacent markets, sometimes to the disadvantage of competitors (ADB 2021). For example, Amazon is an e-commerce platform operator that also sells its own products on the platform, and is a leading provider of cloud services through Amazon Web Services. In Southeast Asia, Grab used its market stronghold in ride hailing to enter other markets such as digital payments (GrabPay), food delivery (GrabFood), and point-to-point parcel delivery (GrabExpress).

This chapter examines the factors and strategies, challenges, and barriers to the application of competition policy in the digital platforms market. New approaches are recommended as policy makers seek to promote competition and encourage innovation, limit concentration of market power, and protect consumer welfare.

7.2. Competition Law and Policy for Digital Platforms

Competition law and policy aim to ensure and promote free markets. In principle, markets with free and fair competition are expected to deliver greater consumer welfare, encourage innovation and economic efficiency, and help create a more dynamic and growing economy. Consumers pay lower prices, get better quality, and have more choices. Market efficiency reduces the need for complicated interventions and costly regulation.

A combination of characteristics inherent in digital platforms has underscored the appropriateness of traditional competition policy tools for this market. Yet, the possible distortionary effects of these same characteristics highlight the need to rethink competition law and policy in the context of digital platforms.

7.3. Characteristics of Digital Platform Markets

Digital platforms are internet-based, multisided markets that connect user groups. Along with multisidedness, digital platforms exhibit strong network effects, enjoy significant economies of scale and scope, and have raised the value of user data (Figure 7.1). These characteristics together result in digital platform companies with significant market power and the ability to dictate the rules of the game in the market ecosystems where they operate. This raises a concern for competition policy as firms in dominant positions may engage in anti-competitive behavior that stifles innovation, and reduces consumer welfare and overall economic growth.

Multisidedness and Network Effects

Rochet and Tirole (2006) define multisided markets as those wherein platforms enable interactions between end users to get multiple sides "on board" by appropriately charging each side while attempting to make a profit. Unlike a one-sided market, where only one price level can be observed, multisided markets feature a "price structure," or the ratio of prices between user groups, which platform operators must balance to increase the number of users. Table 7.1 provides a few examples of multisided platforms with asymmetric pricing between user types.

Figure 7.1: Market Characteristics That Could Stifle Competition

Network effects: Value of the platform is positively correlated with the number of users.

Extreme returns to scale: Returns of producing digital goods and services are, in time, very large compared to its cost of production.

Data intensiveness: Perhaps the most important byproduct of using digital platforms is the amount of data captured, e.g., targeted recommendations, behavioral nudges.

Switching costs: Real or perceived costs incurred by a consumer when changing suppliers for similar goods or services.

Source: Bernabe (2020).

Table 7.1: Pricing Structure in Multisided Platforms

Multisided Platform	Money Side	Subsidy Side	Typical Price on Subsidy Side
Video game consoles	Game publishers pay royalty	Consumers pay marginal cost or less for console	Below cost
Physical newspapers	Advertisers pay	Readers usually pay less than the marginal cost of printing and distribution and sometimes pay nothing	Below cost
Online marketplaces	Sellers often pay commission	Buyers usually do not pay	Free
Job recruiters and online job boards	Employers pay for postings or recruitment	Job seekers do not pay	Free
Search engines	Businesses pay for advertisements	Searchers do not pay	Free

Source: Evans and Schmalensee (2016).

The dynamics of pricing in multisided platforms create difficulties in applying traditional competition tools used to measure market outcomes such as price levels. As Table 1 shows, it is not unusual for businesses to price products at zero. This asymmetric pricing can create confusion when using traditional competition policy concepts, as a zero or negative-pricing strategy could be incorrectly interpreted as anti-competitive or predatory behavior. On the money-making side, where prices may be higher than non-digital alternatives—such as commissions paid by sellers—competition analysis might again wrongly diagnose these as a signal of excessive pricing and an exercise of market power.

Multisided business models also result in strong network effects, particularly indirect effects. Network effects exist in two broad categories: direct and indirect. Direct network effects occur when the value of a platform increases with the rise in the number of users. An example is the old telephone networks where customers preferred the network where most of their contacts could be found. Notably, these telephone networks tended to encourage monopolies until regulations were implemented to promote competition through mandatory interconnection among different networks.

Indirect network effects are present when the value ascribed to a platform by one user type increases when the number of another type of user increases. This is observed in online marketplaces where a platform becomes more attractive for buyers if there are more merchants and vice versa. Another example is ride-hailing services—passengers prefer platforms with more vehicles or drivers, while drivers in turn prefer platforms with more passengers. These network effects provide immense benefits to "first-movers" who are able to quickly reach critical mass. These also, in turn, make it relatively more difficult for the newer players to establish a foothold in the market and to introduce more competition (ADB 2021). Thus, both types of network effects often cause more market concentration.

Economies of Scale and Scope

Economies of scale occur when a business becomes more cost-efficient as it increases the scale of its operations. Digital platforms often entail significant fixed costs in setting up but have almost negligible marginal costs in providing each additional unit of output, thus exhibiting scale economies. An additional advantage for incumbents and first-movers able to scale up their operations is their collection of massive amounts of data. Incumbent advantages are further reinforced by the practice of integration wherein big digital platforms expand vertically or to adjacent markets, effectively suppressing competition from new and smaller players in multiple markets.

Data Intensiveness

The ability of platform operators to collect, analyze, and use massive amounts of data is crucial to enabling digital platforms to deliver greater value to users and ward off competition. Indeed, the way data is utilized in a digital platform economy is both a privacy and competition issue, especially when accounting for network effects.

Ezrachi and Stucke (2018) identify several market distortions from the rise of what they call "data-opolies." One is that dominant incumbents can use their ownership and control of the flow of excessive amounts of information and data to the detriment of consumers and competitors, as the market, and consequently regulators, have yet to establish the price or value of data. This degrades product quality and increases information asymmetry, which some argue is equivalent to paying an excessive price for a product or service. Another is that control of a key platform allows exclusionary behavior, as the platform operator can push its own products and services to users and advertisers. Another distortion is negative innovation, where market leaders invent ways that harm consumers and markets, such as exploitative techniques to increase user engagement or exclude competitors. Coherent policy on data management and competition is needed to limit proliferation of these harmful market distortions.

7.4. Rethinking Competition Policy in the Context of Digital Platforms

Interventions promoting competition must be consistent with competition policy's underlying goal to promote consumer welfare through efficient markets. Any recalibration should thus ideally avoid suppression of the value created by technological advancements, network effects, and scale economies.

Competition policy recognizes that actual competition among fragmented players may not be practical or efficient in certain markets, such as in most digital platform markets, due to network effects and scale economies. Tirole (2020) argues that contestability can be maintained by ensuring "dynamic competition." Due to network externalities, rather than inducing the entry of competitors, incumbents can be provoked into acting competitively by the perceived threat of entrants into the market. As long as markets are contestable, incumbents continue to offer competitively priced, high-quality, and innovative products to protect their market share against potential competitors, thus ensuring consumer welfare.

Analysis of Mergers and Acquisitions

Much like traditional enterprises, digital platforms compete and pursue cross-country expansion plans through mergers and acquisitions of stakes. Grab's acquisition of the operations of Uber in Southeast Asia significantly increased the former's share in the digital platform-based transportation service market in the region, drawing heavy regulatory scrutiny from competition authorities. The transaction saw Uber exit its operations in Southeast Asia but retain a 27.5% stake in Grab's operation. Uber's operations in Armenia, Azerbaijan, Belarus, Georgia, Kazakhstan, and the Russian Federation were also merged with Yandex.Taxi in 2018 (Yandex.Taxi n.d.).

Larger and global players likewise employ acquisitions to either penetrate local markets inclined toward homegrown platforms or to increase local market presence. In some cases, they maintain multiple brands or labels, blurring perception of market power. When Alibaba acquired a controlling stake in Lazada in 2016 (Alibaba Group 2016), it effectively defused the power of a strong regional competitor and, together with Aliexpress, gained access to six of the largest Southeast Asian economies. Facebook's acquisition of Instagram and WhatsApp still generates discussion on whether the traditional tools used by competition authorities are appropriate for multisided digital platforms.

Recognizing that breakups of large firms are administratively and politically costly, competition authorities need to recalibrate their merger analysis toolkit and consider other relevant economic concepts. For instance, price theory or the analytical tool used to predict prices post-merger should explicitly consider the multisided nature of digital platforms so as not to misdiagnose price movements in one side of a market as representative of the total welfare effects of a merger.

The Centre on Regulation in Europe, in its recent publication *Digital Markets and Online Platforms: New Perspectives on Regulation and Competition Law*, recommends key actions that competition authorities should consider in updating their approach to merger analysis (Kramer 2020). First, the efficiency effects of mergers should be explicitly and simultaneously analyzed with theories of harm. This recognizes the efficiency-improving effects, due to network effects, of increasing the size of firms. Second, focus should move away from actual or existing competition and shift toward analyzing potential competition and innovation capabilities. Third, focus on the "balance-of-harm" that could befall parties to the dispute, while taking into account the risks and costs of assessment and enforcement errors.[4] Fourth, update the burden of proof in merger regulation to allow for presumptions. These presumptions can be rebutted by the parties involved with the merger, effectively reverting the burden of proof to firms instead of competition authorities. Mergers with likely welfare-enhancing effects are cleared or those with welfare-reducing effects blocked without the need for detailed and resource-intensive case analysis. Finally, to avoid analysis paralysis, consider introducing confidential divestiture plans in cases of high uncertainty so that mergers with highly ambiguous competition effects can be cleared yet allowing competition authorities to reverse the clearance if it later becomes apparent that the cleared merger has merger-specific anti-competitive effects.

Moving Beyond Enforcement through Ex Ante Policies

The dominance of a few large digital platform companies and the difficulty that government authorities have had in arresting their ever-increasing dominance has made it apparent that traditional *ex post* enforcement of competition laws may be inadequate in multisided digital platform markets with network effects. This has renewed interest in *ex ante* policies that seek to prevent anti-competitive outcomes before they happen. One *ex ante* instrument currently available to competition authorities is merger regulation, which by itself may not be enough.

---

4   The "balance-of-harms" approach—as proposed in the Digital Competition Expert Panel report (Furman et al. 2019) to update the United Kingdom's competition framework— aims to account for the scale and the likelihood of harm in merger cases in terms of potential competition and innovation. The report argues that "a more economic approach to assessing mergers would be to weigh both the likelihood and the magnitude of the impact of the merger." This leads to "mergers being blocked when they are expected to do more harm than good", following the balance-of-harms approach.

The adoption of rules that incentivize incumbents to behave competitively despite their advantageous positions is consistent with achieving competitive market outcomes while retaining the benefits of network effects. Instead of penalizing dominance and artificially creating a fragmented but inefficient market, *ex ante* policies that ensure contestability may be more appropriate. Figure 7.2 lists some of the policy areas where government support is crucial in promoting competition in the digital economy.

Figure 7.2: Promoting Competition in the Digital Economy

Government Support of Digital Entrepreneurship

- Local businesses equipped to participate in the digital economy
- Policies minimizing barriers to entries and expansion
- Accessibility to resources (financial and technological) needed to participate in the digital space
- Public–private collaboration in organizing capability-enhancing activities (e.g., hackathons, trainings, networking, and partnership opportunities, etc.)

Cohesive and Pro-Competitive Data-Sharing Rules: Taking advantage of inherent network effects and reducing barriers from a few firms' control of data

More user data control
- Ensures rules promote consumer control over personal data and data generated through their activities
- Eases platform switching by reducing overhead costs

Increased data portability
- With regard to data collection and storage
- Includes the following standards: Universal or portable formats, accountability, and guarantees of accuracy

Trustworthy data ecosystem
- Clear, reliable, and consumer-centric policies
- Ensures user data is not used adversely and businesses handle data responsibly
- First two rules will be ineffective without data owner consent

Sources: Authors and Bernabe (2020).

One way to ensure contestability is through "multi-homing" or by restricting exclusivity arrangements. Multi-homing means that users can join and use multiple platforms at minimal switching costs (Box 7.1). In digital platform markets where incumbents enjoy a certain degree of dominance, it may be difficult for newer players to gain enough foothold in the market to be considered an effective competitor. An example could be in ride-hailing platforms, where an incumbent can set exclusivity arrangements to lock-in their drivers. Thus, a prospective entrant, even with potentially better services

Box 7.1: Multi-Homing and Market Dominance

"Multi-homing" refers to the ability of users and service providers to simultaneously avail of goods or services provided by multiple platforms, and possibly their corresponding complementary components. Multi-homing becomes especially pertinent in platform markets with high concentration, as a mechanism to prevent market dominance of select firms. It becomes possible for one to freely multi-home when costs to do so are low.

Chisholm and Jung (2016) particularly warn against market dominance and the inability to multi-home across platforms. As explained in the subsequent bullet points, the incumbents' dominance may be reinforced by certain types of contractual restrictions, the constraints faced by users in moving their data to other platforms, and dominant players' exclusive access to proprietary data, among other things.

- *Contractual restrictions.* Contractual restrictions are commonly embodied in wide-scoping most favored nation (MFN) clauses and exclusivity and tying provisions.[a] European competition authorities work with broad MFN clauses as those that "require suppliers and retailers to publish on a price comparison tool of online marketplace the same or better price and conditions as those published on any other sales channel." They also work with narrow causes that "require suppliers and retailers to publish on a price comparison tool or online marketplace the same or better price and conditions as those published on its own (direct) website" (Chappatte and O'Connell 2019). Transportation network companies and other platforms also have exclusivity clauses, which tend to discourage multi-homing.

- *Lack of capacity of customers to transfer existing profiles to a different competing platform.* The users facing this constraint are thus effectively locked-in, which reduces opportunities for engagement by other companies or platforms. The inability to multi-home can result in high transactions costs and disincentivize switching, in addition to large network effects.

- *Dominant players' exclusive access to proprietary data.* Access to individual-level information, such as commonly searched items and historical transactions, advantages incumbent players in understanding consumer behavior. It allows them to better tailor advertisements and promotions to target markets. In some cases, multi-homing policies less effectively promote competition because of a firm's overwhelming market dominance, in addition to its data advantage, as the Grab experience in ride hailing in the Philippines demonstrates.

---

[a] A common citation of the use of a wide MFN clause is in the hotel booking market, particularly the Bundeskartellamnt (Federal Cartel Office) case against Booking.com in December 2015 (See: Chappatte and O'Connell 2019; Bryan Cave Leighton Paisner LLP 2019). As a result of the Federal Cartel Office's finding, Booking.com limited its agreements with hotels to "narrow" MFN clauses, although it subsequently challenged this as well on appeal. Narrow MFN clauses prohibit hotels from offering prices and conditions better booking and cancellation conditions or terms of availability—on their own websites or through offline distribution channels more favorable than what Booking.com offered. On appeal, the Düsseldorf Higher Regional Court quashed the initial decision by the office in June 2019 because narrow MFN clauses were found to be consistent with competition law as they would permit a "fair and balanced contractual exchange of services between the portal and the hotels". As such, Booking.com's provision was required to subvert a "disloyal re-channeling" of portal customer bookings if the hotel were to establish more desirable prices and terms on their own online and offline media. A similar ruling was later issued by the Swedish court, bringing the jurisprudence in these countries in line with most other jurisdictions in Europe.

Source: ADB (2021).

and terms, would find it difficult to entice enough drivers to subsequently attract more passengers. However, a more sizable passenger base generated by multi-homing will induce more drivers to service various platforms. By allowing drivers and passengers to multi-home, barriers to entry are reduced and contestability is introduced or preserved. In line with this perspective, the Philippine Competition Authority mandated Grab to engage in nonexclusive arrangements with drivers and operators when the company acquired Uber (PCC 2018).

Relatedly, interoperability is a tool that can also promote and facilitate multi-homing. Interoperability is the ease with which one system or platform integrates with another in access, exchange, and use of data (Box 7.2). For instance, ApplePay and Paypal can be used to pay for transactions in Rakuten's e-commerce platform even if RakutenPay is also available. In some cases, transfer of funds is also possible between e-wallets from different digital payment platforms.

Authorities have previously employed the interoperability tool to address the dominance of incumbents. In the case of Microsoft, the European Commission expressed concerns about the tying of the firm's web browser Internet Explorer to Windows, which is its largest customer product in the PC operating system market. In 2019, as part of its commitments, Microsoft agreed to establish broad interoperability information disclosures to allow interconnection between Windows and third-party products.

The use of protocol interoperability suggests the need to construct standards to guide the development of complementary services, on a merit basis, to promote competition (Crémer, de Montjoye, and Schweitzer 2019). However, enforcement of these standards must be timed with prudence so that they do not hamper and distort market conditions and impede innovation.

While *ex ante* tools aim to induce pro-competitive behavior of firms, another approach is to empower consumers in their interactions with digital platforms. This can be done through data access and privacy rules. The magnitude of the collection and use of data is a crucial issue, which can lead to the development of new business models that deliver more value and offer innovative products and services to consumers. But it is also a mechanism to maintain or amplify market dominance while potentially subjecting clients to privacy risks. This shows the importance of integrating the design of competition law and its implementation with the protection of consumer rights and data privacy.

Box 7.2: Interoperability of Systems

Crémer, de Montjoye, and Schweitzer (2019) identified three kinds of interoperability (Table). Protocol interoperability refers to the capacity of two types of products or services to create an interlinkage and subsequently supply complementary services. It is the concept most frequently referred to in competition policy. Data interoperability is similar to data portability, but the former offers potential real-time and continuous availability of personal or machine user data. Notably, systems that observe protocol interoperability lead to the accessibility of data, but the reverse is not true. Meanwhile, full protocol interoperability is defined as the processes and criteria which permit the interoperability of two substitutable systems.

Characteristics of the Three Types of Interoperability

Type	Description	Advantages	Disadvantages	Real-World Applications
Protocol interoperability	Ability of two services or products to fully interconnect with one another and provide complementary services Can exist within the context of platforms	Allows for the development of complementary services and competition on the quality of those services	Competitive risks which arise from possible de facto standard-setting of firms required in this type of interoperability's implementation	Operating systems (platforms), online service with their complementary services, phones and charges (e.g., charging protocols)
Data interoperability	Roughly identical to data portability, but with continuous, potentially real-time access to personal or machine user data Relies on privileged Application Programming Interfaces (APIs) when users authorize a service B to access existing data through service A's API	Can enable the offering of a complementary service Allows users to avail of non-bundled services Can promote multi-homing Possible to reduce security risks and costs through sufficient technical and legal standards and data protection laws	In the context of platforms, may require substitution of some platforms' functionalities Security issues, particularly ensuring that users who have agreed to data sharing, can control the subsequent use of the shared data	Add-ons to platforms such as Gmail, access to vehicle data, or access to the Internet of Things data

continued on next page

Box 7.2 *continued*

Type	Description	Advantages	Disadvantages	Real-World Applications
	Can exist within the context of platforms or as a network of services complementary to one another; this type of interoperability may prompt the offering of a complementary service Always requires some form of protocol interoperability		Higher costs relative to data portability May be prone to anti-competitive information exchange depending of data type and access modalities	
Full protocol interoperability	Ensures two or more substitute services interoperate	Positive network effects can be shared among direct competitors, or decrease lock-in effects rooted from network effects, thus may possibly be an efficient instrument to address concentration	Must be imposed with caution Requires stronger integration and standardization, relative to protocol interoperability, across several competing platforms, which implies possible significant preclusion of a firm's ability to innovate and differentiate the various services it provides Network effects for this type of interoperability depend on the number of users of all the services and the standardization is higher given that several services must all agree on a common standard Since it necessitates coordination among firms, it may lead to collusive behavior	Messaging systems, mobile phone networks, e-mails, file formats

Source: Crémer, de Montjoye, and Schweitzer (2019).

Generally, in promoting competition in digital platforms, consumers need to be empowered with control over their data generated through their digital activities. When data privacy rules are enforced, consumers can trust the market with their data. Consumers will face lower switching costs, and entry of new businesses is eased as they can now access, with their consent, the data being held by dominant incumbents.

Asian economies are following the European Union (EU) model in this respect. Blackmore (2019) observes that while the direction and priorities differ across jurisdictions in Asia and the Pacific economies, a "consistent strengthening of data protection laws throughout the region" is occurring following the EU's General Data Protection Regulation (GDPR) standards. However, the strengthening of consumer protection and data privacy rules has also increased the operating costs of firms, which could dampen competition.

Finally, competition authorities will need to figure out how to handle "walled gardens" in digital platform markets (Box 7.3). A small number of firms have now become dominant, managing multiple powerful platforms and acting as "gatekeepers" in the digital economy. The concept of walled gardens describes an ecosystem where dominant incumbents, such as monopolies, duopolies, and oligopolies, control several aspects of a platform system. As a closed structure, it walls in current and potential users because these incumbent-operated platforms already have a large existing consumer base. Primarily, consumers suffer within the walled gardens as they inhibit consumers moving to alternative platforms due to high switching costs. In the same vein, such "walling" precludes entry of new players who may introduce better-quality products, more innovation, and business models that could improve consumer experience. While this ecosystem prevails, not only are users "locked in" and potential competitors "locked out" of the walled garden, but the advancement of technologies and business models also suffer slower growth or even stagnation.

Competition Policy and Cooperation

In enforcing *ex ante* regulation, competition authorities cannot operate in a vacuum. They will need to cooperate with other policy-setting and regulatory agencies to make sure that rules and regulations complement each other (Figure 7.3). While competition authorities hold the main responsibility for promoting market competition, digital platforms have a unique and complex set of characteristics that requires a multifaceted approach. An example of the

Box 7.3: GCash Walled Garden

Presently, GCash is the biggest digital money and electronic wallet platform in the Philippines.[a] The volume of registrations on the app doubled between April and June of 2020 (during the coronavirus pandemic),[b] while transactions rose by 700% year-on-year in May 2020,[c] primarily from bank cash-ins and online bills payment.[d] Aside from these unprecedented figures, GCash has become the number one downloaded app on both Android and iOS app stores consequently strengthening its leadership position also in terms of app penetration.

The user data that GCash collects include mobile numbers, location, bank account numbers, transaction details, and know-your-customer information, as required by the Bangko Sentral ng Pilipinas, the central bank. Such confidential data and information are kept by GCash and are not shared with other actors on the platform, such as banks and merchants, despite being connected through payment systems like InstaPay and PESONet. While these are not yet directly monetized by GCash, the massive consumer data at their disposal allow them to introduce other tailored products in their platform, such as a short-term credit line through GCash partner banks.

Data monetization may not also necessarily entail disposal or transfer of raw user data. In the case of GCash, its GScore feature, which produces user credit scores based on the data collected by and stored in the system, is identified as a possible mode to go about the monetization process. While already aggregated, these user credit scores can arguably still be valuable to institutions involved in credit intermediation and related activities.

---

[a] GCash regards itself as a lifestyle and financial app offering a full suite of various services such as buying load, paying bills and lifestyle payments, and sending money and/or local and global remittances, among others.
[b] Based on an interview with Ron Testa, vice-president of strategy, GCash in July 2020.
[c] Globe Telecom, Inc. 2020. Filipinos More Inclined to Use Digital Finance: GCash Transactions Balloon by 700% YoY in May. Globe Newsroom. 22 June. https://www.globe.com.ph/about-us/newsroom/917ventures/gcash-transactions-700percent-yoy-May.html.
[d] Bank cash-ins refer to the transferring of funds from existing bank accounts, over-the-counter stations, and remittance partners to a user's GCash account.

Sources: Authors and ADB (2021).

---

need for interagency coordination is in data privacy rules where the technical domain expertise of privacy and technology agencies will help inform decisions on which specific instruments are feasible for implementation.

Given the pronounced cross-border dimension of digital platforms, multilateral cooperation is crucial in strengthening competition laws, in setting policies, and in improving the capacities of regulatory agencies. Cross-country competition cooperation is vital in regulating standards and in enforcing rules on data privacy, trade protection, industrial policies, and taxation, among other areas. Likewise, cooperation helps mitigate unwanted consequences of policy changes on the investment climate and innovation, as well as adversarial counter measures. Additionally, national authorities in the region, with diverse experiences in handling digital economy issues, can benefit from working closely. They can also adapt elements of best practices from countries that have already dealt with similar issues that they are facing.

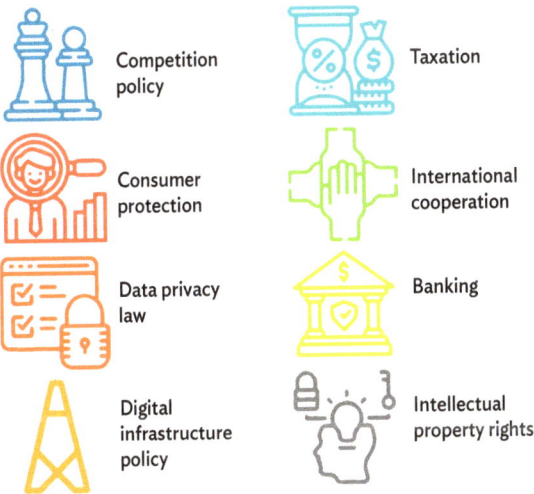

Figure 7.3: Supporting Policies and Regulations in the Digital Economy

Competition policy does not operate in a vacuum; regulations must be complementary, consistent, and multifaceted.

Competition policy

Taxation

Consumer protection

International cooperation

Data privacy law

Banking

Digital infrastructure policy

Intellectual property rights

Source: Bernabe (2020).

7.5. A Short Case Study on Digital Payments

State of Play and Policy Issues

Digital payment platform activity is growing rapidly around the world. For example, in 2019 an estimated 2.1 billion people used e-wallets, from just 500 million in 2017 (de Sartiges et al. 2020). Digital payment flows have three main components: (i) the initial source of funds (e.g., traditional or mobile bank or trading platform for financial assets), (ii) the payment option (e.g., digital wallet, which can be a bank wallet or a third-party wallet, or credit/debit card), and (iii) the payment network that allows movement of funds from one digital wallet to another or to a bank account. Identifying the nodes in the digital payment transaction flow (Figure 7.4) is important in viewing the competition landscape.

Recent trends indicate that while some payment platforms focus solely on payment services, others that started in other service segments have developed their own payment solutions within their platforms. In Asia, e-commerce platforms like Lazada and Shopee have developed their own e-wallets and payment networks to facilitate transactions on their platforms. However, their e-wallets cannot be used outside the home platform. In comparison, GrabPay's e-wallet allows payment for purchases outside the home platform, similar to Alipay, WeChat Pay, Paytm, KakaoPay, GCash, and PayMaya.

Several jurisdictions have recognized the importance of digital payment platforms in improving financial access of consumers. Given the complex ecosystem surrounding digital payments, various policies and regulations have been adopted to maximize the benefits from digital payment platforms while also addressing concerns such as privacy. Two main policy thrusts have been pursued to promote the expansion of digital payments: those relating to data privacy and management and those relating to interoperability.

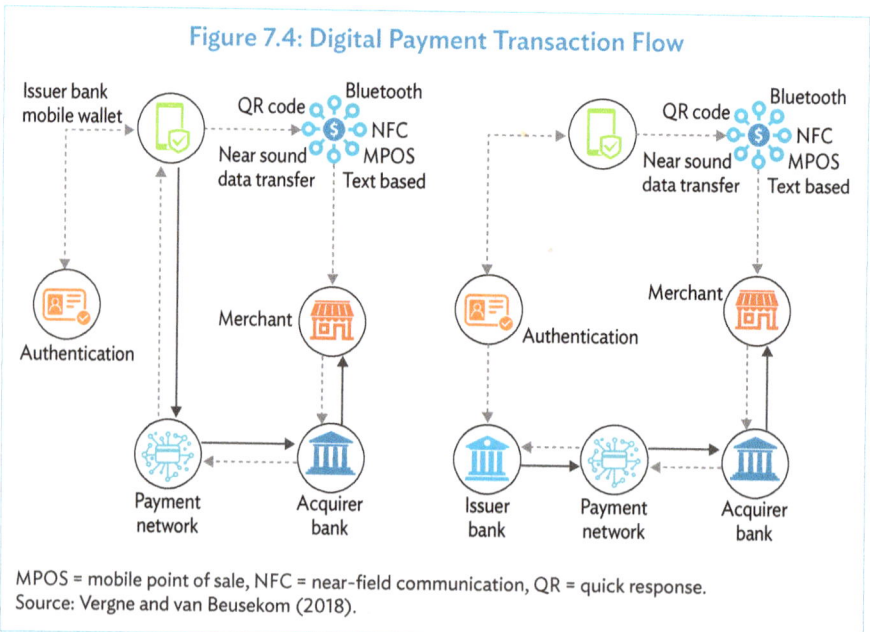

Figure 7.4: Digital Payment Transaction Flow

MPOS = mobile point of sale, NFC = near-field communication, QR = quick response.
Source: Vergne and van Beusekom (2018).

Data privacy and security are key to increasing adoption of financial technologies. Collaboration between the public and private sectors is necessary not only to increase adoption, but also to ensure that fundamental privacy rights are protected. Some of the most well-known examples of data privacy and security rules are the EU's GDPR and Payment Services Directive, and the US Consumer Financial Protection Bureau's Consumer Protection Principles for Data Sharing. Asian economies have also started adopting their own data security rules, such as the PRC's cybersecurity laws and Malaysia's personal data protection laws, which incorporate many principles outlined in the GDPR.

To preserve the benefits of network effects while promoting innovation through competition, policies that ensure interoperability among several systems have been adopted. Examples of this include the United Kingdom's Open Banking Initiative, the Hong Kong Monetary Authority's Open API Framework, and the Monetary Authority of Singapore's API Playbook.

The challenge in designing a coherent and pro-competitive data access policy is to enable the market to take full advantage of inherent network effects in digital platforms while ensuring that entry barriers stemming from control of data by a few players are minimized if not eliminated.

Digital Payments and the National ID System in the Philippines

Cash remains the preferred mode of transaction in the Philippines, although the COVID-19 pandemic has helped accelerate the use of digital payments. According to the Bangko Sentral ng Pilipinas (2019) Financial Inclusion Survey, 75% of public sector and 88% of private sector workers are still largely paid in cash. Trust is an issue, and a recurring theme in several jurisdictions' efforts to increase competition and expand access to banking and financial services is to create a high-trust ecosystem. Trust is a bilateral concern—customers must be able to trust service providers to keep their data secure, while service providers must be able to manage risks through an ability to verify customer identity.

One requirement of know-your-customer processes followed by banks and other financial institutions is valid ID from potential clients. This requirement is a common problem for many Filipinos without valid ID. Lacking ID and other personal documents, many Filipinos are left unbanked and with little to no ability to access financial services. This issue came to the fore during the COVID-19 pandemic, as digital payment service providers saw a surge in transaction volume and new user registration.[5] Most new users were technology-savvy millennials who already had bank accounts, but with limited intake of customers from the unbanked and underserved demographic.

The implementation of a national ID system is intended to significantly facilitate affordable and widespread access to financial services (i.e., fund transfers, remittances, payments) by increasing convenience and compliance with valid ID requirements. A valid ID for most, if not all, Filipinos will allow them to create a digital identity which they can use to access other digital services. A national ID system is indeed promising, but its benefits rely on the ability of the market to establish and operationalize a system in which any data generated and stored remains private, secure, and customer-centric.[6]

7.6. Conclusion

With digital platforms still evolving in many economies in Asia and the Pacific, competition is uneven across countries and sectors. Traditional factors continue to influence competition among digital platforms. Factors such as network effects, multisidedness, and agility in adopting innovative practices and business models, as well as mergers and stake acquisitions, are pressing concerns. The collection and use of big data are another prominent issue. Data are utilized to ward off competitors. In some cases, data transferability is a material determinant of switching costs, stifling competition.

In regulating digital platforms, competition authorities need to work closely with other policy-setting and regulatory agencies to ensure that rules are complementary and consistent with each other. Promoting competition in digital platforms fundamentally necessitates appropriate and relevant competition policy and effective regional cooperation frameworks as well as well-defined and actionable consumer protection and data privacy rules.

---

[5] Based on an interview with Jonathan Bates and Krhizzy Pasigan of GrabPay Philippines in July 2020; and with Ron Testa of GCash in July 2020.

[6] Customer-centric in the context of a data ecosystem is a broad term referring to rules and practices that put customers at the forefront in terms of accuracy, transparency, access, security, and rights (e.g., consent, right to be forgotten, ability to dispute, etc.), among others.

Under-enforcement due to a lack of understanding and outdated tools will have adverse consequences, and government intervention will become increasingly difficult if digital platforms continue to become more concentrated and dominant companies become too powerful to regulate. On the other hand, over-enforcement will stifle innovation and suppress value creation resulting from network effects and scale economies. Competition authorities need to decisively update analytical and regulatory instruments that balance promotion of competition while continuing to reap the benefits of digital platforms.

References

Alibaba Group. 2016. Alibaba Acquires Controlling Stake in E-commerce Platform Lazada. *News release.* https://www.alibabagroup.com/en/news/press_pdf/p160412.pdf.

Asian Development Bank (ADB). 2021. *Asian Economic Integration Report 2021: Making Digital Platforms Work for Asia and the Pacific.* Manila. http://dx.doi.org/10.22617/TCS210048-2.

Bangko Sentral ng Pilipinas. 2019. *2019 Financial Inclusion Survey.* Manila. https://www.bsp.gov.ph/Inclusive%20Finance/Financial%20Inclusion%20Reports%20and%20Publications/2019/2019FISTopline Report.pdf.

Bernabe, J. R. 2020. Competition in Digital Platforms. *Presentation.* Making Digital Platforms Work for Asia. 25-26 July. Manila: Asian Development Bank.

Blackmore, N. 2019. Moving Towards Europe: Recent Trends in Asia-Pacific Data Protection Law. *Kennedys Law LLP.* 7 October. Melbourne. https://www.kennedyslaw.com/thought-leadership/article/moving-towards-europe-recent-trends-in-asia-pacific-data-protection-law.

Bryan Cave Leighton Paisner LLP. (2019). *Price Parity Clauses and Booking. com – a More Unified Approach or a Reminder of Diverging Opinions?* https://www.bclplaw.com/en-US/insights/price-parity-clauses-and-booking-com-a-more-unified-approach-or.html.

Chappatte, P. and K. O'Connell. 2019. European Union–E-commerce: Most Favoured Nation Clauses. *Global Competition Review.* https://globalcompetitionreview.com/insight/e-commerce-competition-enforcement-guide-second-edition/1209644/european-union-%E2%80%93-e-commerce-most-favoured-nation-clauses.

Chisholm, A. and N. Jung. 2016. Platform Regulation – Ex-Ante versus Ex-Post Intervention: Evolving Out Antitrust Tools and Practices to Meet the Challenges. *Competition Policy International.* 21 March. https://www.competitionpolicyinternational.com/platform-regulation-ex-ante-versus-ex-post-intervention-evolving-our-antitrust-tools-and-practices-to-meet-the-challenges/.

Crémer, J., Y. A. de Montjoye, and H. Schweitzer. 2019. *Competition Policy for the Digital Era*. Brussels: European Commission.

de Sartiges, D., A. Bharadwaj, I. Khan, J. Tasiaux, and P. Witschi. 2020. Southeast Asian Consumers Are Driving a Digital Payment Revolution. *Boston Consulting Group*. 20 May. Boston. https://www.bcg.com/publications/2020/southeast-asian-consumers-digital-payment-revolutions.

Evans, D. S. and R. Schmalensee. 2016. *Matchmakers: The New Economics of Multisided Platforms*. Boston: Harvard Business Review Press.

Ezrachi, A. and M. E. Stucke. 2018. eDistortions: How Data-Opolies Are Dissipating the Internet's Potential. Digital Platforms and Concentration. pp. 5–7. Chicago Booth School of Business.

Furman, J., D. Coyle, A. Fletcher, P. Marsden, and D. McAuley. 2019. *Unlocking Digital Competition: Report of the Digital Competition Expert Panel*. London: HM Treasury. https://assets.publishing.service.gov.uk/government/uploads/system/uploads/attachment_data/file/785547/unlocking_digital_competition_furman_review_web.pdf.

Iprice Group. n.d. Year-End Report on Southeast Asia's Map of E-Commerce 2019.

Kramer, J., ed. 2020. *Digital Markets and Online Platforms: New Perspectives on Regulation and Competition Law*. Brussels: Centre on Regulation in Europe.

Philippine Competition Commission (PCC). 2018. *2018 PCC Annual Report: Disrupting Unfair Market Competition*. Manila. https://www.phcc.gov.ph/wp-content/uploads/2017/08/2018-Annual-Report-4mb-may-21.pdf.

Rochet, J. C. and J. Tirole. 2006. Two-Sided Markets: A Progress Report. *The Rand Journal of Economics*. 37 (3): pp. 645–667.

Tirole, J. 2020. Competition and the Industrial Challenge for the Digital Age. Paper.

Vergne, C. and J. D. van Beusekom. 2018. Digital-World Consumers Expect Banks to Securely Step Up Their Technology Game. *Capgemini*. Paris. https://worldpaymentsreport.com/2018/10/digital-world-consumers-expect-banks-to-securely-step-up-their-technology-game/.

Yandex.Taxi. n.d. "About Company". Webpage. https://taxi.yandex.com/company/ (accessed July 2020).

Digitalization of Work and the Role of Universal Basic Income in Developing Asia

Ma. Diyina Gem Arbo and Aiko Kikkawa

8.1. Introduction

Many countries still lag on extending social protection to vulnerable segments of their populations, leaving many people exposed to poverty, inequality, and social exclusion. About 61.1% of the population in Asia and the Pacific remains uncovered by at least one form of social protection (ILO 2017). This situation is largely attributed to widespread informal employment in the region, which stood at 59.2% of non-agriculture employment in 2016 (ILO 2018a). Social protection coverage in developing Asia and the Pacific is not extended to all labor market participants (Campbell forthcoming). Only a few informal workers secure themselves through contributory schemes while the rest continue to rely on the limited and often targeted noncontributory schemes of governments (ILO 2018b).

At present, digitalization has not only made some jobs redundant by automation but also created new ways for individuals to participate in the labor market. This includes the digital platform economy, where individuals offer their labor and are contracted, typically, for a short duration (Campbell forthcoming). While one objective of the platform economy is to make idle resources productive, unemployed individuals in developing Asia tend to use it as a principal source of income. This may add to the numbers of people who work informally and leave them without social protection coverage.

Along with informal employment, poverty and economic inequality, population aging, and gender inequality generate an even greater need for inclusive social security systems in developing Asia. This has prompted some Asian countries to consider reforming public social security programs.

One discussion has focused on universal and unconditional cash-based assistance called universal basic income (UBI). Some see UBI as "the most radical social protection scheme" among all types of social protection programs (Ortiz et al. 2018). Usually, it involves an unconditional transfer of cash to all individuals in a population, which can be contrasted to prevailing social protection that provide *conditional, targeted, and in-kind* transfers. The main rationale for universal transfers rests on eliminating exclusion and inclusion errors and transaction costs associated with targeted transfers.

In a nutshell, UBI has the potential to deliver

- a guaranteed provision of benefits for all, including informal workers, unlike prevailing social protection programs either tied to employment or provided only to targeted groups;

- a quicker disbursement of benefits without the need for means-testing; and

- an overall improvement in work conditions because workers have the option to "quit" when they have suitable cash income.

However, concerns remain over the financial resources needed for a UBI, its redistributive effects, and its tendency to encourage informal workers to stay in informal employment.

This chapter

i. presents the emerging trends of platform-based work and the implications for social protection;

ii. discusses key UBI features, particularly in addressing new social protection challenges and its viability as an alternative to prevailing social protection programs in developing economies;

iii. reviews Mongolia's UBI scheme, the only full-fledged, nationwide UBI program implemented in Asia, and variants of the program in the region;

iv. provides an analytical framework for the assessment of UBI impacts, which can be useful for developing Asian economies in determining UBI feasibility; and

v. reviews empirical studies on selected Asian and developed countries.

8.2. Changing World of Work and Social Protection Implications in Developing Asia

Emergence of the Platform Economy

The rise of the platform economy in the region has generated modern forms of employment. Workers in these types of jobs enjoy a lot of flexibility, but also face issues related to regular income and social security. Digital platforms can be categorized by the online markets they create (Schmidt 2017). Figure 8.1 indicates that the labor generated through digital platforms is categorized into either cloud work or gig work, depending on whether the services and tasks are bound to a specific location or person.

Figure 8.1: Categorization of Digital Markets in the Platform Economy

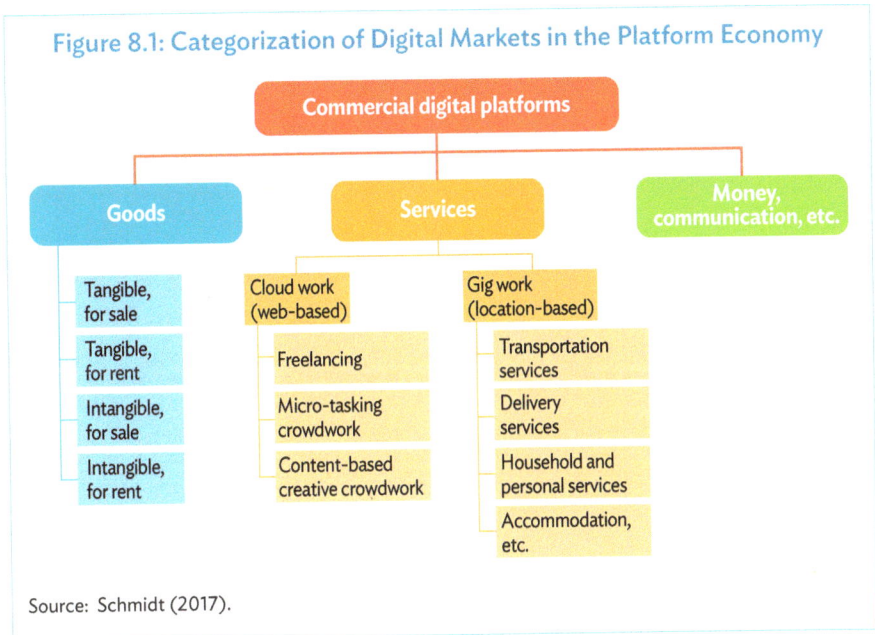

Source: Schmidt (2017).

Cloud work is web-based digital labor subdivided into freelancing, micro-tasking crowdwork, and contest-based creative crowdwork. Typically, workers find work engagements through digital platforms while workers, clients, and platforms are in different countries. In freelancing, a worker is selected based on skills and is engaged in a specific task for a pre-determined payment.[1]

Crowdwork involves several workers. In micro-tasking crowdwork, a group of unspecified crowd workers attend to different tiny repetitive tasks required by a single project.[2] In contest-based creative crowdwork involving several workers performing creative tasks, workers compete for remuneration.[3]

In both types of crowdwork, rejection of work output is possible. Using automated evaluation, an individual's output in a micro-tasking crowdwork can be rejected and thus receives no payment if it is observed to be different from the output of other project members. Similarly, in content-based creative crowdwork, payment is conditional on a worker's output being selected (ADB-ILO forthcoming (a), ADB-ILO forthcoming (b), and Schmidt 2017).

Aside from nonpayment, rejections may reduce chances of obtaining new tasks or lead to deactivation from the platform (Berg et al. 2018).[4] In an International Labour Organization (ILO) survey that covered workers in 75 countries participating in five micro-tasking platforms,[5] almost 9 out of 10 workers have had work rejected or payment refused. In such cases, workers endure longer periods of no income. In 2017, a typical crowdworker earned an average of $3.31 per hour, accounting for both paid and unpaid hours, based on the survey results.

Official data on the total number of crowdworkers are not typically collected in official labor force surveys; nevertheless, estimates based on ad hoc surveys and related efforts try to fill this information gap. In the Philippines, freelancers and crowdworkers are estimated to number around 1.5 million (PayPal 2018), representing 3.4% of the labor force and 7.1% of informal

---

[1] Among platforms, freelancer.com, upwork.com, guru.com, talent.hubstaff.com, getcraft.com, and many others including domestic digital platforms are available in the Philippines and Indonesia (ADB-ILO forthcoming-a and forthcoming-b).

[2] Amazon Mechanical Turk is available in the Philippines and Indonesia (ADB-ILO forthcoming-a and forthcoming-b).

[3] Among platforms, designcrowd.com, crowdspring.com, 99designs.com and others are available in the Philippines and Indonesia (ADB-ILO 2020).

[4] On microworkers, workers with approval rates of less than 75% are disqualified to participate in new tasks for the next 30 days.

[5] AMT, Prolific Academic, Clickworker, CrowdFlower, and Microworkers.

employment (ADB-ILO forthcoming [b]).[6] In an ad hoc effort to gather data on the number of crowd workers by The iLabour Project to produce the Online Labour Index,[7] three Asian countries were found to lead on supplying labor for online gig work (Figure 8.2). This pattern continues over time with fluctuations (Figure 8.3).

Figure 8.2: Top 15 Home Countries of Crowdworkers, June 2021
(% of total number of workers)

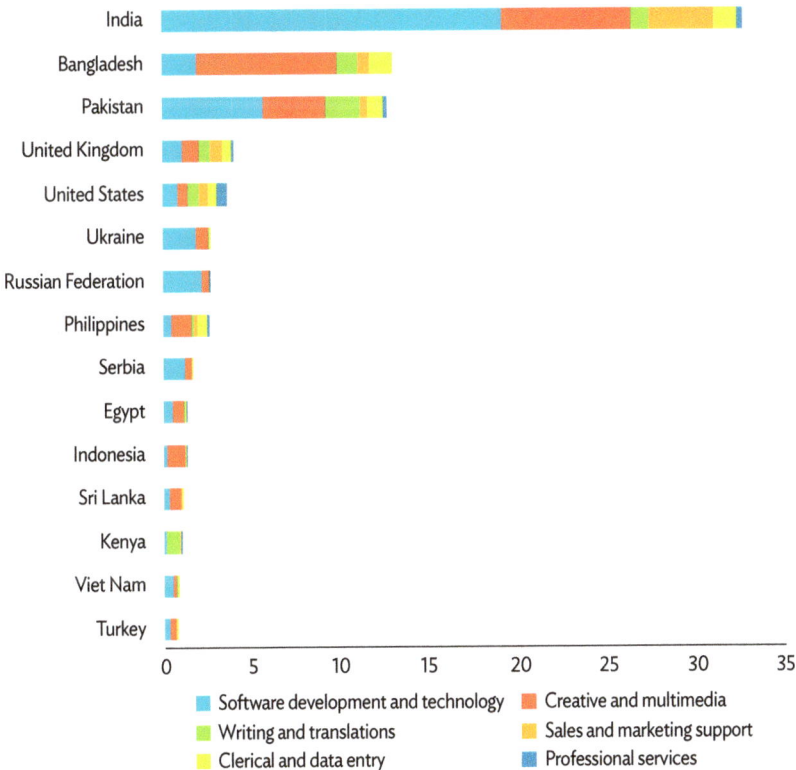

Note: Data is collected periodically (once every 24 hours) by sampling workers from four major online labour platforms: Fiverr, Freelancer, Guru, and PeoplePerHour.
Source: The iLabour Project, Oxford Internet Institute, https://ilabour.oii.ox.ac.uk/online-labour-index/ (accessed July 2021).

---

[6]   Apart from general survey design issues such as representativeness, ad hoc surveys raise additional reliability and comparability issues (Schwellnus et al. 2019) .
[7]   The Online Labour Index measures utilization of online labor platforms over time and across countries and occupations.

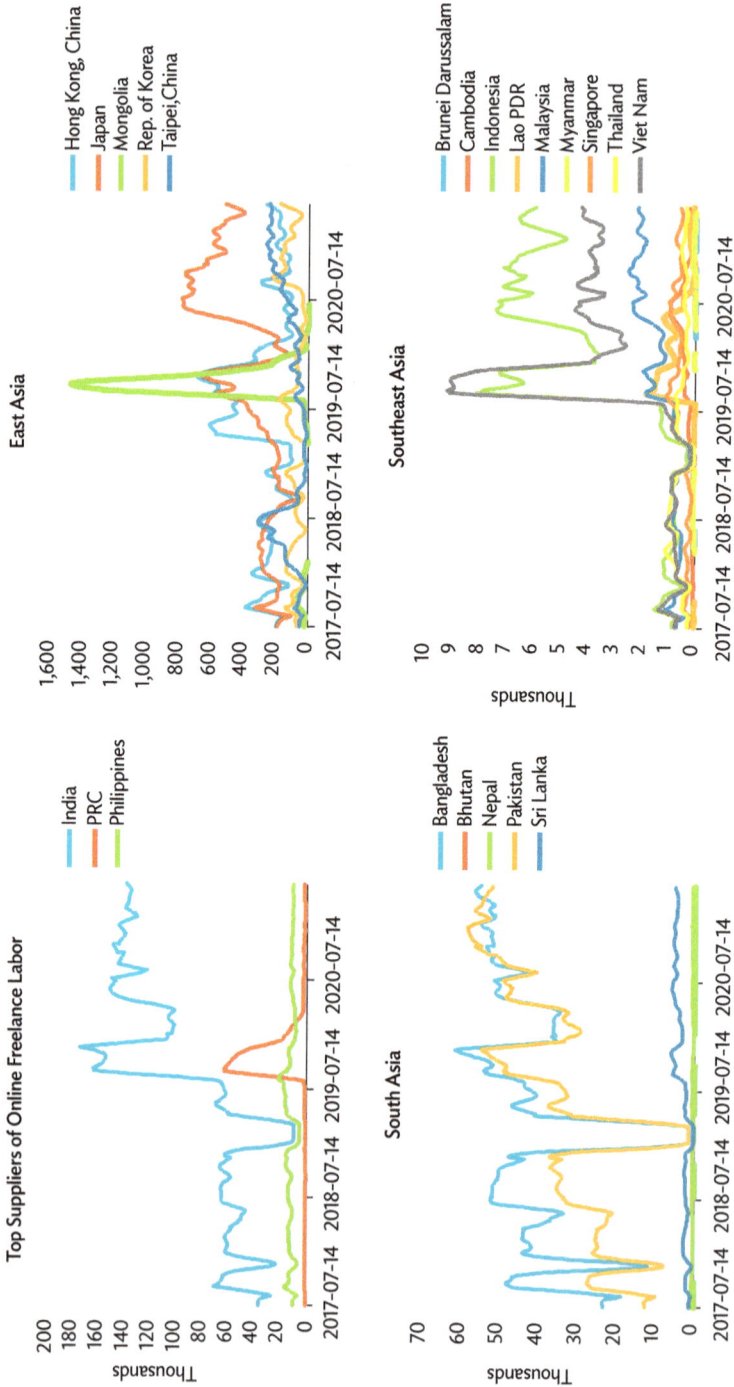

Figure 8.3: Number of Crowdworkers by Economy, July 2017 to June 2021
(28-day moving average of daily number of crowdworkers)

Lao PDR = Lao People's Democratic Republic, PRC = People's Republic of China.
Source: Online Labour Index, Oxford Internet Institute, https://ilabour.oii.ox.ac.uk/online-labour-index/ (accessed July 2021).

Based on the sample, an average of 258 workers in East Asian economies (excluding the PRC), 14,282 workers in South Asian economies (excluding India), and 1,564 workers in Southeast Asian economies (excluding the Philippines), supply online labor and compete for available cloud work projects per day in online platforms (Table 8.1).

Table 8.1: Average Online Labor Supply for Crowdwork per Day, March 2019 to March 2020

Subregion/Country	Average Number of Workers per Day
East Asia (excluding PRC)	258
South Asia (excluding India)	14,282
Southeast Asia (excluding Philippines)	1,564
PRC	20,700
India	103,408
Philippines	13,450

PRC = People's Republic of China.
Source: Author's computation based on data from the Online Labour Index, Oxford Internet Institute, https://ilabour.oii.ox.ac.uk/online-labour-index/ (accessed July 2021).

Persisting Work Informality and Social Protection

The emergence of the platform economy turned some informal jobs and tasks into formal ones, but it has also partly contributed to work informality in Asia and the Pacific. Many digital platform workers who self-enlist in online platforms may be classified as informal workers who often have no or insufficient social security coverage afforded by formal employment arrangements.[8] This highlights the need for inclusive, government-provided social security schemes that are not dependent on employment.

Work informality is high among the self-employed or own-account workers (86.2% of self-employed workers in Asia and the Pacific are informal workers), and more prevalent among youth aged 15–24 as well as those aged 65 and above (both 86.3% of total youth and total elderly employment, respectively) (ILO 2018a). Informal employment, meanwhile, decreases with higher educational level.

---

[8] Only 15 out of 100 driver-partners of Grab benefit from one or more of the company-provided insurance systems (health insurance, life insurance, motor insurance, and prolonged medical leave insurance) (Grab 2019).

Informal workers usually lack coverage from social insurance or contributory schemes due to exclusion from legal coverage, lack of contributory capacity, low and inconsistent earnings, and complicated administrative processes. They also tend to be excluded from social assistance or noncontributory schemes typically targeted to the poor. Hence, the case of the "missing middle" exists (ILO 2017, ILO 2019a, and Ulrichs 2016). Digital platform workers remain vulnerable as fulfillment of contributions is often contingent on having gainful employment. When they do have social protection, it often stems from previous formal employment or from the extension of family members' social protection coverage (ILO 2019a).

Digital platform workers are among those who have faced risk of job loss and employment uncertainty during the COVID-19 pandemic. Indeed, Howson et al. (2021) note that while digital labor platforms are widely promoted to remedy COVID-19-induced unemployment, the pandemic has also exposed platform workers to income loss and infection while being excluded from labor protections. Freelancers and crowdworkers not on location may still conduct remote work online. However, for location-based gig workers, the impacts tend to differ depending on the type of service offered. For example, gig workers involved in household services may have seen a decline in income opportunities given the lockdown measures. Meanwhile, demand increased for transport and delivery gig workers in some countries as most people who self-isolate rely on digital platforms to access goods and services.[9] They have been at the forefront during the pandemic and are among those with relatively high health risks. The impacts of the crisis on digital platform workers have stirred global discussion of health insurance, sick pay, and other work-related benefits; and underscore the need for the extension of social protection (PYMNTS 2020).

Overall, properly functioning social security systems can help address challenges that continue alongside changes in the world of work brought by digitalization. Recently, governments have been adopting a long-term perspective on social protection. In fact, developing Asian economies have explored implementing various social assistance programs such as social support services, noncontributory health insurance, food subsidies, training, fuel and electricity subsidies, unconditional in-kind transfers, school feeding

---

[9] Digital platforms offering delivery services like Grab, Lalamove, Food Panda, etc. supported demand of households during the crisis. Other digital platforms on transport services, like Didi, have disabled this channel and converted to delivery and grocery shopping services (Abacus 2020, Hung 2020, and Sukumaran 2020).

programs, educational fee waiver, and conditional and unconditional cash transfers (IPC-IG and UNICEF 2019). However, limited fiscal space can hinder the extension of social protection; hence, the extension would be subject to the existing social protection priorities.

In this context, some countries in developing Asia have been examining the feasibility of a universal and unconditional cash-based social assistance scheme known as universal basic income.[10] Some have also opted to implement UBI-like social protection measures in the short term to cope with the pandemic.

8.3. Universal Basic Income: An Overview of Advantages and Disadvantages

UBI can be considered a type of social assistance among the whole range of programs with variations in selectivity, conditionality, and the modality of transfer. UBI can provide digital platform workers with a guaranteed income, unlike other social protection programs linked to employment. Despite the lack of employment-associated social protection, UBI can provide these types of workers a cushion during unexpected lifetime shocks. UBI can also offer a quicker way to disburse benefits without the need for means-testing. Further, UBI gives workers the option to quit unsatisfying jobs, given the guaranteed cash income.

The core features of a UBI can be discussed based on three dimensions: *universality, conditionality,* and *modality.*

Universality of UBI guarantees coverage for everyone. However, programs for all elderly people or children are also considered universal. In this context, universality means that eligibility does not involve any other requirement aside from age (Gentilini et al. 2020). From here on, this chapter will refer to UBI for certain age groups as "quasi-UBI." The universality of UBI upholds transparency in the public expenditure system, while preventing benefit fraud and non-reporting on income (Fitzpatrick 1999).

---

[10] In India, a wide range of proposals have emerged following decades of debate and concern over fragmentation (Banerjee 2016, Bardhan 2017, Ghatak 2016, Joshi 2017, and Ray 2016). UBI proposals from politicians were also part of electoral campaigns in 2019. In the PRC, recent studies were conducted to stir debate on UBI in the country and assess compatibility with the PRC's social and economic system (UNDP China 2020a and 2020b, Zheng et al. 2017). A UBI scheme is also currently ongoing in Macau, China.

Second, UBI involves provision of assistance *without conditions*. Imposition of conditionality is used to influence recipients' behaviors, typically toward nutrition, health, and education. Implementation of conditional social assistance requires institutional and administrative capacity and a proper coordination system across the whole government to monitor compliance.[11] In most developing countries where complex government systems often lack coherence, public development programs need a robust design to perform well. In this regard, UBI may prove compatible with the existing institutional and governance scenario in developing countries in Asia.

Finally, UBI is *cash-based*. Compared to in-kind transfers, cash transfers provide flexibility to individuals. It is also easier for governments to move cash to recipients. With digitalization, the use of electronic cash payments also reduces security concerns. In addition, cash transfers do not require procurement, storage, and physical distribution, making the scheme less prone to red tape and corruption and able to promote greater transparency than other types of social security programs (Gentilini et al. 2020).

Trade-offs on whether to choose UBI over other social protection programs include "generosity versus work disincentives, effective coverage of poor households versus leakages to richer individuals, alternative use of available resources versus fiscal cost, and implementation challenges versus objectives" (Francese and Prady 2018). The macroeconomic effects of UBI should also be considered.

The degree of potential trade-offs may differ across countries, depending on their respective fiscal situation, design of existing social security schemes, and government institutional environment. It is therefore crucial to discuss advantages and disadvantages of UBI by assessing compatibility with existing systems, i.e., social security, taxation, government institutions, and prevailing and emerging forms of employment. Nevertheless, a well-designed UBI may offer solutions to existing problems in targeted and in-kind social protection programs.

---

[11] Conditional cash transfers in the Philippines need to be coordinated with regional government offices, local government units, etc.

8.4. Universal Basic Income and Other Social Assistance Programs in Asia

In Asia, the UBI experience is still very limited. In India, some proposals for a UBI have recently emerged (Banerjee 2016; Banerjee, Niehaus, and Suri 2019; Bardhan 2017; Ghatak 2016; Joshi 2017; Ray 2016) with some UBI pilots implemented in selected regions or villages in the country. Proponents of UBI in India argue that it can reduce distribution leakages, empower individuals by utilizing money, and ultimately provide a more efficient way to alleviate poverty compared to existing schemes. However, critics maintain that UBI could lead to work disincentives, demand a huge fiscal space, and dismantle the whole social protection system in the long term (Aiyar 2018, Drèze 2017, and Ghosh 2017). To contribute to the debate, some studies (Cariappa and Srinivas 2019, Khosla 2018, Mookherjee 2018, and Radhakrishna 2017) have compared various proposals and assessed the merits and demerits of a UBI in India.

Some studies on UBI in the PRC were recently completed (UNDP China 2020b, Zheng et al. 2017). A small-scale UBI scheme called Wealth Partaking Scheme in Macau, China has been ongoing, while a UBI-like scheme recently ran in Hong Kong, China (Chong and Jing 2016 and Kwong 2013). However, UBI discussion in other economies in the region remains limited. In this regard, this chapter aims to contribute to the relatively scarce literature on UBI in developing Asian economies.

Mongolia is the only economy that has implemented a full-fledged UBI scheme at the domestic level.[12] Most of the social assistance programs in developing Asia are targeted schemes that incorporate some but not all three elements of UBI (universality, conditionality, and modality). Mongolia's UBI ran briefly, from 2010–2012, which entitled all citizens to a regular cash transfer funded by the dividends of their copper and other mineral resources (Table 8.2).

---

[12] A small-scale UBI scheme has also been ongoing in Macau, China called the Wealth Partaking Scheme, but studies assessing it are scarce.

Table 8.2: Experience and Lessons Learned from Mongolia's Universal Basic Income Program

Program	Universal Basic Income
Start date	2010; ended in 2012
Program typology	Universal basic income
Main objective	To evenly distribute the dividends of the nation's wealth to all citizens including the poor by providing cash assistance
Target area	Nationwide
Target group	All citizens
Coverage	All citizens
Type of benefit	Cash
Amount of benefit	Togrog (MNT) 70,000 in February 2010; MNT10,000 from August to December 2010; MNT21,000 from January 2011 to June 2012
Program expenditure	MNT324 billion (in the first year)

Note: MNT10,000 = $7.3 as of January 2012.
Source: Yeung and Howes (2015).

This was an upgraded and universalized version of the Child Money Program[13]—a cash transfer program that provided benefits to all eligible children and families with newborn children. However, the program was unsustainable, as its funding source, the Human Development Fund, was vulnerable to metal price fluctuations. Eventually, logistical delays and late payments hounded the program as citizens demanded transparent reporting and scheduled transfer distributions (Yeung and Howes 2015).

After the 2012 elections, the UBI program ceased to operate and the Child Money Program was reinstated (Yeung and Howes 2015). Despite the program closure, evidence suggests that Mongolia's UBI reduced poverty by almost a third and curbed inequality by up to 13% in 2011.[14]

The key policy lessons revolve around ensuring the sustainability of a resources-to-cash scheme. Some suggest that resource-to-cash transfers like

---

[13] The Child Money Program commenced in 2006 as copper and gold mining profits raised government revenues.

[14] Most studies on Mongolia's social assistance scheme are focused on the Child Money Program and not on the 2-year UBI scheme (ILO 2016 and Jackson et al. 2011). Earlier analysis by UNICEF estimated the extent to which the conditional Child Money Program (2005–2006) reduced poverty (Budragchaa et al 2007), and the effect of social transfers on children between 2002 and 2010 (Gankhuyag and Banzarch 2014).

Mongolia's should be taxed to guarantee sustainability (Moss 2011). More importantly, there should be a proper *ex ante* assessment to determine the feasible transfer amount.

8.5. Comparing Universal Basic Income to Targeted Social Assistance Schemes

Most of the weaknesses and limitations of social assistance programs in Asia revolve around targeting and coverage, fiscal cost, and institutional coordination, which UBI may help address. Governments typically adopt multiple social protection programs in their countries to make overall social protection systems inclusive, progressive, and adaptive. They also attempt to achieve other, specific goals through separate programs. Intended goals include income-smoothing, risk-pooling, human capital formation, increasing labor income, and redistributing resource dividends (Gentilini et al. 2020). Another reason for multiple programs is to cater services to specific target groups such as the unemployed, youth, elderly, migrants, and women. Overall, the number of programs in each country may not necessarily indicate inefficiency, as long as they complement each other and are well administered.

Nonetheless, individual targeted schemes can be costly to administer as they typically entail means testing and ongoing collection of data on the poor. For instance, means-testing cost $100 million in Indonesia (2015) and $60 million in Pakistan (2009) (Kidd and Wylde 2011). As the poverty status of individuals changes each year, data needs to be consistently collected on the poor and targeting adjusted to ensure the effectiveness of targeted schemes. However, frequent monitoring is not usually practiced in developing countries. This contributes to exclusion and inclusion errors in targeted schemes (Banerjee Niehaus, and Suri 2019).

One could argue that it may be more efficient to consolidate a multitude of schemes into one single social protection program such as UBI. The universality of UBI guarantees inclusiveness, making sure vulnerable sectors are covered. However, it is also inclusiveness that makes the progressivity of UBI uncertain.

For UBI to contribute effectively to poverty reduction, the transfer amount matters. Transfers can be set at different levels, and higher amounts up to the national poverty line can eventually eradicate poverty. Nevertheless, the transfer amount largely depends on fiscal capacity. Indeed, UBI may be costly for some countries. This emphasizes the need to study the fiscal requirements of a UBI as well as its associated fiscal stress on a per-country basis.

UBI also benefits informal workers by providing them with guaranteed income whenever they are unemployed and during periods when they are employed but without social protection. Informal workers often get insured like formal workers, conditional to meeting minimum income and insurance contribution requirements. However, those who often switch jobs do not automatically fall under the framework of social insurance systems (Gentilini et al. 2020). In this regard, firms are incentivized to hire part-time or temporary workers who are provided with less benefits (OECD 2018). Further, social assistance schemes are often targeted at the poor and do not aptly cover informal workers. With UBI, transfers can act as top-up income during periods of employment, which people can use for any life-cycle shocks, including gaps in employment. Recently, Hong Kong, China and Singapore implemented UBI programs, while some Asian economies resorted to UBI-like measures as a policy response to the economic effects of the ongoing COVID-19 pandemic (Gentilini, Almenfi, and Orton 2020; ILO 2020a; IMF 2020).

Apart from considering the societal benefits of a UBI, thorough assessment remains crucial to determine whether UBI would perform better than an economy's portfolio of social protection schemes. In particular, it is crucial to assess the capacity of current social security systems, compare the administrative cost of managing a universal scheme with that of targeting beneficiaries, and estimate the fiscal space for extending or reforming social security schemes.

8.6. Challenges in Administering a Universal Social Protection Scheme

Current social protection systems in most Asian countries do not have sufficient capacity and experience to operate population-wide schemes such as UBI. For instance, social protection coverage in South Asia and Southeast Asia remains lower than in other subregions. Most social protection schemes are targeted noncontributory schemes and do not cover all life contingencies. Countries such as the Philippines, Thailand, and Viet Nam have more comprehensive contributory schemes, however, less than half of the labor force access these (United Nations 2021).

Administrative weaknesses often contribute to the ineffectiveness of existing social protection schemes. These include issues in beneficiary identification, registration, disbursement, and grievance processes. While most proponents argue that UBI removes administrative costs, the supposed administrative savings from shifting to a UBI depend on existing administrative capacity. In most mature welfare states, UBI tends to free-ride on the strong administrative systems already in place (Wispelaere and Stirton 2011). Arguably, the administrative capacity in many developing Asian economies may not yet be robust enough for a UBI-type program. However, broadening digitalization could enhance feasibility in coming years.

In as much as digitalization of the jobs market strengthens the impetus for UBI, digitalization of administrative systems can also help lessen the management cost of social programs, including the cost of leakage. Gaspar and Rhee (2018) purport that digitalization can make governments fairer and more efficient, including in the delivery of social services. At the same time, stronger e-governance is found to be associated with lower incidence of corruption (Ali et al. 2021, Lupu and Lazăr 2015).

In this respect, the increasing premium placed by the region's policy makers on digitalizing their governance systems is valuable. Based on the recent e-government development index data developed by the United Nations (UN), Asia is ahead of the other regions and only trails Europe, although Oceania is catching up (UN 2020).[15] The data further show that Asian economies have been steadily progressing in this area in recent years.

The rollout of national digital ID systems in a number of developing Asian economies is in line with this predisposition (Thales Group 2021, Lago 2019). National ID systems can structure data collection and validation. They can also support government efforts to ensure that social protection is provided to an individual whose employment, income, health, or civil status changes within life course. And with the data at hand, the system gives policy makers flexibility in the design of social protection interventions.

---

[15] The country groupings are based on the definitions of United Nations (2020).

As with other digital systems, however, digitalization of governance opens the public sector to cybersecurity risks. This calls for sustained improvement in the capacity and stability of the base ICT infrastructure to expand access and ensure reliability of service.

Overall, transforming the existing social protection system to one that supports UBI could help address the lack of social protection that stems from the changing nature of work. However, considerable administrative work remains. Continued digitalization of governance is a critical ingredient in expanding government administrative capacity for improving the feasibility of more universal social protection systems over those currently in place.

8.7. Challenges in Financing Social Protection in Developing Asia

The main objective for countries in the region is to close the social protection gap, but this entails fiscal risks and funding requirements. For example, Handayani, Cichon, and Carraro (2018) analyze the fiscal space in 16 developing Asian economies and find encouraging results.[16] If full spending is considered at the stationary state, an average of 3.5% to 8.5% of GDP of involved countries is needed to close the social protection gap from 2015 to 2030 through targeted or quasi-UBI schemes. Based on the share of the lower estimates of fiscal requirement to total government revenues, achieving the social protection agenda of the Sustainable Development Goals (SDGs) would require huge resource mobilization or re-budgeting among public social expenditure items in the countries studied.

If social protection spending in those countries were to progress gradually from 2015 to 2030,[17] the long-term resource requirement may be brought down to an average of 2.1% to 4.9% of GDP. If dynamic revenue development is considered,[18] the countries to expect major fiscal stress from closing the social protection gap through quasi-UBI schemes are Cambodia,

---

[16] Countries include Azerbaijan, Cambodia, the PRC, India, Indonesia, Kazakhstan, the Lao PDR, Malaysia, Mongolia, Myanmar, Nepal, the Philippines, Sri Lanka, Thailand, Timor-Leste, and Viet Nam.

[17] The maturation function assumes a maturation pattern in which 20% of stationary state expenditure is reached in year 7, 40% in year 8, 60% in year 9, 80% in year 10, and gradual and slow increase to 100% maturity from year 10 to 15.

[18] Indeed, governments can raise revenues from increasing tax rates, reallocating energy subsidies, and reallocating natural resources taxes. For example, Nepal, the Philippines, and Thailand could generate considerable revenues from stricter tax enforcement (Handayani, Cichon, and Carraro 2018).

the Lao People's Democratic Republic (Lao PDR), and Timor-Leste. Countries to experience manageable fiscal stress are Azerbaijan, Malaysia, Mongolia, Nepal, and Viet Nam. Finally, countries without any or with low expected fiscal stress are the PRC, India, Indonesia, Kazakhstan, the Philippines, Sri Lanka, and Thailand. Nevertheless, the results from the dynamic analysis are conditional on long-term financial planning, raising resources immediately, and building reserves and reducing financial deficits (Handayani, Cichon, and Carraro 2018).

Compared to a UBI, universal social protection envisioned under the SDGs would give everyone adequate protection against any life-cycle risks, which does not essentially imply that *everyone* receives a regular benefit. Universal social protection can also be attained through a UBI as long as it has universal coverage and comprehensive and adequate protection (ILO 2019b). However, simply adopting a UBI program does not ensure universal social protection.

Cost estimates in Handayani, Cichon, and Carraro (2018) represent the amount of additional resources needed to close the social protection gap through targeted and quasi-UBI schemes. These would extend social protection in line with the SDGs without providing benefits to all. Therefore, it is expected that a UBI would result in higher cost estimates. To illustrate this, Table 8.3 presents an indicative cost of the additional resources needed to achieve UBI.

The total cost estimate of a UBI (excluding administrative costs) that assumes a basic income transfer equivalent to 100% of the national poverty line for all adults and children (Scenario I)[19] is 23.4% of GDP on average in the 16 countries (Ortiz et al. 2018). Rather than dynamic state estimates, Table 8.3 presents the lower and upper estimates at the stationary state. These are more comparable to UBI cost estimates in Ortiz et al. (2018), which did not consider expenditure maturation from 2015 to 2030 as in Handayani, Cichon, and Carraro (2018). Further, both social protection schemes considered in the two studies achieve social protection in line with the SDGs.

Notably, the two studies differ in expenditure calculation such that, unlike Ortiz et al. (2018), estimates in Handayani, Cichon, and Carraro (2018) include administrative costs. To improve comparability, administrative costs must be deducted from the estimates of required additional resources

---

[19] Scenario II assumes a basic income transfer at 100% of the national poverty line for all adults and 50% of the poverty line for children up to 15 years old. This scenario is not presented here, for ease of comparison.

Table 8.3: Comparison of Estimated Additional Resource Requirement to Achieve Social Protection in Sustainable Development Goals and Universal Basic Income
(% of GDP)

Country	Government Expenditure on Social Assistance and Social Insurance, 2015 (ADB 2019)	Total Cost Estimate of Scenario I UBI (Ortiz et al. 2018)	Indicative Cost of Additional Resources to Achieve Poverty Line UBI Based on (Ortiz et al. 2018)	Lower Cost Estimate of Additional Resources to Achieve SDGs Social Protection at Stationary State (Handayani, Cichon, and Carraro 2018)	Upper Cost Estimate of Additional Resources to Achieve SDGs Social Protection at Stationary State (Handayani, Cichon, and Carraro 2018)	Administrative Cost in the Upper Cost Estimate at Stationary State (Handayani, Cichon, and Carraro 2018)	Upper Cost Estimate Less Administrative Costs at Stationary State (Handayani, Cichon, and Carraro 2018)	Total Cost Estimate of Poverty Line UBI (Gentilini et al. 2020)	Indicative Cost of Additional Resources to Achieve Poverty Line UBI based on (Gentilini et al. 2020)
Azerbaijan	7.60	22.60	15.00	2.62	8.77	0.62	8.15	...	...
Cambodia	0.80	33.90	33.10	7.09	14.08	0.69	13.39	...	...
PRC	7.52	22.80	15.30	0.20	1.75	0.14	1.61	...	...
India	...	26.70	...	3.62	8.27	0.55	7.72	22.00	...
Indonesia	2.00	9.40	7.40	3.67	6.97	0.31	6.66	11.00	9.00
Kazakhstan	...	6.70	...	0.95	3.90	0.28	3.62	10.00	...
Lao PDR	0.80	20.10	19.30	6.47	10.25	0.42	9.83	...	...
Malaysia	4.20	37.10	32.90	0.10	6.01	0.54	5.47	...	...
Mongolia	8.80	3.50	5.30	2.45	7.73	0.49	7.24	...	...
Myanmar	0.10	56.70	56.60	7.25	13.63	0.77	12.86	...	...
Nepal	2.60	35.30	32.70	5.05	14.74	1.02	13.72	36.00	33.40
Philippines	2.90	8.50	5.60	5.94	9.59	0.35	9.24	...	...
Sri Lanka	3.20	9.70	6.50	0.62	2.87	0.20	2.67	...	...
Thailand	4.00	10.80	6.80	0.60	5.13	0.45	4.68	...	...
Timor-Leste	...	48.30	...	7.18	14.72	1.16	13.56	...	...
Viet Nam	6.10	21.70	15.60	1.37	7.37	0.60	6.77	...	...

... = not available, PRC = People's Republic of China, Lao PDR = Lao People's Democratic Republic, SDG = Sustainable Development Goal, UBI = universal basic income.
Sources: ADB (2019), Gentilini et al. (2020), Handayani, Cichon, and Carraro (2018), and Ortiz et al. (2018).

at the stationary state in Handayani, Cichon, and Carraro (2018). However, this can be done only with the upper estimates, as this is only where the analysis explicitly distinguishes the additional administrative costs. Further, the two studies consider expenditure on dissimilar sets of social protection categories. In Handayani, Cichon, and Carraro (2018), spending is included on education, services, and health that counts toward extending social protection. Ortiz et al. (2018) accounts only for spending on cash transfers.

In most countries in the list, except for Mongolia and the Philippines, the indicative cost of extra resources needed for a UBI is higher than both the lower and upper cost estimates of additional financing to close the social protection gap through targeted and quasi-UBI schemes. Moreover, unsurprisingly, deducting the administrative costs from the upper cost estimates only widens the gap between the indicative cost of additional resources for a UBI and the upper cost estimate that assumes a quasi-UBI scheme with transfer amount less than 100% of poverty line. This implies that, for these countries (Azerbaijan, Cambodia, the PRC, the Lao PDR, Malaysia, Nepal, Sri Lanka, Thailand, and Viet Nam), closing the social protection gap without providing poverty line-equivalent transfers to all would likely be more fiscally attainable.

The lower and upper cost estimates in Handayani, Cichon, and Carraro (2018) can also be compared to an indicative cost based on the results in Gentilini et al. (2020). For the developing Asian economies covered in Gentilini et al. (2020), the indicative cost of additional resources for a UBI with transfer amounts equal to the poverty line do not differ greatly from the indicative cost based on Ortiz et al. (2018). Consequently, these indicative costs of additional resources for UBI are greater than the cost estimates of closing the social protection gap through quasi-UBI and targeted schemes. However, notably, the data years for the four countries in Gentilini et al. (2020) are not all the same with the data years (2015) in the other two studies.

To conclude, the results of this back-of-the-envelope calculation on the additional resource requirement to implement a UBI are only indicative. However, the main takeaway from this exercise rests on highlighting the need to answer key questions for government decision-making on whether to extend social protection by improving existing schemes through quasi-UBI and well-targeted schemes or by replacing them with a UBI.

Other studies assessed the viability and the impact of UBI (Table 8.4). In particular, two analyses evaluated UBI relative to existing schemes in terms of poverty and inequality reduction, fiscal costs (excluding administrative and other transaction costs), and financing options, based on partial static equilibrium simulation model, where only households are considered and behavioral responses are not incorporated.[20]

Table 8.4: Non-Exhaustive List of Studies on Universal Basic Income

Study	Method	Research focus	Countries
Nikiforos, Steinbaum, and Zezza (2017)	Levy Institute macro-econometric model	Macroeconomic effects (real GDP, price level, nominal wages, government deficit, employment rate, labor force)	United States (US)
University of Pennsylvania (2018) Penn Wharton Budget Model	Dynamic overlapping generations model	Macroeconomic effects	US
Van der Linden (2004)	Dynamic general equilibrium model	Labor supply effects, welfare effects	Not applicable
Fabre, Pallage, and Zimmermann (2014)	Dynamic general equilibrium model	Welfare effects	US
Yunker (2013)	Small-scale computable general equilibrium model	Welfare effects	US
Francese and Prady (2018) and IMF (2017)	Partial static equilibrium model	Distributional effects, fiscal costs	8 countries
Gentilini et al. (2020)	Partial static equilibrium model	Distributional effects, fiscal costs	10 countries including developing Asian economies
OECD (2017)	Partial static equilibrium model	Distributional effects, fiscal costs	4 OECD countries
Ortiz et al. (2018)	Costing model	Fiscal costs	130 countries
Coady and Prady (2018)	Subsidy cost estimation and incidence analysis	Distributional effects	India
Scutella (2004)	Behavioral microsimulation model	Labor supply effects, welfare effects	Australia
Clavet, Duclos, and Lacroix (2013)	Behavioral microsimulation model	Labor supply effects, welfare effects	Canada

continued on next page

---

[20] The simulations are not intended to give evidence on the macroeconomic effects of a UBI. Rather, the studies try to present a logical approach to understand UBI and its feasibility.

Table 8.4 *continued*

Study	Method	Research focus	Countries
Jessen (2017)	Behavioral microsimulation model	Labor supply effects, welfare effects	Germany
Colombino (2015), and Colombino and Narazani (2013)	Behavioral microsimulation model	Labor supply effects, welfare effects	Italy
Islam and Colombino (2018)	Behavioral microsimulation model	Labor supply effects, welfare effects	6 OECD countries
UNDP China (2020a)	Regression analysis (based on UBI survey and game)	Behavioral effects, willingness to receive UBI	PRC
Brown, Ravallion, and van de Walle (2016)	Regression analysis	Comparison of various program targeting methods	9 African countries
Hanna and Olken (2018)	Simulation model	Comparison of various program targeting methods	Indonesia and Peru
Haushofer and Shapiro (2016)	Experimental model	Impacts on economic outcomes and psychological well-being	Kenya
Blattman, Fiala, and Martinez (2012)	Experimental model	Impacts on employment and poverty	Uganda

GDP = gross domestic product, OECD = Organisation for Economic Co-operation and Development, PRC = People's Republic of China.
Source: Authors and Colombino (2019).

In general, UBI designs with greater generosity (i.e., larger transfer size and fiscal allocation) and larger coverage (i.e., covering all individuals) can reduce poverty and inequality better. Intuitively, fiscal cost is proportional to the generosity level and coverage of a UBI. Findings from Gentilini et al. (2020) suggest that the fiscal cost (not considering administration cost) increases with the generosity level of UBI schemes. In general, the fiscal cost of UBI would put more pressure on low-income countries. IMF (2017) estimates also show that the fiscal cost of a UBI is directly proportional to its coverage size. Therefore, determining the feasibility of a UBI depends on finding an effective, adequate, and progressive UBI design that entails reasonable fiscal cost.

However, a maximal social protection scheme like UBI would require additional resources to ensure adequacy and progressivity. Various financing options should be considered before determining the viability of adopting a UBI. Options include reallocating government budget, increasing tax revenues, lobbying for development aid or transfers, curtailing illicit financial flows, utilizing fiscal and foreign reserves, borrowing from multilateral development banks, and adopting a more accommodating macroeconomic policy. Meanwhile, funding a UBI with a proportional increase in income tax would preserve the progressivity of social programs in these countries. Some studies suggest that regardless of a country's income status, financing a UBI to all individuals through a proportional increase in income tax can lead to more desirable and redistributive outcomes. Based on the two studies (Gentilini et al. 2020 and IMF 2017) that considered taxation options, a UBI funded by an increase in direct taxes, such as an income tax, delivers more redistributive outcomes than a UBI supported by indirect taxes or the same level of fiscal envelope as existing schemes.

Key findings on the country cases based on the previously presented analytical framework on assessing viability of UBI can be summarized as follows (Francese and Prady 2018, Gentilini et al. 2020, and IMF 2017):

i.   When social assistance has substantial coverage and slight progressivity, barriers to access, eligibility and coverage, and delivery should be carefully studied and addressed. A UBI may better be motivated by other objectives other than to alleviate poverty.

ii. When social assistance has high coverage but is not progressive, a UBI may be feasible, especially if it is difficult to improve progressivity within the existing programs. However, the UBI should be combined with progressive financing.

iii. When social assistance has low coverage but is progressive, a UBI may extend coverage but also flatten the distribution, especially if budget neutral. Hence, a more generous UBI design is preferable to ensure adequacy of benefits, particularly at the bottom of the income distribution. UBI may also be considered as a complement to existing schemes to expand coverage and preserve progressivity of baseline programs.

iv. When social assistance is inconsistent and flat or regressive, a UBI may be a good option to extend coverage, especially if financed through progressive income taxation, elimination of energy subsidies, or redistribution of extra revenues.

v. When social assistance has low coverage, progressivity, and generosity due to very limited resources, a UBI may extend coverage but would entail huge financial pressure. Other social assistance schemes may be more compatible than a UBI.

8.8. Conclusion and Recommendation

Digitalization has altered business models and created new types of jobs in developing Asia. However, digital platform workers are typically non-standard workers falling outside of formal labor protection systems. These workers typically do not receive benefits from contributory social protection schemes through employment. As social assistance programs in Asia are mostly targeted for the poor, digital platform workers, like other informal workers, tend to be excluded from such schemes. In this context, UBI can deliver by ensuring the extension of social protection to all individuals, including digital platform workers.

UBI is a unique and maximal form of social assistance that involves an unconditional transfer of uniform amounts of cash to all individuals of a given country on a regular basis. Despite criticism, UBI may be able to play a crucial role in alleviating poverty, ensuring extension of social protection to informal workers including digital platform workers, empowering women, stimulating the macro-economy during crises, and redistributing natural wealth dividends. UBI has the potential to eliminate huge administrative costs and inclusion/exclusion errors associated with targeted social assistance schemes. However, it also faces considerable funding requirements and associated fiscal risks, especially in developing and low-income economies.

Initiatives assessing the potential impacts and viability of UBI remain limited in most developing countries in Asia. Future research studies may focus on Macau, China's Wealth Partaking Scheme, ongoing since 2008. However, data availability and access may be potential issues. Kwong (2013) finds that the Wealth Partaking Scheme provided financial relief to residents, especially during the global economic crisis. Future studies may evaluate the scheme in its effects on labor supply, poverty, as well as the overall macro-economy. Potential research may be conducted to assess the feasibility of UBI in other developing countries in Asia.

Future assessments should fill the information gap on the spillover effects and administrative costs of UBI. Haushofer and Shapiro (2016) and Özler (2018) studied spillover effects of the UBI pilot in Kenya on women's empowerment and consumption, but analysis of past and existing UBI schemes remains limited. Similarly, the literature on UBI rarely focuses on estimating administrative costs. In the US, Colombino (2019) estimates that the administrative cost of a UBI falls around 1%–2% of total UBI cost. In 16 countries in Asia, Handayani, Cichon, and Carraro (2018) estimate the administrative cost of a quasi-UBI scheme to be around 0.1%–1.2% of GDP. Although, one could argue that this estimate might be close to the administrative cost of a full UBI scheme, deeper analysis of the cost of administering a UBI could shed light on the argument that UBI requires less resources to administer than targeted social assistance schemes.

References

Abacus. 2020. Drivers for Ride-Hailing Giant Didi Will Now Go Grocery Shopping for You. 11 March. https://www.scmp.com/tech/article/3074709/drivers-ride-hailing-giant-didi-will-now-go-grocery-shopping-you.

Aiyar, S. S. A. 2018. Universal Basic Income: A Doleful, Wasteful Idea. *Indian Journal of Human Development*. https://doi.org/10.1177/0973703017730511.

Ali, M., S. A. Raza, C. H. Puah, and T. Arsalan. 2021. Does E-government Control Corruption? Evidence from South Asian Countries. *Journal of Financial Crime*. https://doi.org/10.1108/JFC-01-2021-0003.

Asian Development Bank (ADB). 2019. *The Social Protection Indicator for Asia: Assessing Progress*. Manila: ADB. http://dx.doi.org/10.22617/TCS190257-2.

ADB-International Labour Organization (ILO). Forthcoming (a). Challenges and Opportunities for the Extension of Social Protection Arising from the New Forms of Employment in Indonesia (preliminary draft).

Banerjee, A. 2016. The Best Way to Welfare. *The Indian Express*. 18 June. https://indianexpress.com/article/opinion/columns/swiss-voted-against-the-idea-of-a-universal-basic-income-but-the-debate-continues-2859528/.

Banerjee, A., P. Niehaus, and T. Suri. 2019. Universal Basic Income in the Developing World. *National Bureau of Economic Research (NBER) Working Paper* No. 25598. Cambridge, MA. https://doi.org/10.3386/w25598.

Bardhan, P. 2017. Universal Basic Income – Its Special Case for India. *Indian Journal of Human Development*. 11 (2). pp. 141–143. https://doi.org/10.1177/0973703017734719.

Berg, J., M. Furrer, E. Harmon, U. Rani, and M. S. Silberman. 2018. Digital Labour Platforms and the Future of Work: Towards Decent Work in the Online World. ILO report. http://www.ilo.org/global/publications/books/WCMS_645337/lang--en/index.htm.

Blattman, C., N. Fiala, and S. Martinez. 2012. Employment Generation in Rural Africa: Mid-Term Results from an Experimental Evaluation of the Youth Opportunities Program in Northern Uganda. *DIW Berlin Discussion Paper.* https://doi.org/10.2139/ssrn.2030866.

Brown, C., M. Ravallion, and D. van de Walle. 2016. A Poor Means Test? Econometric Targeting in Africa. NBER Working Paper No. 22919. Cambridge, MA. https://doi.org/10.3386/w22919.

Campbell, D. Forthcoming. Work and Social Protection in the Fourth Industrial Revolution. *ADB Sustainable Development Working Paper Series* (preliminary draft). Tokyo.

Cariappa, A. G. A. and A. Srinivas. 2019. Universal Basic Income for India: The Way Towards Right to Equality-A Review. *Indian Journal of Economics and Development.* 15 (1). pp. 142–149. https://doi.org/10.5958/2322-0430.2019.00016.7.

Chong, T. and H. Jing. 2016. An Analysis of the Issues and Potential Alternatives to Macau's 'Wealth Partaking Scheme' (in Chinese). *IGEF Working Paper* No. 43. https://doi.org/10.2139/ssrn.2748393.

Clavet, N. J., J. Y. Duclos, and G. Lacroix. 2013. Fighting Poverty: Assessing the Effect of Guaranteed Minimum Income Proposals in Québec. *Institute of Labor Economics (IZA) Discussion Papers* No. 7283. https://ideas.repec.org/p/iza/izadps/dp7283.html.

Coady, D. and D. Prady. 2018. Universal Basic Income in Developing Countries: Issues, Options, and Illustration for India. *International Monetary Fund Working Papers.* Washington, DC: IMF. https://www.imf.org/en/Publications/WP/Issues/2018/07/31/Universal-Basic-Income-in-Developing-Countries-Issues-Options-and-Illustration-for-India-46079.

Colombino, U. 2015. Five Crossroads on the Way to Basic Income. An Italian Tour. *Italian Economic Journal.* 1 (3). pp. 353–389. https://doi.org/10.1007/s40797-015-0018-3.

Colombino, U. 2019. Is Unconditional Basic Income a Viable Alternative to Other Social Welfare Measures? IZA World of Labor. https://doi.org/10.15185/izawol.128.

Colombino, U., M. Locatelli, E. Narazani, C. O'Donoghue, and I. Shima. 2008. Behavioural and Welfare Effects of Basic Income Policies: A Simulation for European Countries. *EUROMOD Working Papers* EM5/08; Institute for Social and Economic Research. https://ideas.repec.org/p/ese/emodwp/em5-08.html.

Colombino, U. and E. Narazani. 2013. Designing a Universal Income Support Mechanism for Italy: An Exploratory Tour. *Basic Income Studies.* 8 (1). pp. 1–17. https://doi.org/10.1515/bis-2012-0010.

Drèze, J. 2017. Decoding Universal Basic Income. *Indian Journal of Human Development.* 11 (2). pp. 163–166. https://doi.org/10.1177/0973703017733876.

Fabre, A., S. Pallage, and C. Zimmermann. 2014. Universal Basic Income versus Unemployment Insurance. Federal Reserve Bank of St. Louis, working paper. https://doi.org/10.20955/wp.2014.047.

Fitzpatrick, T. 1999. *Freedom and Security: An Introduction to the Basic Income Debate.* In J. Campling, ed. London: Palgrave Macmillan. https://doi.org/10.1057/9780333983287.

Francese, M. and D. Prady. 2018. Universal Basic Income: Debate and Impact Assessment. *IMF Working Papers.* Washington, DC. https://www.imf.org/en/Publications/WP/Issues/2018/12/10/Universal-Basic-Income-Debate-and-Impact-Assessment-46441.

Gaspar, V. and C.Y. Rhee. 2018. The Digital Accelerator: Revving Up Government in Asia. *IMF Blog.* 26 September. Washington, DC. https://blogs.imf.org/2018/09/26/the-digital-accelerator-revving-up-government-in-asia/.

Gentilini, U., M. Almenfi, and I. Orton. 2020. Social Protection and Jobs Responses to COVID-19: A Real-Time Review of Country Measures. Paper, version 2. http://www.ugogentilini.net/wp-content/uploads/2020/03/Social-protection-responses-to-COVID19_March27.pdf.

Gentilini, U., M. E. Grosh, I. P. Rigolini, and R. G. Yemtsov. 2020. *Exploring Universal Basic Income: A Guide to Navigating Concepts, Evidence, and Practices.* Washington, DC: World Bank. http://documents.worldbank.org/curated/en/993911574784667955/Exploring-Universal-Basic-Income-A-Guide-to-Navigating-Concepts-Evidence-and-Practices.

Ghatak, M. 2016. The Price of Basic Income. *The Indian Express*. 1 July. https://indianexpress.com/article/opinion/columns/basic-income-in-india-brexit-referendum-switzerland-basic-income-jan-dhan-yojana-guarantee-employment-programme-mgnrega-2879930/.

Ghosh, J. 2017. A Universal Basic Income in India? *International Development Economics Associates*. 3 February. https://www.networkideas.org/themes/economy-and-society/2017/02/a-universal-basic-income-in-india/ https://scholarworks.alaska.edu/handle/11122/4170.

Grab. 2019. Social Impact Report 2018/2019.

Handayani, S. W., M. Cichon, and L. Carraro. 2018. *Asia's Fiscal Challenge: Financing the Social Protection Agenda of the Sustainable Development Goals*. Manila: ADB. http://dx.doi.org/10.22617/TCS178935-2.

Hanna, R. and B. A. Olken. 2018. Universal Basic Incomes versus Targeted Transfers: Anti-Poverty Programs in Developing Countries. *Journal of Economic Perspectives*. 32 (4). pp. 201–226. https://doi.org/10.1257/jep.32.4.201.

Haushofer, J. and J. Shapiro. 2016. The Short-Term Impact of Unconditional Cash Transfers to the Poor: Experimental Evidence from Kenya. *The Quarterly Journal of Economics*. 131 (4). pp. 1973–2042. https://doi.org/10.1093/qje/qjw025.

Howson, K., F. Ustek Spilda, A. Bertolini, R. Heeks, F. Ferrari, S. Katta, M. Cole, P. Aguera Renese, N. Salem, D. Sutcliffe, S. Steward, and M. Graham 2021. Stripping Back the Mask: Working Conditions on Digital Labour Platforms during the COVID-19 Pandemic. *International Labour Review*. Article. 1 July. https://doi.org/10.1111/ilr.12222.

Hung, J. 2020. Delivery People Are Risking Their Lives to Keep Asia Running. Here's What People Are Doing to Say Thank You. *The Diplomat*. 1 April. https://thediplomat.com/2020/04/delivery-people-are-risking-their-lives-to-keep-asia-running-heres-what-people-are-doing-to-say-thank-you/.

International Labour Organization (ILO). 2016. The Universal Child Money Programme in Mongolia. Fact sheet. Geneva. http://www.ilo.org/beijing/what-we-do/publications/WCMS_534930/lang--en/index.htm.

_____. 2017. World Social Protection Report 2017–19: Universal Social Protection to Achieve the Sustainable Development Goals. Report. Geneva. http://www.ilo.org/global/publications/books/WCMS_604882/lang--en/index.htm.

_____. 2018a. *Women and Men in the Informal Economy: A Statistical Picture. Third Edition.* Geneva: http://www.ilo.org/global/publications/books/WCMS_626831/lang--en/index.htm.

_____. 2018b. Asia-Pacific Employment and Social Outlook 2018. International Labour Organization, Geneva. https://www.ilo.org/asia/publications/apeso/lang--en/index.htm.

_____. 2019a. Extending Social Security to Workers in the Informal Economy: Lessons from International Experience. Guidebook. Geneva. https://socialprotection.org/discover/publications/extending-social-security-workers-informal-economy-lessons-international.

_____. 2019b. Universal Social Protection: Key Concepts and International Framework Social Protection for All Issue Brief. April. Geneva. https://www.social-protection.org/gimi/RessourcePDF.action?id=55517.

_____. 2020a. Social Protection Responses to the COVID-19 Crisis: Country Responses in Asia and the Pacific. Spotlight Brief. Geneva. https://www.ilo.org/wcmsp5/groups/public/---asia/---ro-bangkok/documents/briefingnote/wcms_739587.pdf.

_____. 2020b. ILO Monitor: COVID-19 and the World of Work. Second Edition: Updated Estimates and Analysis. International Labour Organization, Geneva. https://www.ilo.org/wcmsp5/groups/public/---dgreports/---dcomm/documents/briefingnote/wcms_740877.pdf.

International Monetary Fund (IMF). 2017. *IMF Fiscal Monitor: Tackling Inequality.* October. IMF, Washington, DC. https://www.imf.org/en/Publications/FM/Issues/2017/10/05/fiscal-monitor-october-2017.

_____. 2020. Policy Responses to COVID-19. IMF Policy Tracker. Washington, DC. https://www.imf.org/en/Topics/imf-and-covid19/Policy-Responses-to-COVID-19.

International Policy Centre for Inclusive Growth and United Nations Children's Fund (IPC-IG and UNICEF). 2019. *Social Protection in Asia and the Pacific: Inventory of Non-Contributory Programmes*. New York. https://socialprotection.org/discover/publications/social-protection-asia-and-pacific-inventory-non-contributory-programmes.

Islam, N. and U. Colombino. 2018. The Case for NIT+FT in Europe. An Empirical Optimal Taxation Exercise. *Economic Modelling*. 75 (C). pp. 38–69. https://doi.org/10.1016/j.econmod.2018.06.004.

Jackson, C., S. Butters, E. Byambaa, M. Davies, and N. Perkins. 2011. Lessons from Social Protection Programme Implementation in Kenya, Zambia and Mongolia. *IDS Research Reports*. 69: pp. 1–39. https://doi.org/10.1111/j.2040-0217.2011.00069_2.x.

Jessen, R. 2017. Getting the Poor to Work: Three Welfare-Increasing Reforms for a Busy Germany. *FinanzArchiv*. 73 (1). pp. 1–41. https://doi.org/10.1628/001522117X14864674910065.

Joshi, V. 2017. Universal Basic Income Supplement for India: A Proposal. *Indian Journal of Human Development*. 11 (2). pp. 144–149. https://doi.org/10.1177/0973703017730513.

Khosla, S. 2018. *India's Universal Basic Income: Bedeviled by the Details*. Carnegie India. https://carnegieindia.org/2018/02/14/india-s-universal-basic-income-bedeviled-by-details-pub-75500.

Kidd, S. and E. Wylde. 2011. *Targeting the Poorest: An Assessment of the Proxy Means Test Methodology*. Canberra: Australian Agency for International Development.

Kwong, B. K. K. 2013. A Comparative Analysis of the Cash Handout Policy of Hong Kong and Macau. *Journal of Current Chinese Affairs*. 42 (3). pp. 87–100.

Lago, C. 2019. Which Countries are Implementing Digital IDs in SE Asia? *CIO*. 4 January. https://www.cio.com/article/3331296/which-countries-are-implementing-digital-ids-in-se-asia.html.

Lupu, D. and G. Lazăr. 2015. Influence of E-Government on the Level of Corruption in Some EU and Non-EU States. *Procedia Economics and Finance.* 20 (1). pp. 365–371. https://doi.org/10.1016/S2212-5671(15)00085-4.

Mookherjee, D. 2018. Towards a Comprehensive Social Security System: An Assessment of Recent UBI Proposals. *Indian Journal of Human Development.* 11 (2). 173–176. https://doi.org/10.1177/0973703017733880.

Moss, T. 2011. Oil to Cash: Fighting the Resource Curse through Cash Transfers. *Working Papers* 3489. https://ideas.repec.org/p/ess/wpaper/id3489.html.

Nikiforos, M., M. Steinbaum, and G. Zezza. 2017. Modeling the Macroeconomic Effects of a Universal Basic Income. Roosevelt Institute. https://rooseveltinstitute.org/modeling-macroeconomic-effects-ubi/.

Organisation for Economic Co-operation and Development (OECD). 2017. Basic Income as a Policy Option: Technical Background Note Illustrating Costs and Distributional Implications for Selected Countries. Social Protection and Human Rights. Paris. https://socialprotection-humanrights.org/resource/basic-income-policy-option-technical-background-note-illustrating-costs-distributional-implications-selected-countries/.

———. 2018. *The Future of Social Protection: What Works for Non-standard Workers?* Paris: OECD Publishing. https://www.oecd-ilibrary.org/social-issues-migration-health/the-future-of-social-protection_9789264306943-en.

———. 2019. Public Social Spending Is High in Many OECD Countries. Social Expenditure Update 2019. Paris. https://www.oecd.org/social/soc/OECD2019-Social-Expenditure-Update.pdf.

Ortiz, I., C. Behrendt, A. Acuña-Ulate, and N. Q. Anh. 2018. Universal Basic Income Proposals in Light of ILO Standards: Key Issues and Global Costing. *SSRN Electronic Journal.* https://doi.org/10.2139/ssrn.3208737.

Ortiz, I., M. Cummins, and K. Karunanethy. 2015. Fiscal Space for Social Protection and the SDGs Options to Expand Social Investments in 187 Countries. *ILO Working Papers* No. 994877663402676. Geneva. https://ideas.repec.org/p/ilo/ilowps/994877663402676.html.

Özler, B. (2018, March 30). *GiveDirectly Three-Year Impacts, Explained*. World Bank Blogs.

PayPal. 2018. PayPal Global Freelancer Survey. https://www.paypal.com/stories/sea/paypal-global-freelancer-survey.

PYMNTS. 2020. Gig Economy Tracker. https://www.pymnts.com/tracker/gig-economy-tracker-april-2020/.

Radhakrishna, R. 2017. Is India Ready to Implement Universal Basic Income Scheme? *Indian Journal of Human Development*. 11 (2). pp. 200–202. https://doi.org/10.1177/0973703017738666.

Ray, D. 2016. The Universal Basic Share. Ideas For India. 29 September. http://www.ideasforindia.in/topics/poverty-inequality/the-universal-basic-share.html.

Schmidt, F. A. 2017. Digital Labour Markets in the Platform Economy. p. 32. Friedrich-Ebert-Stiftung.

Schwellnus, C., A. Geva, M. Pak, and R. Veiel. 2019. Gig Economy Platforms: Boon or Bane? *OECD Economics Department Working Papers*. Paris. https://doi.org/10.1787/fdb0570b-en.

Scutella, R. 2004. Moves to a Basic Income-Flat Tax System in Australia: Implications for the Distribution Of Income and Supply of Labour. Melbourne Institute of Applied Economic and Social Research. http://minerva-access.unimelb.edu.au/handle/11343/33799.

Sukumaran, T. 2020. Food Delivery Workers Keep Malaysia Connected amid Virus Lockdown. 31 March. https://www.scmp.com/week-asia/health-environment/article/3077719/coronavirus-delivery-workers-keep-malaysia-connected.

Thales Group. 2021. National ID Cards: 2016-2021 Facts and Trends. Updated 6 June 2021. https://www.thalesgroup.com/en/markets/digital-identity-and-security/government/identity/2016-national-id-card-trends.

Ulrichs, M. 2016. Informality, Women and Social Protection: Identifying Barriers to Provide Effective Coverage. *Overseas Development Institute Working Paper* No. 435: p. 55.

United Nations (UN). 2020. *E-Government Survey 2020 Digital Government in the Decade of Action for Sustainable Development.* New York: UN. https://publicadministration.un.org/egovkb/Portals/egovkb/Documents/un/2020-Survey/2020%20UN%20E-Government%20Survey%20(Full%20Report).pdf.

United Nations Development Programme (UNDP) China. 2020a. *Universal Basic Income in China.* UNDP. https://www.cn.undp.org/content/china/en/home/library/innovation-/universal-basic-income-in-china.html.

UNDP China. 2020b. Issue Brief—Universal Basic Income – Findings from China and Implications for Responses in COVID-19. https://www.cn.undp.org/content/china/en/home/library/innovation-/issue-brief---universal-basic-income--findings-from-china---impl.html.

_____. 2021. Social Outlook for Asia and the Pacific: The Protection We Want. Bangkok.

University of Pennsylvania. 2018. Options for Universal Basic Income: Dynamic Modeling. Penn Wharton Budget Model. https://budgetmodel.wharton.upenn.edu/issues/2018/3/29/options-for-universal-basic-income-dynamic-modeling.

Van der Linden, B. 2004. Active Citizen's Income, Unconditional Income and Participation under Imperfect Competition: A Welfare Analysis. *Oxford Economic Papers.* 56 (1). pp. 98–117. https://doi.org/10.1093/oep/56.1.98.

Wispelaere, J. and L. Stirton. 2011. The Administrative Efficiency of Basic Income. *Policy and Politics.* 39: pp. 115–132. https://doi.org/10.1332/030557311X546352.

Yeung, Y. and S. Howes. 2015. Resources-to-Cash: A Cautionary Tale from Mongolia. International Mining for Development Centre Action Research Report.

Yunker, J. A. 2013. The Basic Income Guarantee: A General Equilibrium Evaluation. *Basic Income Studies*. 8 (2). pp. 203–233. https://doi.org/10.1515/bis-2013-0014.

Zheng, Y., M. Guerriero, E. Lopez, and P. Haverman 2017. Universal Basic Income: A Policy Option for China beyond 2020? Working Paper. UNDP China Office.

Digital Platforms and International Taxation in Asia

Rolando Avendano and Peter Rosenkranz

9.1. Introduction

The rise of the digital economy has fundamentally transformed how many companies conduct their operations, multinational corporations in particular.[1] The heavy reliance on data and information and communication technologies, increasingly mobile business processes, and the central role of digital intermediation platforms has underscored the importance of digitally intensive companies to Asian economies. By providing the infrastructure for digital adoption, technological multinational corporations have outgrown their counterparts in other sectors, gained dominance in their own segments, and become hubs for other sectors in the digital economy.

While gaining dominance, technological multinational corporations have also exacerbated the risks to national tax systems. Technological multinational corporations have enjoyed exceptional growth thanks to their reliance on intangibles, such as know-how and intellectual property, strong liquidity, and spending capacity. They can operate in multiple countries without need for physical presence and are more prone to market concentration. Given their business models and financial profiles, technological multinational corporations may also have more incentives to artificially lower taxable income and exploit corporate tax structures to avoid paying their share of income tax.

---

[1] This chapter was prepared as a background paper for ADB (2021). The authors are grateful to Cyn-Young Park, Go Nagata, Aurore Arcambal, Satoru Yamadera, Bruno da Silva, and Ryan Jacildo for helpful comments and suggestions, and thank Monica Melchor for her excellent research assistance. This study was presented at the virtual ADB-ADBI Conference on Digital Platforms in June 2020. The authors are also thankful to the participants of the seminar for their comments and suggestions.

International efforts to respond to this scenario reflect the need to adapt corporate income tax rules and ensure economic activity and value creation. The Organisation for Economic Co-operation and Development (OECD)/G20 Inclusive Framework on Base Erosion Profit Shifting (BEPS) provided a platform for governments to develop standards and instruments to reduce tax avoidance. Other efforts have since been undertaken to improve the coherence of international tax rules. In October 2021, 136 jurisdictions reached a historical agreement on global tax reform on large multinationals. The agreement ensures that multinationals, regardless of their sector, pay 15% in tax in the countries where they operate. Together with achieving minimum taxation on income, the agreement will considerably reduce the incentives of multinational corporations to shift profits to low-tax jurisdictions and strengthen the transparency and predictability for tax administrations and companies.

Regional and international cooperation will be needed to modernize the international tax framework. As a multilateral solution for an agreement on tax rules is reached, international cooperation will be essential for designing and implementing the reforms in domestic and international tax frameworks. Areas for cooperation include knowledge sharing on tax policy and domestic resource mobilization, improving exchange of information for tax purposes, technical assistance for modernizing tax administrations, and collaboration in the implementation of a global minimum tax solution.

9.2. Trends and Challenges of Digitalization in Taxation and International Tax Cooperation and Impact of COVID-19

The consolidation of digital platforms in Asia has accelerated in recent years. Digital platforms are transforming economic structures and disrupting markets. Regional companies like Alibaba, Tencent, and rapidly expanding examples such as Gojek have successfully created businesses and reinvented market arrangements, creating new business models that generate and capture value. Together with digital platforms, there is a spectrum of intermediary structures within the scope of firms operating in the digital economy, with various implications for the formulation of tax policy.

The digital economy presents challenges for the design of international tax systems, given the lower significance of physical presence and uncertainty about adequately accounting for business income. The evolving nature of business processes in the current economic climate has rendered many international tax rules outdated. The digital economy poses three major challenges. First, technological progress and the expanded scope for businesses to operate in an area without a physical presence prompts questions about whether rules centered on physical presence (nexus rules) remain appropriate. Concretely, tax offices in the region do not always have the tools nor the guidelines for revising regulations on permanent establishment status.[2] Second, the extensive use of data and the ability of companies to monetize this raises questions about whether data and the value they generate are appropriately captured for tax purposes. Third, advances in digital products and service delivery have made it more difficult to properly characterize income under newer business models.

As Asian economies rely more on digital products and services, this will bring challenges and opportunities for national tax systems. Most economic sectors are shifting toward a business model dominated by digital functions and capabilities (the "digital asymptote"), underscoring issues for determining economic and physical presence, intangibles, and user-generated value (Aslam and Shah 2020). While a larger share of the digital economy poses numerous challenges, as mentioned above, it can also result in greater traceability and thus more efficient tax systems.

The COVID-19 pandemic has fueled the rise of the digital economy, facilitating widespread adoption and utilization of digital technologies while introducing changes to the corporate landscape. Survey data suggest consumers expect the elevated engagement with digital processes to persist beyond the pandemic. In the People's Republic of China (PRC), over half of respondents have indicated that they will continue to shop more online than before the pandemic (Figure 9.1). Digital payment transactions have also increased sharply in Asia since the COVID-19 outbreak, while tech giants such as Amazon have increased hiring to cope with higher demand. As some

---

2   A permanent establishment broadly denotes the place in a country at or through which a firm carries out its business activities. The concept of a permanent establishment is important when considering the extent to which profits of a firm based on a jurisdiction can be taxed in another jurisdiction. Tax treaties generally provide that the business profits of a foreign enterprise are taxable in a state only to the extent that the foreign enterprise has in that state a permanent establishment to which the profits are attributable. The definition of permanent establishment is therefore crucial in determining whether a nonresident enterprise must pay income tax in another state (OECD 2018).

Figure 9.1: Trends in E-Commerce Consumer Behavior Post-COVID-19, 2020

Percentage who say they expect to shop online more frequently after the outbreak is over

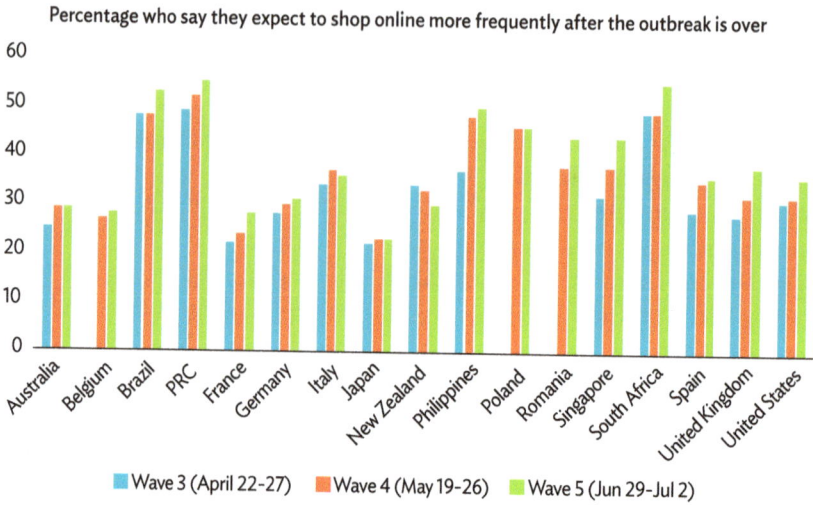

■ Wave 3 (April 22-27)   ■ Wave 4 (May 19-26)   ■ Wave 5 (Jun 29-Jul 2)

PRC = People's Republic of China.
Source: Global Web Index (2020). *Coronavirus Research: July 2020, Multi-Market Research Wave 5.*
https://www.globalwebindex.com/.

platforms have consolidated their positions during the pandemic, such as Alibaba, they are facing competition from emerging players, such as start-up Pinduoduo. The pandemic could have long-lasting impact on the corporate landscape. On the other hand, the crisis could increase firm concentration, with multinationals becoming even more dominant. The pandemic has also raised questions about the applicability of existing tax regimes, such as cross-border components of taxing rights under tax treaty rules and rising tax exemptions due to disruptions to firms' daily operations and constraints related to workforce availability.

Empirical assessments of the effect of base erosion practices suggest a negative impact on tax revenues—a dynamic which growing digitalization may have underscored. Jansky and Palansky (2019) find that annual tax revenue losses triggered by profit-shifting activities amount to $125 billion.[3]

---

[3] This estimate of $125 billion in corporate revenue losses aligns with the lower bound of similar studies by Tørsløv Wier, and Zucman (2018); Cobham and Jansky (2018, 2019); and Clausing (2016).

In their analysis of foreign direct investment (FDI) data of 79 countries, they find that low-income and lower middle-income economies experience the greatest losses in corporate tax revenue, both as a proportion of gross domestic product (GDP) and of total tax revenue. Johansson et al. (2017) estimate $100–$240 billion in annual revenue losses (or 4% to 10% of global corporate tax revenues). Further, Bradbury, Hanappi, and Moore (2018) find a wide range of losses—from $80 billion to $647 billion annually—in their meta-analysis examining efforts to estimate the fiscal impact of FDI-related BEPS. Overall, these exercises suggest that the losses in tax revenue triggered by profit-shifting activities are sizable, with the potential to escalate in line with growing economic digitalization triggered by the pandemic. On the other hand, the OECD two-pillar plan for the reform of international taxation[4] is projected to have a potential annual global net revenue gain of up to $100 billion, or 4% of global income tax revenues, according to initial forecasts.[5] While effects stemming from Pillar 1 would primarily relate to a reallocation of taxable profits, the impact of Pillar 2 through its proposed global minimum tax would translate to an increase in corporate income tax revenues (OECD 2020a).

Policy makers in the region need to consider how enhanced international taxation can help mobilize domestic tax revenues and address development gaps. With big variation between countries, domestic tax collection in developing Asia remains low relative to the OECD average (Figure 9.2). In 21 Asian economies for which comparable data is available, tax revenues as a share of GDP were lower than the OECD average in 2019 (OECD 2021). Value-added taxes still account for a large share of tax revenues, while statutory corporate income tax rates diverge across countries. The uneven composition highlights the different tax revenue profiles and implications relative to the digital economy. These figures are also a reminder of the importance of broadening the tax base and enhancing tax compliance. Strengthening international tax cooperation to increase domestic tax revenues should be important, both in view of a swift recovery from the pandemic and to meet the long-term objective of achieving the Sustainable Development Goals in Asia and the Pacific.

---

[4] These two complementary pillars consist of Pillar 1 considering the reallocation of taxation rights and Pillar 2 on a global anti-base erosion mechanism. The first seeks to modify the allocation of taxing rights through comprehensive and concurrent review of profit allocation and nexus rules. The second is concerned with remaining BEPS issues and minimum taxation.

[5] In addition to accounting for the effects of these reforms, this estimate considers the United States' Global Intangible Low-Taxed Income regime. After excluding this regime, the estimated potential annual net revenue gain would amount to $80 billion, or 3.2% of global corporate income tax revenues (OECD 2020d).

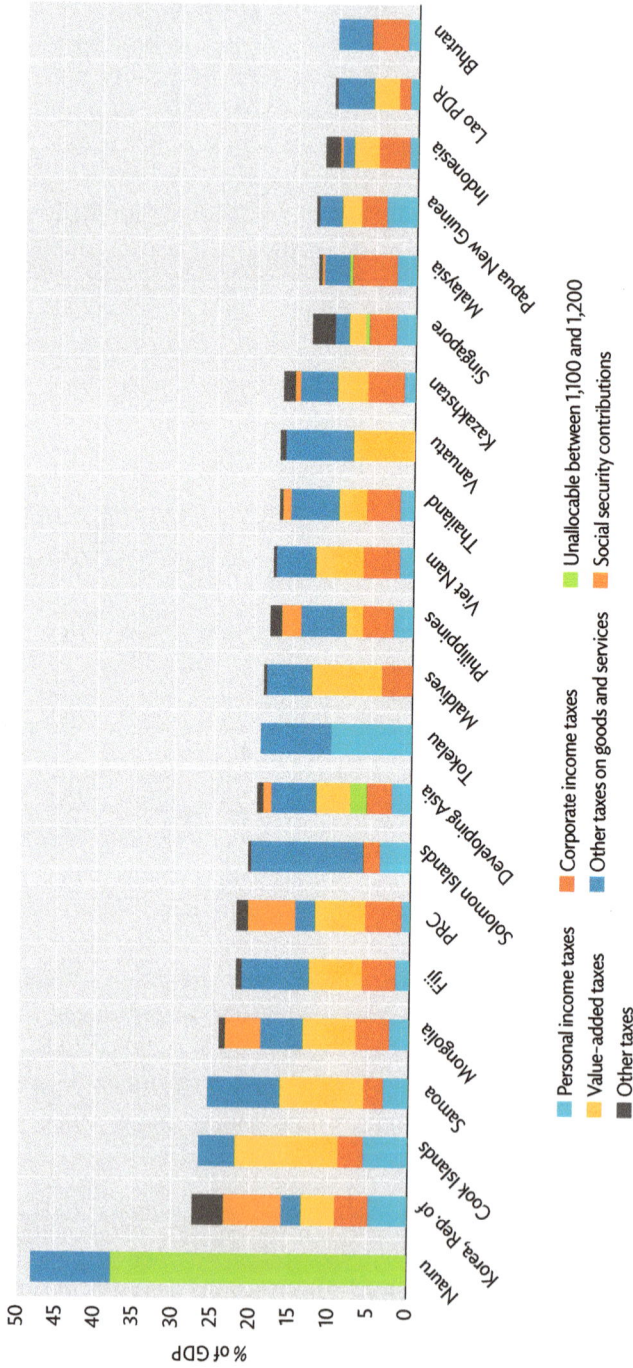

Figure 9.2: Tax-to-GDP Ratios in Developing Asian Economies, 2019

GDP = gross domestic product, PRC = People's Republic of China, Lao PDR = Lao People's Democratic Republic.
Note: The averages for Organisation for Economic Co-operation and Development (OECD) (37 countries) are unweighted. Data for Australia, Japan, the Republic of Korea, New Zealand, and the OECD average are taken from Revenue Statistics 2020 (OECD 2020b). 2018 data are used for Australia, Japan, and the OECD average.
Source: OECD (2021), Revenue Statistics – Asian and Pacific Economies: Comparative tables, OECD Tax Statistics database (accessed September 2021).

9.3. Progress in Regional and Global Initiatives to Address the Tax Challenges of the Digital Economy

Progress is considerable in the Inclusive Framework on BEPS to tackle tax and digitalization issues in recent years.[6] While efforts to reach a multilateral solution to the tax challenges of the digital economy, participation from Asia and the Pacific economies can improve. As of October 2021, 20 Asian Development Bank (ADB) developing member countries (DMCs) had joined the BEPS Inclusive Framework (Figure 9.3). The Inclusive Framework has a commitment from all members to work on (i) nexus and (ii) profit allocation rules that would consider the impacts of digitalization, relating to the principle of aligning profits with economic activities and value creation (OECD 2019a).

Figure 9.3: Regional Composition of the OECD/G20 Inclusive Framework on BEPS

a. By Region (%)

- Western Europe, 22.0
- Africa, 18.0
- Asia-Pacific, 15.0
- Americas, 26.0
- Eastern Europe – Central Asia, 19.0

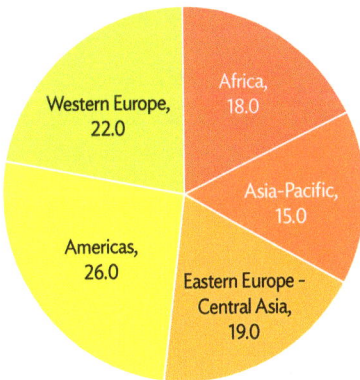

b. By ADB Membership

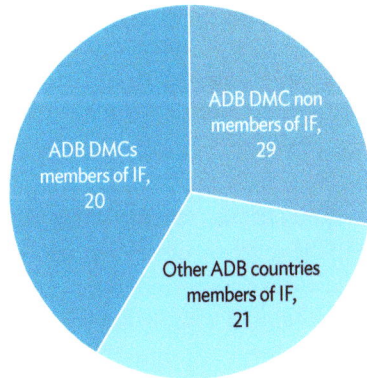

- ADB DMCs members of IF, 20
- ADB DMC non members of IF, 29
- Other ADB countries members of IF, 21

ADB = Asian Development Bank, BEPS = base erosion and profit shifting, DMC = developing member country, G20 = Group of Twenty, IF = OECD/G20 Inclusive Framework on BEPS, OECD = Organisation for Economic Co-operation and Development.
Source: OECD (2021), Addressing the tax challenges arising from digitalization of the economy. July 2021. https://www.oecd.org/tax/beps/brochure-addressing-the-tax-challenges-arising-from-the-digitalisation-of-the-economy-july-2021.pdf.

---

6   The OECD/G20 Inclusive Framework on BEPS was established to ensure interested countries and jurisdictions, including developing economies, can participate on an equal footing in the development of standards on BEPS-related issues. Besides OECD and G20 countries, the inclusive framework includes international organizations as well as regional tax organizations.

The multilateral agreement approved in 2021 is based on two complementary pillars, one to revisit allocations specified by profit and nexus rules (Pillar One), and another one to consider a global anti-base-erosion mechanism—in particular, a global minimum tax (Pillar Two). Another important area of work refers to the challenges of collecting value-added tax (VAT) on online sales of services and intangibles by foreign vendors, which was addressed in the 2015 BEPS Action 1 and reinforced since. Together with these initiatives, international guidelines are being developed, as presented below, to ensure that digital platforms hold full and sole liability for the assessment, collection, and remittance of VAT/goods and services tax (GST) for sales they facilitate online.

Asia's commitment to automatic exchange of information, an important step to curb tax evasion, has shown some progress. As of October 2021, 27 Asian DMCs have joined the Global Forum on Transparency and Exchange of Information for Tax Purposes. While still an ongoing regional effort, tax authorities are taking steps in adopting strong mechanisms for information exchange. Exchange of information agreements represent an important instrument for tracking and assessing transactions across borders. The peer review process evaluates jurisdictions' compliance with the international standard of transparency and exchange of information on request. Asian developing countries have seen progress in some areas surrounding the exchange of information on request and automatic exchange of information (Figure 9.4). The region has pursued progress in this area, including strengthening tax agreements, double taxation treaties, and other exchange of information mechanisms (Figure 9.5).

In response to calls for a global reporting system for digital platforms, the OECD recently developed model rules for reporting by platform operators. The rules are designed for digital platforms to collect information on the income realized by operators and to report the information to tax authorities (OECD 2020c).[7] The model rules have various objectives: to ensure that tax administrations get timely access on high-quality and relevant information on digital transactions, to promote standardization of reporting rules between jurisdictions and help platforms comply with reporting obligations, to promote international cooperation between tax administrations, and to develop a reporting regime that can be used for other tax-related purposes.

---

[7]   The design of model rules for platforms encompasses three broad dimensions. First, a targeted scope, focusing on accommodation, transport, and other personal services. Second, a broader scope of platform operators and sellers to ensure that as many relevant transactions as possible are being reported. Third, due diligence and reporting rules to warrant accuracy while avoiding overburdening procedures.

Figure 9.4: Compliance with Exchange of Information Standards in Developing Asia

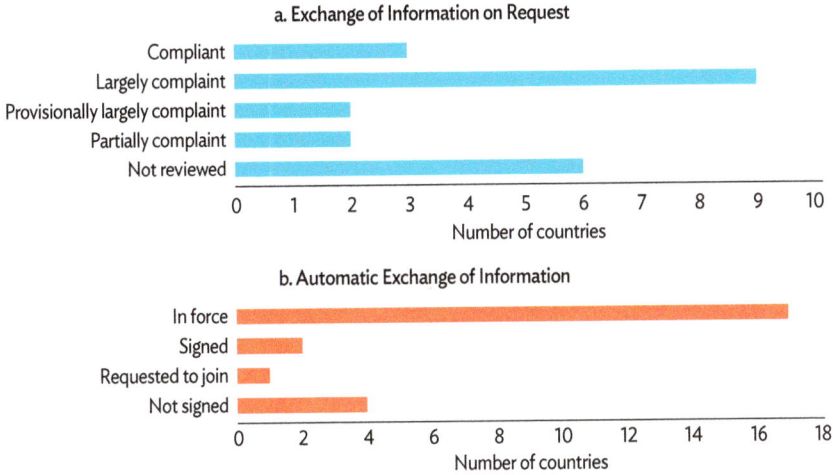

a. Exchange of Information on Request

(Number of countries)

b. Automatic Exchange of Information

(Number of countries)

Note: In panel (a), compliance refers to automatic exchange of information on request, which includes relevant information for the administration or enforcement of the domestic tax laws of a requesting party. In panel (b), compliance refers to the common reporting standard regarding financial accounts on a global level, between tax authorities.
Source: Authors, based on OECD's International Tax Cooperation Map. https://www.oecd.org/tax/international-tax-co-operation-map.htm (accessed July 2020).

Figure 9.5: Proportion of Regional Economies with Signed Double Taxation Treaty

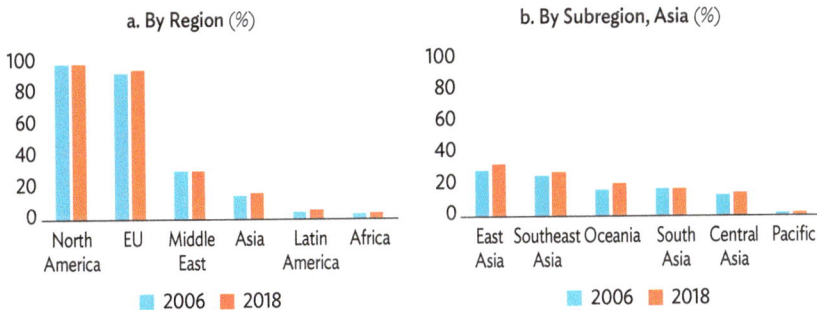

a. By Region (%)

b. By Subregion, Asia (%)

EU = European Union.
Note: Values computed as the average of the indicator in all countries belonging to a region. For instance, the value for Asia in 2006 is an average of the values for all countries in Asia for the year 2006.
Sources: ADB Asia-Pacific Regional Cooperation and Integration Index, based on data from United Nations Conference on Trade and Development. Investment Policy Hub. https://investmentpolicy.unctad.org/international-investment-agreements; and International Bureau of Fiscal Documentation. Tax Treaty Database (both accessed December 2020).

The model rules could provide a framework for involving digital platforms and be complemented by an international legal framework to support the automatic exchange of information between jurisdictions. In parallel, a number of countries in the region are considering extending VAT to capture e-commerce and digital services, which could have significant impact on tax revenue for tax administrations (IMF 2021).

ADB's support to strengthen regional tax systems during the pandemic has focused on improving tax policy and assisting tax administrations in the region. ADB has promoted a holistic approach on tax relief by recommending deferring, lowering, or temporarily waiving taxes to stabilize the economy. At the same time, in collaboration with OECD, ADB is helping DMCs introduce VAT systems on digitalized and cross-border transactions. Support for strengthening tax administrations is offered in several areas: (i) ensuring that operational risks in core business processes of tax administrations are managed during the pandemic, (ii) enhancing compliance risk management, and (iii) supporting digital transformation of tax administrations.

A world reshaped by the pandemic requires addressing domestic resource mobilization with a wider perspective. First, it is important to balance raising tax revenues with promoting investments that contribute to robust recovery from the pandemic. Second, leveraging tax policy measures are needed to support strong growth and improve development outcomes. This also includes adopting a progressive tax system and promoting carbon or other environmental taxes to promote a green recovery. Lastly, it is crucial to protect the tax base from the tax challenges of the digital economy.

In line with these efforts, ADB announced the establishment of the Asia Pacific Tax Hub in 2020. The hub, launched in May 2021, aims to provide an open and inclusive platform for strategic policy dialogue, institutional and capacity development, information exchange through dialogue among DMCs, and knowledge sharing and collaboration and development coordination across partners. Through these aims, the hub hopes to assist developing countries in the region to define differentiated domestic resource mobilization and international tax cooperation goals that take due consideration of their respective country circumstances and level of development (ADB 2020).

9.4. Case Studies in Asia

While global initiatives for addressing tax challenges of the digital economy have made significant progress, the majority of Asian countries have implemented domestic tax reforms in the interim to address challenges in digitalization. Case studies of platform giants in the PRC illustrate challenges in the taxation of digital platforms, which may offer important lessons to other countries in the region, in addition to recent experiences of Asian economies in improving their tax systems in response to digitalization. While domestic measures can help alleviate challenges and support needed domestic resource mobilization in the interim, international coordination and cooperation will eventually be crucial in the digital economy.

Big Tech: Issues, Challenges, and Lessons Learned

The growth of the digital economy across developing Asia and in the PRC has been unprecedented. E-commerce accounted for over a third of retail sales in the PRC in 2019—relative to a little over a 10% in the United States—comprising over half of the global total in that year , and is estimated to reach over 60% in 2022 (Turley and Leung 2019). The platform giants—Baidu, Alibaba, and Tencent—have played a large role in these trends, with the latter two named among the top 10 global companies by market capitalization in March of 2019 (PricewaterhouseCoopers 2019).

Baidu, Alibaba, and Tencent have played a critical role in the rapidly expanding digital economy of the PRC. For instance, the Alibaba e-commerce platform features 10 million active sellers and accounts for 60% of the local e-commerce market. The Tencent and Alibaba digital ecosystems feature *superapps* allowing activities ranging from entertainment and retail to health and education. Baidu, Alibaba, and Tencent command considerable volumes of data that allow them to help partner firms better target their offerings, optimize placement of stores, and streamline supply chains (Turley, Ho, and Leung 2018). As these firms expand to neighboring South Asian and Southeast Asian markets, their geographic reach is growing, allowing e-commerce platforms to become increasingly regional (Turley and Leung 2019). The rapid growth and dominant role of *Alipay* (Alibaba) and *WeChat Pay* (Tencent) in Chinese retail payment systems have prompted the People's Bank of China to consider establishing its own retail (central bank) digital currency, which is being piloted since November 2020.

The challenges these Big Tech firms pose to tax systems span regulatory issues, questions over how to classify digital platforms, and difficulties embedded in tax collection. Institutional constraints have emerged as regulatory frameworks have not kept pace with rapid developments in the digital economy, prompting mismatches between the regulatory classification of ride sharing or transport services, for instance, and the classification for tax purposes. There is also uncertainty whether to treat platforms as either brokers or principals, muddling the nature of the requirements to meet tax obligations, likely contributing to the existing low compliance levels among vendors. The direction domestic policy on platforms and tax collection will take is also yet to be defined. Ambiguities surrounding cross-border transactions raise further complications for taxation, including limited classifications for outbound payments outlined in foreign exchange rules, difficulties in determining whether the consumption of imported digital services occurred beyond PRC borders, and insufficient guidance on permanent establishment—in particular, limited regulations governing mirror servers or user interfaces (Turley and Leung 2019).

The operational structure of Big Tech firms further challenges tax systems. Some may choose to operate under a variable interest entity structure. Under this setup, part of the organization would be located in an offshore holding company, while an onshore or domestic counterpart manages essential key operations. Such an arrangement, though legally sound, would allow transfer of substantial amounts of value outside borders, possibly undermining the domestic country's tax base. These arrangements highlight important challenges to the BEPS Action Plan and draw attention to controversial practices, including use of tax havens, internal transfer pricing, and distortion of the concept of permanent establishment. And while the BEPS Action Plan outlines measures to mitigate such practices, it lacks clear guidelines for implementation or enforcement. Such risks underline the need for clear policies or guidance on variable interest entity structures and measures to address them (Larson 2018).

Selected Examples of Measures to Improve Taxation in the Digital Era in Asia

Permanent Establishment Status

To counter the limitations of permanent establishment guidelines, India has introduced amendments to its domestic nexus rules to accommodate the concept of significant economic presence and account for digital economic activity. In 2019, India adopted a broader definition of the nexus for corporate income tax purposes (OECD 2018). This expanded definition allowed consideration of significant economic presence and enabled taxation of nonresident corporation profits regardless of the extent of the corporation's physical presence in the taxing jurisdiction. Under this amendment, the significant economic presence can be grounded on either: (i) a threshold based on local revenue or (ii) a threshold based on number of local users (OECD 2018). The first allows significant economic presence of a nonresident enterprise to be established if the aggregated payments from goods, services, or property by a nonresident in India exceed a specified amount in a given year. The second allows significant economic presence to be established if the number of local users exceeds a specific target. The two criteria, moreover, account for digital economic activity, including the download of data or software in the transactions covered under the first criterion and encompassing the engagement of users through digital means under the second (OECD 2018).

In Australia, the Multinational Anti-Avoidance Law seeks to deter permanent establishment avoidance by nonresident enterprises belonging to large multinational enterprises. The measure targets a particular trade structure whereby an overseas ("billing") company employs locally based workers (typically a local subsidiary) to provide goods and services to final customers in Australia while limiting the tax levied on the multinational enterprise group in Australia. In practice, such an arrangement is often available to companies offering digital goods and services. Such structures are liable to a reallocation of income after consideration of permanent establishment terms as well as a penalty comprising a proportion of the avoided tax. This measure is expected to generate an additional $77 million in annual corporate tax by increasing Australia's tax base by $5.4 billion annually (OECD 2018).

Improving Domestic Tax Systems and Resource Mobilization

In Malaysia, Singapore, and other countries, electronic systems are used to enhance tax compliance. Malaysia, Singapore, and other jurisdictions have tapped into electronic processes to issue pre-filled returns for some or all sources of personal income. These countries have taken a "deemed acceptance" approach of pre-filled returns following a certain length of time following the notice period (OECD 2018).

Several Asian countries have made progress in the adoption of a VAT in goods and services taxes in relation to cross-border transactions. Table 9.1 illustrates that a number of Asian countries adhere to international standards for VAT/GST guidelines, which is particularly relevant for high-value cross-border transactions in order to broaden the domestic tax base and consequently facilitate domestic resource mobilization.

Additional examples of domestic tax reforms taken by Asian economies include the expansion of the scope of withholding taxes in Malaysia and the Philippines. The two countries have taken steps to broaden royalties, expanding their scope to include payments for the right to use digital images, sound transmissions, and other software (Terada-Hagiwara, Gonzales, and Wang 2019).

As the digital economy grew strongly during the COVID-19 pandemic, the Philippines proposed a VAT and income tax for digital platforms. As public spending is growing, digital transactions are booming and the economy is contracting, such a tax aims at relieving budgetary pressure and enhancing domestic resource mobilization. The main addressees of this proposed tax would be multinational Big Tech companies, such as e-commerce platforms, media service providers, as well as ride-hailing companies, whose services would be subject to VAT. Further, nonresidents providing digital services in the country would be required to establish a local office and thus be subject to income tax.

Table 9.1: Progress in Select Asian Economies in Addressing the Challenges of the Digital Economy
(BEPS Action 1)

Jurisdiction	Cross-Border B2C Supplies of Services and Intangibles		Low-Value Imports
	Applies Principles of the International VAT/GST Guidelines on Cross-Border B2C Supplies of Services and Intangibles	Simplified Registration and Collection Mechanisms	Implementation of Mechanism for Collecting VAT/GST on imports of Low-Value Goods from Online Trade
Hong Kong, China	...	...	...
India	Yes[a]	Yes	No
Indonesia	Under consideration	...	No
Japan	Yes[b]	Yes	No
Kazakhstan	No	No	
Malaysia	Yes[c]	No	...
Philippines	Under consideration	No	No
PRC	Yes[d]	No	No
Republic of Korea	Yes[b]	Yes	No
Singapore	Yes	Yes	Under consideration
Sri Lanka	No	No	
Taipei,China	Yes	Yes	
Thailand	Under consideration		No
Viet Nam	Yes[e]	No	

B2C = business-to-consumer, GST = goods and services tax, PRC = People's Republic of China, VAT = value-added tax.
[a] Adoption of actions based on guidelines in 2017.
[b] Adoption of actions based on guidelines in 2015.
[c] Services tax policy on digital services.
[d] Adoption of actions based on guidelines in 2009.
[e] Adoption of actions based on guidelines in 2020.
Source: ADB (2021).

9.5. Policy Considerations[8]

Many of the key features of the digital economy raise risks for tax policy design, necessitating careful examination by policy makers. Multinational companies can disproportionately benefit from opportunities within national tax and legal systems to artificially reduce or remove tax obligations in different jurisdictions across the entire supply chain. Measures therefore need to be taken to ensure core activities of multinational firms do not gain inappropriately from exceptions from permanent establishment status. Among the key features of the digital economy with implications for tax policy are the central role of intangibles. The growing pervasiveness of data in business operations and the fragmentation of global production networks have also allowed other firms, in particular digitally driven firms, to benefit from these conditions. A further key characteristic posing risk is the ability of digital firms to centralize operations from remote locations and their growing capacity to conduct business activities with minimal personnel, allowing businesses to fragment their operations to avoid taxes.

The predominance of digital transactions could also offer opportunities to national tax authorities. In many cases, the increasing use of digital platforms for economic purposes could significantly facilitate the traceability of taxable transactions. In contrast to cash transactions, digital transactions can be traceable and information can be shared among concerned tax authorities. Tax authorities in some countries have introduced tax credits and other incentives to promote the use of electronic payments. Current discussions on the implementation of VAT/GST guidelines for online sales illustrate the importance of information sharing among platforms and tax authorities. There is, however, a significant gap in the capacity of tax administrations, both technological and operational, to implement these practices. Communication with digital platforms and businesses on their fiscal obligations will also be important if a cooperative compliance model is to be implemented in the future.

---

[8]　This chapter was initially a background paper for the theme chapter of the ADB Asian Economic Integration Report 2021 on *Making Digital Platforms Work for Asia and the Pacific* (ADB 2021). The policy considerations outlined in this section served as inputs to those discussed in the theme chapter.

Proposed measures to address the tax challenges of digitalization include active participation in international forums, adoption of domestic measures in the interim, collection of VAT for customer-to-customer transactions, and improvement in tax administration capacity. While the multilateral agreement on tax rules is implemented, measures that countries can take include active participation in international forums for tax matters and the adoption of domestic measures that comply with a country's international obligations in the interim. A VAT imposed on customer-to-customer transactions can be considered. Yet, while domestic measures can be effective to some extent, a proliferation of unilateral approaches, such as the introduction of a digital services tax, might not be a sustainable approach in the long term. Providing a level playing field among national tax systems in the region is therefore necessary for reducing tax competition and potential loopholes in the future. Importantly, improvements in tax administration capacity for both cross-border and domestic e-commerce transactions can be adopted, including the digitalization of tax invoices; the creation of a centralized and uniform tax administration system; and the introduction of risk-based management, self-assessment, and tax audits to facilitate the collection of tax information and the reduction in compliance costs for taxpayers (Terada-Hagiwara, Gonzales, and Wang 2019).

As regional trade agreements gradually include more elaborate provisions on digital trade and data flows, coordination on the implementation of the Inclusive Framework on BEPS two-pillar solution will be important in the future. Around 27% of the 275 existing regional trade agreements in the World Trade Organization (WTO) explicitly address e-commerce issues, ranging from customs duties, consumer protection, and data privacy (WTO 2017). From this group, about one-third specifies a right to impose an internal tax or charge on digital products. As these agreements include further measures, Asian economies will need to incorporate them into their tax practices.

Measures to strengthen tax systems also need to balance implementation of new tax rules and possible impact on tax incentives for foreign investment inflows. Governments in Asia have been keen to attract foreign direct investment (FDI) for employment, technology adoption, and support to new sectors. They have traditionally balanced measures to attract international investors with the need to ensure a fair share of tax is collected from multinationals. FDI flows are particularly sensitive to corporate tax regimes. In the past, Asian economies, including Indonesia and Thailand, have introduced cuts in statutory tax rates and offered tax incentives to attract FDI. As in OECD economies, evidence in the region suggests that tax regimes, including statutory tax rates but also other tax provisions, are important in explaining FDI allocation (Devereux and Griffith 1998, Muthitacharoen 2019). The potential effects of the new international tax rules on tax incentive regimes will require further assessment in the near future.

Large-scale policy responses to the pandemic will inevitably increase sovereign debt, underpinning the need for efficient tax systems and addressing the tax challenges of the digital economy to assure public debt sustainability in the longer term. It is expected that the sovereign debt-to-GDP ratio in Asia's developing countries will increase 7 percentage points in 2020 over 2019.[9] With the prospect of a significant economic downturn, high debt levels not only pose considerable risks to Asian economies and financial markets but will also weigh on governments' future fiscal space. Consequently, to ensure public debt sustainability and maintain needed public spending post-pandemic, the taxation of the digital economy is even more important for domestic resource mobilization.

Regional and international cooperation and coordination are necessary elements underlying effective response in adapting to existing corporate tax frameworks. Such cooperation should expand beyond OECD and G20 member economies to encompass developing economies. This encapsulates knowledge sharing on the best practices in tax administration and the monitoring of new developments. The G20/OECD Inclusive Framework can facilitate and monitor the implementation of a global solution to end tax avoidance by technological companies. Critically, BEPS Action 1 on the Digital Economy may become a minimum standard in the future, and countries will be assessed on their progress regardless of their membership or participation. The reputational risk for countries is therefore important. Meanwhile, the region continues to strengthen the issue of tax agreements, double taxation treaties, and other mechanisms for exchanging tax information, including the promotion of a unique legal entity identifier for firms in the region. Regional policy forums (such as ASEAN/+3 and Asia-Pacific Economic Forum) and multilateral development banks (such as ADB) can help advance these efforts.

---

[9] Based on the simple average of the difference in the 2020 and 2019 general government gross debt as percentage of GDP for ADB's developing member countries, using data from International Monetary Fund. World Economic Outlook October 2020 Database (accessed 19 November 2020). Does not include Mongolia and Palau as data are unavailable.

Meanwhile, the pandemic provides an opportunity for regional cooperation to regain reform momentum. ADB's recently established the Asia Pacific Tax Hub, geared to help countries strengthen domestic resource mobilization and international tax cooperation.

References

Asian Development Bank (ADB). 2020. Achieving the Sustainable Development Goals by Strengthening Domestic Resource Mobilization and International Tax Cooperation. Speech by ADB President Masatsugu Asakawa. 17 September. https://www.adb.org/news/speeches/achieving-sdgs-strengthening-domestic-resource-mobilization-masatsugu-asakawa.

ADB. 2021. *Asian Economic Integration Report 2021: Making Digital Platforms Work for Asia and the Pacific.* Manila. http://dx.doi.org/10.22617/TCS210048-2.

Aslam, A. and A. Shah. 2020. Tec(h)tonic Shifts: Taxing the "Digital Economy". *IMF Working Papers* WP/20/76. Washington, DC. https://www.imf.org/en/Publications/WP/Issues/2020/05/29/Tec-h-tonic-Shifts-Taxing-the-Digital-Economy-49363.

Bradbury, D., T. Hanappi, and A. Moore. 2018. Estimating the Fiscal Effects of Base Erosion and Profit Shifting: Data Availability and Analytical Issues. *Transnational Corporations.* 25 (2): pp. 91–106.

Clausing, K. A. 2016. The Effect of Profit Shifting on the Corporate Tax Base in the United States and Beyond. *National Tax Journal.* 69 (4): pp. 905–934. https://doi.org/10.17310/ntj.2016.4.09.

Cobham, A., and P. Janský. 2018. Global Distribution of Revenue Loss from Corporate Tax Avoidance: Reestimation and Country Results. *Journal of International Development.* 30 (2): pp. 206–232. https://doi.org/10.1002/jid.3348.

Cobham, A., and P. Janský. 2019. Measuring Misalignment: The Location of US Multinationals' Economic Activity Versus the Location of Their Profits. *Development Policy Review.* 37 (1): pp. 91–110. https://doi.org/10.1111/dpr.12315.

Devereux, M. and Griffith, R. 1998. Taxes and the Location of Production: Evidence from a Panel of US Multinationals. *Journal of Public Economics.* 68 (3): pp. 335–367.

International Monetary Fund (IMF). 2021. Digitalization and Taxation in Asia. *Departmental Paper* No 2021/017. Washington, DC. https://www.imf.org/en/Publications/Departmental-Papers-Policy-Papers/Issues/2021/09/13/Digitalization-and-Taxation-in-Asia-460120.

Janskỳ, P. and M. Palansky. 2019. Estimating the Scale of Profit Shifting and Tax Revenue Losses Related to Foreign Direct Investment. *International Tax and Public Finance*. 26: 1048–1103. https://doi.org/10.1007/s10797-019-09547-8.

Johansson, A., O.B. Skeie, S. Sorbe, and C. Menon. 2017. Tax Planning by Multinational Firms: Firm-level Evidence from a Cross-Country Database. *OECD Economics Department Working Papers* 1355 (64). https://doi.org/10.1787/9ea89b4d-en.

KPMG. 2020. *Taxation of the Digitalized Economy: Developments Summary*. https://tax.kpmg.us/content/dam/tax/en/pdfs/2020/digitalized-economy-taxation-developments-summary.pdf.

Larson, M. 2018. Alibaba's VIE Structure and Erosion of BEPS Goals in China's E-commerce Industry. *Temple International and Comparative Law Journal*. 33 (1): pp. 201–241.

Muthitacharoen, A. 2019. Assessing the Importance of Taxation on Foreign Direct Investment: Evidence from Southeast Asian Developing Countries. *eJournal of Tax Research 2019*. 17 (1): pp. 63–82.

Organisation for Economic Co-operation and Development (OECD) 2017. International VAT/GST Guidelines. Paris: OECD Publishing. http://dx.doi.org/10.1787/9789264271401-en.

——. 2018. *Tax Challenges Arising from Digitalisation — Interim Report 2018: Inclusive Framework on BEPS*. OECD/G20 Base Erosion and Profit Shifting Project. Paris: OECD Publishing. http://dx.doi.org/10.1787/9789264293083-en.

————. 2019a. OECD/G20 Inclusive Framework on BEPS Progress report July 2018 – May 2019. https://www.oecd.org/tax/beps/inclusive-framework-on-beps-progress-report-july-2018-may-2019.htm; http://www.oecd.org/tax/the-role-of-digital-platforms-in-the-collection-of-vat-gst-on-online-sales-e0e2dd2d-en.htm.

————. 2020a. *Tax Challenges Arising from Digitalisation – Economic Impact Assessment.*

————. *Inclusive Framework on BEPS.* Paris: OECD Publishing. http://www.oecd.org/tax/beps/tax-challenges-arising-from-digitalisation-economic-impact-assessment-0e3cc2d4-en.htm.

————. 2020b. *Revenue Statistics in Asian and Pacific Economies 2020.* Paris: OECD Publishing. https://doi.org/10.1787/d47d0ae3-en.

————. 2020c. *Model Rules for Reporting by Platform Operators with respect to Sellers in the Sharing and Gig Economy.* Paris: OECD Publishing. www.oecd.org/tax/exchange-of-tax-information/model-rules-for-reporting-by-platform-operators-with-respect-to-sellers-in-the-sharing-and-gig-economy.htm.

————. (2021) Addressing the tax challenges arising from digitalization of the economy. July 2021. https://www.oecd.org/tax/beps/brochure-addressing-the-tax-challenges-arising-from-the-digitalisation-of-the-economy-july-2021.pdf.

OECD/ADB. 2019. Regional Meeting on Tax and Digitalization for Asia and the Pacific. Asian Development Bank, Manila. https://www.oecd.org/tax/beps/co-chairs-statement-regional-meeting-manila-november-2019.pdf.

PricewaterhouseCoopers. 2019. *Global Top 100 Companies by Market Capitalisation.* https://www.pwc.com/gx/en/audit-services/publications/assets/global-top-100-companies-2019.pdf.

Terada-Hagiwara, A., K. Gonzales, and J. Wang. 2019. Taxation Challenges in a Digital Economy—The Case of the People's Republic of China. *ADB Briefs* 108. Manila. https://www.adb.org/sites/default/files/publication/504616/adb-brief-108-taxation-digital-economy-peoples-republic-china.pdf.

Tørsløv, T. R., L. S. Wier, and G. Zucman. 2018. The Missing Profits of Nations. *National Bureau of Economic Research Working Paper* No. 24701. https://doi.org/10.3386/w24701.

Turley, C., K. Ho, and S. Leung. 2018. A Sisyphean Task? – Tax Plays Catch Up with China's Rapid Digitalisation. *International Tax Review*. https://www.internationaltaxreview.com/article/b1f7n29dkqsyz8/a-sisyphean-task-tax-plays-catch-up-with-chinas-rapid-digitalisation.

Turley, C. and S. Leung. 2019. We Need to Talk About Platforms: Ongoing Tax Challenges in China. *International Tax Review*. https://www.internationaltaxreview.com/article/b1j8y77w953x5t/we-need-to-talk-about-platforms-ongoing-tax-challenges-in-china.

World Trade Organization (WTO). 2017. Provisions on Electronic Commerce in Regional Trade Agreements. *WTO Working Paper* ERSD-2017-11. WTO Economic Research and Statistics Division. https://www.wto.org/english/res_e/reser_e/ersd201711_e.pdf.

www.ingramcontent.com/pod-product-compliance
Lightning Source LLC
Chambersburg PA
CBHW041143230326
41599CB00039BA/7154